# Global Econometrics

# Global Econometrics
Essays in Honor of Lawrence R. Klein

edited by F. Gerard Adams and Bert G. Hickman

The MIT Press
Cambridge, Massachusetts
London, England

© 1983 by
The Massachusetts Institute of Technology

This book was set in Times New Roman by Aşco Trade Typesetting Ltd., Hong Kong, and printed and bound by Halliday Lithograph in the United States of America.

Library of Congress Cataloging in Publication Data

Main entry under title:

Global econometrics.

    Includes bibliographies and indexes.
    1. Econometrics—Addresses, essays, lectures.    2. Klein, Lawrence Robert.    I. Klein, Lawrence Robert.    II. Adams, Francis Gerard, 1929–.    III. Hickman, Bert G., 1924–.
HB139.G58    1983        330′.028        82-18804
ISBN 0-262-01071-2

# Contents

Preface   vii

# Preface

The papers in this collection were pledged in honor of Lawrence Klein's sixtieth birthday, on September 14, 1980.

Good econometric research requires an optimal combination of economic theory, statistical methodology, institutional knowledge, and data analysis. Lawrence Klein is a master of all these phases of econometrics and has contributed importantly to them all throughout his career. For this reason alone it is fitting to entitle this volume *Global Econometrics*, since the interests of the contributors range similarly across economic theory, econometric theory, and applied econometrics. It is also fitting, however, because Klein's influence on econometric modeling has been worldwide. His example, and his frequent participation at home and abroad, stimulated the efflorescence of econometric model building during the past twenty years. In turn, the proliferation of national models laid the basis for the foundation by Klein and others in 1968 of Project LINK, a pioneering international venture to model the world economy by linking the national models through their trading and financial relationships. For these reasons, many of the contributors to this Festschrift are from other countries and many of the subjects deal with other economies or international markets or world models. Be they his students, his present or former university colleagues, or his past or present associates in his many research endeavors, all the contributors share a deep respect for Klein's work and an abiding appreciation of his modesty and warmth.

# Global Econometrics

# I ECONOMIC THEORY

# 1 Rigorous Observational Positivism: Klein's Envelope Aggregation; Thermodynamics and Economic Isomorphisms

Paul A. Samuelson

Twenty or more years ago, Edwin G. Nourse, the first chairman of the Council of Economic Advisers and a respected agricultural economist at the Brookings Institution, wrote to Alvin Hansen to ask "Who originated the word 'macroeconomics'?" Hansen wrote back "I don't know. Probably Samuelson."

I know there is much that I will have to answer for at Saint Peter's Gate. But when I read carbons of this correspondence, I was pretty sure that I was not guilty as charged. Familiar as the distinction between *microeconomics* and *macroeconomics* is today, the expressions are not old ones. I confirmed that *macroeconomics* is not in the index of the first (1948) edition of my textbook *Economics*. I suspected that the word was a coinage of Ragnar Frisch, who was so ingenious in originating and naming concepts. I did a little research in the 1952 *Guide to Econometrica*. Sure enough, there was a classification there involving *macroeconomics*. And, as I vaguely recall, listed under that category were articles from the early 1930s by Frisch, Jan Tinbergen, and others. However, when I perused the bound volumes of those early issues, I discovered that Frisch and Tinbergen seemed not to have actually used the word in question. The compilers of the *Guide* had (properly) used hindsight in making their classification of earlier articles.[1]

So I was stumped. And I was challenged to do some further cursory research on the appearance of *macroeconomics*. Moreover, I realized that *macroeconomics* as used today has two primary meanings. The first deals, for example, with Keynesian notions of effective demand, of fluctuations in output as a whole. At the pre-Keynesian neoclassical level, this first concept involves the notion of the "price level," as distinct from individual prices and price ratios and as determinable by a Fisherian equation of exchange, $MV = PQ$. The second important meaning we now give to *macroeconomics* is at the real level of pure theory. With J. B. Clark, we speak of a society with a production function that produces (aggregate) output out of its total labor, land, and capital. In this second sense, a micro system of general equilibrium that is very simple becomes a macromodel. Trade theory is full of two-good, two-factor models, involving Marshallian bales and indifference contours for a country.

To return to the hunt for origins of the term *macroeconomics*: Its earliest appearance turned up by my desultory explorations was in the second sense of the term—in connection with simple, aggregated micro models. The lead article in the April 1946 *Econometrica*, written by the 25-year-old Lawrence R. Klein, had the word in its title: Macroeconomics and the Theory of Rational Behavior. I am sure more assiduous researchers will turn up references prior to 1946; until they do, Laurie Klein can be regarded as Columbus.

## Envelope Aggregation

Over 35 years later, we can sum up on the 1946 Klein program for aggregation.[2] There are many different kinds of aggregation—some rigorous, some approximate, some erroneous or incomplete. Klein put his emphasis on what I here characterize as *envelope aggregation*.

Let me briefly mention some other kinds of aggregation. Ricardo and other classical writers are sometimes assumed to work with a "dose of labor and capital." This reduces two inputs, $L$ and $K$, to a new single input, $\text{Min}(L/a, K/b) \equiv V$. This so-called Leontief (1936) aggregation is not in Klein's focus.

Hicks (1939) holds the ratio $P_3/P_2$ constant at $\overline{\Pi}$ in demand functions for three goods: $D^i(M; P_1, P_2, P_3)$. Hicks shows that the first good, and the composite spent on the remaining goods, obey well-behaved two-good demand:

$$D^1(M; P_1 \ P_2, \quad \overline{\Pi}P_2) \equiv D^1(M; P_1, P_2),$$

where the latter obeys all of the Slutsky conditions. Again, Klein's focus is not on this.

One last example of aggregation that does not concern Klein can be given. Suppose each of $j = 1, \ldots, J$ persons has a simple propensity-to-consume function: $C_j = a_j + b_j Y_j$. Then, even if the $b$s differ capriciously, suppose that whatever business-cycle forces affect total income, $Y = \sum_j Y_j$, always do so consistently with definite distributional laws: $Y_j = f_j(Y)$. It will follow that total consumption, $C = \sum_j C_j$, obeys an invariant function of total income:

$$C = F(Y) = \sum_j [a_j + b_j f_j(Y)], \tag{1}$$

$$F'(Y) = \sum_j b_j f_j'(Y). \tag{2}$$

The collective marginal propensity to consume depicts no property of a collective mind with thrift propensities; it is merely a definable average of disparate minds. Legitimate as this could be, it is not what Klein has in mind.

What is Klein's concern? He does want to replace multivarious relations between $(x_1, \ldots, x_n)$ and $(y_1, \ldots, y_m)$ by fewer relations between some scalar $X$ and some scalar $Y$—as, for example, $Y = F(X)$. This goal he shares with the other theorists I have mentioned and with the Bureau of Labor Statistics and other government agencies that provide us with statistical measures of aggregates (index numbers of price levels, output or input measures, and the like).

But Klein insists on an additional criterion for his aggregate functions: If economic theory says that the individual firms and families at the microscopic level are maximizers or minimizers who equate market prices of goods or factors to partial derivatives of their respective micro functions, then the surrogate macro functions constructed from these micro functions should have its partial derivatives equaling *its* macro prices. An example is the marginal productivity wage. If each product has

$$q_j = f_j(L_j, \ldots),\tag{3}$$

$$\frac{W}{P_j} = \frac{\partial f_j(L_j, \ldots)}{\partial L_j},\tag{4}$$

then Klein seeks for $\sum q_j = Q$, $\sum L_j = L$, $\ldots$

$$Q = F(L, \ldots),\tag{5}$$

$$\frac{W}{P_Q} = \frac{\partial F(L, \ldots)}{\partial L}.\tag{6}$$

The correspondence between equations 4 and 6 is what is characteristic of envelope aggregation. (I supply this term for it because, as will be seen, an envelope property is what is involved.)

## Motivations

Remember, Klein was a Berkeley undergraduate. Like Francis Dresch, George Danzig, Kenneth May, Ronald Shephard, and many other students of that generation, Klein benefited from the influence of two noneconomists: the mathematician Griffith C. Evans and the statistician Jerszy Neyman. Around 1925, Evans went beyond his specialty of functional analysis to explore mathematical economics (Evans 1930, 1934). His ideas were important for diverse topics: integrability conditions, aggregation and Divisia indexes, and time-phased input-output models (which W. W. Leontief and P. Sraffa were to cultivate in depth). In particular, Klein puzzled over the approach to aggregation along the lines of Divisia indexes by Francis W. Dresch.

Klein was a student of mine at the Massachusetts Institute of Technology. He was MIT's first Ph.D. in economics—and still our fastest, provided you penalize Robert Mundell for graduate study elsewhere than at MIT. Between wartime tasks at the Radiation Laboratory, I was revising for publication my Well's Prize Harvard thesis. *Foundations of Economic Analysis* (Samuelson 1947) contained a chapter on special topics such as aggregation. Already in 1936, on a trip back to Chicago, I had unsuccessfully tried to interest Henry Schultz in Jacobian conditions for rigorous aggregation (functional dependences of separability). Also, I spent countless hours pursuing testable regularities that aggregate demand data ($\Sigma_j q_1^j$, $\Sigma_j q_2^j$, ..., $p_1$, $p_2$, ...) must theoretically obey. Only in relatively recent times did Hugo Sonnenschein (1972) demonstrate how empty of such laws aggregate functions will be if we are not given data on ($I^1, I^2, \ldots$) and if endowment breakdowns of $q_i$ totals by individuals ($\bar{q}_i^j$) cannot be known.

Finally, Klein had gone to the Chicago Cowles Commission from MIT. I suspect that Jacob Marschak and Leo Hurwicz had urged him to try to give his aggregate models greater trustworthiness by trying to anchor them in the individuals' maximizing behavior of economic theory.[3]

Already, A. A. Könus, G. Haberler, H. Staehle, R. G. D. Allen, A. P. Lerner, Leontief, and Frisch had shown the value of basing index numbers on the theory of indifference curves rather than on the mechanical tests of Irving Fisher, F. Y. Edgeworth, W. Persons, the earlier Frisch, and the official compilers of indexes. It was natural for Klein to attempt to bring production theory in line.

I add that, implicitly at least, there had always been envelope aggregation involved in such classical concepts as the total of corn produced for each total of labor applied (under the invisible hand of competition) to diverse acres of land, and in such neoclassical concepts as the supply curve for an industry.

## Crusoe's Exact Case

Provide R. Crusoe with totals of primary factors: $(V_1, V_2, \ldots, V_I)$. They can be allocated among $j = 1, \ldots, J$ different single-good industries:

$$q_j = F^j(V_{1j}, V_{2j}, \ldots), \quad \sum_j V_{ij} \le V_i > 0 \le V_{ij}. \tag{7}$$

Suppose Crusoe has a quasi-concave indicator of the utility of the goods he consumes: $u = u[q_1, \ldots, q_J]$. Then it is an easy envelope theory that we can define for Crusoe a derived utility function that depends only on his factor totals, $(V_1, V_2, \ldots)$.
Thus,

$$U(V_1, V_2, \ldots) = \operatorname*{Max}_{V_{ij}} u[q_1, q_2, \ldots, q_j, \ldots]$$

$$= \operatorname*{Max}_{V_{ij}} u[F^1(V_{11}, V_{21}, \ldots), F^2(V_{12}, V_{22}, \ldots), \ldots] \tag{8}$$

$$\text{s.t.} \sum_j V_{ij} \le V_i \quad (i = 1, 2, \ldots, I).$$

What is important for Klein's requirement is that the slopes of the indifference contours of the constructed aggregate utility yield the factor-price ratios needed to define functional distribution among the factors; that is,

$$\frac{W_2}{W_1} = \frac{\partial U(V_1, V_2, \ldots)/\partial V_2}{\partial U(V_1, V_2, \ldots)/\partial V_1}, \text{ etc.} \tag{9}$$

## Trivial Generalizations of Symmetry

If Crusoe is joined by Friday, with equal ownership of each $V_j$ total, and with $u[q_1, q_2, \ldots]$ tastes of exactly Crusoe's form, then the aggregate $U(V_1, V_2, \ldots)$ that works for the whole can also stand for the representative person.

Classroom expositions often use Santa Claus cases like this one to make the portrayal of complicated general equilibrium look simple. A century ago, Friedrich von Wieser's *Natural Value* improved on the Crusoe metaphor by using the metaphor of the perfect communist state. This led, via V. Pareto, E. Barone, L. von Mises, F. Taylor, A. P. Lerner, O. Lange, F. von Hayek, A. Bergson, and L. Kantorovitch, to fruitful debate on the role of market pricing in socialist planning.

To appreciate when a theorem is not true, realize that indifference curves and factor endowments that differ among people will vitiate the existence of a social surrogate with the sought Klein properties.

## Uniform Homotheticity

Does Klein set out to hunt a unicorn or chimera? Does his quarry exist? In general, no aggregate that is an exact surrogate will exist. Only if we can tolerate some approximations can we, in general, succeed in the hunt. Perhaps an antelope or a cow can approximate to a unicorn. But there are sufficient conditions that ensure exact surrogates. Here is the rock-bottom example.

A Crusoe world with fixed supplies of two goods, $x$ and $y$, could have its sole price ratio predicted by the slope of Crusoe's indifference contour at that point:

$$\frac{P_x}{P_y} = r(x,y) = \frac{\partial u(x,y)/\partial x}{\partial u(x,y)/\partial y}. \tag{10}$$

Now add Friday. Knowing $x^1$, $y^1$, $x^2$, $y^2$, $X = x^1 + x^2$, and $Y = y^1 + y^2$, we cannot in general validly write

$$p_x/p_y = R(X, Y) = R(x^1 + x^2, y^1 + y^2). \tag{11}$$

Reallocating $x^1$ and $x^2$ within the same total of $x^1 + x^2$ will alter real-world $p_x/p_y$, falsifying equation 11, unless the persons' $[r^1(x^1,y^1), r^2(x^2,y^2)]$ marginal-rate-of-substitution functions are of special form. We require

$$p_x/p_y = r^1(x^1,y^1) = r^2(x^2,y^2) \equiv r(x^1 + x^2, y^1 + y^2). \tag{12}$$

If this identity is to hold throughout the $(x,y)$ non-negative orthant, it is necessary and sufficient that

$$r^1(a,b) \equiv r(a/b) \equiv r^2(a,b). \tag{13}$$

This is the singular case of *uniform homothetic* demand. (Both adjectives are required.) William Gorman (1953) and Henri Theil (1957) have presented a weaker condition for aggregative invariance under limited local reallocations of the $(x^1 + x^2, y^1 + y^2)$ totals, namely that the persons have straight-line Engel's paths with the same positive slopes at common price ratios. But, globally throughout the non-negative orthant, the only straight lines that will not be bent by the axes are straight lines through the origin—the uniform homothetic case of Samuelson (1956).

When Klein (1946a, p. 103) suggested Cobb-Douglas-type functions, his instinct was a good one. But, as just seen, it is homotheticity and general homogeneous functions that are in order and not merely the special species of Cobb-Douglas type.

Dresch's use of Divisia indexes can also be shown to have a certain rationale through their connection with homogeneous functions. If Divisia index integrals are to enjoy the indispensable independence-of-path property, they must be applied to homothetic structures.

In particular, let $[p_1, \ldots, p_n]$ be proportional to the gradient of $f(x_1, \ldots, x_J)$,

$$[\partial f(x_1, \ldots, x_J)/\partial x_J] \equiv [f_1(x), \ldots, f_J(x)],$$

where these partials are well defined on $x \geq 0 \neq x$.

The integral

$$\int \sum_j \left( p_j \Big/ \sum_k p_k x_k \right) dx_j = \int \sum_j \left( f_j(x) \Big/ \sum_k f_k(x) x_k \right) dx_j \tag{14}$$

will be the same for every path beginning at $(x_1^0, \ldots, x_J^0)$ and ending at $(x_1^1, \ldots, x_J^1)$ if and only if $f(x)$ can be written in the form

$$f(x_1, \ldots, x_n) \underset{\lambda}{\equiv} \phi[x_1 \psi(x_2/x_1, \ldots, x_J/x_1)], \quad \Phi''[\ ] \gtrless 0. \tag{15}$$

The next section shows the purest case of uniform homotheticity.

## The Santa Claus Case

In connection with the Hicks Festschrift and my memorial notice for Paul Douglas (Samuelson 1968, 1979), I show how simple general equilibrium can become if every dollar is spent in the same way by people who have uniform homothetic tastes.[4]

Suppose individuals, $k = 1, \ldots, K$, have inelastic factor supplies, $V_i^k$, whose $i = 1, \ldots, I$ totals can be allocated among goods $j = 1, \ldots, J$, in amounts $V_{ij}$. These goods have production functions

$$q_j = Q^j(V_{1j}, \ldots, V_{ij}, \ldots, V_{Ij}) \quad (j = 1, \ldots, J), \quad V_{ij} \geq 0, \tag{16}$$

$$\sum_{k=1}^{K} V_i^k = \sum_{j=1}^{J} V_{ij} \quad (i = 1, \ldots, I), \quad V_i^k \geq 0. \tag{17}$$

With uniform homothetic tastes, any person $k$ acts to maximize the first-degree-homogeneous utility function

$$u^k = u[q_1^k, \ldots, q_J^k] \quad (k = 1, \ldots, K). \tag{18}$$

All consumptions end up subject to individual budget restrictions and

$$\sum_{k=1}^{K} q_j^k = q_j = Q^j(V_{1j}, \ldots, V_{Ij}) \quad (j = 1, \ldots, J), \quad q_j^k \geq 0. \tag{19}$$

The multivarious general equilibrium relations, $JI + JK + TJ$ in number,

$$p_j \frac{\partial Q^j(V_{1j}, \ldots)}{\partial V_{ij}} = W_i \quad (i = 1, \ldots, I; j = 1, \ldots, J), \tag{20}$$

$$\frac{\partial u^k[q_1^k, \ldots]/\partial q_j^k}{\partial u^k[q_1^k, \ldots]/\partial q_1^k} = \frac{p_j}{p_1} \quad (k = 1, \ldots, K; j = 2, \ldots, J), \tag{21}$$

$$\sum_{j=1}^{J} p_j q_j^k = \sum_{i=1}^{I} W_i V_i^k \quad (k = 1, \ldots, K), \tag{22}$$

$$\sum_{k=1}^{K} q_j^k = Q^j(V_{1j}, \ldots, K_{Ij}) \quad (j = 1, \ldots, J), \tag{23}$$

can be summarized by the $I$ relations from equation 8's $U(V_1, \ldots)$ function:

$$\frac{\partial U\left(\sum_k V_1^k, \ldots, \sum_k V_I^k\right)}{\partial V_i} = \frac{W_i}{P_U} \quad (i = 1, \ldots, I) \tag{24}$$

where $W_i/P_U$ is the real wage of $V_i$ in terms of the $u[\ ]$ measure of output.

The economy becomes a simple Clark sausage machine for producing real-dollar pleasure out of the given factor supplies. The imputation of real income among factors is given by the marginal product the sausage machine defines for the factors. Successful aggregation can go no further.

The reader may be amused to contemplate the simplest possible case of general equilibrium. It is the double Cobb-Douglas case, where all calculations can be done in one's head. Assume constant imputed marginal product shares for factors $i$ in industry $j$:

$$1 = s_{1j} + \cdots + s_{ij} + \cdots + s_{Ij} \quad (j = 1, \ldots, J). \tag{25}$$

Assume constant fractional shares of expenditure on each of the $J$ goods:

$$e_1 + e_2 + \cdots + e_j + \cdots + e_J = 1. \tag{26}$$

Then

$$U = bV_1^{\Sigma_j s_{1j} e_j} \cdots V_I^{\Sigma_j s_{Ij} e_j}, \tag{27}$$

$$\frac{W_i}{W_1} = \frac{V_1}{V_i} \frac{\sum_j s_{ij}}{\sum_j s_{1j}} \quad (i = 2, \ldots, I), \tag{28}$$

$$\frac{P_j}{P_1} = \frac{q_1}{q_j} \frac{e_j}{e_1} \quad (j = 2, \ldots, J). \tag{29}$$

## The Prose Long Spoken

I go from the strongest case for aggregation to the more general sphere, where a version of envelope aggregation has long been utilized at the implicit level. Every time we add marginal curves laterally to define a resultant marginal curve, we are employing envelope aggregation. I describe two familiar instances.

Marshall analyzes the supply of tea. Suppose tea relies solely on lands good only for it. Each amount of homogeneous labor made available to the tea industry gets optimally allocated (by rent charging . . . ) on the land. The lateral sum of the separate acres' marginal-cost or supply curves provides Marshall's long-and-intermediate-run SS curve for the industry.

Change tea to corn and you have Ricardo's case. The corn industry has what we would call a production function. Aggregation is involved, implicitly by Ricardo and explicitly by post-Wicksell economists. The marginal productivity of the aggregate $(L, Q)$ relation gives the real wage; Ricardian rent can be measured as a triangular-area residual.

## Labor Theory of Value as Attempted Aggregation

When labor alone timelessly hunts deer and beaver, Smith's labor theory of value applies. If boy labor differs from man labor, and both differ from girl and woman labor, Marx tries to rescue Smith's theory by defining each person's labor hour as containing so many units of lowest-common-denominator labor. Thus, if boys have the lowest productivity, Marx would *try* to use their labor as the lowest common denominator: for example, one unit in boy labor, two such input units in man labor, three units in girl labor, and five lowest-common-denominator units in an hour of woman's labor. This way, Mozart has $10^9$ of my units in him.

But such envelope aggregation usually is not valid. I beat Mozart at quaternions. I have $10^3$ Mozart units in me. Which is right: Does Samuelson/Mozart equal 1/1 billion, or 1,000? As soon as the ratio of labor efficiencies becomes an endogenous variable for general equilibrium to resolve, the trick of reducing heterogeneous labor inputs to a lowest common denominator will not work. The labor theory of value is *kaput*. (James Mill, admitting that old trees sell for more than their labor of planting, tried to save the labor theory of value by making "time and capital" honorary congealed labor. That way lies comedy.)

## Methodology of Operational Positivism

Clerk Maxwell wrote down the equations that light and electromagnetism must follow. When physicists complained about the mathematical complexity of Maxwell's exposition, Heinrich Hertz properly chastized them by observing that the content of Maxwell's theory was that of his equations, no more and no less. Similarly, the economic theory of consumption is no more and no less than the Slutsky or revealed-preference restrictions it obeys. Envelope aggregation stands or falls with, and is, the maximizing equilibrium relations that obtain in a competitive market. If Soviet economic planning were capricious, with no resemblance to decentralized pricing or to realization of planning maxima, Klein could never expect the partial derivatives of Soviet aggregates to have any systematic relation to wage shares or goods prices. (There is a moral here for Klein's 1946 hope to handle imperfect competition in the aggregation process: Unless the deviations from perfect competition are very balanced, what envelope aggregation adds to crude aggregation will be very hard to obtain.)

Werner Heisenberg was led to his 1925 matrix mechanics by taking a hard-boiled Machian approach to what it is that we can observe. He thought he was following in Einstein's footsteps, in that Einstein's 1905 Special Theory of Relativity can be formulated antiseptically in terms of axioms on what can be observed: the impossibility of measuring "ether drift"; the constancy of speed of light observed to emanate from a body independently of its own velocity. However, in the last half of his life Einstein increasingly used language that people could be forgiven for interpreting as showing some indifference toward what has been and will be observed. Some Einstein admirers have admired him for these anti-Machian sentiments.

In my youth I did not agree with this. After 45 years of observing what does and does not turn out to be fruitful in economic science, I still dissent. Einstein was right to suspect that simple systems will be found to explain much of physics. He was right to reserve judgment about fragmentary experiments that seemed to contradict details of his beautiful synthesis. He was right to eschew piecemeal patchwork. But he would have been wrong to shrug off important empirical discrepancies that were observed repeatedly. And Bohr and other great contemporaries of Einstein were right to carry on with their probabilistic models in defiance of Einstein's hunch that someone might later come up with a better theory.

Although not every branch of science benefits from an axiomatic approach based on observational relations—successful immunology, for example, seems to have had to proceed largely on an *ad hoc* basis—there are some branches that do. Classical thermodynamics is an archetype. Essentially, it is isomorphic with envelope aggregation. For this reason I put in a self-contained appendix to this chapter an economist's way of formulating the relations of that important subject. Inasmuch as Lawerence Klein has been one of the economists who have provided generalizations of the thermodynamic Le Chatelier principle, this is a fitting place to show how the economist's practice of framing theoretical axioms in terms of strict observables can be carried out for classical thermodynamics, the most chastely elegant branch of physics and chemistry.

## Appendix: Some Axiomatic Foundations For Thermodynamics

### 1. Mechanics

Classical mechanics, from Galileo through Newton, Euler, Lagrange, and Hamilton, deals with motions of apples, planets, pendulums, bicycles, and general systems of particles. Implicit in Galileo's analysis of freely falling bodies, and made explicit by Leibniz, is the law of conservation of (mechanical) energy for a (frictionless) system. A frictionless pendulum has the greatest kinetic energy (squared velocity) at the bottom of its swing, when its potential energy is minimal. The sum of a conservative system's kinetic and potential energies is a constant along any motion, conserving the initial value of that sum.

No observed system is completely without friction. As actual systems lose mechanical energy, a rise in "temperature" occurs. Thus, as a weight moves from rest at a higher altitude to rest at a lower altitude, turning thereby a paddle wheel in a fluid, it increases that fluid's temperature. It loses total mechanical energy, and that loss is offset by a rise in the fluid's temperature.

### 2. Thermodynamics

Classical thermodynamics is the subject that deals with such interactions of mechanics and "temperatures." That part of the subject's development dealt with here is associated with Rumford, Sadi Carnot, Kelvin (William Thomson), Mayer, Joule, Helmholtz, Clausius, Maxwell, Gibbs, Cara-théodory, Born, Tisza, and many others. Although there is extensive overlap between my formulation and those of these authors, mine is idiosyncratic in that the formal relations that are important in analytical economics have motivated my choice of physical axioms and the order of their introduction. In the end, of course, the system derived here is isomorphic with that of conventional phenomenological thermodynamics.

### 3. Program

I have eschewed all reference to statistical mechanics, kinetic theory, quantum mechanics, Brownian motion, and other microscopic observations. This abstention is solely for the purpose of characterizing the logical structure of macroscopic (phenomenological) thermodynamics.

I avoid the word *heat*, not because there is any objection in principle to giving a name to certain differences between *work* and *energy* magnitudes, but to forestall implicit theorizing.

I avoid differentials, exact or inexact, such as $-pdv$, or $-pdv + tds$, $ds$, $dQ$, or $-\int pdv$. I do work with derivatives—partial derivatives like $\partial p/\partial v$, with temperature held constant, and ordinary derivatives like $p'[x]$, where $p[x]$ is a well-defined arc along which the behavior of pressure is specified.

For the most part, I do not employ the language of engineering. When I utilize the area of a closed curve in the (pressure, volume) plane, I do not relate it to the "cycle" some engine might be performing. This does not mean that I share Max Born's repugnance against basing thermodynamics on axioms couched in terms of the impossibility of perpetual-motion machines of various kinds. What's wrong with that, aesthetically or methodologically? The mathematical axioms that I do hypothesize undoubtedly can be put into equivalent engineering language.

Finally, much of thermodynamics might as appropriately be called thermo-*statics*. My approach tries (necessarily without complete success, as it itself makes clear) to deal with equilibrium relations, obviating the need to execute *reversible* motions. The irreducible notion of *irreversible* movements is introduced at the beginning to define certain "insulated" or "adiabatic" contours. Then the results of one short Joule experiment, it is shown, do have to be assumed known at some later stage. Beyond that, no irreversibility phenomena are required, nor for that matter any reversibility phenomena as such.[5] (In section 16, I do digress to show how internal energy functions can be defined solely by observing spontaneous irreversible equalizations of empirical temperature.)

## 4. Walls

Assume that any substance, for example a specified mass of water vapor, can be enclosed in walls that define a measurable volume. The surrounding wall may be of two kinds. The pressures of two substances on each side of a rigid wall need not be equal. When we wish to, we can work with a *nonrigid* wall that lets volume expand or contract to cause internal pressure to come into equality with some measurable external pressure. Similarly, our wall may be insulating or *noninsulating* (thermal conducting). By use of Dewar "thermos" flasks, a fluid that looks to the eye red-hot can persist next to external substances that are blue-hot or cold to the touch. By contrast to such an insulating wall, we have noninsulating walls such that one observes that substances they separate show observable changes in properties until finally they approach compatible states. From such reproducible observations one builds up the notion of "equality of temperature" of two substances and of "inequality of (empirical) temperatures."

In considering nonsimple substances that involve the masses of more than one chemical substance—of $M_1, M_2, \ldots$ rather than $M$ alone—we assume that there are impermeable and semipermeable walls that either do or do not let some of the $M_i$ in an internal system interchange with that external system outside the walls. Again, one learns from observation that two substances inside and outside a wall permeable to $M_i$ will in general not stay unchanged in observable properties; rather, their properties will gradually change until they each come to states of compatible rest—equilibrium states. So just as the primitive notion of "temperature differences" can be built up out of crude observational experience, the primitive notion of Gibb's "differences in chemical potential of each mass" can be built up.

Until later, I ignore multivarious masses and concentrate on simple substances with a single $M$, encloseable in a volume of measurable $V$—for example, $H_2O$ in liquid, gaseous, or solid form.

## 5. Overview

Here is a brief preview of my axiomatic procedure. Axiom 1 posits the existence of what familiar expositions call "isotherms." Axiom 2 posits the existence of a second set of observable contours, the "adiabatics." Axiom 3 posits a proportionality property of pressure-volume areas of the curvilinear parallelograms formed by intersections of the two families of contours. Axiom 2 has something of the conventional second law of thermodynamics in it; axiom 3 adds to the others much of the content of the first and second laws. Although the three axioms do together cover most of what holds for thermostatics (that is, for equilibrium states of compatible rest), they fail to determine a privileged zero-origin for Absolute temperature. Carnot's maximal efficiency between two Kelvin temperatures cannot be deduced from this triad of axioms. Yet the triad does define unique Absolute-temperature differences (called "canonical temperature"), canonical entropy, and canonical internal energy, whose differences *along adiabatics* will agree with

Joule's conventional internal energy (and which, by a unique choice of zero-origin for canonical temperature, we can make agree completely with Joule energy). So, if as axiom 4 I posit knowledge of one irreversible experiment—for example, knowledge of how much altitude an external weight loses in making a paddle wheel turn to stir a fluid enough to raise its pressure a small specified amount, while its volume is held constant—then my four-axiom system comes full circle and has all the properties of conventional macroscopic thermodynamics.[6]

### 6. "Zeroth" Law of Thermodynamics

Maxwell and Fowler emphasized that, if substance A is in temperature equilibrium with both B and C independently, then one can predict before observing the fact that B and C will stay in compatible equilibrium with each other after insulating walls between them are replaced by noninsulating walls. The same logical relationship (of things "equal" to a common thing being "equal" to each other) holds for pressure (and, for that matter, for the chemical potential of mass $M_i$, namely $\mu_i$). Something more is involved here methodologically than the truth that holds for arithmetic scalars: $1 + 5 = 2 + 4$ and $3 + 3 = 2 + 4$ implies that $1 + 5 = 3 + 3$. It is a refutable hypothesis whether every observable state of a substance can be arrayed in a one-dimensional temperature ordering that can be put in unique correspondence to the one-dimensional temperature ordering of any other substance. And likewise with respect to the ways masses $(M_1, M_2, \ldots)$ interact across permeable walls. I leave moot whether the pressure a fluid exerts on its external environment can, by definition, be related from the beginning to the scale of arithmetic numbers so that there is no need for Maxwell's zeroth axiom to be separately assumed to hold for pressures.

### 7. Isotherms

A simple substance of unit mass cannot always have its equilibrium states uniquely defined by points in its (pressure, specific volume) space: $(p, V/M) \equiv (p, v)$. But if we make an inessential simplification of avoiding certain reversal phenomena (such as the reversal of water's contraction of volume at lower temperatures that occurs near its freezing temperature under ordinary room atmospheres), we can use the $(p, v)$ space to frame our needed axioms.

AXIOM 1: There is an observable "equation of state." For any substance whose state is characterized by $(p, v)$ coordinates, there exist one-dimensional contours of states that are compatibly in equilibrium when in contact with each other through rigid noninsulating walls. These loci, called *isotherms*, exist and can be written in the form

$$f(p, v) = \vartheta \quad \text{or} \quad F[f(p, v)] = F[\vartheta], \tag{7.1}$$

$$F'[\vartheta] > 0 \gtreqless F''[\vartheta]. \tag{7.2}$$

Similarly, between two or more substances, each of whose states are respectively characterized by $(p_1, v_1)$, $(p_2, v_2)$, ... coordinates, the equations of state for each imply when all are in contact through noninsulating walls that

$$f_1(p_1, v_1) = f_2(p_2, v_2) = \cdots = \vartheta \tag{7.3}$$

or

$$F[f_1(p_1, v_1)] = F[f_2(p_2, v_2)] = \cdots = F[\vartheta] \tag{7.4}$$

where the arbitrary stretching of one "empirical temperature" into another is given by $F[\vartheta]$, which has the property given in the relation 7.2.

*Remarks:* I could avoid working with even one arbitrary empirical temperature metric—$\vartheta$, $F[\vartheta]$, $f_i(p_i, v_i)$, ...—by working with the observable invariant isotherm slopes:

$$\left(\frac{\partial p_i}{\partial v_i}\right)_{\text{temp}} = R_i(p_i, v_i). \tag{7.5}$$

Also, instead of choosing from $[p, v, \vartheta]$ the pair $[p, v]$ to specify the system's state, we could even more conveniently use $[\vartheta, v]$ as independent variables to specify its state. Then equation 7.3 would be written

$$p_1 = \Pi_1(\vartheta, v_1), \quad p_2 = \Pi_2(\vartheta, v_2), \ldots. \tag{7.6}$$

More complicated systems involving different chemical masses, with variables $(V, M_1, M_2, \ldots, p, \mu_1, \mu_2, \ldots)$, have further equations of state that are in principle identifiable by observation of what is required for states to be compatible in equilibrium when connected by permeable walls.

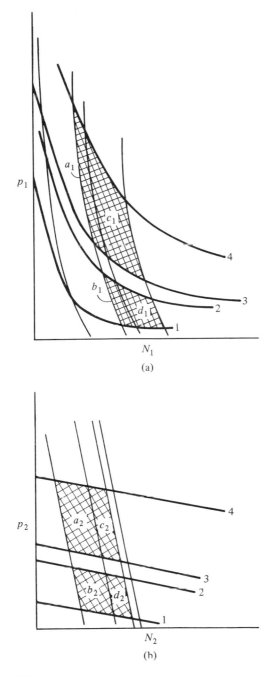

$p_1$

$a_1$

$c_1$

4

$b_1$

3

2

$d_1$

1

$N_1$

(a)

$p_2$

4

$a_2$

$c_2$

3

2

$b_2$

$d_2$

1

$N_2$

(b)

**Figure 1**
The four isotherms marked 1, 2, 3, and 4 for the substance in part a will respectively be in equilibrium with points on the four isotherms for the substance in part b. Each substance's four steeper adiabatics mark off with respective isotherms shaded areas that must have the proportionality property: $a_1/b_1 = c_1/d_1$ and $a_2/b_2 = c_2/d_2$. Also, between substances, areas formed by compatible isotherms must have the proportionality property: $a_1/b_1 = a_2/b_2$.

## 8. Adiabatic Contours

Figures 1a and 1b show dashed contours also. These are definable by specified operational procedures, and may be called adiabatics if none of the connotations familiar with that name are prematurely read into them.

Another name for any one of these contours would be this: Starting from an arbitrary point $(p^0, v^0)$, the other points on its adiabatic contour are those frontier points that bound the region of $(p, v)$ points that can never be reached from $(p^0, v^0)$ when the substance is surrounded by perfectly insulating walls, no matter what mechanical work we do on the system—that is, no matter how we stir its fluids by paddle-wheel motions, or push its piston walls back and forth rapidly or indefinitely slowly.

It is a fact of nature—a fact about "irreversibility," if you wish—that adiabatics exist and can be taken as given by observation. Nature might have been constructed otherwise. So our second axiom asserts the existence of "adiabatic contours."

AXIOM 2: For each simple substance, there exist well-defined adiabatic contours in its $(p_i, v_i)$ space. Thus, for any $(p_i^0, v_i^0)$ initial point, there exist a set of points that could never be reached from it by any mechanical movement of its insulating walls or by any mechanical stirrings of its contents or other processes that can be performed on it by the use of external mechanical work. The remaining points in the $(p_i, v_i)$ space can be reached from $(p_i^0, v_i^0)$ by performing such external mechanical work on it. The limit points of this second "available set" form the one-dimensional adiabatic contour going through $(p_i^0, v_i^0)$.

Mathematically, an empirical numbering of the adiabatics can be defined for each substance by the empirical functions

$$a_1(p_1, v_1) = \text{constants}, \quad a_2(p_2, v_2) = \text{constants}, \ldots \tag{8.1}$$

or by arbitrary monotone stretchings of any such empirical measures:

$$A_1[a_1(p_1, v_1)], A_2[a_2(p_2, v_2)], \ldots \tag{8.2}$$

$$A_i'[\ ] > 0 \gtrless A_i''[\ ] \quad (i = 1, 2, \ldots). \tag{8.3}$$

*Remarks:* To avoid use of an arbitrary empirical numbering of the adiabatic contours, I could have worked with observable invariant adiabatic slopes in the $(p_i, v_i)$ planes, namely with

$$0 \geq \left(\frac{\partial p_i}{\partial v_i}\right)_{ad} = \alpha_i(p_i, v_i) \quad (i = 1, 2, \ldots). \tag{8.4}$$

By use of limitingly slow movements of the surrounding insulating walls—that is, by what are called quasi-static, reversible movements—the exact shapes of the adiabatic contours could be determined experimentally. As an alternative to my exposition, if you had available to you Joule's first law of thermodynamics, ensuring the existence of an internal energy function, $u_i(p_i, v_1)$, then you could deduce the adiabatic slopes of equation 8.4 from the fact that the difference between $u_i$ at two points on the same adiabatic must equal the integral $-\int p_i[x] v_i'[x] dx$, evaluated on the arc of the adiabatic between those points. This implies

$$\alpha_i(p_i, v_i) = \frac{-p_i - \partial u_i(p_i, v_i)/\partial v_i}{\partial u_i(p_i, v_i)/\partial p_i}. \tag{8.5}$$

The existence of the equation of state and its exact functional form, unlike those of the adiabatic, cannot be deduced from mere knowledge of $u_i(p_i, v_i)$—that is to say, it cannot be deduced from the first law of thermodynamics alone.

## 9. The Proportional-Area Property

Axioms 1 and 2, which assert the existence of knowable isotherms and adiabatics, do not exhaust the verifiable regularities of nature. Brute experience shows that isotherms and adiabatics are always related in a singular way involving a proportional-area property.

From the way things are, any four areas on the $(p_i, v_i)$ diagram formed by intersections of any four isotherms with any four adiabatics must be in proportion. Thus, for the marked areas in figures 1a and 1b,

$$\frac{a_1}{b_1} = \frac{c_1}{d_1}, \quad \frac{a_2}{p_2} = \frac{c_2}{d_2}. \tag{9.1}$$

Moreover, if the four temperatures used are compatible ones between the two substances—so that points in each diagram on an isotherm marked with, say, 3 are in compatible thermal equilibrium with each other, and likewise for those on the respective isotherms marked 4—then between substances we must have

$$\frac{a_1}{b_1} = \frac{a_2}{b_2}. \tag{9.2}$$

This is a basic regularity of nature, which among other things could have been deduced from the conventional axioms concerning the first and second laws of thermodynamics. I begin with this observational fact as my axiom 3, which goes as follows.

AXIOM 3: The ("Carnot-circuit") areas defined between specified isotherms and adiabatics, as measured by $\int p[x]v'[x]dx$ integrals taken along the defined $(p[x], v[x])$ arcs, must have the equiproportionality property, both within a simple substance and between any two substances in compatible equilibria.

Axiom 3 is singularly restrictive on the facts. If nature had not displayed it, we should never have expected it to prevail. (To be sure, it would not be easy to imagine how the world would behave if it did admit of perpetual-motion machines of different kinds. A whimsical Einstein might assert that God could hardly have invented a different world, thereby answering Bohr's objection: "Who are we to tell Him his business?")

My overview noted that axioms 1–3 can generate the full set of thermostatic equilibrium relations that obtain in nature. But the point of my present selected order of imposition of axioms is to identify what observable facts of thermodynamics *cannot* be deduced from thermostatic equilibrium relations. In particular, a preferred origin of zero Absolute temperature cannot be deduced from axioms 1–3. We must add to them some subset of the (Carathéodory-Joule) first law of thermodynamics to be able to deduce a privileged Absolute Zero for canonical temperature and to be able to deduce a measurable "heat" and Carnot's coefficient of universal efficiency attainable at best between two specified empirical temperatures.

## 10. Diagrammatic Recapitulation

Figure 1a shows the isotherms and adiabatics for some specified mass of a gas. These contours look like those of a "perfect gas," but that coincidence plays no part in the development. (The facts that adiabatics must be steeper than the isotherms and that neither can be positively sloped constitute one version of the so-called Le Chatelier principle.) Figure 1a verifies the equiproportionality-of-areas property: $a_1/b_1 =$

$a_2/b_2$, and so on. Figure 1b shows isotherms and adiabatics for another simple substance. They are drawn as straight lines for expositional convenience only; but, locally, linearity is an admissible physical case. Again, figure 1b shows the $a_2/b_2 = c_2/d_2$ property of axiom 3.

When the two substances are in contact through noninsulating (rigid) walls, any isotherm of figure 1a is compatible with but one particular isotherm of figure 1b. Points on respective contours marked 1, 2, 3, and 4 in figure 1a are found by observation to be compatible in equilibrium with contours marked 1, 2, 3, and 4 in figure 1b.[7] It will be seen that, between the substances, axiom 3's area property is satisfied: $a_1/b_1$ is indeed equal to $a_2/b_2$ or to $c_2/d_2$.

*Remark:* When the isotherms alone are drawn on the diagram, there is no way to say when "one of them is halfway between two others." I could have used $1^2 = 1$, $2^2 = 4$, $3^2 = 9$, and $4^2 = 16$ to label the isotherms—then 9 would certainly not be "halfway" between 16 and and 4; and, actually, the isotherm marked 3 in figure 1a or 1b is not in any useful sense halfway between those marked 2 and 4.

The same lack of a natural metric holds for the adiabatics drawn by themselves. Only when axiom 3 interrelates them in its special way will our *p-v* areas provide a natural canonical metric for the isotherms (canonical temperature differences) and for the adiabatics (canonical "entropy" differences). (Although each numbered isotherm in figure 1a does relate exactly to the labeled isotherm in 1b, there is complete independence between 1a's and 1b's respective adiabatics.)

Figure 2a shows how the nonmetric empirical ordering, $\vartheta$, can be converted into a privileged metric of canonical temperature, $T_c - T_c^0$:

$$T_c - T_c^0 = \Theta[\vartheta], \quad \Theta'[\ ] > 0 \gtrless 0 \tag{10.1}$$

where the $\Theta[\ ]$ function is made definite by use of the horizontally shaded areas. We may choose our scale unit of canonical temperature arbitrarily—say, by calling the freezing point of water at standard atmospheric pressure 0 and its boiling point 1. (This convention is to hold as applied to other substances than water. Their canonical temperature is 0 when they are in equilibrium with icewater, even if their own melting point is much lower or higher.) Neither substance in figure 1a or 1b is water. Figure 2a's substance is the same as 1b's, as can be seen from its axes being labeled with $(p_2, v_2)$.

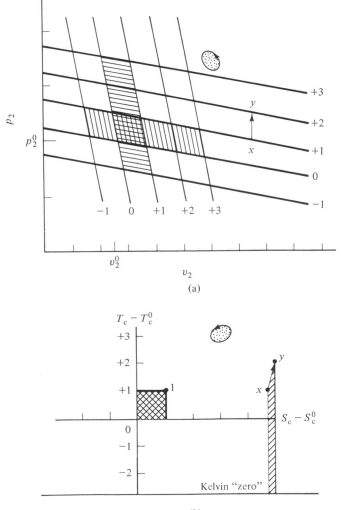

(a)

(b)

**Figure 2**

Part a of this figure is figure 1b, but now with the proportionality-of-area property used to define the metric of equally spaced isotherms and adiabatics. This gives the metrics for canonical temperature (shown in part b on the $T_c - T_c^0$ vertical axis) and canonical entropy (shown in part b on the horizontal axis). The area between the arbitrary "zero" point and the "unity" point must be the same in both diagrams, by construction. Every closed area in part a maps into a closed area in part b with the same area, by construction. Note the dot-shaded circular areas. To find a natural Kelvin "zero" that converts any canonical temperature to unique Absolute temperature, consider external Joule work observed to be required to move from $x$ to $y$ in part a (by frictional stirring or otherwise.) The $xy$ arrow in part b must have the area under it equated to the Joule work measured, which provides the equation for $\bar{\theta}*$ that makes $T_c - T_c^0 + \bar{\theta}*$ equal to $T$.

Pick the $(p_2^0, v_2^0)$ point marked "0" as our arbitrary origin for canonical temperature. Pick the $(p_2^1, v_2^1)$ point marked "1" as our unit-scaling point. The doubly shaded area thus selected gives us our unit for canonical temperature (and, as we will see, for our canonical entropy and canonical "internal energy").

Using the two arbitrarily selected adiabatics, as we measure off the isotherms that divide their areas in equal amounts, as shown by the blocks, we deduce the canonical numberings $+3$, $+2$, $+1$, 0, and $-1$ for the isotherms. These are the defined canonical temperatures, $T - T^0$, for those isotherms; thus, the $\Theta[\vartheta]$ function in equation 10.1 can be defined as accurately as we wish.

Similarly, using the arbitrarily selected base isotherms, we can divide the areas between them into equal blocks of subareas with adiabatic boundaries, as shown by the vertically shaded blocks. Thus, we deduce the canonical numberings for the adiabatics: $+3$, $+2$, $+1$, $+0$, $-1$. Call this $s - s^0$, or, for substance 2, $s_2 - s_2^0$. (If the two substances are plotted with equal areas for their $(0, 1)$ points, entropies will be dimensionally addable across substances.)

## 11. Canonical Internal Energy

Figure 2b plots the canonical $(T_2^c, s_2)$ space. Every point in $(p_2, v_2)$ maps into a unique $(T_2^c, s_2)$, and vice versa. Moreover, by axiom 3's area property, the $(T_2^c, s_2)$ space relates to the $(p_2, v_2)$ space in the exact way to make the area inside any closed curve in 2a exactly equal to the area inside the implied closed curve in figure 2b. More precisely, by construction, the signed area formed by traversing the closed contour in figure 2a in the counterclockwise direction must exactly equal the signed area traversed by going in the counterclockwise direction around the implied closed contour in figure 2b.[8]

Mathematically, around closed arcs that map into each other on $0 \leq x \leq 1$, $(p[x], v[x])$, and $(T_c[x], s[x])$,

$$\int_0^1 p[x] v'[x] dx = \int_0^1 (T_c[x] - T_c^0) s'[x] dx. \tag{11.1}$$

(Here I have omitted the subscript 2 on $p$, $v$, $T_c$, and $s$, since axiom 3 makes this property hold for any substance.)

Around any closed arc of equilibrium-compatible points, the following line integral vanishes independent of path:

$$-\int \{p[x]v'[x]dx + (T_c[x] - T_c^0)s'[x]dx\} = 0. \tag{11.2}$$

Therefore, between any two points, such as $(p^0, v^0) = (p[x^0], v[x^0])$ and $(p, v) = (p[x], v[x])$, the following line integral is independent of the path connecting $(p^0, v^0, T_c^0, s^0)$ and $(p, v, T_c, s)$:

$$u_c^*(p, v) - u_c^*(p^0, v^0)$$

$$= \int_{x^0}^{x} \{-p[y]v'[y] + (T_c[y] - T_c^0)s'[y]\} dy. \tag{11.3}$$

Thus, axiom 3 enables us to define canonical (internal) energy differences as the sum of $\int -pdv$ and $\int (T_c - T_c^0)ds$ line integrals. As equation 11.3 shows, we can express all this as simple definite integrals of a single $x$ variable.

Remark: Instead of specifying $(p^0, v^0)$ and $(p, v)$, we could have picked from $(p, v, T_c, s)$ the specified pair $(v, s)$ and written $u_c^*$ as a function of them; or we could have specified the pair $(T_c, v)$, and written $u_c^*$ as a function of them; or we could have picked the pair $(T_c, p)$ and written the internal energy (of the unit mass) as a function of them. Finally, just as we have been able to use $(p, v)$ as our independent variables in regions where volume-temperature relations do not change direction, we could have picked $(T_c, s)$ as the independent variables to define $u^*$ in that region. Most generally, for a given mass, any one choice from the conjugate pairs $(-p, v)$ and $(T_c, s)$ can be selected as independent variables; the $4 = 2^2$ pairs of independent variables that are always admissible then become $(v, s)$, $(v, T_c)$, $(-p, s)$, and $(-p, T_c)$.

## 12. Nonuniqueness of Canonical Energy Differences

There has been defined no natural, privileged zero for canonical temperature. Instead of $T_c$, we could use $T_c + \Theta$, $-\infty < \Theta < \infty$. Indeed, we can add to equation 11.3's integral an arbitrary linear term $\overline{\Theta}s'[x]$ and still get an (energy) integral that is independent of path. So it is natural to free ourselves from the tyranny of the particular $(p^0, v^0)$ arbitrary origin that we happened to use. Instead of the unique, arbitrary $u^*(p, v)$ of equation 11.3, we can generalize to a one-parameter family of canonical internal energies:

$$u_c(p,v) - u_c(p^0,v^0) = u_c^*(p,v) - u_c^*(p^0,v^0) + \overline{\Theta}(s - s^0)$$

$$= \int \{-p[x]v'[x] + (T_c[x] - T_c^0 + \overline{\Theta})s'[x]\}dx.$$

$$(12.1)$$

A numerical example is illuminating. Consider figure 1a, whose isotherms and adiabatics resemble those of a "perfect gas." These isotherms and adiabatics can be given empirical numbers that respectively satisfy the following formulas:

$$pv = \text{constants} = 9,\tag{12.2}$$

$$pv^3 = \text{constants} = \sigma.\tag{12.3}$$

Axiom 3's area proportionalities can be verified by elementary integrations. This assures us that, after we select a $(p^0, v^0)$ as our local arbitrary origin and a $(p^1, v^1)$ as our arbitrary unity point, we can define canonical temperature and canonical entropy by the following formulas:

$$T_c - T_c^0 = \frac{pv - p^0v^0}{p^1v^1 - p^0v^0},\tag{12.4}$$

$$s - s^0 = \frac{\ln(pv^3) - \ln([p^0][v^0]^3)}{\ln([p^1][v^1]^3) - \ln([p^0][v^0]^3)}.\tag{12.5}$$

Then our $u^*(p, v)$ and our family of canonical internal energy functions can be defined by line integrals that are independent of path and yield

$$u^*(p,v) - u^*(p^0,v^0) = \frac{3}{2}\frac{pv - p^0v^0}{p^1v^1 - p^0v^0},\tag{12.6}$$

$$u_c(p,v) - u_c(p^0,v^0) = u_c^*(p,v) - u^*(p^0,v^0)$$

$$= \frac{3}{2}\frac{pv - p^0v^0}{p^1v^1 - p^0v^0} + \overline{\Theta}\frac{\ln(pv^3/p^0[v^0]^3)}{\ln(p^1[v^1]^3/p^0[v^0]^3)}.\tag{12.7}$$

An engineer confronted with these formulas would simplify them by choosing to set

$$\overline{\Theta} = p^0v^0/(p^1v^1 - p^0v^0).\tag{12.8}$$

Then his canonical energy simplifies to be proportional to the product of $p$ and $v$. But it is purely an accident that he can find for a "perfect gas" such a simplifying choice. How any actual substance (even a rarefied gas) will behave when very cold cannot be predicted from how much its volume shrinks between the boiling and freezing points of water.

Figure 2b shows how arbitrary are the $\int T_c ds$ areas in their dependence on where one bases the horizontal axis by arbitrarily choosing an origin for canonical temperature. The shaded area "under" the curve would have been much larger if a large $\overline{\Theta}$ had been arbitrarily added to $T_c - T_c^0$.

## 13. Joule Internal Energy

Joule's experimental vindication of the first law of thermodynamics can give us a privileged origin for canonical temperature. Joule established that, in moving any enclosed insulated system from one state $(p_1^0, v_1^0)$ to another $(p, v)$, always exactly the same external work (or sacrifice of external mechanical energy) is implied—no matter whether the movement is accomplished quickly or slowly, reversibly or irreversibly, quasi-statically or otherwise, and no matter whether the task is done by stirring fluids against friction, by moving walls against internal pressure, by generating electric currents that pass through resistances and warm up the internal fluids and solids, or by other means. Thus, Joule can in principle supply us with still another internal energy function. Call it $u_J(p, v) - u_J(p^0, v^0)$. It must not be confused with $u_c^*(p, v) - u_c^*(p^0, v^0)$. As yet, we have no warrant for identifying it with any one of the infinity of canonical energy functions defined in equation 12.1.

When I add a fourth axiom to axioms 1–3, I will be able to show that Joule internal energy is in fact one of our family of canonical energies. So, if we have even one small Joule (irreversible) experiment on any one substance or system of substances, we shall be able to identify a privileged $\overline{\Theta}^*$ to provide us with Kelvin's Absolute Zero for temperature. At long last, axioms 1–4 will cover essentially the same ground as conventional thermodynamics. I have shown we can get along with no use of the concept of "heat." Note that I never wrote down "$Q$", or "$dQ$", or "$\dslash Q$", or "$dQ/T$". Though we do not need the "heat" concept for axioms 1–3, axiom 4 restores the right to use it wherever we find it useful.

But first we must add the axiom that, together with axioms 1–3, assures us that there will be a unique choice of $\overline{\Theta}^*$ that converts

$$u_J(p, v) - u_J(p^0, v^0) \equiv u_c^*(p, v) - u_c^*(p^0, v^0) + \overline{\Theta}^*[s - s^0]$$

$$\equiv u_c^*(p, v) - u_c^*(p^0, v^0) + \overline{\Theta}^*[s(p, v) - s(p^0, v^0)]$$

$$(13.1)$$

into a valid entity.

## 14. The Final Axiom

Now, for the first time, consider the measurable amount of external work needed to move the system from one adiabatic to another (possibly to a close-by contour). Let $(p^\dagger, v^\dagger)$ and $(p^{\dagger\dagger}, v^{\dagger\dagger})$ be on different adiabatics, and label the two points so that by external mechanical work operating through the insulated walls of the the system we can move from $(p^\dagger, v^\dagger)$ to $(p^{\dagger\dagger}, v^{\dagger\dagger})$. Select units of work that agree with the units of $\int p\, dv$ integrals. Join the points by arcs

$$(p[x], v[x], (T_c[x] - T^0), s[x]), \quad 0 \le x \le 1$$

and let the work, $W_J[x]$, be an observable measurement.

Warning: How quickly or slowly Joule makes his measurements has nothing to do with the "speed" with which we traverse the arcs or with their geometric "lengths." $W_J[x]$ is taken to be observed. Its derivative, $W_J'[x]$, is taken to be an observable positive number, as for example $W_J'[0]$ at $x = 0$.

AXIOM 4: Select out of the one-parameter infinity of canonical energies the one that has its parameter $\overline{\Theta}*$ in equation 12.1 such that it will agree with the measured Joule energy, $u_J(p, v) - u_J(p^0, v^0)$, or (what is the same thing) with $W_J[x]$, on the arc connecting $(p^\dagger, v^\dagger)$ and $(p^{\dagger\dagger}, v^{\dagger\dagger})$. In particular, if we write $u_c^*(p[x], v[x]) - u_c^*(p^\dagger, v^\dagger)$ as $W_c^*[x]$ and $u_c(p[x], v[x]) - u_c(p^\dagger, v^\dagger)$ as $W_c[x] = W_c[x; \overline{\Theta}] = W_c^*[x] + \overline{\Theta}(s[x] - s^0)$, this imposes the single (point) condition to determine $\overline{\Theta}*$ as the root of

$$W_c'[0] = W_c^{*\prime}[0] + \overline{\Theta}* s'[0] = W_J'[0], \tag{14.1}$$

$$\overline{\Theta}* = (W_J'[0] - W_c^{*\prime}[0])/s'[0]. \tag{14.2}$$

This uniquely identifies the $\overline{\Theta}*$ that converts canonical temperature with its arbitrary origin into Kelvin Absolute temperature, $T$, with its natural origin. Specifically,

$$T = T_c - T_c^0 + \overline{\Theta}*. \tag{14.3}$$

Axioms 1–4 imply that the chosen canonical energy agrees everywhere with the observable Joule energy:

$$u_c[p,v] - u_c^0[p^0,v^0]$$
$$= u_c^*[p,v] - u_c^*[p^0,v^0] + \overline{\Theta}^*[s(p,v) - s(p^0,v^0)]$$
$$\equiv u_J[p,v] - u_J[p^0,v^0]. \tag{14.4}$$

To see why, recall that the adiabatics that Joule's $u_J(p,v)$ would define must be the same ones that our $u_c(p,v)$'s will all define. The isotherms Joule's function will define, by the relation

$$\left(\frac{\partial U_J}{\partial s}\right)_v = T, \tag{14.5}$$

must yield the same observable equations of state defined by

$$\left(\frac{\partial u_c^*}{\partial s}\right)_v = T_c - T_c^0 \quad \text{or} \quad \left(\frac{\partial[u_c^* + \Theta^* s]}{\partial s}\right)_v = T_c - T_c^0 + \overline{\Theta}^*. \tag{14.6}$$

To see that my axioms 1–4 imply testable, refutable restrictions on the observations, note that they could be falsified if any exception to Joule's first law could be observed: If you could go from $(p^\dagger, v^\dagger)$ to $(p^{\dagger\dagger}, v^{\dagger\dagger})$ with two different expenditures of external mechanical work performed on the system surrounded by insulating walls, that would invalidate the system defined by axioms 1–4.

Figure 2b shows how the crucial $\overline{\Theta}^*$ can be determined from a single irreversible measurement. In the beginning we have no Absolute Zero axis at the bottom of figure 2b. We know from any elementary physics text that, on the Celsius scale, it should come at a distance below the melting point of water (marked "0" in figure 2a) that is about 2.7316 times the distance by which the melting point is below the boiling point of water (marked "1" in figure 2a).[9]

Now consider a Joule experiment that takes the system from $x$ to $y$ in figure 2a. Since the volumes are the same in this northward movement, and since by hypothesis the system is surrounded by an insulating wall, suppose that the transition occurs by a paddle wheel's stirring the fluid until it is warmed enough to raise its pressure from $x$ to $y$. We measure how much external work in the form of a falling external weight is needed to turn the paddle wheel the requisite amount. We record the numerical external work, which Joule treats as the increment to his internal energy $u_J$.

By Axiom 4, that numerical work must equal an observable area in figure 2b. The arc $xy$ in figure 2a maps into the arc $xy$ in figure 2b. Under axiom 4, we must put our Absolute Zero axis for $T_c$ (that is, for $T = T_c - T_c^0 + \overline{\Theta}*$) just far enough below $ab$ so that the area $zyxa$ just equals our Joule experiment's numerical work. (Thereafter, axioms 1–4 enable us to predict the numerical results of all-new Joule experiments. The system is far from a tautology; it is a set of falsifiable hypotheses about reality.)

## 15. Additivity

Some axiomatic treatments of thermodynamics stipulate a separate axiom that entropy and energy be additive magnitudes. No fifth axiom to this effect need be stipulated in addition to the present axiom 1–4. Areas are addable. It comes as a theorem of the axiom system that entropies and internal energies are addable. Thus, twice the mass, $M$, at unchanged pressure ($p$) and unchanged temperature ($\vartheta$ or $T$), will imply twice the canonical entropies and energies. First-degree homogeneity applies to all the extensive functions:

$$S = Ms, \quad U_c = Mu_c, \quad V = Mv. \tag{15.1}$$

More specific,

$$s - s^0 = s(p, T) = (S - S^0)/M, \tag{15.2}$$

$$u_c - u_c^0 = u_c(p, T) = (U_c - U_c^0)/M, \tag{15.3}$$

$$v = v(p, T) = V/M. \tag{15.4}$$

Also, consider different masses of the same substance, $\overline{M}'$ and $\overline{M}''$, each contained with fixed volumes by rigid impermeable walls. If, first, the walls are insulating, the observed pressures and specific volumes, ($p', v'$; $p'', v''$), are independent. What can we predict for equilibrium if, now, the rigid wall separating the two masses of the same substance is made to be noninsulating? Although the two subsystems' pressures can still differ, their temperatures must, in equilibrium, be equal. From the empirical equations of state, for $V'/M' = \overline{v}'$ and $V''/M'' = \overline{v}''$ given, we have

$$\vartheta = f(\overline{v}', p') = f(\overline{v}'', p''). \tag{15.5}$$

Here we have three unknowns $(\vartheta, p', p'')$, two known parameters $(\bar{v}', \bar{v}'')$, and only two equations. From the data given we are unable to determine a unique $(p', p'')$ equilibrium. A one-dimensional continuum of admissible equilibria is determined by equation 15.5. Those same $(p', p'')$ equilibria can be generated by an alternative formulation involving the canonical entropies and canonical energies of the two subsystems.

Every total of canonical entropies, $S' + S''$, must divide itself between the two subsystems so as to minimize the summed internal energies, $U' + U''$. The equilibria configurations of equation 15.5 all belong to the minimizing solution of the following problem:

$$\underset{p', p''}{\text{Min}} \left[ \bar{M}' u_c^*(p', \bar{v}') + \bar{M}'' u_c^*(p'', \bar{v}'') \right]$$

$$\text{subject to } \bar{M}' s(p', \bar{v}') + \bar{M}'' s(p'', \bar{v}'')$$

$$= S \, (= S' + S''). \tag{15.6}$$

Call the minimized value $\mathscr{W}_c^*(\bar{V}'/\bar{M}', \bar{V}''/\bar{M}'', S, \bar{M}', \bar{M}'')$. Then, for every assigned total $S$, we have equilibrium solutions for $(p', p'', T_c - T_c^0)$ given by the envelope relations

$$p' = - \frac{\partial \mathscr{W}_c^*(\bar{v}', \bar{v}'', S, \bar{M}', \bar{M}'')}{\partial \bar{v}'},$$

$$p'' = - \frac{\partial \mathscr{W}_c^*(\bar{v}', \bar{v}'', S, \bar{M}', \bar{M}'')}{\partial \bar{v}''}, \tag{15.7}$$

$$T_c - T_c^0 = \frac{\partial \mathscr{W}_c^*(\bar{v}', \bar{v}'', S, \bar{M}', \bar{M}'')}{\partial S}.$$

If we like, we can replace $u_c^*[\ ]$ by $u_c[\ ] = u^* + \bar{\Theta}(s - s^0)$. This adds to $\mathscr{W}^*(\ )$ the term $\bar{\Theta}(S - S^0)$, and to $T_c - T_c^0$ the term $\bar{\Theta}$. If $\bar{\Theta} = \bar{\Theta}^*$, so that $u_c(\ )$ becomes Joule's $u_J(\ )$, the same formalism holds.

## 16. Time Rise in Entropy

Instead of minimizing $U' + U''$ for fixed $S' + S''$, so long as $\bar{\Theta}$ is enough positive to keep $T - T^0 + \bar{\Theta}$ positive we can as well maximize entropy, $S' + S''$, for fixed total energy, $U' + U''$, and generate the same equilibria. Which is a better formulation? At the level of thermostatics it makes no difference, since the same infinity of $(p', p'', T_c - T_c^0)$ points represent the possible equilibria respecting the equation of state and the assigned specific volumes. But it does make a difference if dynamically we are to be able to predict the actual unique terminal state that a prescribed initial state will spontaneously lead to.

For temporal movements, from a prior equilibrium to a new equilibrium achieved dynamically spontaneously and under assurance that no external work has been done on the combined system, the combined total Joule internal energy of the system may be dynamically assumed to remain constant in time. If that can be stipulated—and to do so takes us outside of the thermostatics here axiomatized—then it will be seen to be more convenient to maximize summed entropy for the assigned initial summed Joule internal energy. (Warning: Now we must use $u_J(\ )$'s, not any old one of the $u_c(\ )$'s.)

Return to the system just discussed, which has masses $\overline{M}'$ and $\overline{M}''$ of the same substance. First, it has them in rigid, impermeable insulating walls that define fixed specific volumes $(\overline{v}', \overline{v}'')$ and permit unequal temperatures. Our four unknowns begin at $(p'_a, \vartheta'_a; p''_a, \vartheta''_a)$.

Now let the connecting wall be made noninsulating. Eventually, in brute fact, the system will change dynamically, from initial a, until it comes to rest at a rendezvous terminal equilibrium, b $(p'_b, \vartheta'_b = \vartheta''_b, p''_b)$. Axioms 1–4 do not have enough dynamic content to answer this specific question about behavior over real time. But if we are told dynamically that summed Joule internal energy cannot change in the absence of external work done on the system, that will provide the minimal new knowledge about dynamic behavior over time to enable us to reduce equation 15.5's or 15.7's one-dimensional continuum of admissible equilibrium rendezvous to the single true physical rendezvous.

How? If the minimized $U'_J + U''_J$ in equation 15.5 must have the same total as the given initial $U'_J + U''_J$, namely $\overline{M}' u_J(\overline{v}', p'_a) + \overline{M}'' u_J(\overline{v}'', p''_a)$— for the reason that external mechanical energy has not been changed— then we can solve for the unique $S$ in equations 15.6 and 15.7 that satisfies this requirement. That is, we can solve for $S_b$ the implicit equation

$$\mathscr{W}_J(v', v'', S, \overline{M}', \overline{M}'') = \overline{M}' u_J(\overline{v}', p'_a) + \overline{M}'' u_J(\overline{v}', p''_a). \tag{16.1}$$

Then, putting this $S_b$ into equation 15.7 gives us our unique terminal equilibrium state $(p'_b, p''_b, \vartheta_b)$.

Rather than solve an implicit equation, we can more elegantly utilize the maximum-entropy formulation:

$$\mathscr{S}(\bar{v}', \bar{v}'', \bar{U}_{\mathrm{J}}, \bar{M}', \bar{M}'') = \operatorname*{Max}_{p', p''}[\bar{M}'s(p', \bar{v}') + \bar{M}''s(p'', \bar{v}'')] \tag{16.2}$$

subject to

$$\bar{M}'u_{\mathrm{J}}(p', \bar{v}') + \bar{M}''u_{\mathrm{J}}(p'', \bar{v}'') = \bar{M}'u_{\mathrm{J}}(p'_{\mathrm{a}}, \bar{v}') + \bar{M}''u_{\mathrm{J}}(p''_{\mathrm{a}}, v''_{\mathrm{a}}) = \bar{U}_{\mathrm{J}}.$$

Then the following envelope relations give our proper unique terminal equilibrium:

$$p'_{\mathrm{b}} = \frac{\partial \mathscr{S}(\bar{v}', \bar{v}'', \bar{U}_{\mathrm{J}}, \bar{M}', \bar{M}'')/\partial \bar{v}'}{\partial \mathscr{S}(\bar{v}', \bar{v}'', \bar{U}_{\mathrm{J}}, \bar{M}', \bar{M}'')/\partial \bar{U}_{\mathrm{J}}}, \tag{16.3}$$

$$p''_{\mathrm{b}} = \frac{\partial \mathscr{S}(\bar{v}', \bar{v}'', \bar{U}_{\mathrm{J}}, \bar{M}', \bar{M}'')/\partial v''}{\partial \mathscr{S}(\bar{v}', \bar{v}'', \bar{U}_{\mathrm{J}}, \bar{M}', \bar{M}'')/\partial \bar{U}_{\mathrm{J}}}, \tag{16.4}$$

$$T^{-1} = \partial \mathscr{S}(\bar{v}, \bar{v}, \bar{U}_{\mathrm{J}}, \bar{M}', \bar{M}'')/\partial \bar{U}_{\mathrm{J}}. \tag{16.5}$$

The same formalism would enable us to predict where the system will reach a third equilibrium if, after it is at rest at b, we unlock its rigid separating wall and let its subvolumes adjust until pressure equality obtains as well as temperature equality. The variables $v'$ and $v''$ then adjust to maximize $S' + S''$ for unchanged $U'_{\mathrm{J}} + U''_{\mathrm{J}}$ and $V' + V''$.

## 17. Nonsimple Systems

So far I have been considering simple substances. Each is simple because its state depends only on the variables $V, S, M$, with intensive properties that depend only on specific variables $(V/M, S/M) = (v, m)$. Readers of Born and Carathéodory will suspect that my two-variable systems enabled me to avoid the complexity of Pfaffian differential expressions and the problem of whether they satisfy "integrability conditions" and can be made to be proportional to exact differentials. That suspicion is only partially justified. Thus, as soon as I consider equilibria between two or more simple substances, each contained within its impermeable walls or even between subsystems that involve a single simple substance, my functions are already in a space of variables with dimensionality much greater than 2. If I wrote down the usual Pfaffian for such systems, they would indeed be testable for integrability conditions of the type that interested Carathéodory explicitly and conventional physicists implicitly. The point I must make is this: Axioms 1–3 do imply, as theorems, the requisite independence-of-path integrals in the higher-than-two-dimensional spaces.

Still, a word is needed for systems that are neither themselves simple substances nor equilibrium combinations of enclosed simple substances. Thus, consider chemical problems where two or more different chemical masses ($M_1$ for hydrogen and $M_2$ for oxygen, for example) interact. They (and their implied chemical compounds) share a volume and provide the observer with a fluid whose pressure and (empirical) temperature depend on more than two specific variables. Thus, 7.3's equation of state might now have to be written as

$$\vartheta = F(p; V, M_1, M_2) \equiv F(p; 1, M_1/V, M_2/V). \tag{17.1}$$

Now that we have added a new intrinsic variable, a second independent equation of state will be observable. In conventional terms, what Gibbs called "chemical potentials"—$(\mu_1, \mu_2)$, corresponding respectively to $(M_1, M_2)$—are new variables an observer could measure. (Remark: Conventionally, the measurable Joule energy function would be used, but here axioms 1–4 could be used after natural generalizations.)

The second independent equation of state might be observed as

$$\lambda_1 = \phi(p; V, M_1, M_2) = \phi(p; 1, M_1/V, M_2/V). \tag{17.2}$$

Finally, brute experimentation could be taken as establishing adiabatic contours in the $(p, M_1/V, M_2/V)$ space. For any point $(p^0, m_1^0, m_2^0)$ in that space, two mutually exclusive sets of $(p, m_1, m_2)$ are determinable. The first set is the points that cannot be reached from $(p^0, m_1^0, m_2^0)$ by any expenditure of external mechanical work; the second set is those points that can be so reached. (The process of reaching them involves what is conventionally called an irreversible process, but that need not detain us.) The frontier separating these sets (whose points technically belong to the first set) defines the adiabatic contours.

The existence of these adiabatics is a question of physics, not of Pfaffian mathematics. We might just as well axiomatize their existence, as I did in the two-dimensional case, where there never arises the mathematical "integrability conditions" (to ensure the existence of an "integrating factor" that converts a Pfaffian differential form into an "exact differential").

The adiabatic contours, assumed given to the logician by empirical observations, are of the form

$$A(p; M_1/V, M_2/V, \dots) = \text{constants} = \overline{A}. \tag{17.3}$$

With even empirical numberings of the contours eschewed, adiabatic contours can be defined by their observable slope functions:

$$\left(\frac{\partial p}{\partial m_1}\right)_{\text{ad}} = A^1(p, m_1, m_2),$$

$$\left(\frac{\partial p}{\partial m_2}\right)_{\text{ad}} = A^2(p, m_1, m_2), \qquad (17.3')$$

. . . .

From axiom 2's postulated existence of equation 17.3, we have implied the following integrability conditions:

$$\alpha_{ji} = \alpha_{ij} = \frac{\partial A^i(p; m_1, m_2, \ldots)}{\partial m_i} - A^j(p; m_1, m_2, \ldots) \frac{\partial A^i(p; m_1, m_2, \ldots)}{\partial p}$$

$$(17.4)$$

where $[\alpha_{ij}]$ is assured to be an observably symmetric matrix.

Here is a sketch of how the new axiom system must go for nonsimple as well as simple systems.

AXIOM 1:   Independent equations of state are observable, and are as numerous as different chemical masses.

AXIOM 2:   A set of adiabatic contours is observable, as in equation 17.3.

AXIOM 3:   The different contours of axioms 1 and 2 cannot be independent of each other, but instead must be interrelated so that generalized areas and volumes respect observable proportionality conditions. These imply that conjugate canonical entropy and canonical temperature variables $[S_c - S_c^0, T_c - T_c^0]$ are definable by path-independent integrals

$$\int (T_c[x] - T_c^0) S_c'[x] dx - \int \left( p[x] dV + \sum_{j=1}^{J} \lambda_j[x] M_j'[x] \right) dx \qquad (17.5)$$

independent of the arc path that joins $(p^0, V^0, M_1^0, M_2^0, \ldots, M_J^0)$ to $(p, V, M_1, M_2, \ldots, M_J)$. The important point is that the $(T_c, S)$ variables so defined must be invariant monotone stretchings of the observable (arbitrarily defined) empirical numberings of the respective isotherms and adiabatics of equations 17.1 and 17.3[10]

Space prevents me from considering other nonsimple systems. Besides chemical systems, magnetic and electric systems and still more general systems can also be made subject to thermodynamic axioms. We augment the extensive variables $(V, S, M_1, M_2, \ldots)$ to any set $(Y_1, Y_2, Y_3, Y_4, Y_5, \ldots)$; at the same time the former's conjugate intensive variables

$(-p, T, \mu_1, \mu_2, \dots)$ are augmented to the general set of variables conjugate to $(Y_1, Y_2, \dots)$, namely $(y_1, y_2, \dots)$. Legendre transformations, and various formalisms involving mixed functions

$$\phi(Y_1, \dots, Y_r; y_{r+1}, \dots, y_J) - \sum_1^r y_j Y_j + \sum_{r+1}^j Y_j y_j,$$

can be shown to apply. The letter and spirit of my three or four Axioms require only various natural adaptations.

## 18. Conclusion

Space limits force heuristic brevity. In the end, one's admiration for conventional pre-Carathéodory thermodynamics is enhanced. And it is gratifying to see that this most elegant paradigm of nature, thermostatics and thermodynamics, can be antiseptically formulated solely in terms of the observable measurements. It is now clear that, by an independent path, economic theory has arrived at an isomorphic logical structure.

## Acknowledgments

I owe thanks to the National Science Foundation for financial aid and to Aase Huggins for editorial assistance.

## Notes

1. Frisch and Tinbergen had used the closely related word *macrodynamics*. In physics, particularly in relating thermodynamics and statistical mechanics, *microscopic* and *macroscopic* had been familiar since the mid-nineteenth century at least. Thus, Maxwell, Boltzmann, Poincaré, Lohnschmidt, Zermelo, Ehrenfest, and others wrestled with the paradox that objects that are subject to time-reversible laws at the microscopic level somehow seem at the macroscopic level to be characterized by time-asymmetric properties (such as necessary increase in entropy with the passage of time). I can remember arguing in Gottfried Haberler's 1936 Harvard seminar how Carl Menger's methodological dictum, that economic theory must build on individual's behavior, might be valid at the microscopic level without contradicting the possible usefulness of macroscopic regularities. Professor Hendrik Houthakker has verified my surmise of a reference to macroeconomics antedating 1946, namely Pieter de Wolff (1941).

2. Klein (1946a) evoked useful replies from Kenneth May (1946) and Shou Shan Pu (1946), to which he replied in Klein 1946b. At about the same time, independently, Leontief (1946, 1947) was exploring requirements for weak and strong separability. Subsequently a vast literature on aggregation emerged, associated with R. M. Solow, H. A. J. Green, H. Theil, W. M. Gorman, P. A. Samuelson, F. M. Fisher, J. V. Robinson, John Chipman, and many others.

3. I am not able to judge whether the empirical reliability has or has not been greater for macro models that try to follow economic theory in specifying their relations. Some *ad hoc* models without theoretical underpinnings have worked tolerably well. Some models based on theory have performed badly. What the preponderance of experience has been I do not know.

4. If stochastic elements are involved, tastes for risk would have also to be uniformly homothetic; since each person has only 24 hours a day, it would seem to be hard to make tastes for leisure (as against work) fit into a homothetic framework.

5. In theoretical economics there is no "irreversibility" concept, which is one reason Georgescu-Roegen (1971) is critical of conventional economics. I have benefited over the years from discussions with MIT colleagues, particularly Laszlo Tisza and the late Joseph Keenan. Edwin Bidwell Wilson, Willard Gibb's last assistant, was my teacher at Harvard, and to him I owe my interest in the formal relations between economics and thermodynamics. Although I learned of the Carathéodory formulation years after my own ideas were formed, his approach is the one I find most congenial, even though I think there is some merit in considering at least once the present alternative to it. My present exposition overlaps, but goes beyond, my axiomatic appendix on thermodynamics in the Harold Hotelling *Festschrift* (Samuelson 1960). For the Carathéodory approach, see Carathéodory 1909, 1925; Born 1921, 1949; and Wilson 1957. The last takes notice of Norman Ramsey's "negative temperature" (negative $T^{-1}$) for spin systems, a possibility here ignored.

6. Of course, Nernst's so-called third law of thermodynamics requires separate stipulation concerning how the contours behave as the system becomes ever colder.

7. It could even be the case that, in figure 1b, the numbers 1, 2, 3, and 4 could be *reversed* in order: the colder 1b's substance, the greater could be its volumes at fixed pressures—as with water near its freezing point.

8. Must the closed arc be traversed limitingly slowly, so that the movement is a quasi-static reversible one? Such a question comes naturally to those familiar with the conventional axiomatic treatments. But once one understands the alternative present approach, one sees that all we are doing is measuring magnitudes defined by paired equilibrium states. Our computer can run the arcs as quickly as it pleases; there is no necessary correspondence between the $-\int p\,dv$ calculations and any real-time "cycle" of any physical "engine." The reversibility-irreversibility issue has no further relevance once we are given adiabatic contours. (This does not mean that axiom 4 will not reintroduce at least one physical measurement along what is an irreversible movement in real time. When a paddle wheel does work against friction and changes a fluid's temperature, you cannot physically reverse that action. But what does a well-defined integral $\int f(x)\,dx$ care about that?)

9. Warning: Figures 1b and 2a do not refer to water. For example, water would have horizontal isotherms around its "O" melting temperature where ice and water coexist as phases, rather than having the negatively sloped parallel isotherms shown in figure 2a. Nonetheless, for the actual substance shown in 2a, the zero and unity reference states have been selected to be those that would be in temperature and pressure equilibrium with water at freezing and evaporating points under standard atmospheric pressure.

10. I have here taken the Gibbs $(\lambda_1, \ldots, \lambda_5)$ as observable magnitudes. More fundamentally, we might treat them the way we do empirical temperature, $\vartheta$. When any equation of state 17.2 is not satisfied, we observe a dynamic flow of mass through semipermeable or permeable walls; static equilibrium is observed only when equation 17.2 is satisfied. So we can infer an empirical scale of each $\lambda_j$, namely

$$\vartheta_j = \Theta_j[\lambda_j], \quad \Theta_j'[\ ] > 0 \gtreqless \Theta_j''[\ ], \quad (j = 0, 1, \ldots, J).$$

Expanding the $\vartheta_0 = \vartheta$, empirical temperature specification of axiom 3, we would have to specify logical conditions that guarantee independence of path for integrals of the form

$$\int \left( -p[x]V'[x] + \sum_1^j \Theta_j^{-1}[\vartheta_j]M_j[x] + \Theta_0^{-1}[\vartheta]G'[\bar{A}] \right) dx.$$

These are generalized proportionality-of-area properties. Such properties are "in-the-large integrability condition." So in the end the present approach does seem to reduce to much the same logic as the admirable Carathéodory system. Multiplying axioms is not a sign of decadence or inelegance; the point is to unbundle the separable contents of the final axiom system—to show the independence of the separate axioms and recognize the wider models that would satisfy various subsets of the axioms.

## Bibliography

Born, M. 1921. Critical reflections on the traditional exposition of thermodynamics. *Phys. Z.* 22 : 218, 249, 282.

Born, M. 1949. *Natural Philosophy of Cause and Chance.* Oxford: Clarendon. Chapter 5, appendixes 6–10.

Carathéodory, C. 1909. Investigations on the foundation of thermodynamics. *Math. Ann.* 67 : 355.

Carathéodory, C. 1925. The determination of the internal energy and the absolute temperature by means of reversible processes. *S. B. Preuss. Akad. Wiss.* 39.

de Wolff, P. 1941. Income elasticity of demand, a micro-economic and a macro-economic interpretation. *Economic Journal* 51 : 140–145.

Evans, G. C. 1930. *Introduction to Mathematical Economics.* New York: McGraw-Hill.

Evans, G. C. 1934. Maximum production studied in a simplified economic system. *Econometrica* 2 : 37–50.

Georgescu-Roegen, N. 1971. *The Entropy Law and the Economic Process.* Cambridge, Mass.: Harvard University Press.

Gorman, W. M. 1953. Community preference fields. *Econometrica* 21 : 63–80.

Hatsopoulos, G. N., and J. H. Keenan. 1965. *Principles of General Thermodynamics.* New York: Wiley.

Hicks, J. R. 1939. *Value and Capital.* Oxford: Clarendon.

Klein, L. R. 1946a. Macroeconomics and the theory of rational behavior. *Econometrica* 14 : 93–108.

Klein, L. R. 1946b. Remarks on the theory of aggregation *Econometrica* 14 : 303–312.

Leontief, W. W. 1936. Composite commodities and the problem of index numbers. *Econometrica* 4 : 39–59.

Leontief, W. W. 1946. A note on the interrelation of subsets of independent variables of a continuous function with continuous first derivatives. *Bull. Am. Math. Soc.* 53 : 343–350.

Leontief, W. W. 1947. Introduction to a theory of the internal structure of functional relationships. *Econometrica* 15 : 361–373.

May. K. O. 1946. The aggregation problem for a one-industry model. *Econometrica* 14 : 285–298.

Pu, Shou Shan. 1946. A note on macroeconomics. *Econometrica* 14 : 229–302.

Samuelson, P. A. 1947. *Foundations of Economic Analysis.* Cambridge, Mass.: Harvard University Press

Samuelson, P. A. 1956. Social indifference curves. *Q. J. Econ.* 70: 1–22.

Samuelson, P. A. 1960. Structure of a minimum system. In Hotelling *Festschrift*, ed. R. W. Pfouts. Charlotte: University of North Carolina Press. Reproduced as chapter 44 in *Collected Scientific Papers of Paul A. Samuelson* (Cambridge, Mass.: MIT Press, 1966).

Samuelson, P. A. 1966. *Collected Scientific Papers.* Cambridge, Mass.: MIT Press. Volume 1, chapters 42, 43, 44, appendix to chapter 44.

Samuelson, P. A. 1968. Two generalizations of the elasticity of substitution. In *Value, Capital and Growth* (Hicks *Festschrift*), ed. J. N. Wolfe. Edinburgh University Press.

Samuelson, P. A. 1979. Paul Douglas's measurement of production functions and marginal productivities. *J. Pol. Econ.* 87: 923–939.

Sonnenschein, H. 1972. Market excess demand functions. *Econometrica* 40: 549–563.

Theil, H. 1957. Linear aggregation in input-output analysis. *Econometrica* 25: 346–349.

Tisza, L. 1966. *Generalized Thermodynamics.* Cambridge, Mass.: MIT Press.

Wilson, A. H. 1957. *Thermodynamics and Statistical Mechanics.* Cambridge University Press. Chapter 4.

# 2 Equilibrium Business-Cycle Models: An Appraisal

Albert Ando

For most older students of business cycles, the term represents the tendency of economic activities to fluctuate in a recognizably cyclical rather than purely random pattern over time. Such a tendency has persisted as long as we have data to trace it. This tendency seems fairly obvious to anyone who plots a time series representing the level of economic activity (such as gross national product or a production index), somehow detrended, against time. The National Bureau of Economic Research has documented this observation extensively. I reproduce here as an example (figure 1) a graph, prepared by Martin Bailey (1978), that happens to be conveniently available. As Bailey notes, the graph suggests that the order of magnitude of fluctuations relative to the average level of GNP has been lower for the years after the second world war than for the years before the war. However, the persistence of the cyclical fluctuations throughout the period 1901–1975 seems unmistakable. Klein (1982) summarizes it as follows: "Types of periodic or cyclical movement are often found in economic systems. They may be seasonal cycles, with an annual period; inventory cycles, with a short 2–3 year

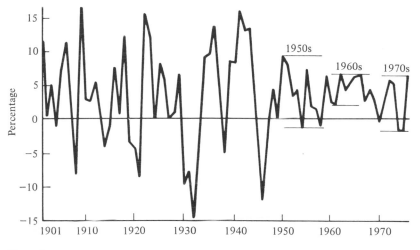

**Figure 1**
Rate of growth of real gross national product, 1901–1976. Sources: U.S. Bureau of the Census, Historical Statistics of the United States: Colonial Time to 1970, part 1 (Government Printing Office, 1975), series F3; Economic Report of the President, January 1977, p. 188; *Survey of Current Business*, volume 57 (July 1977), table 1.2.

period; Juglar cycles, with an 8–10 year period; and long Kondratieff or Kuznets cycles, with a 20 year period. The average of all these different cycles over the business history of America, covering more than 100 years, comes to approximately 4 years."

Until fairly recently, the literature on business cycles, including large-scale econometric models, reflected this interpretation of empirical data by focusing much attention on (mathematical) systems that are capable of generating time series with regular and sustained cyclical patterns. There are two distinct mathematical structures that meet this requirement: limit cycles generated by an explosive dynamic system coupled with reflecting barriers at the ceiling and the floor, and large, linear, inherently stable dynamic systems subjected to steady, additive, white-noise disturbances satisfying the conditions of what has become known as harmonic limit theorems (Otsuki 1971; Moran 1950).

If one adopts the point of view that one of these systems—or perhaps a mixture of the two (as I believe)—is the likely structure capable of describing business cycles, there is a natural supposition that the more accurately and completely we describe the dynamic behavior of economic agents and institutions, the better our theory of business cycles will be. This then leads us into formidable, unending empirical investigations that are likely to produce very large, complex systems rather than any simple, intuitively obvious explanation of business cycles.

Skepticism about the existence of the regular cyclical patterns outlined above was raised by those who have estimated the power spectra of a number of economic time series and found that, except for those associated with seasonal variations, they typically have the monotonically declining shape from the left to right, which implies that regular cyclical fluctuations of these series are not identifiable (Granger 1966). Some theorists of business cycles have taken this type of statistical evidence seriously and used it as an empirical justification for a major redirection in theories of business cycles. Thus, according to Robert Lucas, who has pioneered a recent attempt at reformulating business-cycle theory that has become known as "equilibrium business-cycle modeling,"

Technically, movement about trend in gross national product in any country can be described by a stochastically disturbed difference equation of very low order. These movements do not exhibit uniformity of either period or amplitude, which is to say, they do not resemble the deterministic wave motions which sometimes arise in the natural sciences.

Those regularities which are observed are in the co-movements among different aggregate time series.[1]

This alternative view of time-series data on the aggregate economy suggests that the model of business cycles should be much simpler than we had thought. Under the earlier interpretation of the data, an essential part of the business-cycle theory is to determine all important dynamic adjustment processes in the economy, with an understanding that there are many such processes (which implies that the description of business cycles would involve a large, complex dynamic system). Under the Granger-Lucas interpretation of history, a model needs to contain only one or two simple dynamic adjustment processes. It appears to suggest that we could construct a model of business cycles in which almost everything is in equilibrium except one or two critical processes. This is a tempting idea for economists because, in economics, the theories for equilibrium states are much more polished than those for dynamic adjustment processes. The development of equilibrium business-cycle models is, therefore, intimately related to this interpretation of aggregate time-series data.

I do not believe that the shape of estimated power spectra is by any means conclusive evidence on the nature of dynamic systems generating these time series. This is especially true of long cycles such as Kuznets cycles, because the whole length of time series tested is typically too short to give us much confidence for estimates of power spectra at frequencies corresponding to these long cycles. Moreover, in my view, the structure of the U.S. economy contains a number of significant nonlinearities, and local linear approximations to such a structure may be stable or unstable depending on the initial conditions. Historical time series, therefore, will contain segments that can be approximated by a stable linear transformation of white noise, and other segments that are more like limit cycles generated by nonstationary processes coupled with reflecting barriers which cannot be characterized by power spectra. Finally, the type of statistical hypotheses involved makes it inherently difficult to define alternate hypotheses, and therefore the power of tests is either undefined or very weak. I therefore believe that the results summarized by Granger are suggestive but not sufficient to enable one to judge the types of processes generating economic time series.

The challenge of the equilibrium business-cycle models to those theories that were dominant between the 1930s and the 1960s, therefore, must be evaluated on other grounds. Proponents of equilibrium business-cycle models (or "classical macroeconomics") appear to claim that the existing large-scale econometric models are inconsistent in some fundamental way with the implications of rational behavior (that is, behavior characterized by optimization of some well-defined criterion function given the relevant constraints) and hence worthless. The fact that, in most econometric models, in at least some markets, a gap is allowed to develop between demand and supply without prices moving sufficiently and instantaneously to bring them into equilibrium is also considered to be a fatal defect of these models. Furthermore, proponents of these models claim to have formulated a better theoretical framework for understanding the modern, mixed economies.[2]

Therefore, I shall comment in some detail on the essential structure of equilibrium business-cycle models, and attempt to assess the merits and defects of these models. I will examine them according to the criteria of their authors, namely that behavioral equations be rigorously derivable from the optimizing behavior of economic agents and that equilibrium conditions be strictly satisfied. I find that these criteria are far from being met by equilibrium business-cycle models proposed to date.

Proponents of the equilibrium business-cycle models emphasize the simultaneous presence of real and monetary disturbances in the economy and the inability of economic agents to distinguish between the two through observed price movements as the basic cause of economic fluctuations. I believe that the recognition of this mechanism is a valid and important insight, and that all future business-cycle models must take cognizance of this mechanism, but it is difficult to see how this mechanism can be the only significant cause of economic fluctuations, as proponents of the equilibrium business-cycle models seem to insist (Lucas 1981, p. 564). Many other dynamic adjustment processes, many of which have been studied by Klein throughout his career, are equally important determinants of the nature of business cycles in modern mixed economies.

## Equilibrium Business-Cycle Models: The Micro Theory

As their name implies, the models under discussion attempt to interpret historical data using a model in which the price moves sufficiently to equate demand and supply of aggregate output in every period. Of course, apparent equality of demand and supply of a good that is storable to any extent can be achieved by accommodating changes of inventory in every period. Presumably, equilibrium business-cycle theorists mean more than this accounting identity; they must mean that the level of inventory at the end of the period and the price of the good for the period are so adjusted with each other that there is neither further tendency for price to move nor for the level of inventory to change.

If the demand and supply functions of a particular commodity are subject to continuous random shocks while equality of demand and supply in every period is required, observed quantity and price should exhibit some variation over time, but there is no obvious reason why the time series on quantity and price should be positively correlated. There is also no obvious reason why the rate of change of the aggregate nominal price and the level of aggregate output should be positively correlated over time. Theorists of equilibrium business-cycle models, however, recognize the existence of a correlation between the level of aggregate output and the rate of change of the aggregate nominal price, and they have taken as the primary challenge the need to explain this correlation using a model in which demand and supply of aggregate output are continuously equated.

Historically, this strand of theory developed in two distinct stages. The first development was the well-known paper in which Lucas (1972) constructed a simple, stochastic model of an economy in which the neutrality of money (in a sense that will be defined later) is preserved while movements over time of the absolute level of price and output, if they both occur, are correlated. The second stage was the development of the so-called aggregate supply function, purportedly based on this abstract model of Lucas, and on whose specific form most of the important properties of the equilibrium business-cycle models depend. Since we wish to ascertain whether or not the macro version of equilibrium business-cycle theory is in fact rigorously based on the rational behavior of economic agents and nothing else, as claimed by its proponents, it is useful to summarize those features of the Lucas theory that form the foundation of the macro models.

Lucas's theory is framed in the "islands" economy popularized earlier by Phelps (1969). In Lucas's version, only one homogeneous good is produced, which is not storable. The only means of carrying purchasing power from one period to the next is by holding "money." [3] All individuals are identical, and they live for two periods. In the first period they work to produce output, and they consume some of it and exchange the rest for money in order to carry the purchasing power into the second period. In the second period they simply exchange the money in their possession for output produced by the then younger generation, and consume what they can purchase; that is, in the second period, they cannot work to produce output. There is no possibility of inheritance or gifts, so that any money owned by members of the older generation at the beginning of the period will be used to purchase output for consumption.[4] Money is issued by the state as described below, and the state has no function other than the issuance of money. Since there is no capital or other input into production, the relationship between output and the labor input can be thought of as proportional, and the proportionality factor is the same in all islands.

The essence of the islands economy is that no interaction among islands is possible within a single period. There cannot be transportation of commodities or individuals, transfer of assets, exchange of information, or, of course, trading among islands.

In Lucas's model, three interventions take place between any two periods. First, there is a monetary intervention, which takes the form of a distribution of additional (positive or negative) money; the total amount of money distributed follows a well-defined stochastic process over time, and it is distributed only to the members of the older generation in the same proportion as the initial holdings of money the individuals carried from the previous period, so that it in no way affects the distribution of resources among members of the older generation. Second, members of the older generation, who own all of the money supply and therefore (in this model) control the nominal demand for the economy, are redistributed among islands so that the nominal demand is completely equalized among islands at the beginning of each period. Third, members of the younger generation, who control the real supply of goods, are distributed among islands according to a well-defined probability distribution.

In addition, although Lucas does not say so explicitly, it must also be assumed that members of the younger generation are informed at the beginning of the first period of their lives how much money supply existed at the end of the previous period, although they are not informed how much additional money is injected into the economy between the end of the previous period and the beginning of the current period. Unless this information on the initial amount of money is provided to them, members of the younger generation cannot utilize the knowledge they are supposed to possess of the distribution by which the net addition to the money supply is generated in each period in the way they are described to.[5]

The point of all these arrangements is that individual members of the younger generation in this society are placed, in any one period, in the situation where each must decide how much to produce and to sell, and how much money to carry over to the next period, knowing the market price on his island but nothing about what is happening on other islands—in particular, what the prices are on the other islands. In other words, the price signal is not sufficient for each member of the younger generation to distinguish how much of the current changes in the price he faces is due to the purely monetary disturbance (additional supply of money injected by the government at the beginning of the period) and how much is due to the real disturbance (the proportion of the younger generation allocated to his island).

The second point, equally important but not clearly noted in the literature, is that the redistribution of members of the older generation described above, together with the assumption that money is the only asset that can be carried over from one period to the next, makes all conditions in period $t$-1 irrelevant for the macro solution of period $t$ except insofar as data for past periods give economic agents information about the comparison between the size of the variance of the monetary disturbance and that of the real disturbance. But any finite number of observations cannot provide additional information on the relative size of these variances—if it did, then one would have to suppose that the distribution generating these disturbances changes over time, and this would profoundly alter the model constructed by Lucas.[6]

Given this setup, Lucas shows the following:

• If all disturbances are strictly monetary; that is, if the allocation of the young generation among islands is constant over time, then the price is proportional to the money supply in every period (irrespective of whether the change in the money supply is expected or unexpected), and money is neutral in the classical sense.

• If the money supply is absolutely fixed at a given level while the real disturbances are present (that is, the distribution of the young generation among islands is newly drawn every period), then the disturbance will have real consequences.

• If both types of disturbances are present, then output will respond to both types of disturbances because individuals cannot distinguish which types of disturbances is causing changes in price that they observe in their own island. We will then observe, in the aggregate, a positive correlation between the level of prices and the level of output, the degree of correlation depending upon the characteristics of the joint probability distribution generating the real and monetary disturbances.

This result depends on the detailed structure of Lucas's model, which guarantees that the substitution effect rather than the income effect dominates the younger generation's response to its perception of the relative price changes and that the total expenditure in the economy is exogenously given. Otherwise, the sign of the correlation could not be determined.

Lucas's theory is elegant and quite suggestive, but its limitations as a basis on which to build a dynamic macroeconomic theory must be clearly recognized. Fundamentally, Lucas's theory is a theory of a stationary state, and the only novel result, the one concerning the positive correlation between output and the price level, is quite sensitive to details of his assumptions. I shall emphasize here four aspects of Lucas' theory that are important in relating it to the subsequent macroeconomic models that have developed.

1. Lucas carefully structures his analysis so that the links between the current period and all preceding periods are strictly limited to two well-defined ones. One is the distribution of money among the members of a generation, which is preserved when a generation ends its working period and enters its consuming period by Lucas's specification that any new distribution of money (positive or negative) be strictly proportional to the amount accumulated by individuals during their working period. But this preservation of distribution has no consequence at all for markets and the economy as a whole, because of the further assumption that members of the older generation are redistributed among all markets in such a way that the amounts of money allocated to each market are completely equalized among all markets. Therefore, this first link is no link at all.

The second link arises from the fact that agents in each market impute the observed changes in the price in that market to real and monetary causes according to their understanding of the relative size of the variances of the monetary and real disturbances, which is in turn supposed to be estimated on the basis of past observations. But both the monetary disturbances (the additional supply of money) and the real disturbances (the distribution of members of the younger generation among all markets) are generated by a joint stationary stochastic process that is assumed to be known to economic agents. Therefore, strictly speaking, realizations in any finite number of recent periods should have no effects on the decision processes of agents in the current period; this makes the second link also superfluous. One must conclude, therefore, that Lucas's model is concerned only with stationary states of the economy.[7]

2. The sense in which the neutrality of money in the long run holds when both the real and the monetary disturbances are present is very restricted. It holds for a change of the unit of account, so that the distribution of the supply of money remains unchanged except for the scale. But any other change in the rules regulating the money supply will have real effects, because the essence of Lucas's result is that the relative size of the variance of the monetary disturbance and that of the real disturbance (and, in principle, higher moments of the joint distribution of these two random variables) will determine the ways in which monetary disturbance will have real effects on the economy. In particular, an increase in the mean level of the money supply without corresponding adjustments of other moments including its variance will have real effects on the economy.[8]

This second point may be thought of as an implication of the first point, and is not surprising if we recall the nature of the neutrality of money in the nonstochastic environment. The neutrality of money then depended, in addition to the homogeneity properties of the equilibrium solutions, on the set of assumptions guaranteeing that the distributional effects did not occur and that initial conditions, such as the real value of the initial endowments (both assets and liabilities) of individuals, remained unchanged when the quantity of money supply was changed. The presence of any asset or liability that is defined in nominal terms and is capable of being carried over more than a single period is a possible cause of nonhomogeneity, and hence it can introduce a non-neutrality. The only plausible situation in which neutrality of money is valid must therefore be stationary states, in which, by assumption, all contracts defined in nominal terms had time to be completely renegotiated and all initial conditions themselves were reequilibrated. In Lucas's model, a careful set of assumptions ensures that these troublesome initial conditions are not relevant, and the only source of non-neutrality is the inability of economic agents to distinguish between real and monetary disturbances through observed prices. The seriousness of this inability is determined by the second and higher moments of the joint distribution of the monetary and real disturbances. Hence, these higher moments may be thought of as a part of the initial conditions or of the environment, and any monetary disturbance that affects relations among these moments or between them and the mean will have real effects on the economy.

3. In Lucas's model, an expenditure decision by an individual agent is a reflection of his supply decision in the preceding period, but for the economy as a whole it is strictly exogenous by the assumption that the velocity of money per period is unity and that the aggregate supply of money is exogenously given by a stationary stochastic process. This assumption suits admirably well the purpose of modeling the supply of labor in a stationary stochastic environment, but for this very reason it makes Lucas's model unsuitable as a basis on which to build a dynamic macro model. To suppose that the velocity is constant and unity per period under all circumstances is to assume away the essential problem of the role of money in an economy.

4. The positive correlation between the level of aggregate output and the rate of change of its price is implied by Lucas's model only because this model assumes the exogeneity of the total expenditure described above and also assumes an unusual set of restrictions on the utility function of individuals to guarantee that the substitution effects will dominate the response of the supply to variation in the price. This set of restrictions, namely that the Pratt measure of relative risk aversion be between 0 and 1.0,[9] casts serious doubts on the plausibility of Lucas's model as an explanation of the empirically observed positive correlation between the level of output and the rate of inflation, since most empirical estimates of this measure are between 2.0 and 6.0.[10]

In theoretical analysis, one often needs a set of highly restrictive assumptions in order to obtain a good insight into a specific problem. In that spirit, Lucas's model must be considered a highly successful attempt to characterize the supply behavior of labor in a stationary stochastic environment in which monetary and real disturbances cannot be distinguished completely by observing prices alone. To explore the implications of his findings in actual economies is a very different type of analysis, and some of the restrictive assumptions must be relaxed for such a purpose. In my judgment, three generalizations are absolutely essential.

First, the dynamic response behavior of labor supply must be specified, so that the model can describe the response over time of supply to a change in the parameters of the probability distribution generating the monetary and real disturbances.

Second, some form of genuine demand structure must be specified, and this must include the possibility of a transfer of real resources from one period to another, at least through inventories and preferably through capital goods. Without such a possibility, the requirement that demand must equal supply makes the role of aggregate demand almost necessarily subsidiary in determining the characteristics of the economy. After all, Walras's law holds even in a single-good economy; that is, the total payment to factors of production is equal to the total income available for spending, and if total income must be spent on current production there is not much room for interesting discussion. The slight and apparent maneuverability introduced by the presence of money is of little substance in this context.

Third, dynamic response patterns of production—through capital formation and production, employment, and inventory decision rules, on the one hand, and dynamic response patterns of final demand, reflecting long term planning of expenditure patterns by households as well as institutional and contractual constraints, on the other hand—must be recognized.

Only when equilibrium business-cycle models recognize most of these basic dynamic features of macroeconomic systems while satisfying the requirement that demand and supply of output be in equilibrium in every period can we intelligently appraise the advantages and disadvantages of these models relative to others. These points should be kept in mind as we proceed.

The next section will review some of the macro equilibrium business-cycle models that are purportedly based on the theoretical structure of Lucas's 1972 analysis, with the emphasis on discriminating between those features of these aggregate models that are indeed implied by Lucas's 1972 analysis and other features that are consequences of changes in Lucas's original assumptions or of additional hypotheses superimposed on the original ones. This second group of assumptions and hypotheses turns out to be at least as important as Lucas's 1972 model in shaping equilibrium business-cycle models. We must therefore inquire on what basis we are asked to accept these assumptions and hypotheses. Are they to be accepted because they are based on a well-conceived formulation of rational behavior of individuals and firms, or are they to be accepted because they are well supported by empirical evidence? How are they related to the list of necessary generalizations that I listed a little earlier? Indeed, are these set of assumptions clearly better in some sense than those that underlie typical large-scale econometric models?

## Aggregate Equilibrium Business-Cycle Models

Before taking up a sampling of equilibrium business-cycle models that have appeared in the literature, I must clarify the spirit in which these models have been offered. Advocates of these models have not claimed that they are completely satisfactory and ready for use as the framework of macroeconomic policy analysis. However, Lucas (1977, p. 25) wrote the following:

... it is fairly clear that there is nothing in the behavior of observed economic time series which precludes ordering them in equilibrium terms, and enough theoretical examples exist to lend confidence to the hope that this can be done in an explicit and rigourous way. To date, however, no equilibrium model has been developed which meets these standards and which, at the same time could pass the test posed by the Adelmans [1959]. My own guess would be that success in this sense is five, but not twenty-five years off.

He then added, in a note, "Proceeding further out on this limb, it is likely that such a 'successful' model will be a close descendant of Sargent's [1976a]." I believe it is fair to assume from these statements that, in Lucas's view, models such as Sargent's should be taken fairly seriously except for well-defined and specific difficulties.

Much more recently, however, Lucas seems to be taking a somewhat different position, as the following quotation indicates:

These papers together (Sargent and Wallace [1975], Sargent [1976a], and Sargent [1976b]) show that a class of models in which systematic activist monetary and fiscal policy has *no* ability to stabilize the economy has exactly the same ability to fit time series as do standard, Keynesian models in which monetary and fiscal policy has very great powers to do this. This is a counter-example, of course, and as these authors insist, it is not a proof that systematic monetary policy does not matter in the U.S. economy. (Lucas 1981, p. 563)

In other words, we are not to take the substance of these models too seriously, but to view their role as being confined to demonstrating a point of econometric methodology: that often apparent empirical support for a large-scale econometric model is in fact meaningless.

I believe that the issue of econometric methodology is almost completely separate from the choice of the basic economic structure that serves as a starting point for an econometric analysis of a macro economy. In this paper, my focus is on the question of whether or not the structure embodied in simple examples of equilibrium business-cycle models that have been published so far is a promising starting point for studying the basic characteristics of a macro economy, when it is properly modified and elaborated. I shall deal with the question of econometric methodology in a separate paper under preparation.[11]

Lucas's original article contained, at the end, what appears to be an aggregate supply function. But his article provided little explanation of how the aggregate supply function was derived from the micro analysis in the first part of the article, and the only explicit derivation of the aggregate supply function that I am aware of is given again by Lucas—in a much simpler context—in Lucas 1973. This latter derivation, therefore, is a critical link between Lucas's original micro analysis and the later development of classical macroeconomics, and it deserves our attention at this point.

Lucas's starting point in this derivation is the supply function for market $z$, given by

$$y_{ct}(z) = \gamma[P_t(z) - E(P_t|I_t(z))] + \lambda y_{c,t-1}(z), \tag{1a}$$

$$y_{nt} = \alpha + \beta t, \tag{1b}$$

$$y_t(z) = y_{nt} + y_{ct}(z) \tag{1c}$$

where $y_t(z)$ is the logarithm of the supply in market $z$, $y_{nt}$ is the secular component of $y_t(z)$, $y_{ct}(z)$ is the cyclical component of $y_t(z)$, $P_t(z)$ is the logarithm of the actual price prevailing in market $z$, $P_t$ is the mean of $P_t(z)$ over all markets, $I_t(z)$ is the information available in $z$ in period $t$ concerning $P_t$, $t$ is time, and $\alpha$, $\beta$, $\gamma$, and $\lambda$ are constants.

Equations 1 look perfectly reasonable at first glance, but there are several serious questions concerning them. First, in Lucas's micro model, the only reason why the price $P_t(z)$ deviates from $P_t$ is because the distribution of members of the younger generation among markets is random, while the distribution of demand among markets is uniform. On the other hand, equation 1b implies that the supply is identical for all markets except for deviations of $P_t(z)$ from $E(P_t)$ (except for $\lambda y_{c,t-1}(z)$, on which I will comment momentarily). Therefore, in terms of the 1972 theory, there is no cause whatever for deviation of individual $P_t(z)$ from $P_t$. One may be able to salvage the situation by introducing a stochastic term in equation 1b, which is in accordance with the spirit of the 1972 theory. In that case, however, the distribution of $P_t(z)$ given $P_t$ is completely determined by the distribution of the stochastic term in equation 1b, given the form of equation 1a and the assumption in the 1972 theory (which is presumably carried over to the present formulation) that the total expenditure is identical for all $z$ and is determined independent of $P_t(z)$. In other words, the distribution of $P_t(z)$ given $P_t$ is endogenous to the model, and it cannot be arbitrarily assumed.

Second, the term $\lambda y_{c,t-1}$ in equation 1a is an arbitrary addition, and has nothing to do with the 1972 theory. The best we can say about the relationship between the set of equations 1 above and the 1972 theory, I believe, is that it is impressionistic.

One might be tempted to ask why I should be so fussy about the logical relation of Lucas's simple 1973 construction to his 1972 theory. Is it not legitimate to take a suggestive idea contained in the 1972 theory and formulate a simple but practical hypothesis utilizing this idea? I am afraid that the answer to this question must be clearly negative, because the basic issue here is the claim by the new classical macroeconomists and the equilibrium-business-cycle theorists that their models are rigorously derived from the "sound theoretical foundation" of the rational behavior of individuals, whereas all other macroeconomic models are fatally flawed by partial reliance on arbitrary and *ad hoc* propositions. It is this claim, and not the convincing empirical evidence, that has brought the new classical macroeconomics to the prominence it enjoys today. This claim, in the end, is based on Lucas's 1972 theory, and it is therefore crucial whether or not the aggregate supply function, which plays the central role in new classical economics, can be logically derived from Lucas's 1972 theory. It should also be recalled that Lucas's 1972 theory can imply positive correlation between $y$ and $[P_t(z) - E(P_t|I_t(z))]$ only under a very stringent set of assumptions that are unlikely to be empirically valid.

Once it is admitted that equations 1 are not logically implied by Lucas's 1972 theory, then they must be justified on other grounds, and it is difficult to see how one can take them seriously. To begin with, Lucas never makes clear whether these equations refer to the supply of labor, or of all the factors of production, or of output. Depending on one's choice of what $y$ refers to, substantially different formulations of supply suggest themselves. Suppose that $y$ refers to labor. Questions that may be asked of equations 1 might then include the following:

• Are we to understand the price effects to be net of substitution and income effects, or are they strictly the substitution effects?

• What is the justification for the sole dynamic mechanism represented by the term $y_{c,t-1}(z)$? I do not think that it can be easily justified by the rationality of behavior, and it is a poor approximation empirically.

• Surely, there must be other variables (such as population structure, other income, and net worth of households) that belong in a determination of the equilibrium supply of labor, and still others (such as the difficulty or ease of finding jobs) that affect the dynamics of the supply response.

• Suppose for the moment that we accept the basic formulation of equations 1. If we, for instance, interpret different "markets" as those for persons with different skills and in different professions, surely it is unreasonable to suppose that the elasticity $\gamma$ and the adjustment parameter $\lambda$ are both identical for all groups. Indeed, these two parameters are probably related to each other. This point has an important implication for the aggregation procedure discussed below.

• Equations 1 are written so that $y_{c,t}(z)$ is homogeneous of degree zero in all prices. This, of course, was one of the features of the 1972 theory, but the question of if and how this type of homogeneity may be disturbed during the dynamic adjustment process is the most critical aspect of the specification of dynamic adjustment processes. One cannot make the question go away by simply ignoring it. Notice also that each agent is supposed to compare the logarithm of the price in his own market against the mean of logarithm in all other markets—that is, he is supposed to compare the price in his own market against the geometric mean of prices in all other markets. Not only is this behavior quite unlikely on an intuitive basis, but I also do not know any reasonable setup where a demand function derived by optimizing some criteria function subject to a linear budget constraint takes this form, even as an approximation.[12]

Before dealing with the question of aggregation, I must comment on the nature of the process generating the general price level, $P_t$, and the localized prices in each market, $P_t(z)$. Lucas says that the "prior" distribution of $P_t$ is normal with mean $\bar{P}_t$ (depending in a known way on history) and constant variance $\sigma^2$, while the distribution of $z_t$ [deviation of $P_t(z)$ from $P_t$], given $P_t$, is also normal with mean zero and constant variance $\tau^2$. With this setup, it follows that the mean of $P_t$ posterior to having observed $P_t(z)$ is given by

$$E(P_t|I_t(z)) = E(P_t|P_t(z), \bar{P}_t) = (1 - \theta)P_t(z) + \theta\bar{P}_t \tag{2}$$

where $\theta = \tau^2/(\sigma^2 + \tau^2)$.

Interpretation of this formulation is not quite the standard Bayesian updating process. The decision maker is interested in the realization $P_t$ in period $t$, not in process parameters as in the usual Bayesian analysis.[13] (I will return to this point after summarizing the demand side.)

Lucas then substitutes equation 2 into equations 1 and integrates the resulting equation over the distribution of $z$ to obtain an aggregate supply function of the form

$$y_t = y_{nt} + \theta\gamma[P_t - \bar{P}_t] - \lambda[y_{t-1} - y_{n,t-1}] \tag{3}$$

where $y_t$ is the sum of logarithm of supplies over all markets, $y_{nt}$ is the sum of logarithms of trend outputs in all markets, $P_t$ is the mean of the logarithm of prices in all markets, $\bar{P}_t$ is the mean of the (subjective) distribution of $P_t$ prior to observing $P_t(z)$, and $\theta$, $\gamma$, $\lambda$ are constants (described above).

Since equations 1 were completely linear in logarithms, the aggregation over all markets appears mechanically straightforward. It, of course, relies critically on the assumption that $\gamma$, $\theta$, and $\lambda$ are all identical for all markets. Outside the island model of Lucas's 1972 theory, it is hard to imagine that the price elasticities of supply in all markets are the same. It is also hard to imagine that the variances of prices in different markets given the general price level are the same for all markets. If $\gamma$ and $\theta$ are not the same for all markets, then the aggregate supply function cannot be expressed as a simple function of the aggregate price, but in the context of the model under discussion the homogeneity of the aggregate supply with respect to all prices can be preserved. If $\lambda$ is not the same for all markets, then an extremely complex dynamics will be introduced into the system. Since the term was introduced into equations 1 on a completely *ad hoc* basis, I shall not be concerned with this problem, although it should be noted that dynamic properties of any system using equations 1 are critically dependent on the *ad hoc* assumption that $\lambda$ is the same in all markets.

The most critical problem with equation 3 is that the variables in terms of which it is stated are all sums and means of logarithms of the corresponding variables for individual markets. This raises difficulties at several levels. First, since the statement that "the geometric sum of supplies in all markets is equal to the geometric sum of demands in all markets" is not the same as the statement that "the arithmetic sum of supplies in all markets is equal to the arithmetic sum of demands in all markets," the price that brings about one of these equalities will not be the same as the price that brings about the other. Hence, at this point the definition of "the price that equilibrates markets" is not clear. Second, these geometric sums and means do not correspond at all to any aggregate data on prices and quantities, and it is hard to see how an equation like 3 can be empirically implemented.

However, it might be argued that, under certain conditions, means of logarithms are a good enough approximation for logarithms of means. The acceptability of such an approximation will depend upon the distribution of variables being aggregated. If we accept Lucas's assumption that all basic variables are approximately log-normally distributed, then the condition under which this approximation approaches some acceptable accuracy is that the variance of the distribution of the micro variable approaches zero. But as the variances of the distributions of micro variables approach zero, Lucas's original model reverts back to a simple demand-and-supply model with perfect information, and his analysis loses its basic purpose and message. In addition, there is reason to believe that the variance of the measure of output cannot be small no matter which empirical counterpart to Lucas's islands or markets we choose to look at. This point can be more easily understood when one clarifies the unit in terms of which output in different markets must be measured. The choice of the unit is no problem for Lucas's island economy because in it output in all islands is the same, so that it can be measured in the physical unit. But in a real economy, outputs in different markets are not the same.

Therefore, in order that we be able to talk about the distribution of prices over different markets and to sum supplies of labor and output over all markets, labor or output in all markets must be measured in the unit of the quantities of "one dollar's worth in the base period." The distribution of output measured in this unit is roughly the distribution of total expenditures over different markets, and anyone can inspect data to see that it is very widely dispersed. Hence, the variance of the distribution of output among markets must be substantial, and therefore the mean of the logarithm and the logarithm of the mean cannot be good approximations to each other.

How is it possible, then, to utilize equation 3? It will depend on the formulation of the demand side, which in Lucas's aggregate model is given by

$$y_t' + P_t' = x_t \tag{4}$$

where $x_t$ is "an exogenous shift variable—equal to the observable log of nominal GNP" and $\{\Delta x_t\}$ is "a sequence of independent normal variates with mean $\delta$ and variance $\sigma_x^2$." (Lucas 1973)

Presumably, nominal GNP is exogenous because it is assumed that nominal GNP is proportional to (or at least uniquely determined by) the money supply, which is taken as exogenous. Let us for the moment accept this devious assumption. Then $y_t'$ and $P_t'$ should be understood to be the log of GNP in constant dollars and the log of its deflator. We may or may not wish to question the appropriateness of the official definitions of these variables, but they are an arithmetic sum and an arithmetic mean of some type and certainly not a geometric sum and a geometric mean over many goods and services. If they were a geometric sum and geometric mean, then an identity such as 4 could not hold.

In this situation, it is no simple matter to establish the relationship between $y_t$ and $P_t$ appearing in equation 3 and $y_t'$ and $P_t'$ appearing in equation 4. Given that these variables are logarithms, if they are approximately normally distributed the constancy of the variances will imply that the differences between pairs $y_t$ and $y_t'$ and $P_t$ and $P_t'$ will remain constant over time. But this is unlikely, because, as I suggested above, in reality the elasticity $\lambda$ cannot be the same for all markets, and hence price and output in different markets will respond differently to the same set of shocks over time. This means that there can be no simple relationship between $y_t$ and $y_t'$, even approximately, without our being able to explain movements over time of the variances of output and prices over markets. But the theoretical structure under review has nothing to say about the movements of variances over time, and hence it is impossible to relate $y_t$ to $y_t'$ and $P_t$ to $P_t'$.

Lucas and other proponents of equilibrium business-cycle theory ignore this complex question, equate $y_t$ with $y_t'$ and $P_t$ with $P_t'$, and proceed to solve equations 3 and 4 together for these variables. Literally, they are computing the geometric sum of supplies over different markets and the arithmetic sum of demand over all markets, and then insisting that the level of the price be so determined as to equate these two different types of sums and at the same time that the difference between the geometric mean of prices of various goods and services be equal to their arithmetic mean as well. It would be surprising if such a solution existed. Empirically, proponents of those theories simply reinterpret equation 3 as though it were formulated in terms of the logarithms of the arithmetic sums and means rather than in terms of sums and means of logarithms, disregarding the theory under which it was derived in the first place.

We must conclude, therefore, that Lucas's simple 1973 model is not what equilibrium business-cycle theorists say it is. Equation 3 as given above is not derivable from Lucas's 1972 theory, and therefore his 1973 model is not based on any explicit optimizing or rational behavior of economic agents. Nor is it an equilibrium model, because either it equates two concepts that by definition cannot be equal or it further distorts the aggregate supply function (equation 3).

One further point needs to be made. Given the structure of the model—disregarding for the moment the discrepancies between $y_t$ and $y_t'$ and between $P_t$ and $P_t'$—current output and current price are determined, once $x_t$ and $y_{nt}$ are given, totally independent of the past if the parameter $\lambda$ is zero. Indeed, if $\lambda$ is zero, the expected value of $P_t$, $\bar{P}_t$, is simply given by

$$P_t = x_{t-1} + \delta - y_{nt} \tag{5}$$

and past values of the $P$'s and the $y$'s are of no additional value in predicting $P_t$ or $y_t$. I believe that this point makes it further obvious that models of this type are strictly stationary-state models, and that dynamics is introduced only through the arbitrary addition of lagged values such as $\lambda y_{t-1}$ or an autoregressive error scheme, which is not an integral part of the theory. (See note 13.)

I have taken up Lucas's 1973 model for a detailed review because it is the one closest to his basic theory of 1972, and also because its basic structure is simple and easy to see through. In doing so, however, I may be subject to criticism that I am belaboring an old point, and that I should have taken up a later, more developed model in order to do justice to the basic nature of equilibrium business-cycle models. The model presented by Sargent (1976a) is an obvious candidate for this purpose, because Lucas singles this model out as the one closest to the eventual satisfactory business-cycle model that he expects to emerge within a few years from this strand of literature.[14]

(Models in which prices do not completely clear markets, for reasons such as long-term contracts, are outside the scope of this review, and I do not propose to pass any judgment on these models. Taken literally, they are not within the spirit of equilibrium models, whose essence is that prices move without constraints to equilibrate markets.[15,16])

Sargent's model looks more elaborate than the earlier one of Lucas, but the difference is more apparent than real. Though he starts out with the labor-force-participation equation, he assumes proportionality between employment and output and does not distinguish between the wage rate and the price of output. Sargent's equations relating to supply can therefore be reduced to the same equations as 3 above, except that his will contain more elaborate lag structures. But these lag structures are outside the basic theory of the classical equilibrium models of business cycles—they are simply an *ad hoc* addition introduced to accommodate existing data.

Sargent asserts that the dependent variable in his supply function is the logarithm of the sum of output in all markets, but he does not derive this function from a micro hypothesis about the rational behavior of suppliers, and the only reference he gives as a basis for his supply function is the Lucas paper I have been discussing in detail. Thus, Sargent does not resolve the problem that the mean of logarithms and the logarithm of the mean are equated in a single model without any justification.

On the demand side, Sargent lists two equations instead of Lucas's one. They are the following:

$$R_t = R_{t-1} + \zeta(z_t - E_{t-1}z_t) + u_{4t}, \tag{6}$$

$$m_t - P_t = b_1 R_t + b_2 y_t + b_3(m_{t-1} - P_{t-1}) + u_{5t} \tag{7}$$

where $R_t$ is the nominal, long-term rate of interest, $z_t$ is a vector of exogenous variables in the (exogenous) "$IS$" curve, $m_t$ is the logarithm of money supply (exogenous), and $u_{jt}$ are mutually and serially independent random disturbances with zero mean.

I do not wish to deal with the complex issue of whether or not the martingale assumption for the nominal long-term rate can be accepted on an empirical basis, but I believe it is fair to say that the question has by no means been settled in favor of it. In the context of his model, Sargent (1976a, p. 208) apparently looks at equation 6 above as an abbreviated way of expressing the *IS*-curve relationship, as his definition of the exogenous variable $z_t$ indicates. It is not at all clear, however, how the *IS*-curve relationship can be solved for the nominal long-term rate, rather than for the real rate, without reference to monetary conditions in the economy, even in the stationary state.

Equation 7, which Sargent labels "the portfolio balance schedule," appears to me to be a mixture of the transactions demand for money and a poorly formulated asset-demand equation. As far as I can tell, there are only two assets that economic agents can hold in order to carry purchasing power from one period to the next. One is money, whose value is fixed in nominal terms and which pays no interest. The second instrument must be a perpetuity whose income payments are fixed in nominal terms, since the only rate of return introduced by Sargent is a nominal, long-term rate.[17] If this is so, then it is hard to see how one can justify the basic form of equation 7 as the description of portfolio-choice behavior. If agents are permitted to alter their portfolio once every period, then the relevant rate for the choice between money and the perpetuity is the one-period holding rate (which includes capital gains and losses), and not the market yield, as assumed by Sargent. But if the portfolio-planning horizon of individuals is not one period, what exactly is the portfolio-decision problem faced by agents in Sargent's model?

Since the alternative asset to money is the perpetuity, whose income payments are fixed in nominal terms, it is difficult to see how such an income stream, fixed in nominal terms, should not introduce a significant nonhomogeneity in prices to Sargent's model. Sargent does not explain how he can ignore this question, which should be of critical importance to his purpose.

It does not seem necessary to go much further in order to conclude that equations 6 and 7 are not derived rigorously from any sensible optimizing behavior of economic agents. However, an additional point gives a little insight into the basic motivation for these models. Sargent introduces the only dynamic element in equation 7 in the form of $(m_{t-1} - P_{t-1})$. In the literature of inventory control, whose theory parallels almost exactly that for the transactions demand for money, there is an extensive discussion of dynamic adjustment processes, but I know of no adjustment cost structure that would justify such a form.[18] By rearrangement of terms, equation 7 can be expressed as

$$\Delta P_t = -b_1 R_t - b_2 y_t + (1 - b_3)(m_{t-1} - P_{t-1}) + \Delta m_t + n_{5t}. \qquad (7')$$

This expression makes it clear that, according to equation 7, price must move proportionately with the money supply, with other things equal. (Note that $R_t$ is given by equation 6, and is independent of $P_t$, $y_t$, and $m_t$.) The proportionality then adjusts slowly to other things, such as real output and the long-term nominal rate of interest.

I must conclude therefore that the dynamic adjustment process introduced into equation 7 was chosen strictly for the purpose of preserving the homogeneity between money and prices in the short run. This is the only form of dynamics that serves this purpose, and therefore it is chosen here although there is no justification for this form of dynamics relative to any other.

To recapitulate, Sargent's model expands the original Lucas model by elaborating the demand side, but this elaborated description of the demand side of the economy is incoherent and contains a number of logical contradictions. In particular, Sargent's equations (6 and 7 here) cannot be derived from anything like a set of assumptions describing the consistent, rational behavior of individual economic agents. All the difficulties of Lucas's 1973 model, such as the requirement that the aggregate supply (which is the sum of the logarithms of its components) and the aggregate demand (which is the logarithm of the arithmetic sum of its components) be equated with each other, remain. Moreover, we do not know who is paying or receiving interest payments on bonds, nor how these payments are related to anything. More generally, neither the budget constraints nor the balance-sheet constraint, which bind all economic agents, are observed carefully in these models. Thus, Sargent's classical model of business cycles cannot serve as a useful starting point for further research on this subject.

What have we learned from the literature on equilibrium business-cycle models? Lucas's original 1972 work gave us, in the simplest possible context, a potentially useful insight into the consequences of the imperfect transmission of information by prices on supplies of factors of production (particularly labor) in the presence of stationary stochastic disturbances on both the real and the monetary side. I have stressed the point that Lucas's analysis applies to strictly stationary states by design. It might be interpreted as a modification of the general equilibrium analysis in the presence of uncertainty but with all contingency markets formulated by Arrow and Debreu. Lucas's analysis may be thought of as an inquiry into the consequence of missing some special type of contingency markets in an extremely simplified context.

The subsequent rapid development of macroeconomic analysis purportedly based on this abstract theory of Lucas did not attempt to integrate the insight obtained from Lucas' original analysis into a dynamic model, or to supplement it in the direction that I described above as necessary. Instead, advocates of this strand of analysis proceeded to take a quantum jump and treat Lucas's model as though it contained all that was worth knowing about the economy for the purpose of macroeconomic analysis, including dynamic adjustment processes. Faced with the necessity of bridging the gap between crudely aggregated versions of this stark model and the data generated by the real economy, the new classical macroeconomists deemed it permissible (without discussion) to introduce dynamic elements through any distributed lag processes so long as they met two criteria: that they did not disturb the homogeneity of the system with respect to all prices even in the short run, except through unanticipated price variations, and that demand for and the supply of current output be equated through the movement of current prices in every period, however large the movement of prices must be for this purpose. The latter requirement, however, turned out to be quite elusive. Sometimes it was not met at all; in other cases it was met by distorting the so-called aggregate supply function sufficiently to make the relation between it and the 1972 theory of Lucas essentially nonexistent.

## Concluding Remarks

When one attempts to describe dynamic processes of the economy carefully, it immediately becomes apparent that any characterization of the rational behavior of economic agents conditional on any realistic set of initial conditions involves important nonhomogeneities with respect to prices. Wages and prices are often set by long-term contracts. More obvious, practically all financial contracts are fixed in nominal terms, and some of them cover very long periods. Though formal theories are only beginning to be formulated that attempt to "explain" why some contracts cover long periods while others do not,[19] the presence of these long-term contracts, formal or informal, is a fact, and we cannot assume them away simply because we have no formal explanation for their existence. Equally important is the time it takes to design, produce, and emplace most capital goods, both equipment and structure, after the need for them is determined. This simple fact makes the current decisions of economic agents a function of past prices, and therefore introduces a short-run nonhomogeneity of the system with respect to current prices.

Once these possibilities of nonhomogeneity in behavioral equations with respect to current prices are recognized, many complex issues associated with short-run dynamics must be faced. In particular, it is likely that the short-run price elasticities of demand and supply are much smaller than those in the long run, and hence that prices will have to move much more in response to quantity shocks in any market in order to equilibrate demand and supply in that market than the long run, comparative static elasticities of demand and supply imply. Indeed, it may be impossible for prices to move enough to equilibrate the market, and this raises the possibility of excess demand or supply persisting in some markets. For such an economy, it is quite possible that the short-run dynamic adjustment processes may exhibit substantial instability. I share the judgment of Tobin (1975) that the recognition of the seriousness of this possible instability is the essence of Keynesian economics, and that any theory of business cycles must come to grips with this question.[20]

My conclusion, therefore, is that macro equilibrium business-cycle models have little to say about how economic fluctuations are generated in modern mixed economies. This does not mean that the incomplete information-transmission mechanism studied by Lucas in his 1972 paper should not play an important role in the generation of business cycles observed in real economies. However, this cannot be the only mechanism. In order that Lucas's original idea be exploited fully in explaining the complex phenomena of business cycles, it must be placed in the context with description of other, critical structures of the economy contributing to the determination of the dynamic characteristics of a macroeconomic system, and its specific role in this broader context must be explored both theoretically and empirically. Macro equilibrium business-cycle models developed since the publication of Lucas's 1972 paper have had nothing to say on this point.

Any effort to improve our understanding of economic fluctuations in modern mixed economies will inevitably involve detailed empirical studies of short-run dynamic adjustment mechanisms as well as equilibrium conditions, and improvements in our data and our methods for this purpose are urgently needed.[21] On the issue of market equilibrium, I believe that interactions between demand and supply (not necessarily their equality) for outputs as well as for factor inputs are more satisfactorily described in the better econometric models than they are in any of the so-called equilibrium business-cycle models, though they too need improvement.[22]

There is no alternative to hard and detailed studies of every aspect of the modern mixed economy, and imaginative theoretical construction and judicious empirical analysis must go hand in hand. The equilibrium business-cycle theory is not acceptable, because it attempts to exalt a simple idea to the complete and exclusive explanation of the workings of the economy, and does so without any empirical support.

## Acknowledgments

I am grateful for comments I have received from Jared Enzler, Stephen Goldfeld, Lewis Johnson, Franco Modigliani, George Moore, Ian Novos, and Robert Shiller.

## Notes

1. Lucas 1977, p. 9. I assume here that by the phrase "stochastically disturbed" Lucas means that the equation has an additive, white-noise disturbance term. If such an additive disturbance term has a complex moving average and/or autoregressive features, then it means little that the explicitly specified part of the system is a difference equation of very low order.

2. This is the message that was clearly conveyed by Lucas 1977 and Lucas and Sargent 1978. In very recent writings, Lucas (1980, 1981) appears to put a different interpretation on the basic message one is expected to receive from equilibrium business-cycle models.

3. This assumption, when it is combined with the assumptions described below that imply that all money is in the hands of members of the older generation, who must exchange it all during the period into output and consume what they purchase, guarantees that the velocity of money in this society per period is unity. For this purpose, we can exclude from our consideration output produced and consumed by the younger generation, which does not go through the market. See the following paragraph in the text.

4. Since the possibility of saturation is excluded, no one wishes to die with a positive money balance at the end of his life.

5. One may be struck by the artificiality of the setup at this point. Since the ratio of the new money given to every member of the older generation relative to the amount of money he carried over from the previous period is the same for all members, and since this fact is supposedly known, all members of the older generation know exactly by how much the money supply is increased for the current period. This being the case, it is hard to imagine how members of the younger generation can remain ignorant of this information. Evidently, members of older and younger generations never communicate in this economy. However, in the game we are playing here, the question of whether or not a particular assumption is reasonable or realistic is not relevant at this point.

6. Either the underlying stochastic processes generating monetary and real disturbances are completely known to economic agents or else they are not known completely and agents are learning about their nature from the accumulation of data over time. In the former case, any finite number of additional observations would not add any new information, and therefore additional assumptions are irrelevant. In the latter case, any authority that can alter the nature of stochastic processes (a change in the policy rule) will be able to alter the time pattern of the equilibrium solution, and money will not be neutral independent of initial conditions. Presumably, this is not what Lucas had in mind in writing his 1972 paper.

7. See note 6. If economic agents obtain substantial information from a finite number of past observations about the nature of the stochastic processes generating disturbances, then anyone who controls the nature of the stochastic processes can alter it without all economic agents learning his actions immediately, and thus monetary policy will have real effects. On the other hand, if economic agents always learn any change in the policy rule (the process generating the monetary disturbances) immediately, then Lucas must explain what it is that agents are learning from a finite amount of past data.

8. This point was also made, more formally and from a somewhat different point of view, by Azariadis (1981).

9. Lucas himself sets down the condition clearly. The utility of members of the younger generation is given by

$$U(c,n) + E[V(c')]$$

where $c$ is the current consumption, $n$ is the current supply of labor, and $c'$ is the future consumption. The assumptions in question (given by Lucas's equations 3.3 and 3.4) are

$$V''(c')c' + V'(c') > 0,$$

$$\frac{c'V''(c')}{V'(c')} \le -a < 0.$$

Since $V'(c')$ must be strictly positive for finite $c'$, we can write the first of these equations as

$$\frac{c'V''(c')}{V'(c')} + 1 > 0,$$

or

$$\frac{c'V''(c')}{V'(c')} < 1.$$

That Lucas was well aware of the significance of this assumption is clear from his comment in note 5 on page 107 of Lucas 1972. Examples of cases in which the Platt measure of risk aversion is outside the range defined above, resulting in the Phillips curve sloping the "wrong" way, is provided by Kennickell (1981).

10. For a discussion of empirical evidence on the Platt measure of risk aversion, see, for example, Friend and Blume 1975 and Friend and Hasbrouck 1981. Lucas cannot be faulted for not being aware of these empirical findings, because they came after his paper in question had been written.

11. Lucas (1981, p. 564) berates Tobin for addressing "a platform synthesized from a miscellany of illustrative models" and not concentrating exclusively on the question of whether or not the Keynesian macroeconometric models are of value in providing reliable estimates of the effects of alternative monetary and fiscal policies. Most of us will agree that a proper scientific discussion can proceed only when alternative theories are subjected to critical reviews on an equal basis, and the defects of equilibrium models pose just as serious a question as do the defects of macroeconometric models. Since there is no fully developed equilibrium model in the literature, for the purposes of discussion, there is no alternative to constructing a "platform synthesized from a miscellany of illustrative models." If illustrative models are not serious enough even for this purpose, then perhaps there is nothing to discuss. See also Tobin 1980a and 1980b.

12. My comment applies strictly to the case in which the aggregate price index is the mean of logarithms of individual prices, not to the case in which it is the logarithm of the arithmetic mean of prices.

13. In the standard Bayesian analysis, the mean of the prior distribution, $(\bar{P_t})$ is updated when the sample outcome $P_t$ becomes known. As I will argue below, if we take Lucas's basic theoretical structure as the basis for this macroanalysis then this is not the case.

14. See quotation from Lucas 1977 cited above. See also Lucas 1977, p. 25.

15. On this point, I appeal to the authority of Lucas. In reference to one group of these models (Phelps and Taylor 1977; Taylor 1979; Fischer 1977, Lucas (1981, p. 564) states: "None of these model offers an explanation as to why people should choose to bind themselves to contracts which seem to be in no one's self-interest, and my conjecture is that when reasons for this are found they will reduce to the kind of informational difficulties already stressed in my 1972 article, for example. But even if true, this has yet to be shown, so that at present these models must be viewed as a genuinely different route by which the puzzle motivating the new classicals may be resolved."

16. Another model that I exclude from this review is that of Lucas 1975. Though Lucas attempts to deal with an important issue of the role of capital in it, the structure of this model is not very transparent, and it does not clarify issues raised here.

17. If the alternative to money is a long-term bond with a fixed maturity, then, as time goes on, there will exist in the economy bonds of all maturities and a corresponding range of interest rates.

18. A formulation of the inventory-adjustment process parallel to Sargent's will lead to the following absurd result, which is against the whole purpose of holding inventory: Suppose that, in one period, sales are lower than normal, and the inventory-sales ratio is exceptionally high. Now suppose further that, in the following period, sales turn out to be much higher than normal. Then, since the rules say that the inventory-sales ratio can adjust only slowly, the firm must accumulate the inventory at an extraordinarily rapid rate in order to maintain the higher-than-normal inventory-sales ratio.

19. For a survey of these theories, see Azariadis 1979.

20. The presences of an oligopolistic structure in many markets, of capital goods with differing adjustment costs, and of storable goods having different cost structures for storing and for adjusting production levels over time introduce further complex dynamics, but are beyond the scope of this paper.

21. The question of econometric methodology raised by Lucas (1976)—namely, whether or not it is possible to estimate the type of behavioral equations often encountered in econometric models in the presence of changes in policy rules that act as constraints on economic agents—is a separate issue that I will discuss in a paper under preparation.

22. Malinvaud (1980) stresses the need to model "market pressures" rather than the equalization of demand and supply through price movements alone.

## Bibliography

Adelman, I., and F. L. Adelman. 1959. The dynamic properties of the Klein-Goldberger model. *Econometrica* 27 (October): 596–625.

Azariadis, C. 1979. Implicit Contracts and Related Topics: A Survey. Department of Economics, University of Pennsylvania. CARESS Working Paper 79–17.

Azariadis, C. 1981. A Reexamination of Natural Rate Theory. Department of Economics, University of Pennsylvania. CARESS Working Paper 79–01. Revised February 1981.

Bailey, M. 1978. Stabilization Policy and Private Economic Behavior. Brookings Papers on Economic Activity, no. 1.

Barro, R. J. 1982. The Equilibrium Approach to Business Cycles. In *Money, Expectations and Business Cycles: Essays in Macroeconomics*. New York: Academic.

Fischer, S. 1977. Long-term contracts, rational expectations, and the optimal money supply rule. *J. Pol. Econ.* 85: 191–205.

Friend, I., and M. E. Blume. 1975. The demand for risky assets. *American Economic Review* 65 (December): 900–922.

Friend, I., and J. Hasbrouck. 1981. Effects of Inflation on the Profitability and Valuation of U. S. Corporations. Working Paper 3–81, Rodney White Center for Financial Research, University of Pennsylvania.

Granger, C. W. 1966. The typical spectral shape of an economic variable. *Econometrica* 34 (January): 150–161.

Kennickell, A. 1981. A Note on Lucas and Azariadis. (Manuscript.)

Klein, L. R. 1982. Lectures in Econometrics. To be published.

Lucas, R. E. 1972. Expectations and the neutrality of money. *Journal of Economic Theory* 4 (April): 103–124.

Lucas, R. E. 1973. Some international evidence on output-inflation tradeoffs. *American Economic Review* 63 (June): 326–334.

Lucas, R. E. 1975. An equilibrium model of the business cycle. *Journal of Political Economy* 83 (December): 1113–1144.

Lucas, R. E. 1976. Econometric Policy Evaluation: A Critique. Carnegie-Rochester Conferences on Public Policy (supplement to *Journal of Monetary Economics*): 19–46.

Lucas, R. E. 1977. Understanding Business Cycles. Carnegie-Rochester Conference on Public Policy (supplement to *Journal of Monetary Economics*): 7–33.

Lucas, R. E. 1980. Methods and problems in business cycle theory. *Journal of Money, Credit and Banking* 12 (November): 696–715.

Lucas, R. E. 1981. Tobin and monetarism: A review article. *Journal of Economic Literature* 19 (June): 558–567.

Lucas, R. E., and T. J. Sargent. 1978. After Keynesian macroeconomics. In After the Phillips Curve: Persistence of High Inflation and High Unemployment. Conference Series no. 19, Federal Reserve Bank of Boston.

Malinvaud, E. 1981. Econometrics faced with the needs of macroeconomic policy. *Econometrica* 49: 1363–1376.

Moran, J. P. 1950. The oscillatory behavior of moving averages. *Proceedings of the Cambridge Philosophical Society* 46: 272–280.

Otsuki, M. 1971. Oscillations in stochastic simulations of linear systems. *Economic Studies Quarterly* 22 (December): 54–71.

Phelps, E. S. 1969. Introductory chapter. In E. S. Phelps et al., *Microeconomic Foundations of Employment and Inflation Theory*. New York: Norton, 1969.

Phelps, E. S., and J. B. Taylor. 1977. Stabilizing powers of monetary policy under rational expectations. *Journal of Political Economy* 85: 163–190.

Sargent, T. J. 1976a. A classical macroeconometric model for the United States. *Journal of Political Economy* 84 (April): 207–238.

Sargent, T. J. 1976b. The observational equivalence of natural and unnatural rate theories of macroeconomics. *Journal of Political Economy* 84: 631–640.

Sargent, T. J., and N. Wallace. 1975. Rational expectations, the optimal monetary investment, and optimal money supply rule. *Journal of Political Economy* 83 (April): 241–254.

Taylor, J. B. 1979. Estimation and control of a macroeconomic model with rational expectation. *Econometrica* 47: 1267–1286.

Tobin, J. 1975. Keynesian models of recession and depression. *AEA Papers and Proceedings*, 195–202.

Tobin, J. 1980a. "Are new classical models plausible enough to guide policy?" *Journal of Money, Credit and Banking* 12 (November): 788–799.

Tobin, J. 1980b. *Asset Accumulations and Economic Activity: Reflections on Contemporary Macroeconomic Theory*. University of Chicago Press.

# 3 Socially Optimal Income Distributions

Lawrence J. Lau

Suppose that an economy consists of identical individuals, each of whom has the same utility function of income, $u(M)$, which is strictly monotonic and (not necessarily strictly) concave. Suppose further that the social-welfare function of the economy,[1] $W$, is given by the sum of the utilities over all individuals in the economy, so that

$$W = \int_0^\infty u(M)f(M)dM \tag{1}$$

where $f(M)$ is the probability density function of income.[2] A socially optimal income distribution is defined to be a distribution whose probability density function, $f(M)$, maximizes $W$ in equation 1 subject to the given aggregate income constraint of the economy:

$$\overline{M} = \int_0^\infty Mf(M)dM. \tag{2}$$

Maximization of social welfare $W$ given by equation 1 subject to the aggregate-income constraint given by equation 2 is an optimal-control problem. One can attempt to solve this problem formally. However, it is straightforward to observe that the concavity of $u(M)$ implies, by Jensen's (1906) inequality, that

$$\int_0^\infty u(M)f(M)dM \leqq u(\overline{M})$$

for every probability density function $f(M)$ (in fact, for every probability measure) satisfying

$$\int_0^\infty Mf(M)dM = \overline{M}.$$

But if $f(M)$ is chosen so that it has all its probability density concentrated at $M = \overline{M}$, denoted $\delta(\overline{M})$ (see note 3)—that is, so that it is a distribution in the sense of Schwartz 1966 centered at $\overline{M}$—then

$$\int_0^\infty u(M)\delta(\overline{M})dM = u(\overline{M}).$$

We conclude that the point mass probability density function located at the mean, which implies a perfectly egalitarian income distribution, maximizes social welfare.[4] This is a well-known result for economies with social-welfare functions additive in the individual utility functions that are identical and concave.

It will be shown that, if the utility of an individual depends on not only his income but also his relative position in the income distribution, then, even if all individual utility functions are identical and strictly concave in the respective own incomes, the egalitarian income distribution is not necessarily a socially optimal income distribution. In fact, all continuously differentiable income-distribution functions are potentially optimal income distributions with appropriate choices of the individual utility functions.

## Statement of the Problem

Let the utility function of an individual be given by

$$u = u(M, F(M))$$

where $u(M, F(M))$ is a finite, real-valued function of two non-negative variables, $M$ is the income of the individual, and $F(M)$ is the value of the distribution function of income in the economy evaluated at the level of the income of the individual. In this paper the distribution function of a random variable $m$ is taken to be

$$F(M) = \text{Prob}[m < M]. \tag{3}$$

For continuous distributions, this definition coincides with the conventional definition

$$F(M) = \text{Prob}[m \leq M]. \tag{4}$$

For discrete and mixed discrete-continuous distributions, our definition differs from the conventional definition by the probability density concentrated at $M$.

$F(M)$ thus takes values between zero and unity. In other words, the utility of the individual depends on the level of his income and the proportion of the population in the economy having an income less than his. The latter variable may be considered to be a measure of his relative income position in the economy. It is assumed that individual utility is monotonically increasing in both arguments, that is, utility increases with income and with relative income position. This assumption may be regarded as a version of the relative-income hypothesis.[5] In addition, it is assumed that individual utility is concave in income, holding relative income position constant.

The modification of the definition of a distribution function is not completely innocuous. It has the effect of making $F(M)$ equal to zero, the minimum value, for a perfectly egalitarian income distribution at the level of equal income $M$. Without this modification, $F(M)$ would have been equal to unity, the maximum value. Thus we assume implicitly that, with income held constant, an individual prefers having some other individuals with incomes lower than his to having none. This creates a bias against an egalitarian distribution of income.

The interesting questions are whether, given that all individual utility functions are identical and have the form $u(M, F(M))$, there is a distribution of income that maximizes social welfare

$$W = \int_0^\infty u(M, F(M)) F'(M) dM \tag{5}$$

subject to the aggregate income constraint

$$\overline{M} = \int_0^\infty M F'(M) dM,$$

and, if there is such a distribution, whether it is the egalitarian distribution or some other distribution.

## A Two-Person Example

We first consider a two-person example to illustrate some of the issues involved. Let there be two individuals in the economy. Each individual's utility function is given by

$$u(M_i, F(M_i)) = \alpha M_i + \beta M_i F(M_i) \quad (i = 1, 2) \tag{6}$$

where $\alpha$ and $\beta$ are non-negative constants. Let the aggregate income constraint be

$$M_1 + M_2 = 1. \tag{7}$$

Social welfare is given by

$$W = \alpha(M_1 + M_2) + \beta(M_1 F(M_1) + M_2 F(M_2)), \tag{8}$$

which, because of the aggregate income constraint, becomes

$$W = \alpha + \beta(M_1 F(M_1) + (1 - M_1)F(1 - M_1)). \tag{9}$$

We seek to maximize $W$ with respect to a choice of $F(\cdot)$. In this simple example, $F(\cdot)$ can only take the following form:

$$F(M) = \begin{cases} 0 & (M \leq \frac{1}{2}) \\ \frac{1}{2} & (\frac{1}{2} < M \leq 1) \\ 1 & (1 < M). \end{cases}$$

Under an egalitarian income distribution, the income of either individual is equal to $\frac{1}{2}$, so that $F(M_1) = F(M_2) = 0$. Thus,

$$W = \alpha. \tag{10}$$

If one of the individuals, say the first, is given a greater income, then

$$W = \alpha + \beta M_1/2, \tag{11}$$

from which we deduce that $W$ can be maximized by giving all the income to the first individual so that

$$W = \alpha + \beta/2. \tag{12}$$

By symmetry, the same social welfare can be achieved by giving all the income to the second individual. Thus, we have an example in which the socially optimal income distribution is one of extreme inequality. Although this extreme inequality is an artifact of the constancy of the marginal utility of individual incomes, it does demonstrate that a socially optimal income distribution is not necessarily egalitarian. More general cases will be considered in the next section.

## The Case of a Continuous Income Distribution

Next, consider the case in which the number of individuals is sufficiently large that the distribution of income can be taken to be continuous. Social welfare $W$ is given by

$$\int_0^\infty u(M, F(M))F'(M)dM. \tag{13}$$

Society wishes to maximize $W$ with respect to $F(M)$ (or, equivalently, $F'(M)$) subject to the aggregate-income constraint

$$\overline{M} = \int_0^\infty M F'(M) dM. \tag{14}$$

If $F'(M)$ is assumed to exist and to be continuous, this may be regarded as a calculus-of-variations problem. Euler's equation implies that

$$\frac{\partial u}{\partial F}(M, F(M))F'(M) - \frac{d}{dM}[u(M, F(M)) - \lambda M] = 0,$$

or

$$\frac{\partial u}{\partial M}(M, F(M)) - \lambda = 0, \tag{15}$$

where $\lambda$ is the Lagrange multiplier corresponding to the aggregate-income constraint.

Equation 15 defines $F(M)$ implicitly as a function of $M$ and $\lambda$. With this function given, equation 14 can be used to determine $\lambda$ if necessary. In addition, $F(M)$ must satisfy the boundary conditions $F(0) = 0$ and $F(\infty) = 1$ (as well as non-negativity and monotonicity conditions). Furthermore, the second-order and higher-order conditions for a maximum must also be verified.[6]

## Example 1

Let the individual utility function be given by

$$u(M, F(M)) = -e^{-M} + M F(M),$$

and let the aggregate income constraint be given by

$$\int_0^\infty M F'(M) dM = 1.$$

Equation 15 becomes

$$e^{-M} + F(M) = \lambda.$$

Hence,

$$F(M) = \lambda - e^{-M}.$$

By applying the boundary conditions $F(0) = 0$ and $F(\infty) = 1$, we deduce that $\lambda = 1$. Finally, we verify that the aggregate-income constraint is satisfied:

$$\int_0^\infty Me^{-M}dM = 1.$$

Thus, we conclude that the socially optimal income distribution for this particular concave utility function is the exponential distribution

$$F(M) = 1 - e^{-M},$$

$$F'(M) = e^{-M}.$$

The social welfare for this optimal income distribution can be computed as

$$W = \int_0^\infty [-e^{-M} + M F(M)]F'(M)dM$$

$$= \int_0^\infty [-e^{-2M} + M(1 - e^{-M})e^{-M}]dM$$

$$= -\tfrac{1}{2} + 1 - \int_0^\infty Me^{-2M}dM$$

$$-\tfrac{1}{4}.$$

By comparison, an egalitarian income distribution results in a social welfare equal to (where $\delta(\cdot)$ is the Dirac delta function)

$$W = \int_0^\infty (-e^{-M})\delta(1)dM,$$

$$= -e^{-1},$$

which is clearly less than $\tfrac{1}{4}$.

**Example 2**

Let the individual utility function be given by

$$u(M, F(M)) = \ln M\{-\ln[1 - F(M)]\}.$$

Let the aggregate-income constraint be given by

$$\int_0^\infty M F'(M)dM = 1.$$

Equation 15 becomes

$$\frac{1}{M}\{-\ln[1 - F(M)]\} = \lambda,$$

or

$$1 - F(M) = e^{-\lambda M},$$

or

$$F(M) = 1 - e^{-\lambda M}.$$

This function satisfies the boundary conditions identically. Substituting this function into the aggregate-income constraint, we can determine $\lambda$, the value of the Lagrange multiplier:

$$\int_0^\infty M\lambda e^{-\lambda M} dM = \frac{1}{\lambda}$$

$$= 1.$$

Thus, $\lambda = 1$.

The social welfare can be computed (Gradshteyn and Ryzhik 1965, p. 576) as

$$\int_0^\infty M \ln M e^{-M} dM = 1 - C$$

where $C$ is Euler's constant ($= 0.577215\ldots$). By comparison, under an egalitarian income distribution, social welfare is equal to zero.

Note that although the individual utility functions are different in examples 1 and 2, the optimal income distributions are the same.

**Example 3**

Let the individual utility function be given by

$$u(M, F(M)) = -e^{-2M}(M + 1) + M F(M).$$

Let the aggregate-income constraint be given by

$$\int_0^\infty M F'(M) dM = 1.$$

Equation 15 becomes

$$2e^{-2M}(M+1) - e^{-2M} + F(M) = \lambda,$$

or

$$F(M) = \lambda - e^{-2M}(2M+1).$$

The boundary conditions require that $\lambda = 1$, so

$$F(M) = 1 - e^{-2M}(2M+1),$$

$$F'(M) = 2e^{-2M}(2M).$$

These may be recognized as the distribution and probability density functions of the Erlang (or gamma) distribution. It may be verified that

$$\int_0^\infty M2e^{-2M}(2M)dM = 1,$$

so the aggregate-income constraint is satisfied. The Erlang distribution is considerably more flexible than the exponential in that it can have a nonzero mode.

Can any general principles be induced from these examples? First, from Euler's equation (15), we find that the marginal utility of income, with the relative income position held constant, is equalized across all individuals even though income is not necessarily equalized. This situation can occur because, if the marginal utility of income decreases with income but increases with relative income position, it is possible to increase an individual's income (which also raises his relative income position) while holding his marginal utility of income constant. Likewise, it is possible to decrease an individual's income (which increases his marginal utility of income but lowers his relative income position) while holding his marginal utility of income constant. Thus, equal marginal utilities of income in this case, even with identical strictly concave individual utility functions, do not necessarily imply the optimality of an egalitarian income distribution.

Second, the optimal income distribution function is determined by equation 15:

$$u_M(M, F(M)) = \lambda.$$

The boundary conditions on $F(M)$ imply that $u_M(0,0) = u_M(\infty, 1)$ if they both exist and are finite. This condition must be satisfied by $u(M, F(M))$. In addition, $F(M)$, being a distribution function, must be monotonically increasing in $M$. Thus, by the implicit-function theorem,

$$\frac{dF(M)}{dM} = -\frac{(\partial/\partial M)u_M(M, F(M))}{(\partial/\partial F)u_M(M, F(M))}$$

$$= -\frac{u_{MM}(M, F(M))}{u_{MF}(M, F(M))}.$$

By concavity, $u_{MM}(M, F(M)) \leqq 0$. Thus, in order for $dF(M)/dM$ to be non-negative, $u_{MF}(M, F(M))$ must be non-negative. We conclude that, in order that there exist a continuous and differentiable socially optimal income distribution function,

$$u_{MF}(M, F(M)) \geqq 0.$$

This is not to say that there exists no socially optimal income distribution if $u_{MF}(M, F(M)) < 0$; there is simply no continuously differentiable one. (Bear in mind that an egalitarian income-distribution function is not continuously differentiable.)

To understand intuitively why this may be the case, consider the situation in which the initial distribution of income is egalitarian, and thus every individual has the same marginal utility of income. If the income of one individual is increased by the same amount as the income of another individual is decreased (thus preserving the aggregate-income constraint), the marginal utility of the former individual will decrease, and the marginal utility of the latter individual will increase, on account of both changes in incomes and in relative income positions, if any. Thus the rule of equal marginal utility will be violated at the optimum. We conclude that, if $u_{MF}(M, F(M)) < 0$, the egalitarian income distribution is an optimal income distribution if the rule of equal marginal utility holds.

Third, if the marginal utility of income, given the relative income position, is independent of individual income, that is, if

$$\frac{\partial u}{\partial M}(M, F(M)) = u_M(F(M)),$$

then equation 15 becomes

$$u_M(F(M)) = \lambda. \tag{16}$$

Equation 16 violates the boundary conditions on $F(M)$. We conclude that if the marginal utility of income is a constant for given relative income position, the socially optimal distribution of income cannot be continuously differentiable. (Recall the two-person example above.)

Fourth, if the marginal utility of income, given the relative income position, is independent of the relative income position, then Euler's equation does not determine $F(M)$. In fact, it can be shown that an egalitarian income distribution is always optimal for this case. (This will be done in the following section.)

Fifth, note that in examples 1 and 2, although the individual utility functions are different, the optimal income distributions are the same. (In the following section the equivalence class of utility functions for which the optimal income distributions are the same will be characterized.)

## Invariance of Optimal Income Distribution

If the marginal utility of income given the relative income position is independent of the relative income position, that is, if

$$\frac{\partial u}{\partial M}(M, F(M)) = u_M(M), \tag{17}$$

the egalitarian income distribution is always optimal. Equation 17 is implied by and implies that the individual utility function has the form

$$u(M, F(M)) = u_1(M) + u_2(F(M)).$$

Thus, we need to show that social welfare,

$$W = \int_0^\infty [u_1(M) + u_2(F(M))]F'(M)dM,$$

is always maximized by an egalitarian income distribution. We need the following lemma.

LEMMA 1:   Let $F(x)$ be any arbitrary continuous distribution function of a random variable $x$ of finite dimension, and let $f(z)$ be a finite real-valued function of a single non-negative variable. Then $\int f(F(x))dF$ is a constant for any given function $f(z)$ independent of the choice of the distribution of $F(x)$.

PROOF:   By a change of variable[7] $u = F(x)$,

$$\int f(F(x))dF = \int_0^1 f(u)du,$$

which is independent of the choice of the distribution function $F(x)$. Q.E.D.

We are now in a position to prove the following theorem.

THEOREM 1:   Let the individual utility function, which is a finite real-valued function, be given by

$$u(M, F(M)) = u_1(M) + u_2(F(M)).$$

Then, subject to the aggregate-income constraint, any continuous distribution function $F^*(M)$ that maximizes

$$\int u_1(M)dF$$

also maximizes

$$\int [u_1(M) + u_2(F(M))]dF.$$

In addition, if $u(M, F(M))$ is concave in $M$ given $F(M)$, the egalitarian income distribution maximizes social welfare.

PROOF:   By Lemma 1,

$$\int u_2(F(M))dF$$

is a constant independent of $F(M)$. Thus, the distribution that maximizes $\int u_1(M)dF$ also maximizes $\int u_1(M)dF + \int u_2(F(M))dF$. In addition, if $u_1(M)$ is concave, the egalitarian income distribution maximizes $\int u_1(M)dF$. Q.E.D.

Lemma 1 also implies that any income distribution that maximizes $\int_0^\infty u(M, F(M))F'(M)dM$ also maximizes $\int_0^\infty [u(M, F(M)) + u^*(F(M))]$ $F'(M)dM$ for any arbitrary function $u^*(\cdot)$. Thus, the optimal income distribution (whatever it may be) is invariant to the addition of an arbitrary function of the relative income position alone to the individual utility function.

What types of transformation of the individual utility function will leave the optimal income distribution invariant? We already know that addition of a function depending on $F(M)$ alone will leave the optimal income distribution invariant. What other types of transformations are possible?

Return to Euler's equation:

$$\frac{\partial u}{\partial M}(M, F(M)) = \lambda.$$

Suppose there is another individual utility function $u^*(M, F(M))$ for which $F(M)$ is also the optimal income distribution. It is necessary and sufficient that

$$\frac{dF(M)}{dM} = -\frac{u_{MM}(M, F)}{u_{MF}(M, F)} = -\frac{u^*_{MM}(M, F)}{u^*_{MF}(M, F)} \tag{18}$$

for all admissible values of $M$ and $F$ satisfying Euler's equation. Equation 18 is implied by

$$u^*_M(M, F) = g(u_M(M, F)) \tag{19}$$

where $g(\cdot)$ is a monotonically increasing and differentiable real-valued function of a single variable.[8] Equation 19 may be integrated to yield

$$u^*(M, F) = \int g(u_M(M, F))dM + h(F) \tag{20}$$

where $h(\cdot)$ is an arbitrary real-valued function of a single variable. We have therefore proved the following.

THEOREM 2: Let the individual utility function, which is a finite real-valued function of two non-negative variables, be given by $u(M, F(M))$. Let $F^*(M)$ be any continuously differentiable income-distribution function that maximizes social welfare, defined as

$$W = \int_0^\infty u(M, F(M))F'(M)dM,$$

subject to the aggregate-income constraint

$$\overline{M} = \int_0^\infty M F'(M)dM.$$

Then $F^*(M)$ also maximizes

$$W = \int_0^\infty u^*(M, F(M))F'(M)dM$$

subject to

$$\overline{M} = \int_0^\infty M F'(M)dM$$

where $u^*(M, F(M))$ is any individual utility function that can be written in the form

$$u^*(M, F(M)) = \int g(u_M(M, F(M)))dM + h(F(M))$$

where $g(\cdot)$ is a monotonically increasing and differentiable real-valued function of a single variable and $h(\cdot)$ is an arbitrary real-valued function of a single variable.

A linear transformation of the individual utility function leaves the optimal income distribution unchanged. However, a monotonic but non-linear transformation of the individual utility function does not in general leave the optimal income distribution unchanged.

## The "Inverse-Optimal" Problem

Is it possible to find, for every continuously differentiable distribution function $F(M)$, an individual utility function and hence a social-welfare function for which the given income distribution function is optimal?

Again, look at Euler's equation:

$$\frac{\partial u}{\partial M}(M, F(M)) = \lambda.$$

Given any distribution function $G(M)$, we can first compute the implied aggregate income:

$$\int_0^\infty M\,G'(M)\,dM = \overline{M}.$$

Let the marginal utility function be given by

$$\frac{\partial u}{\partial M}(M, F) = 1 - G(M) + F. \tag{21}$$

This function is non-negative, decreasing in own income, and increasing in relative income position, and hence satisfies all the requirements for a marginal utility function admitting a continuously differentiable optimal income distribution. In addition, if we set $\lambda = 1$, then equation 21 implies that $F = G(M)$. The implied utility function takes the form

$$u(M, F(M)) = M - \int_0^M G(M')\,dM' + M\,F(M), \tag{22}$$

from which it can be verified that $\lambda = (\partial u/\partial M)(M, G(M)) = 1$. Thus, we have proved the following.

THEOREM 3: Any continuously differentiable income distribution function $F(M)$ satisfying an aggregate-income constraint is potentially a socially optimal income distribution for a social-welfare function expressible as the sum of appropriately chosen identical individual utility functions $u(M, F(M))$ that are twice continuously differentiable, monotonically increasing in $M$ and $F$, and concave in $M$ and have positive second cross-partial derivatives.

## Concluding Remarks

The individual utility function has been allowed here to depend not only on absolute level of own income but also on relative income position in the population. It is hypothesized that, with the level of own income held constant, an individual's utility increases with increases in relative income position. It has been shown that, with such a specification of individual utility functions, social welfare—defined as the sum of these utility functions over all individuals—is not necessarily maximized by the egalitarian income distribution even if all utility functions are identical and concave (or even strictly concave) and selfish (that is, if only own income and own income position matter to the individual).

Although the optimal income distribution is not egalitarian, it is not inequitable. It is "fair" in the sense that every individual in the economy faces the same probability distribution of income and has an equal chance and equal opportunity. The society determines only the shape of the optimal income distribution. Which individual receives what income remains to be determined randomly in accordance with the probability distribution. In addition, the expected utility of the individual (assuming that the individual utility function is also the von Neumann–Morgenstern utility function), which turns out to be identical to social welfare, is higher under the optimal income distribution than under an egalitarian income distribution at a fixed mean income.

There are several directions in which this research can be extended. First, in much of the analysis here the optimal income distribution function is only optimal within the class of continuously differentiable distribution functions. This restriction allowed the use of standard calculus-of-variations techniques. It is desirable to relax this restriction by employing more powerful optimization methods. Second, since it has been shown that all continuous income-distribution functions are potentially optimal for some appropriate choice of the individual utility function, it is important to establish the empirical relevance of this type of individual utility function, perhaps through survey techniques, and to ascertain the degree of dependence of individual marginal utility on the relative income position, if any. In this regard, additional work establishing the equivalence classes of individual utility functions corresponding to common empirical income distribution will be very useful. Third, one can introduce additional arguments that depend on the income-distribution function into the individual utility functions. Examples of such additional arguments include the variance, the skewness, the minimum income, and the lowest decile point. The resulting socially optimal income distribution will reflect the individual's preferences over these characteristics of the income distribution functions as well.

## Acknowledgments

I am grateful to T. W. Anderson, D. Andrews, K. J. Arrow, R. Finn, P. Hammond, M. Patel, E. Sheshinski, and B. Van Zummeren for helpful discussions. This research was partially supported by the National Science Foundation under grant no. SOC77-11105 at Stanford University.

# Notes

1. One can assume that this is the social-welfare function of a dictator or that it is arrived at through social consensus.

2. Here the term *probability density function* is used in a generalized sense. $f(M)dM$ should be interpreted as a probability measure. The lowest possible income is taken to be zero. However, the present analysis is unaffected if zero is replaced by $-\infty$.

3. This is also referred to as the Dirac delta function. (See Dirac 1926–1927.)

4. It is, of course, not necessarily the only maximizer unless the individual utility functions are strictly concave.

5. The relative income hypothesis is due to Duesenberry (1952). See also Easterlin 1974. In our formulation only the rank by income matters to the individual, not the whole income distribution.

6. See for example Bliss 1925 for second-order and higher-order conditions for a maximum.

7. This change of variable was suggested by T. W. Anderson. See Goldman and Uzawa 1964.

8. However, equation 19 is not implied by equation 18, because equation 18 does not need to hold for all $M$ and $F$.

# Bibliography

Bliss, G. A. 1925. *Calculus of Variations*. Chicago: Open Court.

Dirac, P. A. M. 1926–1927. The physical interpretation of the quantum dynamics. *Proceedings of the Royal Society* A 113: 621–641.

Duesenberry, J. S. 1952. *Income, Saving and the Theory of Consumer Behavior*. Cambridge, Mass.: Harvard University Press.

Easterlin, R. A. 1974. Does economic growth improve the human lot: Some empirical evidence. In *Nations and Households in Economic Growth: Essays in Honor of Moses Abramovitz*, P. A. David and M. W. Reder, eds. New York: Academic.

Goldman, S. M. and H. Uzawa. 1964. A note on separability in demand analysis. *Econometrica* 32: 387–398.

Gradshteyn, I. S., and I. W. Ryzhik. 1965. *Table of Integrals, Series, and Products*, fourth edition, tr. A. Jeffrey. New York: Academic.

Jenson, J L., W. V. 1906. Sur les fonctions convexes et les inegalities entre les valeurs moyennes. *Acta Mathematica* 30: 175–193.

Schwartz, L. 1966. *Théorie des distributions*. Paris: Hermann.

# 4 Inflation and the Composition of Deficit Finance

Nissan Liviatan

Since the seminal contribution of Blinder and Solow (1973) economists have debated the question of whether the long-run multiplier of bond-financed deficit is more inflationary than that of money-financed deficit. These studies, for example Tobin and Buiter 1976, are based on the assumption that in the long run the government budget is balanced. Indeed this must be the case when the price level and population are constant. However, when we consider a growing, full-employment, inflationary economy, then it is possible to maintain a permanent deficit financed by the "inflation tax" and by population growth.

The long-term macroeconomics under the latter situation are analyzed in Turnovsky 1978 and Smith 1979. One basic question that arises in these papers concerns the long-term effect of changes in the composition of the deficit on the inflation rate. Both Turnovsky and Smith find that an increase in the proportion ($\gamma$) of new money (relative to new bonds) in deficit financing tends to be deflationary. (Smith analyzes the ratio $\gamma$ directly, whereas Turnovsky varies the stock of government bonds as a policy parameter.)

The foregoing models differ not only in their analytic structures but also in their approaches to the nature of government policy. When discussing long-term deficit financing, one has to specify what is the government's policy toward the other parameters under its control. Turnovsky assumes that the government holds constant its expenditures on goods and services ($g$). Smith assumes that it holds constant $g$ plus real net debt interest, which amounts to fixing the total deficit when taxes are constant (in this he follows the choice advocated in Tobin and Buiter 1976; I refer here to the G′ concept defined on page 61 of Smith 1979).

Generally, one would expect that the alternative assumptions used by these authors should lead to different results, since under the constant-deficit policy (CDP) any change in interest payments on government debt must be offset by an appropriate change in $g$ or in taxes, whereas under Turnovsky's assumption no such offsetting is required. Note also that under the latter assumption the composition ($\gamma$) of the deficit and the size of the deficit are changed simultaneously (which is not the case in the alternative approach). I shall therefore refer to this case as the variable-deficit policy, or VDP.

It is not my purpose to advocate the use of one of these assumptions in preference to the other—both are legitimate. But I wish to emphasize that they should yield different implications when examined under the same analytic structure (which is not the case for the two foregoing papers). Carl Christ (1979) has pointed out that different approaches of the kind described above tend to yield qualitatively different results in the comparative analysis of long-term multipliers of bond-financed versus money-financed government expenditures. Why should not the same be true for the analysis of the composition of deficit financing?

I will show here that there is indeed a fundamental difference between the foregoing approaches with respect to long-term open-market operations. In order to simplify the analysis of dynamics (which becomes rather messy with *ad hoc* models) and to avoid the arbitrary characteristics of the *ad hoc* models mentioned above, I adapt the optimization model of Sidrauski (1967) to the present purposes. A basic implication of using the Sidrauski model under the VDP and some separability assumptions is that it renders the behavior of the financial sector completely independent of the production sector, not only across steady states but during the transition phase as well.[1] The same is true for the CDP when it is formulated in an appropriate way. This simplifies the analysis drastically.

The main result of our analysis is that, across steady states, an increase in $\gamma$ is deflationary under the VDP (this conforms to Turnovsky's results) and inflationary under the CDP (contrary to the conclusion of Smith). In the final section the problem is analyzed in terms of comparative dynamics.

## The Model

The model assumes a representative family with an infinitely long horizon which maximizes a discounted utility integral, based on per-capita variables, of the form

$$\int_0^\infty e^{-\delta t} u\{c(t), m(t)\}\, dt \quad (\delta > 0) \tag{1}$$

subject to the constraints

$$\dot{a}(t) = \rho(t)a(t) + (1 - \tau)[y^L(t) + s(t)] - [c(t) + i(t)m(t)] \equiv \tilde{y}_t - \tilde{c}_t$$

and                                                                                   (2)

$$a(0) = a_0.$$

In this problem $u(\cdot)$ is an instantaneous utility function with per-capita consumption $c$ and real balances $m$ $(= M/pL)$ as its arguments ($M$ is nominal balances, $p$ is price level, and $L$ is population size). The sum of material wealth per capita is represented by $a = m + b + k$ where $b$ represents the real value of government's indexed bonds[2] and $k$ the value of physical capital. There is a single tax which is a fixed proportion ($\tau$) of income. $s(t)$ represents real transfer payments from government to the private sector, and $y^L$ represents exogenous labor income. $\rho$ is defined as $\rho = (1 - \tau)r - n$ with $r$ the real interest rate and $n$ the rate of population growth. While $\rho$ can be called "the net real rate of interest," we may describe $i$ as the "net nominal rate of interest," defined as $i = (1 - \tau)r + \pi$ where $\pi$ is the expected rate of inflation ($\dot{P}/P$). (Note that $i = \rho + \pi + n$.)

The change in material wealth ($\dot{a}$) can be expressed as the difference between income from assets and labor ($\tilde{y}_t$) and the total value of consumption ($\tilde{c}$) including consumption of liquidity services ($im$). We may write equation 2 alternatively as

$$\dot{a}(t) = (1 - \tau)r(t)[b(t) + k(t)] - n(b + k)$$
$$- (n + \pi)m - c(t) + (1 - \tau)[y^L(t) + s(t)] \tag{2'}$$

where $n(b + k)$ and $(nm)$ are "depreciation terms" when we deal with per-capita variables and $\pi m$ is the inflationary depreciation of money. Note that $b$ and $k$ appear as identical assets from the point of view of the consumer's portfolio; they are of course different assets from the viewpoint of the economy.

All the variables are viewed as functions of time ($t$). However, since we shall be considering steady states only (except in the last section), we may regard the variables that are exogenous to the consumer as fixed over time, so that $\rho(t) = \rho$, $Y^L(t) = Y^L$, $s(t) = s$, and $i(t) = i$. The first-order optimality conditions imply

$$u_m/u_c = i, \tag{3}$$

$$-\dot{u}_c/u_c = \rho - \delta. \tag{4}$$

Since in a steady state all the variables in per-capita terms are constant, we may drop the $t$ variable and infer from equation 4 that

$$\rho = \delta = \text{constant}. \tag{5}$$

In order to derive explicit solutions for the demand functions let us assume a logarithmic utility function

$$u(c, m) \equiv \beta_1 \ln c + \beta_2 \ln m \tag{6}$$

We may then obtain for steady scates (with $\dot{a} = 0$) the demand functions

$$c = \delta_1 \left( a + \frac{(y^L + s)(1 - \tau)}{\rho} \right), \quad \delta_1 = \frac{\beta_1}{\beta_1 + \beta_2} \delta \tag{7}$$

$$m = \frac{\delta_2}{i} \left( a + \frac{(y^L + s)(1 - \tau)}{\rho} \right), \quad \delta_2 = \frac{\beta_2}{\beta_1 + \beta_2} \delta \tag{8}$$

where the expressions in large parentheses represent consumers' wealth. The demand for $(b + k)$ is derived from equation 8 and the definition of $a$.

The productive sector of this economy operates with a neoclassical production function $y = f(k)$ where $y$ is per-capita output. This is a one-sector economy where $y$ and $k$ relate to the same commodity. The marginal productivity conditions require

$$f'(k) = r \tag{9}$$

where the real interest rate $r$ is also equal, in a steady state, to the rental value. In a competitive economy we must also have

$$y = rk + y^L. \tag{10}$$

Since in steady states $\rho = \delta$ is constant, it follows that $r$, and hence (by equation 9) $k$, are constant; consequently $y$ and $y^L$ are also constant. This is true as long as the tax rate $\tau$ is held constant.

Let us turn to the government sector. We assume that the government's budget consists of real expenditures $(g)$, transfer payments $(s)$, interest payments on government bonds $(rb)$, and a proportional income tax which yields $\tau(y + rb + s)$. Two additional features that relate to deficit financing are the printing of new money $(\dot{M}/PL)$ and the issuing of new bonds $(\dot{B}/L)$, which can be expressed in steady states as $(n + \pi)m$ and $nb$ respectively. The government budget in steady states is then given by[3]

$$(1 - \tau)s + (g - \tau y) + (1 - \tau)rb = m(n + \pi) + nb. \tag{11}$$

In order to close the model we need two additional relationships. First we have to take into consideration the fact that the activities in the three sectors are linked through the national income accounts by

$$y = c + nk + g. \tag{12}$$

Second, we have to specify the government's policy with respect to the variables under its control. We shall assume that the tax rate $(\tau)$ is always held constant; similarly, $g$ and $s$ are treated as constant policy parameters. Another policy parameter is the ratio of the two components of the deficit,

$$\gamma = \frac{\dot{M}/pL}{B/L} = \frac{m(n + \pi)}{bn}. \tag{13}$$

When $g$ and $s$ are constant, so must be $D \equiv g - \tau y + (1 - \tau)s$, since in steady states $y$ is determined by the constant parameters $\delta$, $n$, and $\tau$. It then follows that when $g$ and $s$ are constant there is a one-to-one correspondence between $\gamma$ and $b$:

$$\gamma = \frac{m(n + \pi)}{nb} = \frac{D}{nb} + \frac{[(1 - \tau)r - n]b}{nb} = \frac{D}{nb} + \frac{\rho}{n}. \tag{14}$$

If $D > 0$ and $b > 0$ (as is assumed throughout), then $\gamma$ and $b$ are negatively related. Under these conditions we may speak interchangeably of a policy of increasing $\gamma$ or of reducing $b$.

## The General Equilibrium Rate of Inflation

The general equilibrium of the economy in steady states is described by means of the money and commodity markets and the government budget. Our system consists of

$$y - nk - g = \delta_1 \left( m + b + k + \frac{(s + y^L)(1 - \tau)}{\rho} \right), \tag{15}$$

$$m = \frac{\delta_2}{\rho + n + \pi} \left( m + b + k + \frac{(s + y^L)(1 - \tau)}{\rho} \right), \tag{16}$$

and[4]

$$(1 - \tau)s + (g - \tau y) + \rho b = m(n + \pi). \tag{17}$$

Equation 15 is the equilibrium condition for the commodity market where $y - nk - g$ can be considered as the supply of $c$ (by equation 12) and the right-hand side is the demand for $c$ given by equation 7. Equation 16 is the equilibrium for the money market given by equation 8 and using $i = (1 - \tau)r + \pi = \rho + n + \pi$.

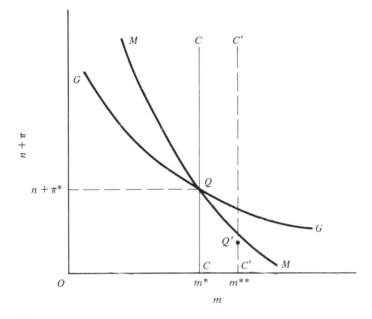

**Figure 1**

Using the relationships given earlier, we can verify that any one of the equations given above is determined by the remaining two. Thus we have a Walras law which states that equilibrium is determined by any pair of the three equations. Because $y$, $k$, and $\rho$ are determined by $\delta$, $\tau$, and $n$ whereas $g$ and $b$ (or $\gamma$) are given by government policy, we have $\pi$ and $m$ as the endogenous variables of the system.

The simultaneous determination of these variables is depicted in figure 1. The $GG$ curve represents the government budget equation (17) which exhibits unitary elasticity in the $(n + \pi, m)$ plane. The money-market equilibrium (equation 16) is described by $MM$ where the elasticity of $m$ with respect to $n + \pi$ is less than unity. This can be seen by solving equation 16 for $m$, which yields the equation for $MM$:

$$m \equiv \frac{\delta_2}{\delta_1 + (n + \pi)}(b + K); \qquad K \equiv k + \frac{(s + y^L)(1 - \tau)}{\rho}, \tag{18}$$

where $\delta_1 + \delta_2 = \delta = \rho$. The commodity-market equilibrium (equation 15) is independent of $\pi$ and yields a unique solution for $m$. Because of the dependence noted above, the three curves must intersect at the point $(m^*, n + \pi^*)$, which corresponds to the full equilibrium.

Consider now the effect of increasing the proportion of the given deficit financed by new money ($\gamma$), which is equivalent, as we saw earlier, to a reduction in $b$. By equation 15, $m + b$ is a constant, so a reduction in $b$ must be matched by an equal increase in $m$. Hence $CC$ is shifted to $C'C'$. Since a reduction in $b$ shifts $GG$ and $MM$ downward, the equilibrium point must shift from $Q$ to $Q'$. In general, $Q'$ must lie within the region defined by $CQM$. It follows therefore that an increase in the proportion of the deficit financed by new money has a deflationary effect on the economy. Alternatively, an increase in the proportion of the deficit financed by the issue of new bonds is inflationary. This analysis is confined to the case where the only variable item in the government's incomes and expenditures is $rb$. Thus we have dealt with the VDP.

## The Constant-Deficit Policy

The foregoing analysis was based on the crucial assumption that $s$ and $g$ are held constant as $\gamma$ varies. According to this approach, as $\gamma$ increases and $b$ falls, the total deficit,

$$\tilde{D} \equiv g - \tau y + (1 - \tau)rb + (1 - \tau)s,$$

is reduced. This approach seems to suggest that the government has a more definite idea of its desired level of $g$ and $s$ than of what its $b$ ought to be. (It is assumed, and we shall continue to assume for convenience, that $\tau$ is constant.)

An alternative approach mentioned in the introduction is that the government holds $\tilde{D}$ constant while $\gamma$ varies. Here the government has a target value of the deficit. An extreme case of this approach is the principle of balanced budget, where $\tilde{D} = 0$ under all circumstances. Here we adopt the modified approach according to which $\tilde{D}$ is constant and positive. Let us examine the implication of this assumption for the effect of $\gamma$.

Since $\tilde{D} > 0$, the relation between $\gamma$ and $b$ is still negative, as can be seen from

$$\gamma = \frac{m(n + \pi)}{nb} = \frac{\tilde{D}}{nb} - 1.$$

Now, in order to maintain $\tilde{D}$ constant while $rb$ varies, the government has to offset the foregoing changes by a compensating variation in either $s$ or $g$. For the steady states, these alternative compensation methods lead to the same sort of results as far as $\pi$ is concerned. However, for the subsequent dynamic analysis it is more convenient to assume that the compensating item is $s$. We then have

$$\tilde{D} = g - \tau y + (1 \quad \tau)rb + (1 - \tau)s$$

$$= (n + \pi)m + nb$$

$$= \text{constant.} \tag{17'}$$

A reduction in $b$ (following an increase in $\gamma$) can then be offset, in order to keep $\tilde{D}$ constant, by an increase in $s$ without affecting $g$ or $c$. In this case we have from equation 17′, with $\tilde{D}$ fixed,

$$ds = - rdb. \tag{19}$$

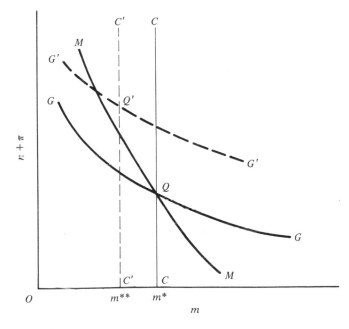

**Figure 2**

Since $c$ is constant, wealth must also be constant, which implies

$$dm + db + \frac{(1 - \tau)ds}{\rho} = 0. \tag{20}$$

Combining the last two equations yields

$$\frac{dm}{db} = \frac{(1 - \tau)r}{\rho} - 1 = \frac{n}{\rho} > 0. \tag{21}$$

It follows that an increase in $\gamma$, which reduces $b$, involves a reduction in $m$. Hence the $CC$ curve must shift to the left as in figure 2. Since a reduction in $b$, with $\tilde{D}$ constant, raises the $GG$ curve in figure 2 (based on 17'), we may infer that an increase in $\gamma$ raises the long-run rate of inflation and reduces real balances, as in figure 2. (Now the $MM$ curve shifts upward.[5])

## An Intuitive Explanation

An intuitive explanation for the different effects of a change in $\gamma$ on $\pi$ may run as follows. Under the VDP we may express equation 17 as

$$(1 - \tau)s + g - \tau y + \rho b = m(n + \pi).$$

Thus a reduction in $b$ (following an increase in $\gamma$) reduces the real value of the new money printed $[m(n + \pi)]$. The reduced need to print money follows from the fact that the reduction in net interest payments $(1 - \tau)rb$ exceeds the reduction in the issue of new bonds $nb$. Now, since the elasticity of $m$ with respect to $n + \pi$ is less than unitary, the reduction in $m(n + \pi)$ implies also a reduction in $\pi$. Thus an increase in $\gamma$ leads to a reduction in $\pi$ as a result of a reduction in the injection of new money (in real terms).

Under the alternative CDP we have

$$\tilde{D} = m(n + \pi) + nb = \text{constant}.$$

Hence a reduction in $b$ must be offset by an increase in the printing of new money, $m(n + \pi)$, to maintain a constant deficit. In other words, the need to use the inflation tax increases. By the same reasoning as before, this leads to an increase in the steady-state level of $\pi$.

## Impact Effects and Dynamics

The foregoing alternative approaches have different implications not only for the long run but for the short run as well. I shall show that for the VDP a permanent increase in $\gamma$ has no impact effect on the current price level or on the rate of inflation. For the alternative CDP the increase in $\gamma$ has an immediate inflationary effect in terms of both the current price level and its rate of change. In the following analysis we shall also derive the complete dynamic paths following the displacement in $\gamma$.

Consider first the VDP. Using equations 2', 3, 4, 13, and 12 in its dynamic version, we obtain

$$\dot{m} + (n + \pi)m = \gamma(\dot{b} + nb), \tag{22}$$

$$\frac{c}{m}\frac{\beta_2}{\beta_1} = \rho + n + \pi, \tag{23}$$

$$\frac{\dot{c}}{c} = \rho - \delta, \tag{24}$$

$$\dot{k} + \dot{b} = [(1 - \tau)r - n](b + k) - [(n + \pi)m + \dot{m}]$$
$$+ y^L(1 - \tau) - c + s(1 - \tau), \tag{25}$$

$$\dot{k} = f(k) - nk - g - c, \tag{26}$$

which is a system of differential equations in $k$, $c$, $m$, and $b$ (after we eliminate $\pi$ by means of equation 23). Note that equations 24 and 26 form a separable dynamic system for the physical sector of the economy (the standard "optimal growth" model).

In the foregoing system the initial values of $b$ and $k$ (at $t_0$) are given exogenously by $b_0$ and $k_0$. These values cannot be changed discontinuously after (say) a change in $\gamma$. The "initial values" that can be changed discontinuously after an exogenous shock are $c_0$ and $m_0$. The former can be changed to conform with the consumers' optimum; the latter by market forces through a change in the current price level ($p_0$).

Assume that at $t_0$ there is a unique pair ($c_0, m_0$) that is admissible in our system, meaning essentially that the price level is uniquely determined. This pair ($c_0, m_0$) is assumed to be the unique pair that guarantees the convergence to the steady-state solution. Formally, assume that the steady state in our system corresponds to a "saddle point."

Suppose we start at a steady-state solution and increase $\gamma$ arbitrarily to a new constant level (say from $\gamma_0$ to $\gamma_1$). For the seperable physical part of the system, the initial value $c_0$ following the change in $\gamma$ must be set at the original steady-state value $c^*$ (that is, $c$ remains unchanged) and is maintained there throughout the adjustment process. In this case it follows from equation 26 that $k$ will be constant at $k^*$ and so will $\rho$. It is then only the financial part of the system, involving $b$ and $m$, that will constitute our effective dynamic system.

When $k$, $c$, and $s$ are constant, the dynamic system can be reduced to

$$\dot{b} = \left(\frac{\rho - \gamma n}{1 + \gamma}\right)b + \frac{1}{1 + \gamma}[\rho k + (y^L + s)(1 - \tau) - c], \tag{27}$$

$$\dot{m} = \gamma\left(\frac{\rho - \gamma n}{1 + \gamma} + n\right)b + \rho m + \frac{\gamma}{1 + \gamma}[\rho k + (y^L + s)(1 - \tau)]$$

$$- \left(\frac{\gamma}{1 + \gamma} + \frac{\beta_2}{\beta_1}\right)c. \tag{28}$$

The homogeneous system corresponding to $m$ and $b$ given by equations 27 and 28 can be written (in terms of deviations from equilibrium) as

$$\dot{b} = a_{11}b + a_{12}m, \tag{29}$$

$$\dot{m} = a_{21}b + a_{22}m, \tag{30}$$

$$a_{11} = \frac{\rho - \gamma n}{1 + \gamma}, \qquad a_{12} = 0$$

$$a_{21} = \gamma\left(\frac{\rho - \gamma n}{1 + \gamma} + n\right), \qquad a_{22} = \rho.$$

Note that

$$a_{21} = \frac{\gamma}{1 + \gamma}(1 - \tau)r > 0,$$

and

$$a_{22} > 0.$$

It can be seen that this system is dynamically unstable in the usual sense of this term.[6] In fact, according to our earlier assumption about the steady state, we require that the foregoing system possess the saddle-

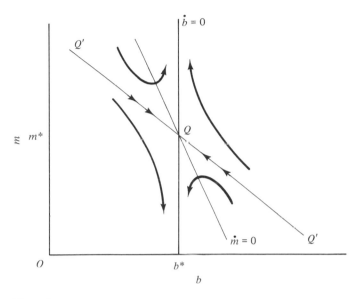

**Figure 3**

point property, which implies that $a_{11}a_{22} < 0$ and hence that $a_{11} < 0$ or $\gamma > \rho/n$, which follows from equation 14. "Stability" in this framework means that the initial value of $m$ must be chosen according to the stable trajectory to be discussed below.

In view of the foregoing remarks, we may draw the phase diagram in the $(m, b)$ space as in figure 3, where only $Q'Q'$ is a stable trajectory going into the steady-state point $Q$, as it should be under the saddle-point assumption. An important property of this trajectory is that its slope coefficient equals $-1$. This must be the case since the assumption of constant $c$ and $k$ implies a constant level of consumers' wealth, which in turn implies that $m + b$ must remain constant.[7] This implies that the equation for $Q'Q'$ is $m - m^* = (b - b^*)$, in terms of the original variables, or

$$m = (m^* + b^*) - b. \tag{31}$$

Suppose that we start at the initial steady state with $\gamma_0$ and increase it to a new constant level $\gamma_1$. This will cause an increase in $m^*$ and a reduction in $b^*$, but $m^* + b^*$ will remain constant, as we have seen. It then follows from equation 31 that the stable trajectory $Q'Q'$ in figure 4 will

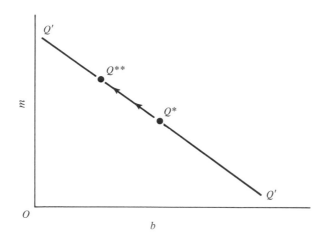

**Figure 4**

remain unchanged, while the steady-state equilibrium point will shift from $Q^*$ to $Q^{**}$. The dynamic adjustment process will then take place along the segment $Q^*Q^{**}$ of $Q'Q'$, as indicated by the arrows in figure 4.

Since the impact effect leaves $m_0$ at $m^*$, there can be no effect of $\gamma$ on the current price level. Furthermore, since in the first instant $c$ and $m$ are unaffected, we see from equation 23 that $\pi$ is unaffected as well. This confirms a statement made in the beginning of this section. As time evolves, $m$ increases along $Q^*Q^{**}$ so that, by equation 23, $\pi$ is reduced gradually to its new steady-state level.

Let us turn now to the dynamic system under the constant-deficit policy, where any change in $rb$ is offset by $s$.[8] Again our starting point is the steady state with $\gamma_0$. As $\gamma_0$ increases to $\gamma_1$ we know from our earlier analysis that $m^*$ and $b^*$ decrease while the physical part of the system remains unchanged (and so does $\rho$).

Equation 25 is now represented as

$$\dot{k} + \dot{b} = (1 - \tau)(rb + s) - nb - \gamma(\dot{b} + nb) + \rho k + (1 - \tau)y^L - c. \quad (25')$$

Note, however, that since any change in $rb$ is offset by $s$ it follows that $rb + s$ is a constant during the adjustment process. Assuming that $c$ and $k$ are constant (when our starting point is a steady state), we can express equation 25' in terms of deviations from full equilibrium, as[9]

$$\dot{b} = -nb + 0 \cdot m. \quad (32)$$

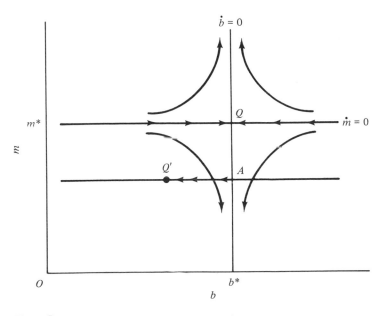

**Figure 5**

The dynamic equation for $\dot{m}$ is, in view of equation 23,

$$\dot{m} = 0 \cdot b + \rho m. \qquad (33)$$

Because of the zero values for the off-diagonal elements, the stable trajectory of our saddle-point system is horizontal and coincides with the $\dot{m} = 0$ line as in figure 5. As $\gamma$ increases from $\gamma_0$ to $\gamma_1$, we know that the steady values of $m$ and $b$ decline, so the full equilibrium point shifts from $Q$ to $Q'$ while the stable trajectory shifts to the horizontal line through $Q'$.

The impact effect of the increase in $\gamma$ is a shift from $Q$ to $A$, which implies an increase in the current price level and, by equation 23, an increase in the rate of inflation. The latter increase in $\pi$ is precisely the same as in full equilibrium, because $m$ is constant along the adjustment path. Hence under the constant deficit policy the short-run and long-run effects coincide.

Since we assume that $c$ remains constant throughout the adjustment process, it must also be the case that wealth is constant. It can indeed be verified that the path implied by

$$\dot{b} = -nb, \qquad \dot{m} = 0 \qquad (34)$$

(which corresponds to equations 32 and 33 and figure 5) maintains total consumers' wealth constant. To see this, define consumers' wealth ($W$) as

$$w = m + b + k^* + \frac{y^{L^*}(1 - \tau)}{\rho^*} + \int_t^\infty e^{-\rho^*(v-t)}(1 - \tau)s(v)\,dv, \qquad (35)$$

where $k^*$, $y^{L^*}$, and $\rho^*$ correspond to the steady state. By the constant-deficit assumption we have

$$s(v)(1 - \tau) = Q - (1 - \tau)rb(v) \qquad (Q \equiv \tilde{D} - g + \tau y^* = \text{constant}). \quad (36)$$

In terms of the original variables, equation 34 can be written as

$$\dot{b} = -n(b - b^*), \qquad (37)$$

which can be solved to yield

$$b(v) = b^* + (b_t - b^*)e^{-n(v-t)}. \qquad (38)$$

Differentiating equation 35 with respect to time gives

$$\dot{w} = \dot{m} + \dot{b} - (1 - \tau)s(t) + \rho \int_t^\infty e^{-\rho(v-t)}s(v)\,dv. \qquad (39)$$

Substituting equations 36 and 38 in equation 39 yields

$$\dot{w} = \dot{m} + \dot{b} + n(b_t - b^*). \qquad (40)$$

However, equations 34 and 37 imply that equation 40 is identically zero, which proves the proposition.

The foregoing results indicate that, with a constant deficit, printing money rather than bonds is a more inflationary method of deficit financing. This is true not only in the long run but in the short run as well. This certainly conforms with the traditional view. It does not mean, however, that the assumption of a constant deficit is in any way more realistic that the variable-deficit assumption, which yields fundamentally different results.

## Acknowledgment

I am indebted to Stan Fischer for useful comments.

# Notes

1. This is at variance with the results of Fischer 1979. The difference is due mainly to Fischer's assumption that the rate of money expansion is constant, whereas in our analysis it is determined endogenously.

2. The analysis is essentially the same for nonindexed bonds, because in steady states the nominal interest rate offsets automatically the inflation tax on these bonds. I use indexed bonds because it simplifies the analysis. See note 3.

3. For $n = \pi = 0$ it is impossible to maintain a positive deficit permanently. Note also that $b$ is not uniquely determined, given $y$ and $\tau$, because of the inflation tax $(n + \pi)m$. Unlike that of Barro 1974, the system is therefore not invariant to $b$. This is the difference between a monetary and a barter system.

4. If we have nonindexed bonds ($b'$) in addition to the indexed ones, the left-hand side of equation 17 will include net interest expenditures of $[(1 - \tau)r + \pi]b'$, while the right-hand side will include a "depreciation" term $(n + \pi)b'$. Hence the net contribution of $b'$ to the inflation tax is $\rho b'$, as with indexed bonds.

5. This is because a reduction of one unit in $b$ requires an increase in $s$ of $r$ units to keep $rb + s = $ constant. The net change in wealth is then

$$-1 + \frac{(1 - \tau)r}{\rho} = \frac{n}{\rho} > 0.$$

Hence, for a given $m$, the $\pi$ in equation 16 must increase, implying that $MM$ rises.

6. One condition of stability requires that the determinant of equations 29 and 30 be positive, which implies that $a_{11} > 0$. However, in this case $a_{11} + a_{22} > 0$, which violates the other requirement of stability.

7. The slope coefficient of the $\dot{m} = 0$ line, in absolute value, or

$$\left| \frac{dm}{db} \right| = \frac{a_{21}}{a_{22}}$$

$$= \frac{\gamma}{\rho} \left( \frac{\rho - \gamma n}{1 + \gamma} \right) + n$$

$$= \frac{\gamma \rho + \gamma n}{\gamma \rho + \rho},$$

is greater than 1 since $\gamma n > \rho$. This implies that the slope of $\dot{m} = 0$ is steeper than that of $Q'Q'$.

8. If $rb$ is offset by $g$, then the dynamic process must involve the nonfinancial sector. This is not the case when the offsetting is by $s$.

9. In the following derivations we use the assumption that the deficit $\tilde{D}$ is constant so that, by equation 22, both $\dot{m} + (n + \pi)m$ and $\dot{b} + nb$ are constant during the dynamic process.

# Bibliography

Barro, R. J. 1974. Are government bonds net wealth? *J. Pol. Econ.* 82: 1095–1118.

Blinder, A. S., and R. M. Solow. 1973. Does fiscal policy matter? *J. Publ. Econ.* 2. 319 337.

Christ, C. F. 1979. On fiscal and monetary policies and the government budget restraint. *Am. Econ. Rev.* 69: 527–540.

Fischer, S. 1979. Capital accumulation on the transition path in a monetary optimizing model. *Econometrica* 47: 1433–1439.

Sidrauski, M. 1967. Rational choice and patterns of growth in a monetary economy. *Am. Econ. Rev.* (Proc.) 57: 534–544.

Smith, G. 1979. The long run consequences of monetary and fiscal policies when the government budget is not balanced. *J. Publ. Econ.* 11: 59–79.

Turnovsky, S. J. 1978. Macroeconomic dynamics and growth in a monetary economy. *J. Money, Credit, Banking* 10: 1–26.

Tobin, J., and W. Buiter. 1976. Long run effects of fiscal and monetary policy on aggregate demand. In *Monetarism (Studies in Monetary Economics)*. Amsterdam: North-Holland.

# II ECONOMETRIC METHODOLOGY

# 5 Comparison of the Densities of the TSLS and LIMLK Estimators for Simultaneous Equations

T. W. Anderson
Naoto Kunitomo
Takamitsu Sawa

Two procedures that have been proposed for estimating the coefficients of a single equation in a system of simultaneous equations are the limited-information maximum-likelihood (LIML) estimator and the two-stage least-squares (TSLS) estimator. It is of interest to compare the sampling distributions of the estimators in various situations. However, the distributions and densities are in general very complicated. The simplest case to consider is when there are two endogenous variables in the equation and only exogenous (nonstochastic) variables are predetermined. Nevertheless, the distributions and densities of the LIML estimator of the coefficient of one endogenous variable are so complicated that the features of the distributions and densities are difficult to understand and they are not useful for computation. (The densities are triply infinite series.) Accordingly, we turn our attention to an estimator that is defined in a similar fashion except that the estimated covariance matrix of the error terms is replaced by the matrix itself. We call this estimator the limited-information maximum-likelihood estimator with covariance matrix known (LIMLK).

The density and the distribution of the LIMLK estimator can be put in fairly simple terms (Anderson and Sawa 1982). For moderately large values of the noncentrality parameter (which may be considered proportional to the sample size) an easy, adequate approximation to the distribution is available. For both the LIMLK and TSLS estimators we can program a computer (or even a desk calculator) to turn out numerical values of the distributions and densities.

The purpose of this chapter is to compare the LIMLK and TSLS estimators graphically. We present graphs of the densities in 27 cases. These cases fairly well cover the range of variation of the key parameters. Other cases of interest can be reduced to these or to interpolations of these.

The LIMLK estimator can be considered a limit of the LIML estimator as the number of degrees of freedom in the estimator of the covariance matrix tends to infinity. Other computations (Anderson, Kunitomo, and Sawa 1982) show that the distribution of the LIML estimator does not depend very much on this number of degrees of freedom (except for a large number of excluded exogenous variables). Hence, the features

of the comparisons made here for the LIMLK estimator apply to the
LIML estimator as well.

## Models and Estimators

Consider the TSLS and LIMLK estimators of the structural parameter
$\beta$ in the equation

$$\mathbf{y}_1 = \beta \mathbf{y}_2 + \mathbf{Z}_1 \mathbf{\gamma}_1 + \mathbf{u}$$

where $\mathbf{y}_1$ and $\mathbf{y}_2$ are $T$-component (column) vectors of $T$ observations
on two endogenous variables, $\mathbf{Z}_1$ is a $T \times K_1$ matrix of observations on
$K_1$ exogenous variables, $\beta$ is a scalar parameter, $\mathbf{\gamma}_1$ is a $K_1$-component
vector of parameters, and $\mathbf{u}$ is a $T$-component vector of (unobservable)
disturbances. The reduced form of the system of structural equation
includes

$$(\mathbf{y}_1 \ \ \mathbf{y}_2) = (\mathbf{Z}_1 \ \ \mathbf{Z}_2) \begin{pmatrix} \pi_{11} & \pi_{12} \\ \pi_{21} & \pi_{22} \end{pmatrix} + (\mathbf{v}_1 \ \ \mathbf{v}_2)$$

where $\mathbf{Z}_2$ is a $T \times K_2$ matrix of observations on $K_2$ exogenous variables
that are excluded from the structural equation that concerns us, $\pi_{11}$
and $\pi_{12}$ are $K_1$-component vectors and $\pi_{21}$ and $\pi_{22}$ are $K_2$-component
vectors of reduced-form coefficients, and $(\mathbf{v}_1 \ \ \mathbf{v}_2)$ is a $T \times 2$ matrix of
(unobservable) disturbances. We make the following conventional as-
sumptions.

ASSUMPTION 1: The rows of $(\mathbf{v}_1 \ \ \mathbf{v}_2)$ are independently normally distributed, each row having mean $\mathbf{0}$ and (nonsingular) covariance matrix

$$\mathbf{\Omega} = \begin{pmatrix} \omega_{11} & \omega_{12} \\ \omega_{21} & \omega_{22} \end{pmatrix}.$$

Since $\mathbf{u} = \mathbf{v}_1 - \beta \mathbf{v}_2$, the variance of each component of $\mathbf{u}$ is

$$\sigma^2 = \omega_{11} - 2\beta\omega_{12} + \beta^2\omega_{22}.$$

ASSUMPTION 2: The $T \times K$ matrix $\mathbf{Z}$ consists of known numbers and
is of rank $K$, and $T > K$.

ASSUMPTION 3: The matrix $(\pi_{21} \ \ \pi_{22})$ is of rank 1, and $\pi_{22}$ has at least
one nonzero component.

The estimator of $\Pi = (\pi_{ij})$ is

$$P = \begin{pmatrix} Z_1'Z_1 & Z_1'Z_2 \\ Z_2'Z_1 & Z_2'Z_2 \end{pmatrix}^{-1} \begin{pmatrix} Z_1'y_1 & Z_1'y_2 \\ Z_2'y_1 & Z_2'y_2 \end{pmatrix} = \begin{pmatrix} p_{11} & p_{12} \\ p_{21} & p_{22} \end{pmatrix}.$$

The estimator of $\Omega$ can be

$$\hat{\Omega} = \frac{1}{T}(Y - ZP)'(Y - ZP) = (\hat{\omega}_{ij})$$

where $Y = (y_1 \ y_2)$ and $Z = (Z_1 \ Z_2)$. Let

$$A_{22.1} = Z_2'Z_2 - Z_2'Z_1(Z_1'Z_1)^{-1}Z_1'Z_2.$$

The TSLS estimator of $\beta$ is

$$\hat{\beta}_{TSLS} = \frac{p_{21}'A_{22.1}p_{22}}{p_{22}'A_{22.1}p_{22}}.$$

The LIML estimator is the negative of the ratio of the second to the first component of $b$ satisfying $(G - \lambda_1\hat{\Omega})b = 0$, where $\lambda_1$ is the smaller root of $|G - \lambda\hat{\Omega}| = 0$ and

$$G = \begin{pmatrix} p_{21}' \\ p_{22}' \end{pmatrix} A_{22.1}(p_{21} \ p_{22}) = (g_{ij}).$$

The LIMLK estimator of $\beta$ (when the covariance matrix is known) is the negative of the ratio of the second to the first component of $b$ satisfying

$$(G - \lambda_1^*\Omega)b = 0,$$

where $\lambda_1^*$ is the smaller root of

$$|G - \lambda\Omega| = 0.$$

Let

$$\delta^2 = \frac{\pi_{22}'A_{22.1}\pi_{22}}{\omega_{22}},$$

$$\alpha = \frac{\omega_{22}\beta - \omega_{12}}{|\Omega|^{1/2}} = \left(\beta - \frac{\omega_{12}}{\omega_{22}}\right)\left(\frac{\omega_{22}}{\omega_{11} - (\omega_{12}^2/\omega_{22})}\right)^{1/2},$$

$$\hat{\alpha} = \frac{\omega_{22}\hat{\beta} - \omega_{12}}{|\Omega|^{1/2}} = \left(\hat{\beta} - \frac{\omega_{12}}{\omega_{22}}\right)\left(\frac{\omega_{22}}{\omega_{11} - (\omega_{12}^2/\omega_{22})}\right)^{1/2}$$

where $\hat{\beta}$ is the TSLS, LIML, or LIMLK estimator. Then the limiting distribution of

$$\frac{(\pi'_{22}\mathbf{A}_{22.1}\pi_{22})^{1/2}}{\sigma}(\hat{\beta} - \beta) = \frac{\delta}{(1 + \alpha^2)^{1/2}}(\hat{\alpha} - \alpha)$$

is normal with mean 0 and variance 1. The exact distribution of this quantity depends only on $K_2$, $\delta^2$, and $\alpha$ (and $T - K$ for LIML). In principle, tables, graphs, and mathematical expressions of the distributions and densities of this quantity for all values of $K_2$, $\delta^2$, and $\alpha$ (and $T - K$ for LIML) can be converted into similar information about $\hat{\beta}$ for any $K_2$, $\beta$, $\gamma$, and $\Omega$ (and $T - K$ for LIML). Hence, we shall present and discuss graphs of the densities of the above quantity for various values of $K_2$, $\delta^2$, and $\alpha$.

The density of $\hat{\beta}$ tends to be centered at $\beta$, and its spread is roughly proportional to $\sigma/(\pi'_{22}\mathbf{A}_{22.1}\pi_{22})^{1/2}$. The sample size $T$ enters only through $\mathbf{A}_{22.1}$, that is, through $\mathbf{Z}'\mathbf{Z}$.

The ordinary least-squares (OLS) estimator of $(\beta \ \gamma'_1)'$ is the solution of

$$\begin{pmatrix} \mathbf{y}'_2\mathbf{y}_1 \\ \mathbf{Z}'_1\mathbf{y}_1 \end{pmatrix} = \begin{pmatrix} \mathbf{y}'_2\mathbf{y}_2 & \mathbf{y}'_2\mathbf{Z}_1 \\ \mathbf{Z}'_1\mathbf{y}_2 & \mathbf{Z}'_1\mathbf{Z}_1 \end{pmatrix}\begin{pmatrix} \hat{\beta} \\ \hat{\gamma}_1 \end{pmatrix}.$$

The distribution of the ordinary least-squares estimator $\hat{\beta} = (g_{21} + \hat{\omega}_{21})/(g_{22} + \hat{\omega}_{22})$ is the same as that of the TSLS estimator except that $K_2$ is replaced by $T - K_1$. Its asymptotic distribution, however, is different.

As shown by Anderson (1976), the TSLS and LIMLK estimators are mathematically equivalent to the least-squares and maximum-likelihood estimators of the slope coefficient in a linear functional relationship. Let the pairs $(x_g, y_g)$ be independently normally distributed, each pair with covariance matrix $\tau^2\mathbf{I}$, and suppose $\mathscr{E}x_g = \mu_g$ and $\mathscr{E}y_g = v_g$, $g = 1, \ldots, N$ where $v_g = \gamma + \alpha\mu_g$. The maximum-likelihood estimator of $\alpha$ is

$$\hat{\alpha} = \frac{s_{yy} - s_{xx} + [(s_{yy} - s_{xx})^2 + 4s_{xy}^2]^{1/2}}{2s_{xy}}$$

$$= \frac{2s_{xy}}{[(s_{yy} - s_{xx})^2 + 4s_{xy}^2]^{1/2} + s_{xx} - s_{yy}}$$

where

$$s_{xx} = \sum_{g=1}^{N}(x_g - \bar{x})^2,$$

$$S_{yy} = \sum_{g=1}^{N} (y_g - \bar{y})^2,$$

$$S_{xy} = \sum_{g=1}^{N} (x_g - \bar{x})(y_g - \bar{y}),$$

$$\bar{x} = \frac{1}{N} \sum_{g=1}^{N} x_g,$$

$$\bar{y} = \frac{1}{N} \sum_{g=1}^{N} y_g.$$

The least-squares estimator (minimizing the sum of squared residuals in the $y$ direction) is $s_{xy}/s_{xx}$. The "number of degrees of freedom" is $K_2 = N - 1$, and the noncentrality parameter is

$$\delta^2 = \frac{1}{\tau^2} \sum_{g=1}^{N} (\mu_g - \bar{\mu})^2$$

where $\bar{\mu} = \sum_{g=1}^{N} \mu_g$.

## Comparison of Distributions

The graphs at the end of the chapter give the densities of the normalized TSLS and LIMLK estimators for $\alpha = 0.0$, 1.0, and 5.0, $K_2 = 3$, 10, and 30, and $\delta^2 = 30$, 100, and 1,000. The graphs for negative values of $\alpha$ are the mirror images of those for the corresponding positive values of $\alpha$. The behavior at intermediate values of $\alpha$, $K_2$, and $\delta^2$ can be obtained by interpolation. (We have inspected the graphs for $\alpha = 0.0$, 0.5, 1.0, 2.0, and 5.0, $K_2 = 3$, 10, and 30, and $\delta^2 = 30$, 50, 100, 300, and 1,000.) The behavior at larger values of these quantities can be inferred by extrapolation. The value of $\delta^2 = 30$ is the smallest value for which our computing method is accurate for all values of $\alpha$ and $K_2$; for smaller values of $\delta^2$ and large values of $\alpha$ and/or $K_2$, a more laborious computing method would have to be used.

As $\delta^2$ increases, the distribution of either normalized estimator approaches the normal distribution with mean 0 and variance 1. The speed of approach can be seen by inspection of the graphs. At $\alpha = 0.0$ the densities are symmetric and look rather normal. The densities of the TSLS estimator are a little less spread out than the standard normal for large values of $K_2$ and small values of $\delta^2$, and the densities of the LIMLK estimator are a little more spread out. In every case, however, when $\delta^2 = 1,000$ (and $\alpha = 0.0$) the density is indistinguishable from the standard normal.

For $\alpha > 0.0$ the most significant feature of the graphs is that in each case the density of the TSLS estimator is shifted to the left while the density of the LIMLK estimator is pretty well centered at 0. The median of the normalized TSLS estimator is negative, and the median of the normalized LIMLK estimator is approximately 0. The shift of the density of the normalized TSLS estimator to the left increases with $\alpha$ and $K_2$ and decreases with $\delta^2$. In the most extreme case here, namely $\alpha = 5.0$, $K_2 = 30$, and $\delta^2 = 30$, the median is about $-2.75$. In that case the density of the normalized LIMLK estimator with a median of approximately 0 hardly overlaps with the density of the normalized TSLS estimator. In this case and in others the TSLS estimator almost surely underestimates the parameter.

The densities tend to be fairly symmetric about suitable points. However, for positive $\alpha$ there is a slight tendency for the right tail to be longer than the left tail; this tendency increases with $\alpha$ and $K_2$ and decreases with $\delta^2$.

For $\alpha \neq 0.0$ the spread of the normalized LIMLK estimator is greater than that of the normalized TSLS estimator. This reflects the fact that the moments of the LIMLK estimator do not exist. However, the greater variability of the LIMLK estimator is more than offset by the bias of the TSLS estimator.

What values of $\alpha$, $K_2$, and $\delta^2$ are likely to occur in practice? Anderson, Morimune, and Sawa (1978) studied the values of estimates of these parameters in a number of studies published between 1949 and 1974. They found "typical" values of $\alpha \approx 1.0$, $K_2 \approx 3$, and $\delta^2/TK_2 \approx 1$. In more recent studies $K_2$ is likely to be considerably greater than 3 and $\delta^2/TK_2$ to be smaller (because of correlation between exogenous variables).

The conclusion we draw from this study is that the LIML estimator should be used unless $K_2$ is small or there is reason to believe that $\alpha$ is close to 0 or $\delta^2$ is very large. Note that $\alpha$ depends on the difference between the structural coefficient $\beta$ and the error regression of one component of $\mathbf{v}_1$ on the corresponding component of $\mathbf{v}_2$.

These observations do not disagree with the inferences one draws from comparison of the moments of the asymptotic expansions of the distributions (see Anderson 1974 and Anderson and Sawa 1973, for example). If we consider the expansion to order $1/\delta^2$, the mean and the variance of the normalized TSLS estimator are, respectively,

$$-\frac{\alpha(K_2 - 2)}{\delta(1 + \alpha^2)^{1/2}}$$

and

$$1 - \frac{4(K_2 - 3)\alpha^2 + K_2 - 4}{\delta^2(1 + \alpha^2)}$$

and the mean and the variance of the normalized LIMLK estimator are, respectively,

$$\frac{\alpha}{\delta(1 + \alpha^2)^{1/2}}$$

and

$$1 + \frac{8\alpha^2 + K_2 + 2}{\delta^2(1 + \alpha^2)}.$$

Tables of the distribution of the TSLS estimator are given in Anderson and Sawa 1977b and 1979, and tables of the distribution of the LIMLK estimator in Anderson and Sawa 1977a and 1978.

## Methods of Computation

The distribution of the TSLS estimator can be converted to the distribution of the doubly noncentral $F$ (which is proportional to the ratio of two independent noncentral $\chi^2$ variables, say $A/B$). For small $\delta^2$ the doubly infinite series in the density can be integrated term by term to yield numerical values of the distribution. For larger $\delta^2$ we can write $A/B < x$ as $A^{1/3} - x^{1/3} B^{1/3} \leq 0$. Using the methods of Muldholkar, Chaubey, and Lin (1976), we obtain a very accurate expansion of the distribution. We consider our tables of the cumulative distribution functions (CDFs) accurate at least to the third decimal place. (See Anderson and Sawa 1979.) The density is approximated by numerical differentiation of the CDF.

As explained in Anderson and Sawa 1982, for large $\delta^2$ the CDF of the normalized LIMLK estimator, or $[\delta/(1 + \alpha^2)^{1/2}](\hat{\alpha} - \alpha)$, is almost exactly the CDF of a doubly noncentral $F$. As in the case of the TSLS estimator, the distribution of this quantity can be calculated quite accurately.

## Acknowledgments

This work was supported by National Science Foundation grant SES79-13976 at the Institute for Mathematical Studies in the Social Sciences, Stanford University.

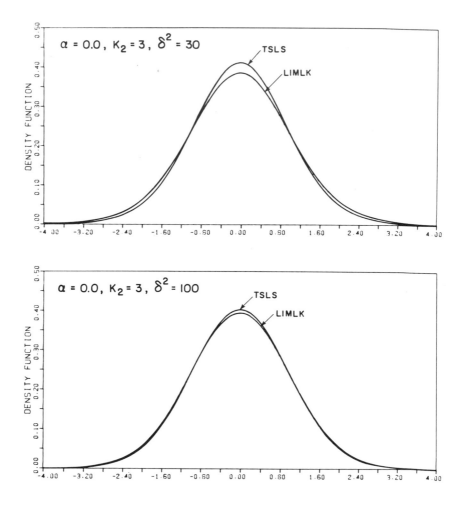

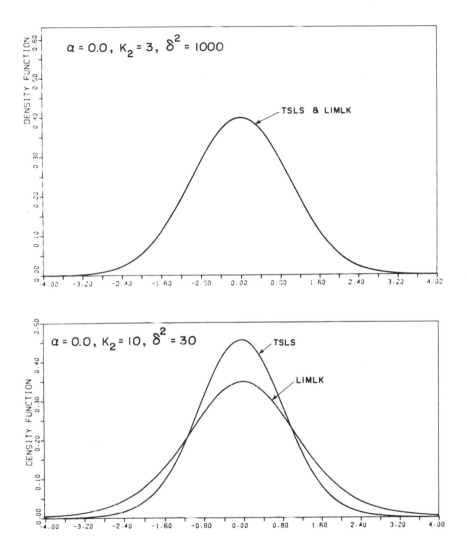

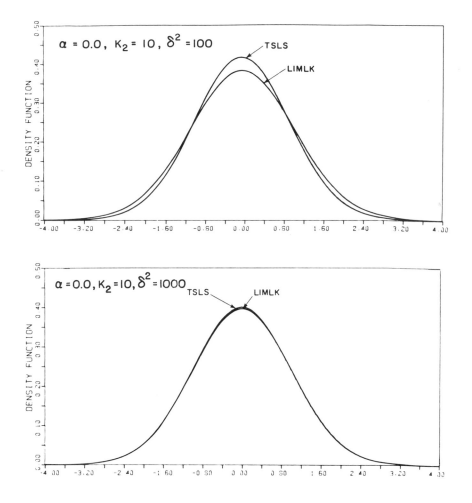

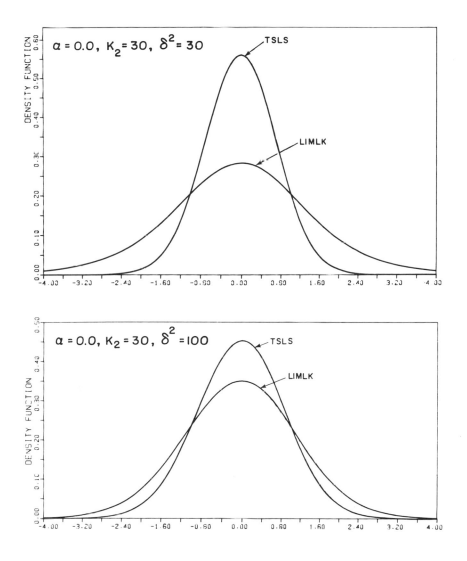

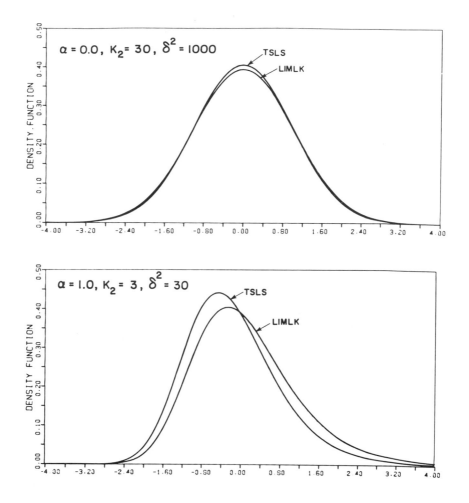

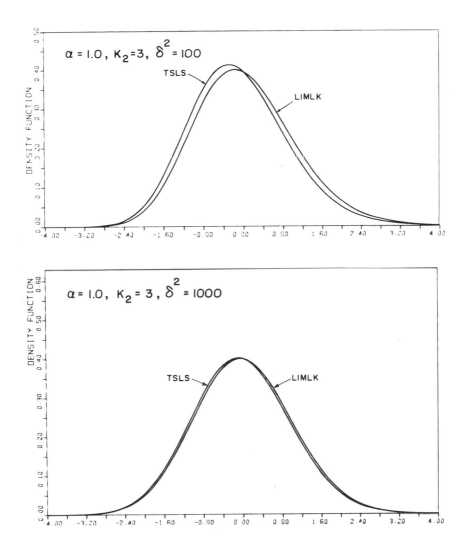

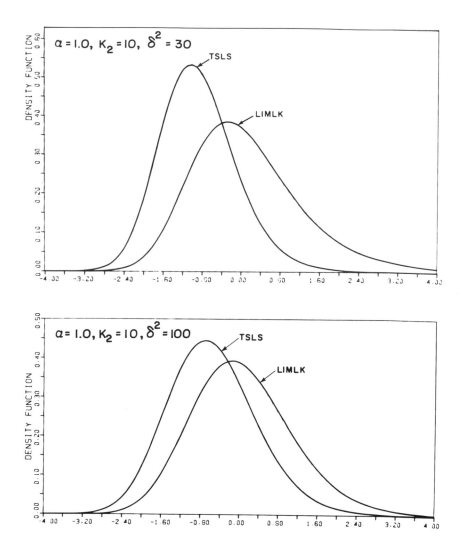

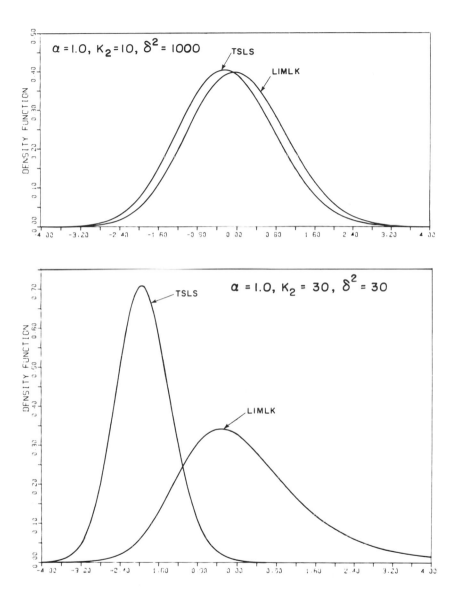

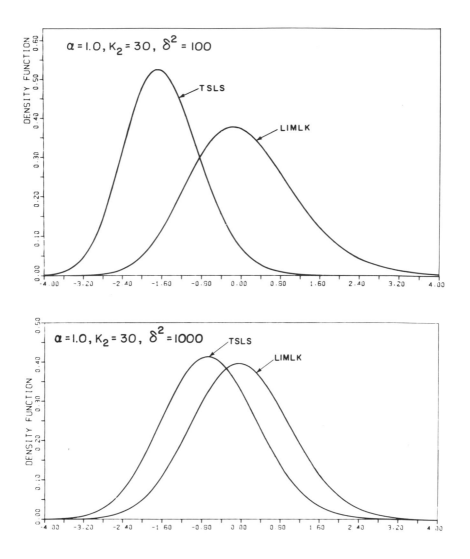

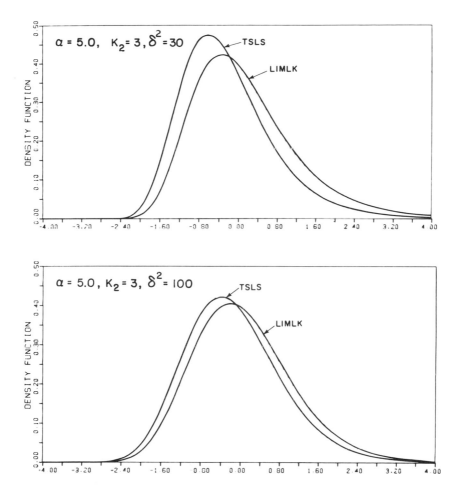

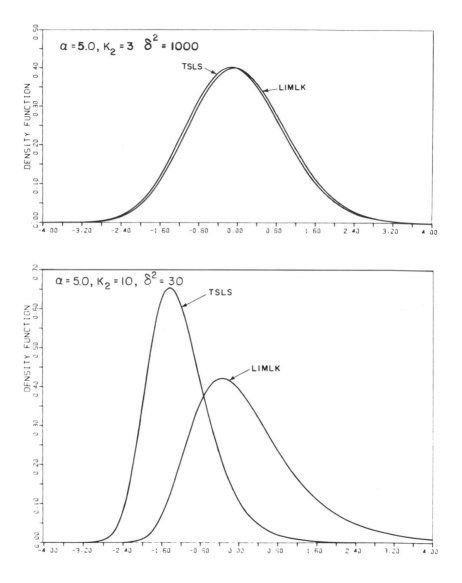

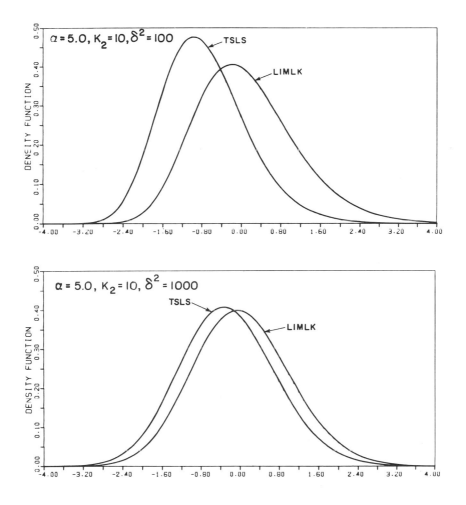

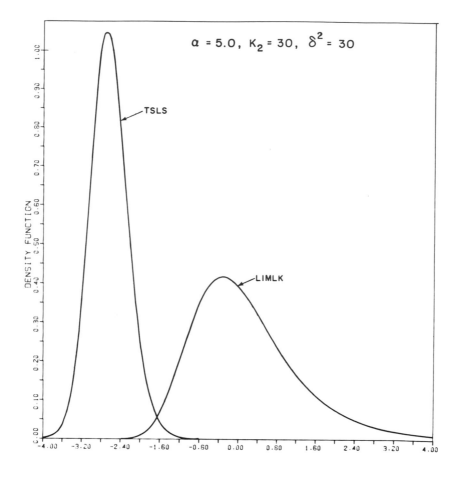

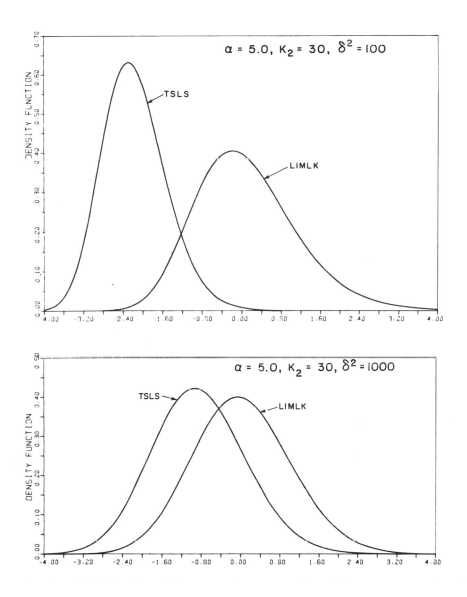

# Bibliography

Anderson, T. W. 1974. An Asymptotic expansion of the distribution of the limited information maximum likelihood estimate of the coefficient in a simultaneous equation system. *Journal of the American Statistical Association* 69: 565–573.

Anderson, T. W. 1976. Estimation of linear functional relationships: Approximate distributions and connections with simultaneous equations in econometrics. *Journal of the Royal Statistical Association* B 38: 1–36.

Anderson, T. W., N. Kunitomo, and T. Sawa. 1982. Evaluation of the distribution function of the limited information maximum likelihood estimator. *Econometrica* 50: 1000–1027.

Anderson, T. W., K. Morimune, and T. Sawa. 1978. The Numerical Values of Some Key Parameters in Econometric Models. Technical report 270, Economics Series, Institute for Mathematical Studies in the Social Sciences, Stanford University.

Anderson, T. W., and T. Sawa. 1973. Distribution of estimates of coefficients of a single equation in a simultaneous system and their asymptotic expansions. *Econometrica* 41: 683–714.

Anderson, T. W., and T. Sawa. 1977a. Tables of the Distribution of the Maximum Likelihood Estimate of the Slope Coefficient and Approximation. Technical report 234, Economics Series, IMSSS, Stanford University.

Anderson, T. W., and T. Sawa. 1977b. Numerical Evaluation of the Exact and Approximate Distribution Functions of the Two-Stage Least Squares Estimate. Technical report 239, Economics Series, IMSSS, Stanford University.

Anderson, T. W., and T. Sawa. 1978. Tables of the Exact Distribution of the Limited Information Maximum Likelihood Estimator when the Covariance Matrix Is Known. Technical report 275, Economics Series, IMSSS, Stanford University.

Anderson, T. W., and T. Sawa. 1979. Evaluation of the distribution function of the two-stage least squares estimate. *Econometrica* 47: 163–182.

Anderson, T. W., and T. Sawa. 1982. Exact and approximate distributions of the maximum likelihood estimate of a slope coefficient. *Journal of the Royal Statistical Society* B 44: 52–62.

Mudholkar, G. S., Y. P. Chaubey, and Ching-Chuong Lin. 1976. Some approximations for the noncentral F-distribution. *Technometrics* 18: 351–358.

# 6 The Asymptotic Relative Inefficiency of Partially Restricted Reduced Forms

Phoebus J. Dhrymes

In his contribution to the volume honoring Harold Hotelling, Lawrence Klein (1960) made a number of important observations on the problem of efficient estimation of the reduced form of simultaneous equations systems. The full implications of his observations were not realized until much later. It is, thus, fitting that a volume similarly honoring Klein's many and varied contributions to econometrics should address the same subject.

The problem of efficiently estimating the reduced form of a simultaneous-equations model given all information available to us was recognized as one of the central problems from the very beginning of modern econometrics. Theil (1955) argued—somewhat incorrectly, as it turned out—that least-squares estimators of structural parameters, although "biased," exhibited smaller (no greater) variability than LIML estimators and on that account ought to be preferred for forecasting. At about the same time, T. C. Liu (1955) was arguing in favor of the unrestricted reduced form on the grounds that econometric systems tend to be under-identified—everything depends on everything else, more or less—and that since this estimator gives the "largest" maximum of the likelihood function it is to be preferred for use in forecasting over other procedures. Thereafter, Goldberger, Nagar, and Odeh (1969) provided a Taylor-series approximation for the standard error of what have come to be called restricted reduced forms induced by structural parameter estimators. Finally, in Dhrymes 1973 the problem was solved definitively by obtaining the relevant limiting distributions and showing that restricted reduced forms induced by full-information structural estimators are efficient whereas those induced by limited-information estimators are not necessarily efficient relative to the unrestricted reduced form estimators favored by Liu and others.

This chapter examines the asymptotic properties of partially restricted reduced form estimators investigated by Kakwani and Court (1972) and several others.

## Notation and Conventions

The general linear structural econometric model (GLSEM) is given by

$$y_{t.}B^* = x_{t.}C + u_{t.}, \quad t = 1, 2, \ldots, T \tag{1}$$

where $y_{t\cdot}$ and $x_{t\cdot}$ are, respectively, $1 \times m$ and $1 \times G$ and represent the current endogenous and predetermined variables of the system. We operate under the following assumptions.

ASSUMPTION 1:  The matrix $B^*$ is nonsingular.

ASSUMPTION 2:  By assumption, or otherwise, it is asserted that

$$\text{(p)} \lim_{T \to \infty} \frac{X'X}{T} = M, \quad M > 0$$

where $X = (x_{t\cdot})$, $t = 1, 2, \ldots, T$.

ASSUMPTION 3:  If the system is dynamic, it is stable.

ASSUMPTION 4:  The equations of the system are all identified by exclusion restrictions.

ASSUMPTION 5:  The error process $\{u_{t\cdot}' : t = 0, \pm 1, \pm 2, \ldots\}$ is one of i.i.d. random variables with $E(u_{t\cdot}') = 0$, $\mathrm{Cov}(u_{t\cdot}') = \Sigma$, $\Sigma > 0$, and (at least) bounded third order moments.

ASSUMPTION 5′:  The system does not contain identities. (This is actually implied by the nonsingularity of $\Sigma$ in assumption 5.)

We shall, also, typically operate under the following conventions.

CONVENTION 1 (normalization):  It is possible to, and we do, set equal to unity the coefficient of $y_i$ in the $i$th equation ($i = 1, 2, \ldots, m$).

CONVENTION 2:  In the right-hand side of the $i$th equation there are $m_i$ current endogenous variables and $G_i$ predetermined variables (serving as explanatory variables).

REMARK 1:  Convention 1 means that we can write

$$B^* = I - B \tag{2}$$

such that

$$B = (b_{ij}), \quad i, j = 1, 2, \ldots, m$$
$$b_{ii} = 0, \quad i = 1, 2, \ldots, m. \tag{3}$$

If we write the entire system as

$$Y = YB + XC + U, \tag{4}$$

then giving effect to assumption 4 and convention 2 we can write for the $i$th equation

$$y_{\cdot i} = Y_i \beta_{\cdot i} + X_i \gamma_{\cdot i} + u_{\cdot i}, \quad i = 1, 2, \ldots, m \tag{5}$$

where $Y_i$ is a $T \times m_i$ submatrix of $Y$ and $X_i$ is a $T \times G_i$ submatrix of $X$,

$$Y = (y_{\cdot 1}, y_{\cdot 2}, \ldots, y_{\cdot m}), \quad X = (x_{\cdot 1}, x_{\cdot 2}, \ldots, x_{\cdot G}) \tag{6}$$

and $y_{\cdot i}$ and $x_{\cdot j}$ are the $i$th and $j$th columns of $Y$ and $X$, respectively. Finally, $\beta_{\cdot i}$ and $\gamma_{\cdot i}$ are the $m_i \times 1$ and $G_i \times 1$ subvectors of $b_{\cdot i}$ and $c_{\cdot i}$, respectively, containing the elements not set by *a priori* information to zero.

Let $L_{1i}$ be a permutation of $m_i$ of the columns of $I_m$ corresponding to the $m_i$ explanatory current endogenous variables appearing in the $i$th equation. Similarly, let $L_{2i}$ be a permutation of $G_i$ of the columns of $I_G$ corresponding to the $G_i$ explanatory predetermined variables appearing in the $i$th equation. Thus we can write

$$Yb_{\cdot i} = Y_i \beta_{\cdot i} = YL_{1i} \beta_{\cdot i},$$

which implies

$$Y_i = YL_{1i}, \quad b_{\cdot i} = L_{1i} \beta_{\cdot i}, \quad i = 1, 2, \ldots, m. \tag{7}$$

Similarly,

$$Xc_{\cdot i} = X_i \gamma_{\cdot i} = XL_{2i} \gamma_{\cdot i},$$

which implies

$$X_i = XL_{2i}, \quad c_{\cdot i} = L_{2i} \gamma_{\cdot i}, \quad i = 1, 2, \ldots, m. \tag{8}$$

## Restricted and Unrestricted Reduced Forms

Returning to equation 1, note that in view of assumption 1 we can obtain the reduced form

$$Y = X\Pi + V, \quad \Pi = CD, \quad V = UD, \quad D = (I - B)^{-1}. \tag{9}$$

In effect the reduced form (RF) is the one appropriate for forecasting, and the question is how can it best be estimated. One obvious procedure is to estimate by ordinary least squares (OLS), ignoring the *a priori* information conveyed by the structural system. I note, in passing, that a system like 9 ignoring the manner in which $\Pi$ is composed of $C$ and $D$—on which assumption 4 imposes exclusion restrictions—could result from a multitude of structural models containing at least the $m$ endogenous variables in $Y$ and (exactly) the $G$ predetermined variables in $X$.

In an earlier paper (Dhrymes 1973) I considered the natural way in which the *a priori* restrictions implied by assumption 4 may be used in obtaining an estimator of $\Pi$. There are of course many other ways in which such restrictions may be imposed in whole or in part. For example, Kakwani and Court (1972) implicitly derive estimators for the reduced form coefficients corresponding to, say, the first endogenous variable by examining the identity $\Pi B^* = C$ insofar as it pertains to the first structural equation, that is,

$$\Pi b_{.1}^* = c_{.1}. \tag{10}$$

By convention 1,

$$b_{.1}^* = \begin{pmatrix} 1 \\ 0 \\ \vdots \\ 0 \end{pmatrix} - b_{.1}.$$

Hence, $\Pi b_{.1}^* = \pi_{.1} - \Pi b_{.1}$, and consequently

$$\pi_{.1} = \Pi b_{.1} + c_{.1}. \tag{11}$$

Using the apparatus of equations 7 and 8, we obtain

$$\pi_{.1} = \Pi L_{11} \beta_{.1} + L_{21} \gamma_{.1}$$

$$= \Pi_1 \beta_{.1} + L_{21} \gamma_{.1}$$

$$= (\Pi_1, L_{21}) \delta_{.1} \tag{12}$$

where

$$\delta_{.1} = \begin{pmatrix} \beta_{.1} \\ \gamma_{.1} \end{pmatrix}$$

and $\Pi_1$ is implicitly defined by the reduced-form representation of the current endogenous variables appearing as explanatory variables in the first structural equation, that is,

$$Y_1 = X\Pi_1 + V_1. \tag{13}$$

Since $L_{21}$ is a known matrix and we will have to estimate $\Pi_1$ (implicitly) by the two-stage least-squares procedure in obtaining an estimator of $\delta_{.1}$, Kakwani and Court (1972) proposed that we could define an estimator

$$\tilde{\pi}_{.1} = (\hat{\Pi}_1, L_{21})\tilde{\delta}_{.1} \tag{14}$$

where $\hat{\Pi}_1 = (X'X)^{-1}X'Y_1$ and $\tilde{\delta}_{.1}$ is, say, the two-stage least-squares estimator of $\delta_{.1}$.

REMARK 2: This procedure, which came to be known as the partially restricted reduced form (PRRF) approach, has the advantage of enabling us to produce a forecasting equation for a given endogenous variable without having to estimate the entire system.

I shall now analyze this procedure and derive the limiting properties of the estimators it yields. Finally, I shall attempt to compare them with the properties of the estimators derived in Dhrymes 1973.

## Limiting Distribution of PRRF Estimators

Applying the above procedure to the entire system, we find, in the obvious notation,

$$\pi_{.i} = S_i\delta_{.i}, \quad i = 1, 2, \ldots, m \tag{15}$$

where

$$S_i = (\Pi_i, L_{2i}), \quad i = 1, 2, \ldots, m.$$

REMARK 3: Recall that $\Pi_i$ is implicitly defined by

$$Y_i = X\Pi_i + V_i$$

where the $i$th structural equation is

$$y_{.i} = Z_i\delta_{.i} + u_{.i}, \quad Z_i = (Y_i, X_i), \quad \delta_{.i} = \begin{pmatrix} \beta_{.i} \\ \gamma_{.i} \end{pmatrix}. \tag{16}$$

By the identifiability condition we have

$$\text{rank}(\Pi_i) = m_i.$$

Hence,

$$\text{rank}(S_i) = m_i + G_i. \tag{17}$$

Further, recall that $S_i$ is $G \times (m_i + G_i)$ and, consequently, that it is of full rank.

Let

$$\pi = (\pi'_{.1}, \pi'_{.2}, \ldots, \pi'_{.m})' \tag{18}$$

where evidently $\pi_{.i}$ is the $i$th column of $\Pi$; define further

$$S = \text{diag}(S_1, S_2, \ldots, S_m), \quad \delta = (\delta'_{.1}, \delta'_{.2}, \ldots, \delta'_{.m})'. \tag{19}$$

Then the PRRF estimator of the system is given by

$$\tilde{\pi} = \hat{S}\tilde{\delta} \tag{20}$$

in the obvious notation. Moreover,

$$(\tilde{\pi} - \pi)_{\text{PRRF}} = \hat{S}\tilde{\delta} - S\delta$$

$$= \hat{S}\tilde{\delta} - \hat{S}\delta + (\hat{S} - S)\delta.$$

Because

$$\hat{S} - S = \text{diag}(\hat{S}_1 - S_1, \hat{S}_2 - S_2, \ldots, \hat{S}_m - S_m),$$

the $i$th subvector of $(\hat{S} - S)\delta$ is

$$(\hat{\Pi}_i - \Pi_i, 0)\begin{pmatrix} \beta_{.i} \\ \gamma_{.i} \end{pmatrix} = (\hat{\Pi}_i - \Pi_i)\beta_{.i}$$

$$= (\hat{\Pi} - \Pi)b_{.i}. \tag{21}$$

Hence

$$(\hat{S} - S)\delta = (B' \otimes I)\,\text{vec}(\hat{\Pi} - \Pi)$$

$$= (B'D' \otimes I)[I \otimes (X'X)^{-1}](I \otimes X')u \tag{22}$$

where $u = \text{vec}(U)$. It follows immediately that

$$\sqrt{T}(\tilde{\pi} - \pi)_{\text{PRRF}} \sim [SA_* + (B'D' \otimes I)(I \otimes M^{-1})]\frac{1}{\sqrt{T}}(I \otimes X')u \tag{23}$$

where $A_*$ is given by

$$A_{*2SLS} = (S^{*\prime}S^*)^{-1}S^\prime \tag{24}$$

when $\tilde{\delta}$ is obtained by the two-stage least-squares method and by

$$A_{*3SLS} = (S^{*\prime}\Phi^{-1}S^*)^{-1}S^\prime\Phi^{-1} \tag{25}$$

when $\tilde{\delta}$ is obtained by the three-stage least-squares method.

In equations 24 and 25,

$$\Phi = \Sigma \otimes I_G, \quad S^* = (I \otimes \bar{R}^\prime)S, \quad \text{and} \quad M = \bar{R}\bar{R}^\prime. \tag{26}$$

We have therefore the following.

THEOREM 1: Under assumptions 1–5′, the PRRF estimators induced by 2SLS (LIML) and 3SLS (FIML) structural estimators have, respectively, the limiting distributions

$$\sqrt{T}(\tilde{\pi} - \pi)_{PRRF\,(2SLS)} \sim N(0, H_2)$$

and

$$\sqrt{T}(\tilde{\pi} - \pi)_{PRRF\,(3SLS)} \sim N(0, H_3)$$

where

$$H_2 = (D^\prime \otimes \bar{R}^{\prime\,-1})[A_2 + (B^\prime \otimes I)(I - A_2)]$$
$$\times \Phi[A_2 + (I - A_2)(B \otimes I)](D \otimes \bar{R}^{-1}),$$
$$H_3 = (D^\prime \otimes \bar{R}^{\prime\,-1})[A_3\Phi^{-1} + (B^\prime \otimes I)(I - A_3\Phi^{-1})]$$
$$\times \Phi[\Phi^{-1}A_3 + (I - \Phi^{-1}A_3)(B \otimes I)](D \otimes \bar{R}^{-1}),$$
$$A_2 = S^*(S^{*\prime}S^*)^{-1}S^{*\prime},$$

and

$$A_3 = S^*(S^{*\prime}\Phi^{-1}S^*)^{-1}S^{*\prime}.$$

PROOF: The conclusion follows quite easily if one notes that by one of the standard central limit theorems

$$\frac{1}{\sqrt{T}}(I \otimes X^\prime)u = \frac{1}{\sqrt{T}}\sum_{t=1}^{T}(I \otimes x_{t\cdot}^\prime)u_{t\cdot}^\prime \sim N(0, \Sigma \otimes M).$$

Q.E.D.

COROLLARY 1: The covariance matrices above can also be expressed as

$$H_3 = (D' \otimes \bar{R}'^{-1})F_3\Phi F_3'(D \otimes \bar{R}^{-1}),$$

$$F_3 = [A_3 + (B' \otimes I)(\Phi - A_3)]\Phi^{-1},$$

$$H_2 = (D' \otimes \bar{R}'^{-1})[F_3 + (D'^{-1} \otimes I)F]\Phi[F_3' + F'(D^{-1} \otimes I)](D \otimes \bar{R}^{-1})$$

where $F$ is defined by

$$A_2 = A_3\Phi^{-1} + F.$$

PROOF: Because $A_2 S^* = S^*$ and $A_3\Phi^{-1}S^* = S^*$,

$$FS^* = 0, \quad FA_2 = 0, \quad FA_3 = 0.$$

Moreover, we can easily verify, by substitution, the representation in the corollary.

In the subsequent discussion, the following two mathematical results, will be useful.

LEMMA 1: The matrix $\Phi - A_3$ is positive semidefinite.

PROOF: Consider the characteristic roots of $A_3$ in the metric of $\Phi$:

$$|\lambda\Phi - A_3| = 0,$$

whose characteristic roots are exactly those of

$$|\lambda I - A_3\Phi^{-1}| = 0. \tag{27}$$

But the nonzero roots of equation 27 are exactly those of

$$|\mu I - (S^{*\prime}\Phi^{-1}S^*)^{-1}S^{*\prime}\Phi^{-1}S^*| = 0. \tag{28}$$

The roots of equation 28, however, are unity—repeated $K = \Sigma_{i=1}^{m}(m_i + G_i)$ times. Hence equation 28 has $K$ unit roots and $mG - K$ zero roots. It follows (see proposition 63 of Dhrymes 1978) that there exists a nonsingular matrix $P$ such that $\Phi = PP'$ and $A_3 = P\Lambda P'$, where $\Lambda = \text{diag}(\lambda_1, \lambda_2, \ldots, \lambda_{mG})$ are the roots of equation 27. Consequently,

$$\Phi - A_3 = PP' - P\Lambda P' = P\begin{bmatrix} I_{mG-K} & 0 \\ 0 & 0 \end{bmatrix}P' \geq 0.$$

Q.E.D.

LEMMA 2: The matrix

$$Q = \begin{bmatrix} 0 & \Phi \\ \Phi & \Phi \end{bmatrix}$$

is indefinite.

PROOF: Let $P$ be a matrix decomposing $\Phi$ as in lemma 1. Then

$$(I_2 \otimes P^{-1})Q(I_2 \otimes P'^{-1}) = \begin{bmatrix} 0 & I_{mG} \\ I_{mG} & I_{mG} \end{bmatrix}.$$

Since $I_2 \otimes P^{-1}$ is nonsingular, it will suffice to show that

$$\begin{bmatrix} 0 & I \\ I & I \end{bmatrix}$$

is indefinite. Let $(\alpha', \beta')$ be two $mG$-element row vectors. Then

$$\phi = [\alpha', \beta'] \begin{bmatrix} 0 & I \\ I & I \end{bmatrix} \begin{bmatrix} \alpha \\ \beta \end{bmatrix} = 2\alpha'\beta + \beta'\beta.$$

Clearly, if

$$\alpha = 0, \quad \beta \neq 0,$$

then

$$\phi > 0$$

Take $\alpha = -\beta$ and $\beta \neq 0$ and note that

$$\phi = -\beta'\beta < 0.$$

Finally, take $\alpha = -\frac{1}{2}\beta$ and $\beta \neq 0$ and note that

$$\psi = 0.$$

Q.E.D.

THEOREM 2: In general, the matrix $H_2 - H_3$ is indefinite.

PROOF: Using the representation of the two matrices as given in corollary 1, we find

$$H_2 - H_3 = (D' \otimes \bar{R}'^{-1})[(B' \otimes I), (D'^{-1} \otimes I)F]$$

$$\times \begin{bmatrix} 0 & \Phi \\ \Phi & \Phi \end{bmatrix} \begin{bmatrix} B \otimes I \\ F'(D^{-1} \otimes I) \end{bmatrix} (D \otimes \bar{R}^{-1}).$$

By lemma 2, the matrix

$$\begin{bmatrix} 0 & \Phi \\ \Phi & \Phi \end{bmatrix}$$

is indefinite; the conclusion, then, follows unless something special obtains with respect to $B$ or $F$.

COROLLARY 2: If all equations of the system are just identified, then $H_2 - H_3 = 0$.

PROOF: Under the conditions of the corollary,

$$S*(S*^{-1}\Phi^{-1}S*)^{-1}S*' = \Phi,$$

and

$$S*(S*'S*)^{-1}S*' = I.$$

Hence

$$A_2 = A_3\Phi^{-1},$$

and

$$F = 0.$$

Q.E.D.

COROLLARY 3: If $\sigma_{ij} = 0$, $(i \neq j)$, then

$$H_2 = H_3.$$

PROOF: By direct computation, we verify

$$S*(S*'\Phi^{-1}S*)^{-1}S*'\Phi^{-1} = S*(S*'S*)^{-1}S*'$$

which implies

$$F = 0.$$

Q.E.D.

REMARK 4: The term "in general" in the statement of theorem 4 is to be interpreted in the sense of "in the absence of any other more specific information it is presumed that. ..." Evidently, if $B$ is singular and we restrict our attention to vectors in the (column) null space of $(B \otimes I)$, then so restricted $H_2 - H_3$ is positive semidefinite. On the other hand, since by lemma 2 the matrix $Q$ is indefinite, it is possible that there exist vectors $\zeta$ such that

$$\zeta'(H_2 - H_3)\zeta = (\alpha', \beta') \begin{bmatrix} 0 & \Phi \\ \Phi & \Phi \end{bmatrix} \begin{bmatrix} \alpha \\ \beta \end{bmatrix} < 0$$

where

$$\alpha = (B \otimes I)(D \otimes \bar{R}^{-1})\zeta, \quad \beta = F'(D^{-1} \otimes I)(D \otimes \bar{R}^{-1})\zeta.$$

## Comparison with Other RF Estimators

Here, in particular, we are interested in comparing the PRRF and the RRF estimators obtained in Dhrymes 1973. As observed therein, since asymptotically 2SLS and 3SLS are equivalent to single-equation LIML and FIML estimators, respectively, the comparison will be exhaustive in view of the results obtained in the preceding section. Recall the following.

THEOREM 3: Under assumptions 1–5', the limiting distributions of the unrestricted reduced form (UNRF) OLS, 2SLS (LIML), and 3SLS (FIML) induced restricted reduced form (RRF) estimators of the parameters of the model in equation 1 are given by

$$\sqrt{T}(\tilde{\pi} - \pi)_{\text{UNRF (OLS)}} \sim N(0, G_0),$$

$$\sqrt{T}(\tilde{\pi} - \pi)_{\text{RRF (2SLS)}} \sim N(0, G_2),$$

$$\sqrt{T}(\tilde{\pi} - \pi)_{\text{RRF (3SLS)}} \sim N(0, G_3),$$

where

$$G_0 = (D' \otimes \bar{R}'^{-1})\Phi(D \otimes \bar{R}^{-1}),$$

$$G_2 = (D' \otimes \bar{R}'^{-1})[A_3 + F\Phi F'](D \otimes \bar{R}^{-1}),$$

$$G_3 = (D' \otimes \bar{R}'^{-1})A_3(D \otimes \bar{R}^{-1}).$$

PROOF: See Dhrymes 1973.

THEOREM 4:   Under the conditions of theorem 3, in general,

$$G_0 - G_3 \geq 0, \quad G_2 - G_3 \geq 0$$

with $G_0 - G_2$ indefinite.

PROOF:   See Dhrymes 1973.

COROLLARY 4:   If all equations of the system are just identified, then

$$G_0 = G_2 = G_3.$$

COROLLARY 5:   If $\sigma_{ij} = 0$ $(i \neq j)$, then

$$G_2 = G_3$$

and, consequently,

$$G_0 - G_2 \geq 0,$$

$$G_0 - G_3 \geq 0,$$

that is, both differences are positive semidefinite.

We are now in a position to compare the two sets of procedures for estimating the reduced form. In particular, we have the following.

THEOREM 5:   Consider the model in equation 1 under assumptions 1–5'. Then the RRF estimator induced by full-information estimators of the structural forms, such as 3SLS or FIML, is efficient relative to the PRRF estimator whether induced by limited- or full-information estimators of the structural form.

PROOF:   Recall from lemma 1 that $\Phi - A_3 \geq 0$. We consider now

$$H_3 - G_3 = (D' \otimes \bar{R}'^{-1})[F_3 \Phi F_3' - A_3](D \otimes \bar{R}^{-1}).$$

But $H_3 - G_3 \geq 0$ if and only if

$$0 \leq F_3 \Phi F_3' - A_3 = (B' \otimes I)(\Phi - A_3)\Phi^{-1}(\Phi - A_3)(B \otimes I), \tag{29}$$

which is evidently, at least, positive semidefinite. Moreover,

$$H_2 - G_3 = (D' \otimes \bar{R}'^{-1})[F_3 \Phi F_3' - A_3 + (D'^{-1} \otimes I)F\Phi F_3'$$

$$+ F_3 \Phi F'(D^{-1} \otimes I)$$

$$+ (D'^{-1} \otimes I)F\Phi F'(D^{-1} \otimes I)](D \otimes \bar{R}^{-1}). \tag{30}$$

Using equation 29 we can simplify the matrix in brackets in equation 30 so that

$$(H_2 - G_3) = (D' \otimes \bar{R}'^{-1})[(B' \otimes I) + (D'^{-1} \otimes I)F](\Phi - A_3)$$
$$\times [(B \otimes I) + F'(D^{-1} \otimes I)](D \otimes \bar{R}^{-1}),$$

which is obviously positive semidefinite, in view of lemma 1. Q.E.D.

REMARK 5.   We may rewrite the preceding equation as

$$(H_2 - G_3) = (D' \otimes \bar{R}'^{-1})[F + (B' \otimes I)(I - F)](\Phi - A_3)$$
$$\times [F' + (I - F)(B \otimes I)](D \otimes \bar{R}^{-1}),$$

which is a more convenient representation.

Finally, does the full-information induced PRRF estimator dominate the UNRF (OLS) or the RRF (2SLS) estimators? The answer is provided by the following.

THEOREM 6:   The PRRF estimator induced by the 3SLS (FIML) estimator of the structural parameters of the model in equation 1 under assumptions 1–5' neither dominates nor is dominated by the UNRF (OLS) or the RRF (2SLS) estimators in the sense that the matrices $G_0 - H_3$ and $G_2 - H_3$ are, in general, indefinite.

PROOF:   From theorem 3,

$$G_0 - H_3 = (D' \otimes \bar{R}'^{-1})[\Phi - F_3\Phi F_3'](D \otimes \bar{R}^{-1}),$$
$$G_2 - H_3 = (D' \otimes \bar{R}'^{-1})[A_3 + F\Phi F' - F_3\Phi F_3'](D \otimes \bar{R}^{-1}).$$

We easily establish that

$$F_3\Phi^{-1}F_3' = A_3 + (B' \otimes I)(\Phi - A_3)(B \otimes I).$$

Thus,

$$(G_0 - H_3) = (D' \otimes \bar{R}'^{-1})[(\Phi - A_3) - (B' \otimes I)(\Phi - A_3)(B \otimes I)]$$
$$\times (D \otimes \bar{R}^{-1}),$$
$$(G_2 - H_3) = (D' \otimes \bar{R}'^{-1})[F(\Phi - A_3)F' - (B' \otimes I)(\Phi - A_3)(B \otimes I)]$$
$$\times (D \otimes \bar{R}^{-1}).$$

To establish the indefiniteness we need only assure ourselves that there exist vectors $\alpha$ and $\beta$ such that

$$\alpha' F(\Phi - A_3) F' \alpha = 0 \quad \text{but} \quad \alpha'(B' \otimes I)(\Phi - A_3)(B \otimes I)\alpha \neq 0$$

and

$$\beta' F(\Phi - A_3) F' \beta \neq 0, \quad \beta'(B' \otimes I)(\Phi - A_3)(B \otimes I)\beta = 0.$$

In general, such vectors will exist, since $F$, though it depends on the data and $\Phi$, does not depend on $B$ explicitly. Q.E.D.

COROLLARY 6: When all equations of the system in equation 1 are just identified, then the PRRF (3SLS) estimator is equivalent to the UNRF (OLS) estimator and to the RRF (2SLS) and RRF (3SLS) estimators.

PROOF: Under the conditions of the corollary, $\Phi - A_3 = 0$.

COROLLARY 7: If $\sigma_{ij} = 0$ (all $i \neq j$), then the RRF (2SLS) dominates the PRRF (3SLS) estimator in the sense that $(G_2 - H_3) \leq 0$.

PROOF: Under the conditions of the corollary, $\Phi - A_3 \geq 0$ but $F = 0$. Hence,

$$(G_2 - H_3) = -(D' \otimes \bar{R}'^{-1})(B' \otimes I)(\Phi - A_3)(B \otimes I)(D \otimes \bar{R}^{-1}) \leq 0.$$
Q.E.D.

COROLLARY 8: The RRF (2SLS) estimator neither dominates nor is dominated by the PRRF (2SLS) estimator in the sense that $(H_2 - G_2)$ is indefinite.

PROOF: Using the representation in remark 5 and in theorem 3, we find

$$(H_2 - G_2) = (D' \otimes \bar{R}'^{-1})[F + (B' \otimes I)(I - F)](\Phi - A_3)$$
$$\times [F' + (I - F')(B \otimes I)]$$
$$- F(\Phi - A_3)F'(D \otimes \bar{R}^{-1}),$$

which will, in general, be an indefinite one. Q.E.D.

REMARK 6: The preceding representation makes clear that in the limited-information case the presumption would favor the RRF over the PRRF estimators in the sense that "small" $F$ would tend to imply $H_2 - G_2 \geq 0$. For example, if $\sigma_{ij} = 0$ (all $i \neq j$), then $F = 0$, so that clearly $H_2 - G_2$

$\geq 0$. Then, by continuity, even for "small" nonzero covariances the same would tend to hold.

## Conclusions

In this chapter I have derived the limiting distributions of the PRRF estimator induced by 2SLS (LIML) and 3SLS (FIML). In comparing these with other estimators of the reduced form I have established the following:

In the class of PRRF estimators, obtaining the underlying structural parameters by (more) efficient procedures (such as 3SLS) does not necessarily induce greater efficiency.

The full-information induced PRRF estimator is not necessarily efficient relative to the unrestricted estimator.

The full-information induced PRRF estimator is not necessarily efficient relative to the limited-information induced RRF estimator. In fact, when the covariance matrix of errors of the system is diagonal the latter dominates the former.

The full-information induced RRF estimator dominates all PRRF estimators.

## Bibliography

Dhrymes, Phoebus J. 1973. Restricted and unrestricted reduced forms: Asymptotic distribution and relative efficiency. *Econometrica* 41: 119–134.

Dhrymes, Phoebus J. 1978. *Mathematics for Econometrics*. New York: Springer.

Goldberger, A. S., A. L. Nagar, and H. S. Odeh. 1969. The covariance matrices of reduced form coefficients and of forecasts for a structural econometric model. *Econometrica* 29: 556–573.

Kakwani, N. C., and R. H. Court. 1972. Reduced form coefficient estimation and forecasting from a simultaneous equations model. *Australian Journal of Statistics* 14: 143–160.

Klein, L. R. 1960. The efficiency of estimation in econometric models. In R. W. Pfouts, ed., *Essays in Economics and Econometrics*. Chapel Hill: University of North Carolina Press.

Liu, T. C. 1955. A simple forecasting model of the U.S. economy. IMF Staff Papers 4: 464–476.

Theil, H. 1955. Report of the Uppsala Meeting, August 2–4, 1954. *Econometrica* 23: 204–205.

# 7 The Existence of Moments of FIML and Other Restricted Reduced-Form Estimates

Michael D. McCarthy

Over thirty years ago the theorists of the Cowles Commission suggested full-information maximum-likelihood (FIML) procedures, which are essentially reduced-form procedures, as the proper way to approach simultaneous-equation estimation. Lawrence R. Klein (1950) was the first to implement these procedures in estimating an econometric model of the United States economy. Computational problems associated with FIML procedures led to their rejection in favor of ordinary, two-stage, and three-stage least-squares procedures. The purpose of this chapter is to demonstrate that FIML procedures and other "direct reduced-form" approaches are unambiguously to be preferred to the currently popular estimation procedures from the viewpoint of finite sample moments' properties. With today's computing power, perhaps the time has come to reconsider FIML procedures and their relatives for econometric model estimation.

Let me define four types of reduced-form estimators for the usual textbook econometric model—that is, one that is linear in the variables and in the parameters:

1. Unrestricted reduced forms (URF).

2. Solved reduced forms (SRF) obtained by first estimating the structural coefficients of the model by single-equation methods such as OLS or "$k$" class procedures, or even by the 3SLS method, and then inverting the estimated dependent variable coefficient matrix to obtain an estimate of the reduced-form coefficients.

3. Direct reduced-form (DRF) estimators, which make use of any over-identifying restrictions that hold. This group includes FIML procedures and many others.

4. Partially restricted reduced forms (PRRF). In this case, if we are given estimates of the coefficients of a given structural equation, we can form a reduced form for that equation by replacing the right-hand-side endo-genous variables by their predicted values from a first-stage least-squares regression, replacing the structural coefficients by their estimates, setting the structural errors equal to zero, and collecting coefficient terms in the exogenous variables of the system.

According to the usual textbook assumptions, the first type of reduced-form estimator will possess moments to the degree that the dependent variables possess moments. It is generally known, however, that if there are any overidentifying restrictions the second type of reduced-form estimator will not possess moments. (On this subject see, for example, McCarthy 1972.) If the structural estimates used in computing the reduced form are restricted by the dictates of economic theory, this problem may not arise. However, this is a troublesome result that calls for additional remedies. The purpose of this chapter is to point out that this problem does not arise with the type 3 and type 4 reduced-form estimators.

The problem with the type 2 reduced-form estimators arises from the fact that the model "builder" has no control on the determinant of the estimated dependent variable coefficient matrix, which one must invert to compute the reduced form. This determinant can take a zero value (in a very inconvenient way) with positive probability density associated with all points in the neighborhood of zero. In the case of the types 3 and 4 reduced-form estimators, however, this cannot happen. In the absence of such a complication, intuition would suggest that the moments' properties of the reduced-form coefficient estimators of types 3 and 4 would be dictated solely by the moments' properties of the model errors.

## FIML Procedures and their Relatives

This section deals with the "two-equation" case, but the setup is such that a generalization is obvious. It is shown that the moments of the FIML reduced-form coefficient estimates exist at least to the extent that the dependent variables possess moments. The argument hinges on the simple observation that the FIML reduced-form coefficient estimates (as functions of the model errors) are bounded on any closed and bounded subset of the possible model errors. Let the reduced-form model be

$$Y_i = X\Pi_i + u_i, \qquad i = 1, 2 \tag{1}$$

where $Y_i$ is a matrix of order $T \times 1$ of $T$ observations on the $i$th endogenous variable, and $X$, of rank $K$, is a matrix of $T$ observations on $K$ exogenous variables in the complete system. Each column of $X$ represents the sample observations on an exogenous variable that enters at least one structural equation. The vectors $\Pi_1$ and $\Pi_2$ represent the true solved reduced-form coefficient values, and $u_1$ and $u_2$ represent the usual error vectors.

In what follows, I shall work with the condensed likelihood function for the reduced form. The determinant involved is

$$|\hat{u}'\hat{u}| = \hat{u}'_1\hat{u}_1 \cdot \hat{u}'_2\hat{u}_2 - (\hat{u}'_1\hat{u}_2)^2, \tag{2}$$

where $\hat{u}_i = Y_i - X\hat{\Pi}_i$ ($i = 1, 2$) and $\hat{\Pi}_i$ represents the FIML solution for $\Pi_i$.

At this point I also define

$$\Pi = \begin{pmatrix} \Pi_1 \\ \Pi_2 \end{pmatrix}, \qquad \hat{\Pi} = \begin{pmatrix} \hat{\Pi}_1 \\ \hat{\Pi}_2 \end{pmatrix}, \qquad \hat{\Pi}_L = \begin{pmatrix} \hat{\Pi}_{1L} \\ \hat{\Pi}_{2L} \end{pmatrix}$$

for later use. The terms $\hat{\Pi}_{iL}$ ($i = 1, 2$) represent the ordinary least-squares estimates of $\Pi_1$ and $\Pi_2$. Also, $Y' = [Y'_1\ Y'_2]$ and $u' = [u'_1 u'_2]$.

In the case of overidentifying restrictions (in both equations), the reduced-form coefficients of $\hat{\Pi}_1$ are related to $\hat{\Pi}_2$ as follows:

$$\hat{\Pi}_1 = \begin{bmatrix} \hat{\Pi}_{11} \\ \hat{\Pi}_{21} \\ \hat{\Pi}_{31} \end{bmatrix} = \begin{bmatrix} \hat{\Pi}_{12} & 0 & 0 \\ 0 & \hat{\Pi}_{22} & 0 \\ 0 & 0 & I \end{bmatrix} \begin{bmatrix} c_1 \\ c_2 \\ \hat{\Pi}_{31} \end{bmatrix} \tag{3}$$

where $\hat{\Pi}_{12}$ represents a column vector of estimated coefficients from the reduced form for $Y_2$ that correspond to exogenous variables excluded from, say, the first structural equation, and $\hat{\Pi}_{22}$ plays the corresponding role for the exogenous variables excluded from the second structural equation. The terms $c_1$ and $c_2$ are scalars, and the identity term corresponds to the exogenous variables common to both structural equations. In short, the overidentifying restrictions are given by

$$\hat{\Pi}_{11} = c_1\hat{\Pi}_{12}, \qquad \hat{\Pi}_{21} = c_2\hat{\Pi}_{22}. \tag{3'}$$

The problem at hand is to minimize the Lagrangian expression

$$Z = \ln|\hat{u}'\hat{u}| + 2\lambda'_1(\hat{\Pi}_{11} - c_1\hat{\Pi}_{12}) + 2\lambda'_2(\hat{\Pi}_{21} - c_2\hat{\Pi}_{22}) \tag{4}$$

with respect to the elements of $\hat{\Pi}$, $\lambda'_1$, $\lambda'_2$, $c_1$, and $c_2$, where $\lambda'_1$ and $\lambda'_2$ are row vectors of Lagrangian multipliers of order $1 \times k_1$ and $1 \times k_2$ corresponding to the overidentifying restrictions. (I have made no assumption about normalcy of the model errors.)

The derivation of the solution to the problem parallels that used by Theil (1971) for the restricted single-equation case. Accordingly, I represent the solution as follows:

$$\lambda = \begin{bmatrix} \lambda_1 \\ \lambda_2 \end{bmatrix} = [R'FR]^{-1}R'(\hat{\Pi} - \hat{\Pi}_L) = -[R'FR]^{-1}R'\hat{\Pi}_L \tag{5}$$

where

$$R' = \begin{bmatrix} -I_{k_1} & 0 & 0 & | & c_1 I_{k_1} & 0 & 0 \\ 0 & -I_{k_2} & 0 & | & 0 & c_2 I_{k_2} & 0 \end{bmatrix} = [R_1' \mid R_2'],$$

$$F = \begin{bmatrix} \hat{u}_1'\hat{u}_1[X'X]^{-1} & \hat{u}_1'\hat{u}_2[X'X]^{-1} \\ \hat{u}_1'\hat{u}_2[X'X]^{-1} & \hat{u}_2'\hat{u}_2[X'X]^{-1} \end{bmatrix}.$$

The zero columns in $R'$ represent variables common to both structural equations. The term $I_{k_i}$ represents the identity matrix of order $k_i$. Also,

$$(\hat{\Pi} - \hat{\Pi}_L) = FR[R'FR]^{-1}R'(\hat{\Pi} - \hat{\Pi}_L) = -FR[R'FR]^{-1}R'\hat{\Pi}_L, \tag{6}$$

$$R'\hat{\Pi} = 0, \tag{7}$$

$$\lambda_1'\hat{\Pi}_{12} = \lambda_2'\hat{\Pi}_{22} = 0, \tag{8}$$

and

$$\lambda_i'\hat{\Pi}_{i1} = 0, \quad \text{if } c_i \neq 0. \tag{8'}$$

Let $\hat{\Pi}_0$, $\lambda_0$, and $c_0 = [c_{10}c_{20}]$ represent the solutions to equations 5–8 that correspond to $Y_0$, and observe that, for $\delta > 0$, $Y = \delta Y_0$ yields as solutions $\delta\hat{\Pi}_0$, $\lambda_0/\delta$, and $C_0$. (Use the facts that, if $\hat{\Pi}$ and $Y_0$ are changed by a factor $\delta$, then $\hat{u}_i'\hat{u}_j$ becomes

$$(\delta Y_{i0} - X\delta\hat{\Pi}_{i0})'(\delta Y_{j0} - X\delta\hat{\Pi}_{j0}) = \delta^2(Y_{i0} - X\hat{\Pi}_{i0})'(Y_{j0} - X\hat{\Pi}_{j0}).$$

This implies that multiplying $Y_0$ by $\delta$ multiplies $FR$ and $R'FR$ by $\delta^2$.)

Consider the set of $Y$ vectors, $S_0$, such that $Y_0 \in S_0$ implies that $Y_0$ lies on the unit sphere; that is, $Y_0'Y_0 = 1$. The set of $Y$ vectors generated by multiplying an element of $Y_0$ by $\delta$ is given by

$$Y = \delta Y_0. \tag{9}$$

The Jacobian of this transformation is

$$J = \delta^{n-1}\left(1 - \sum_{i=2}^{n} Y_{0i}^2\right)^{-1/2} = \delta^{n-1}K_0(Y_0^*) \tag{10}$$

where the elements of $Y_0$ are constrained by the requirement $\sum_{i=2}^{n} Y_{0i}^2 < 1$, where $n = 2T$, and $Y_0^* = Y_{02}, Y_{03}, \ldots, Y_{0n}$.

In examining the probability density function for $\hat{\Pi}$ and its moments, we need only examine the density and its moments as $Y$ moves in a trajectory defined by $\delta$ and the various points of the unit sphere.

Let $A > 0$ be given, and assume that the transformed $Y$ values defined by $\delta$ and $Y_0^*$ are confined to a set $S^*$, the elements of which satisfy $0 \le \delta \le A$. The elements of $S^*$ are thus bounded, and (because of its structure) $\hat{\Pi}_L$ is a bounded and continuous function of the elements of $S^*$.

THEOREM:    The solution for $\hat{\Pi}$ in the system 5–8 is everywhere a bounded function of the elements of $S^*$.

REMARK:    The "solutions" for $\lambda$, $c_1$, and $c_2$ are *not* everywhere bounded functions of the elements of $S^*$.

PROOF:    An assertion that $\hat{\Pi}$ is not bounded on $S^*$ is immediately countered by the following: Since $Y$ is bounded, if $\hat{\Pi}$ is not bounded at some point $S_0^* \in S^*$, then $\hat{u}_1'\hat{u}_1$ and/or $\hat{u}_2'\hat{u}_2$ are not bounded. However, because of the structure of equation 6, such a situation cannot arise. A numerator-denominator type canceling of the terms $\hat{u}_1'\hat{u}_1$ and/or $\hat{u}_2'\hat{u}_2$ in $FR$ and $[R'FR]^{-1}$ on the right-hand side of equation 6 occurs as these terms become arbitrarily large. The equation system 5–8 is one in which the $\hat{u}_i'\hat{u}_i$ ($i = 1, 2$) can only become unbounded relative to each other and not in any absolute way if $\hat{\Pi}_L$ is bounded.

We can rule out pathological cases in which $S_0^*$ is approached in such a manner that $c_1$ and/or $c_2$ approach zero while $\hat{\Pi}_2$ becomes arbitrarily large. (Imagine a situation in which $\hat{u}_1'\hat{u}_1/\hat{u}_2'\hat{u}_2 \to 0$, because $\hat{\Pi}_2$ becomes large, and in which $c_1$ and/or $c_2$ approaches zero.) To simplify matters (without loss of generality), assume that the $R_i$ matrices are $K \times K$. This implies that there are no exogenous variables common to both equations, and that $R_1 = -I_K$ and

$$R_2 = \begin{bmatrix} c_1 I_{k_1} & 0 \\ 0 & c_2 I_{k_2} \end{bmatrix}$$

where $k_1 + k_2 = K$.

Suppose that $Y_1$ and $Y_2$ are nonzero and that both are linearly independent of $X$. Thus, the FIML solutions for $\hat{\Pi}_1$ and $\hat{\Pi}_2$ are such that $\hat{u}_1 \ne 0$ and $\hat{u}_2 \ne 0$. In this case $X'M_i X$ is positive-definite, where

$$M_i = [I - \hat{u}_i[\hat{u}_i'\hat{u}_i]^{-1}\hat{u}_i'] \text{ and } i = 1, 2.$$

To see this, note that

$$\begin{vmatrix} \hat{u}_i'\hat{u}_i & \hat{u}_i'X \\ X'\hat{u}_i & X'X \end{vmatrix} = |X'X|\hat{u}_i'[I - X[X'X]^{-1}X']\hat{u}_i$$

$$= \hat{u}_i'\hat{u}_i|X'M_iX|.$$

The term $\hat{u}_i'[I - X[X'X]^{-1}X']\hat{u}_i$ must be positive, for otherwise $Y_i$ would be linearly dependent on $X$. By assumption, $|X'X|$ and $\hat{u}_i'\hat{u}_i$ are also positive; hence, $X'M_iX$ is positive-definite. Next, FIML must satisfy the inequality

$$\begin{vmatrix} Y_1'Y_1 & Y_1'Y_2 \\ Y_2'Y_1 & Y_2'Y_2 \end{vmatrix} \geq |\hat{u}'\hat{u}|$$

$$= \hat{u}_1'\hat{u}_1 \cdot \hat{u}_2'M_1\hat{u}_2$$

$$= \hat{u}_1'\hat{u}_1(Y_2'M_1Y_2 - 2Y_2'M_1X\hat{\Pi}_2 + \hat{\Pi}_2'X'M_1X\hat{\Pi}_2). \qquad (2')$$

If $X'M_1X$ is positive-definite in some neighborhood of $S_0^*$, then $\hat{\Pi}_2$ must be bounded in such a neighborhood; otherwise the inequality $2'$ would be violated. A parallel argument leads to the conclusion that $\hat{\Pi}_1$ must be bounded. Suppose next that $Y_1$ is nonzero but linearly dependent on $X$, and $Y_2$ is not linearly dependent on $X$. The FIML solution evidently requires that $\hat{u}_1 = 0$, which ensures that $\hat{\Pi}_1$ is bounded since $Y$ is bounded. In fact, $\hat{\Pi}_1 = \hat{\Pi}_{1L}$. Also, $c_1^{-1}\hat{\Pi}_{11} = \hat{\Pi}_{12}$, and $c_2^{-1}\hat{\Pi}_{21} = \hat{\Pi}_{22}$. (Assume for the moment that $c_1$ and $c_2$ are nonzero.) Premultiplying equation 5 by $\hat{\Pi}_1' = [\hat{\Pi}_{11}'\hat{\Pi}_{21}']$ and using equation $8'$, we have

$$\hat{\Pi}_2'[X'X]\hat{\Pi}_2 - \hat{\Pi}_2'[X'X]\hat{\Pi}_{2L} = 0, \qquad (5')$$

which, since $[X'X]$ is positive-definite, ensures that $\hat{\Pi}_2$ is bounded. This result also apparently holds in the limit as $Y_2$ approaches linear dependence on $X$, and holds for situations in which

$$\lim_{q \to S_0^*} c_i = 0, \quad i = 1, 2.$$

When $c_i \to 0$, evidently $\hat{\Pi}_{i1} \to 0$. The case where $Y_1 = 0$ and $Y_2 \neq 0$ is apparently a situation in which $\hat{\Pi}_1 = 0$, $\hat{\Pi}_2 = \hat{\Pi}_{2L}$, and $c_1 = c_2 = 0$. Finally, if $Y_1 = Y_2 = 0$, then FIML yields $\hat{\Pi}_1 = \hat{\Pi}_2 = 0$, and the $c_i$ are indeterminant.

A conclusion that the solution for $\hat{\Pi}$ is bounded at all points in $S^*$ (a closed and bounded set) implies that the solution achieves its maximum and its minimum on the set.

Consider now the class of probability density functions whose general form is $f(u'Au)$, where $A$ is positive-definite and $f(P) \geq f(P + q)$ for $P \geq 0$ and $q \geq 0$. There is no loss of generality in assuming that $A = I$, since $A$ may always be removed from the analysis by the transform $Z = Bu$ where $A = B'B$. Accordingly, in what follows I will concentrate on probability density functions of the form

$$f = f(u'u) \quad \text{or} \quad f = f(Y'Y - 2Y'\alpha + \alpha'\alpha) \tag{12}$$

where

$$\alpha = \chi\Pi,$$

$$\chi = \begin{bmatrix} X & 0 \\ 0 & X \end{bmatrix}.$$

With the transformation defined by equation 9 and the associated Jacobian 10, the joint probability density function for $\delta$ and $Y_0^*$ is of the form

$$f = \delta^{n-1} K_0(Y_0^*) f(\delta^2 - 2\delta Y_0'\alpha + \alpha'\alpha). \tag{12'}$$

Note that

$$\delta^2 - 2Y_0'\alpha\delta + \alpha'\alpha = (1 - r^2)\delta^2 + [r\delta - (\alpha'\alpha)^{1/2}]^2$$

where, for simplicity of notation, $r = (Y_0'\alpha)/(\alpha'\alpha)^{1/2}$. Since $Y_0$ is on the unit sphere, we are assured that $0 \leq |r| \leq 1$.

Equation 12' then becomes

$$f = \delta^{n-1} K_0(Y_0^*) f(\delta^2(1 - r^2) + [r\delta - (\alpha'\alpha)^{1/2}]^2). \tag{12''}$$

Again, considering the transformation 9, note that the observation that multiplying $Y_0 \in S_0$ by $\delta$ multiplies the FIML solution for $\hat{\Pi}$ by $\delta$ is equivalent to asserting that, with $Y_0^*$ fixed, $\hat{\Pi}$ varies proportionally with $\delta$. That is,

$$\hat{\Pi} = g(Y_0^*)\delta. \tag{13}$$

Let $i\hat{\Pi}$ be the $i$th element of $\hat{\Pi}$ in equation 13, and let the integral of $i\hat{\Pi}^k f(\ )$, with $\delta \geq 0$ fixed, be

$$Z_{ik}|\delta = \delta^{n-1+k} \int_{Y_0^*} g_i(Y_0^*)^k K_0(Y_0^*) f(\delta^2(1-r^2) + [\delta r - (\alpha'\alpha)^{1/2}]^2) dY_0^* \tag{14}$$

where $g_i$ denotes the $i$th element of $g(Y_0^*)$. This integral must exist, since $i\hat{\Pi}$ (and $i\hat{\Pi}^k$) are bounded on the unit sphere, $S_0$. For convenience only we assume that $k$ is even; the case where $k$ is odd creates a minor nuisance.

Next, consider the integral

$$\tilde{Z}_{ik}|\delta = \delta^{n-1+k} \int_{Y_0^*} g_i(Y_0^*)^k K_0(Y_0^*) f(\delta^2(1-r^2)) dY_0^*. \tag{14'}$$

The integral in equation 14' differs from that in equation 14 in that the term $[\delta r - (\alpha'\alpha)^{1/2}]^2$ has been omitted from $f$. Since we assume that $f(P) \geq f(P+q)$ for $P \geq 0$ and $q \geq 0$,

$$\tilde{Z}_{ik}|\delta > Z_{ik}|\delta.$$

(Assuming that the difference

$$f(\delta^2(1-r^2)) - f(\delta^2(1-r^2) + [\delta r - \alpha'\alpha)^{1/2}]^2)$$

is bounded for $\delta \geq 0$ and $0 \leq r \leq 1$, we are assured that the integral in equation 14' converges.)

Suppose that before integrating over the $Y_0^*$ in equations 14 and 14' we had introduced the transformation $\beta = (1-r^2)\delta^2$, and then integrated over $Y_0^*$, taking $\beta$ as given. The preceding argument would have led to the conclusion that

$$\tilde{Z}_{ik|\beta} > Z_{ik|\beta} \tag{15}$$

where $\tilde{Z}_{ik|\beta}$ and $Z_{ik|\beta}$ are defined in a manner paralleling the definitions of $\tilde{Z}_{ik|\delta}$ and $Z_{ik|\delta'}$ and that

$$\tilde{Z}_{ik|\beta} = \frac{\beta^{(n-2+k)/2}}{2} f(\beta) \int \left( \frac{g_i(Y_0^*)}{(1-r^2)^{1/2}} \right)^k K_0(Y_0^*)(1-r^2)^{-n/2} dY_0^*$$

$$= \frac{b}{2} \beta^{(n-2+k)/2} f(\beta) \tag{15'}$$

where $b$ represents the integral on the right-hand side. Now integrate both sides of equation 15 from $\beta = 0$ to infinity. The integral of the right-hand side of equation 15, if it exists, yields

$$Z_{ik} = \int_0^\infty Z_{ik|\beta} d\beta = E(i\hat{\Pi}^k).$$

Existence of the integral on the left-hand side ensures that $E(_i\hat{\Pi}^k)$ exists, but this is equivalent to saying that existence of $E_i\hat{\Pi}^k$ is ensured if $f$ possesses moments to the appropriate order. This is exactly what intuition would suggest. Since there is no explicit inversion of a matrix of random structural coefficient estimates in computing FIML reduced-form coefficient estimates (in contrast to the SRF estimators cited in the introduction), the moments' properties of the FIML estimators are governed in a very straightforward way by the moments' properties of the model errors. In the present case, where $c\beta^{(n-2)/2}f(\beta)$ is thought of as a probability density function and where $c$ is a constant of integration, if the $k$th moment of $\beta^{1/2}$ exists, the $k$th moment of $\hat{\Pi}$ exists.

Finally, it is evident that the above results for FIML extend to LIML partially restricted reduced forms, since LIML is a myopic FIML. We have one example of a "$k$ class" partially restricted reduced-form estimator for which the moments of the reduced form exist.

## The Partially Restricted Reduced Forms

This section notes that the PRRF estimators for the $k$ class of estimators (with $k$ fixed) possess moments to the order that the dependent variables possess moments, provided that $0 \leq k \leq 1$, and provides a simple proof. It is also noted that there is a strong presumption that the PRRF estimators possess moments even if $k > 1$. In fact, the FIML results cited above suggest that this has to be the case, since LIML is a myopic FIML. The notation is changed for convenience.

Suppose that the structural equation being considered is

$$y = YA + XB + u \qquad (16)$$

where $y$ is a $T \times 1$ column vector of $T$ sample observations on some dependent variable, $Y$ is a $T \times G$ matrix of right-hand-side endogenous variables, $X$ is a $T \times n$ matrix of right-hand-side exogenous variables, $A$ and $B$ are unknown coefficients, and $u$ is the familiar error vector. Now the true reduced form for $Y$ is

$$Y = \chi P + \eta \qquad (17)$$

where $\chi$ is a $T \times K$ matrix of all exogenous variables in the system and contains $X$ among its columns, $P$ is a coefficient matrix, and $\eta$ is the reduced-form error matrix for $Y$. The reduced-form predicted value for $Y$ is

$$\hat{Y} = \chi\hat{P} \tag{18}$$

where $\hat{P} = [\chi'\chi]^{-1}\chi'Y$. The reduced-form calculated errors are given by

$$\hat{\eta} = [I - \chi(\chi'\chi)^{-1}\chi']Y,$$

and obviously

$$\hat{Y}'\hat{\eta} = 0.$$

Let $\hat{A}$ and $\hat{B}$ be some estimates of the structural coefficients in equation 16. The PRRF "predicted values" for the sample are obtained by replacing $A$ and $B$ in equation 16 by $\hat{A}$ and $\hat{B}$, replacing $Y$ by $\hat{Y}$ from equation 18,[1] and setting $u = 0$. This yields

$$\hat{y} = \hat{Y}\hat{A} + X\hat{B} - (\hat{Y}|X)\begin{pmatrix}\hat{A}\\\hat{B}\end{pmatrix} \tag{19}$$

as the PRRF predicted values for the sample. To get the PRRF coefficient estimates, we would collect terms in equation 19 in the columns of $\chi$. For future reference we designate the coefficient estimates from such a collection of terms by $\hat{R}$ and write

$$\hat{y} = \chi\hat{R}. \tag{19'}$$

Suppose now that $\hat{A}$ and $\hat{B}$ were obtained by $k$-class procedures. Then we have

$$\begin{bmatrix}\hat{A}\\\hat{B}\end{bmatrix} = \begin{bmatrix}\hat{Y}'\hat{Y} + (1-k)\hat{\eta}'\hat{\eta} & \hat{Y}'X \\ X'\hat{Y} & X'X\end{bmatrix}^{-1} \begin{bmatrix}\hat{Y}' + (1-k)\hat{\eta}' \\ X'\end{bmatrix} y. \tag{20}$$

Now consider the term

$$\hat{u} = y - \begin{bmatrix}\hat{Y} + (1-k)\hat{\eta} & X\end{bmatrix}\begin{bmatrix}\hat{A}\\\hat{B}\end{bmatrix}$$

$$= \left\{I - \begin{bmatrix}\hat{Y} + (1-k)\hat{\eta} & X\end{bmatrix}\begin{bmatrix}\hat{Y}'\hat{Y} + (1-k)\hat{\eta}'\hat{\eta} & \hat{Y}'X \\ X'\hat{Y} & X'X\end{bmatrix}^{-1}\right.$$

$$\left.\times \begin{bmatrix}\hat{Y}' + (1 & k)\hat{\eta}' \\ X'\end{bmatrix}\right\} y.$$

This term differs from the PRRF calculated sample residuals by the term $-(1-k)\hat{\eta}\hat{A}$. Note that

$$
\hat{u}'\hat{u} = y'y - 2y' \left[ \hat{Y} + (1-k)\hat{\eta} \; \middle| \; X \right] \left[ \begin{array}{c|c} \hat{Y}'\hat{Y} + (1-k)\hat{\eta}'\hat{\eta} & \hat{Y}'\hat{X} \\ \hline X'\hat{Y} & X'X \end{array} \right]^{-1}
$$

$$
\times \left[ \begin{array}{c} \hat{Y}' + (1-k)\hat{\eta}' \\ X' \end{array} \right] y
$$

$$
+ [\hat{A}'\hat{B}'] \left[ \begin{array}{c|c} \hat{Y}'\hat{Y} + (1-k)^2\hat{\eta}'\hat{\eta} & \hat{Y}'X \\ \hline X'\hat{Y} & X'X \end{array} \right] \left[ \begin{array}{c} \hat{A} \\ \hat{B} \end{array} \right]. \tag{21}
$$

The middle terms on the right-hand side of equation 21 may be written as

$$
-2y' \left[ \hat{Y} + (1-k)\hat{\eta} \; \middle| \; X \right] \left[ \begin{array}{c|c} \hat{Y}'\hat{Y} + (1-k)\hat{\eta}'\hat{\eta} & \hat{Y}'X \\ \hline X'\hat{Y} & X'X \end{array} \right]^{-1} \left[ \begin{array}{c} \hat{Y}' + (1-k)\hat{\eta}' \\ X' \end{array} \right] y
$$

$$
= -2[\hat{A}'\hat{B}'] \left[ \begin{array}{c|c} \hat{Y}'\hat{Y} + (1-k)\hat{\eta}'\hat{\eta} & \hat{Y}'X \\ \hline X'\hat{Y} & X'X \end{array} \right] \left[ \begin{array}{c} \hat{A} \\ \hat{B} \end{array} \right]. \tag{21'}
$$

This can be verified easily by substituting from equation 20 into the right-hand side of equation 21'. With this simplification we have

$$
\hat{u}'\hat{u} = y'y - 2[\hat{A}'\hat{B}'] \left[ \begin{array}{c|c} \hat{Y}'\hat{Y} + (1-k)\hat{\eta}'\hat{\eta} & \hat{Y}'X \\ \hline X'\hat{Y} & X'X \end{array} \right] \left[ \begin{array}{c} \hat{A} \\ \hat{B} \end{array} \right]
$$

$$
+ [\hat{A}'\hat{B}'] \left[ \begin{array}{c|c} \hat{Y}'\hat{Y} + (1-k)^2\hat{\eta}'\hat{\eta} & \hat{Y}'X \\ \hline X'\hat{Y} & X'X \end{array} \right] \left[ \begin{array}{c} \hat{A} \\ \hat{B} \end{array} \right]
$$

$$
= y'y - \hat{y}'\hat{y} + [(1-k)^2 - 2(1-k)]\hat{A}'\hat{\eta}'\hat{\eta}\hat{A}, \tag{21''}
$$

after collecting terms involving $\hat{\eta}'\hat{\eta}$. (The term $\hat{y}'\hat{y}$ is defined by equation 19 or 19' and is the sum of squared sample predicted values for the variable in question.) Now equation 21" simplifies to

$$
\hat{u}'\hat{u} = y'y - \hat{y}'\hat{y} + (k^2 - 1)\hat{A}'\hat{\eta}'\hat{\eta}\hat{A}, \tag{21'''}
$$

or

$$
y'y = \hat{y}'\hat{y} + (1 - k^2)\hat{A}'\hat{\eta}'\hat{\eta}\hat{A} + \hat{u}'\hat{u}, \tag{21''''}
$$

which, if $0 \le k \le 1$, guarantees that $y'y \ge \hat{y}'\hat{y}$.

This last inequality is sufficient to guarantee that, if $0 \le k \le 1$ and if $Ey'y$ exists, then $E\hat{y}'\hat{y}$ will exist—which implies that the variances of

the PRRF coefficient estimators will exist. To see this we make use of
the fact that, since $[\chi'\chi]^{-1}$ exists,

$$\hat{y}'\hat{y} = \hat{R}'\chi'\chi\hat{R} = c_1\hat{R}_1{}^2 + c_2,$$

where $\hat{R}_1$ is a scalar component of $\hat{R}$, $c_1$ and $c_2$ are positive, and $c_1$
depends only on the columns of $\chi$. If $E\hat{R}_1{}^2$ did not exist, we would have
a contradiction of the assumption that $Ey'y$ existed. The fact that $\hat{y}'\hat{y} =
c_1\hat{R}_1 + c_2$, together with the fact that $(y'y)^N \geq (\hat{y}'\hat{y})^N$ for $N = 1, 2, \ldots$,
can be used to extend the result to higher-order moments. (In the common
textbook case, where the model errors are assumed to be normal, all
moments of $\hat{y}'\hat{y}$ and of the PRRF coefficient estimators will exist.)

Now consider the situation in which $k > 1$. In this case, the term
$(1 - k^2)\hat{A}'\hat{\eta}'\hat{\eta}\hat{A}$ will not be positive, and we could imagine a case in
which the bounding

$$y'y \geq \hat{y}'\hat{y}$$

would not hold. However, the bounding

$$y'y \geq \hat{y}'\hat{y} + (1 - k^2)\hat{A}'\hat{\eta}'\hat{\eta}\hat{A} \tag{22}$$

always holds. Thus, if $Ey'y$ exists, the expected value of the right-hand
side of equation 22 must always exist. If $Ey'y$ exists and the expected
value of one term on the right-hand side of equation 22 does not exist,
then the expected value of the other term does not exist; otherwise we
have a contradiction of the inequality. In short, either the expected values
of both terms exist or the expected values of both do not exist. In the
first case, the variances (and first moments) of $\hat{R}$ exist. Let us consider
the second case. For simplicity, define $s = \hat{y}'\hat{y}$ and $\hat{A}'\hat{\eta}'\hat{\eta}\hat{A} = t$. Thus,

$$y'y \geq s + (1 - k^2)t. \tag{23}$$

The expected value of the right-hand side of equation 23 is given by

$$Z = \int [E(s|t) + (1 - k^2)t] f_t(t) dt,$$

where $E(s|t)$ is the conditional expectation of $s$ given $t$, and $f_t(t)$ is the
marginal density function for $t$. Note that $E(s|t)$ and $(1 - k^2)t$ are func-
tions of $t$ and $k$ only. Suppose that $Et$ did not exist. Since the sum must
possess moments, $E(s|t) = h(t, k)$ must pass to $\infty$ fast enough as $t \to \infty$
that the integral defined by $Z$ will converge regardless of the configuration

of $\chi$. I have not been able to rule out this possibility, but the results for LIML cited in the preceding section suggest that such a coincidence is not to be expected. Accordingly, we conclude, in general, that PRRF moments to the second order will exist if the model errors exist to the second order. The argument may be extended to higher-order moments.

## Note

1. If $k$ were stochastic (say, because of the use of LIML), $\hat{Y}$ would be computed using the LIML coefficient estimates for the reduced form for $Y$ in place of equation 18.

## Bibliography

Klein, L. R. 1950 *Economic Fluctuations in the United States*, 1921–1941. Cowles Commission Monograph II. New York: Wiley.

McCarthy, M. D. 1972. A note on the forecasting properties of two-stage least squares restricted reduced forms. *International Economic Review* 13, no. 3: 751–761.

Theil, H. 1971. *Principles of Econometrics*. New York: Wiley.

# 8 Forecasting Theory for Hierarchical Systems with Applications to Multicountry Models

## Stefan Schleicher

This chapter draws from Project LINK (a multicountry econometric model designed to investigate the interdependence of national economies),[1] from the theory of optimal control in hierarchical systems as developed in system science,[2] and from Kalman filter theory (a general statistical model designed for the estimation of system states that cannot be observed directly).[3] The integrating feature of these resources is that large-scale systems such as multicountry models are characterized by a hierarchical system structure. The chapter investigates to what extent this specific system structure can be utilized for forecasting procedures that are based on decentralized information structures. Although a number of available optimal control procedures make explicit use of hierarchical system structures, no special statistical forecasting theory seems to be available for these systems.

Hierarchical systems are characterized by a number of subsystems which are connected via interaction channels. Because of these interactions, a forecast produced by the individual subsystems generally will not meet some overall system constraints. In the case of a multicountry model of international trade like the LINK system, the import forecasts of the individual countries based on their assumptions about export demand might not add up to the volume of world trade calculated by adding up either country imports or country exports. Therefore, the role of a coordinator has to be defined to take into account the interactions between the subsystems.

## Description of the System

Figure 1 illustrates a general system with a mathematical representation given by the vector-valued function

$$h(y, x, u) = 0. \tag{1}$$

Three categories of variables are involved: $y$, the vector of system output (or endogenous) variables; $x$, the vector of system input (or exogenous) variables; and $u$, the vector of system error (or disturbance) variables. For the sake of generality we will assume that, besides the system error $u$, the system input $x$ is also a random variable. This is particularly true

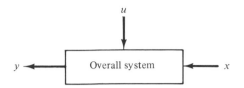

**Figure 1**

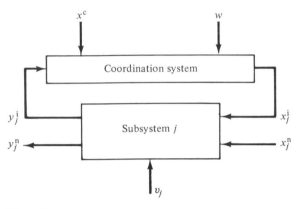

**Figure 2**

if the system is used for forecasting where for most system inputs only imprecise information is available. Obviously the case of a precisely known input is contained in this assumption.

Large-scale systems are characterized by a more or less pronounced hierarchical structure in which subsystems are connected via coordination systems at various hierarchical levels. To understand the general characteristics of a complex hierarchical system it is sufficient to consider the case of a two-level structure. Figure 2 illustrates the relationship between the $j$th subsystem and the coordination system that connects subsystems of the same hierarchical level. The hierarchical system structure suggests the following partition of the system variables:

• Among the endogenous variables $y$, we distinguish between $y^i$ (the vector of interacting endogenous variables) and $y^n$ (the vector of non-interacting endogenous variables), depending on whether they feed back into the coordination system or not.

- Among the exogenous variables $x$, we distinguish between $x^c$ (those that enter only the coordination system and are subject to the control of the coordinator) and $x^i$ and $x^n$ (those that enter only the subsystems and are either interacting or noninteracting exogenous variables).
- Among the stochastic disturbance variables $u$, we distinguish between vector $w$ (which affects only the coordination system) and vector $v$ (which affects only the subsystems).

A subscript $j$ (for the interacting and noninteracting endogenous or exogenous variables or the subsystem disturbance vector $v$) denotes the subvector belonging to the $j$th subsystem.

The $j$th subsystem is described by the vector-valued function

$$f_j(y_j, x_j, v_j) = 0 \tag{2a}$$

where

$$y_j - \begin{bmatrix} y_j^i \\ y_j^n \end{bmatrix}, \quad x_j = \begin{bmatrix} x_j^i \\ x_j^n \end{bmatrix}.$$

The coordination system is described by the vector-valued function

$$g(y^i, x^i, x^c, w) = 0. \tag{2b}$$

## Forecasting Procedures

### Basic Concepts

Forecasting with a general system (equation 1) is equivalent to calculating the probability distribution of the system outputs (endogenous variables) conditioned on the system inputs (endogenous variables) $x$ and the system error (disturbance variable) $u$:

$$P(y|x, u). \tag{3}$$

In case of a hierarchical system (equation 2), the forecast is described by a conditional probability distribution of the endogenous variables of the subsystems $y$ and the interacting exogenous variables $x^i$ conditioned on the noninteracting exogenous variables $x^n$, the exogenous variables of the coordination system $x^c$, the subsystem disturbances $v$, and the coordination-system disturbances $w$:

$$P(y, x^i | x^n, x^c, v, w). \tag{4}$$

Usually only the first and second moments of these distributions are calculated. The optimal forecast finally depends on the chosen loss function for the forecasting error (Granger and Newbold 1977).

A hierarchical system structure raises the question whether the computational complexity can be simplified by splitting up the computational burden between the subsystems and a coordinator.

If there are interdependencies between the subsystems as described by the coordination system, individual subsystem forecasts usually will not be compatible with all the constraints imposed by the coordination system. Then the role has to be defined of a coordinator who collects information from the subsystems, processes this information, and feeds new information back to the subsystems in order to arrive at subsystem forecasts that meet the restrictions imposed by the subsystem interdependencies. In most cases the coordinator and the subsystems represent organizational units, so forecasting methods that divide the computational work between the subsystems and a coordinator seem to be very appealing.

In the following subsections I will introduce three types of forecasting procedures for hierarchical systems. Procedure 1 neglects the hierarchical system structure. Procedure 2 specifies the information exchange between subsystems and coordinator if the subsystems have no extraneous information about their interacting exogenous variables. Procedure 3 allows for such an extraneous information.

The following notational conventions are used. If a variable (either deterministic or stochastic) has to be numerically specified by a subsystem or the coordinator, then this variable will be underlined.

A forecast solution for a variable will be identified by a caret. [Such a forecast will be a probability distribution or moments of a probability distribution as soon as random inputs (random disturbances or stochastic exogenous variables) enter the system.]

**Procedure 1 (Overall System)**

An obvious forecasting procedure for a large system is to have each subsystem mail its equation system and the necessary subsystem inputs to a coordinator, who takes over the task of solving the complete system.

ALGORITHM    Step 1: Each subsystem mails to the coordinator

$f_j$, the complete equation system of the $j$th subsystem (equation 2a),

$\underline{v}_j$, the stochastic characteristics of the corresponding disturbance terms, and

$\underline{x}_j^n$, the (stochastic) assumptions about noninteracting exogenous variables of the $j$th subsystem.

Step 2: The coordinator specifies

$g$, the equation system of the coordination system (equation 2b),

$\underline{w}$, the stochastic characteristics of the corresponding disturbance terms, and

$\underline{x}^c$, the (stochastic) assumptions about the exogenous variables of the coordination system.

Step 3: The coordinator uses the (stochastic) equation system $\{f_1, \ldots, f_n, g\}$ to calculate the forecast for

$\hat{y}^n$, the noninteracting endogenous variables,

$\hat{y}^i$, the interacting endogenous variables, and

$\hat{x}^i$, the interacting exogenous variables.

Step 4: The subsystems receive from the coordinator the portions relevant to them of the overall system forecast obtained in step 3.

REMARKS    One advantage of this forecasting procedure seems to be that the coordinator produces a "complete" solution. The subsystems provide the coordinator with the information specified in step 1 and receive in step 4 the complete forecast for the subsystem. No further calculations are required by the subsystems.

**Procedure 2 (Condensed System)**

The main disadvantage of procedure 1 is the large amount of information to be mailed to the coordinator in step 1. The coordinator consequently has to administer and solve a large equation system with numerous error potentials. Therefore we look for a forecasting procedure that reduces the computational burden of the coordinator and the information exchange with the subsystems.

Since the coordinator only has to know how variations in the interacting exogenous variables of the $j$th subsystem $x_j^i$ affect the interacting endogenous variables $y_j^i$ of this subsystem, we can summarize this information in the interaction functions

$$f_j^i(y_j^i, x_j^i) = 0, \tag{5}$$

which are based on the subsystem assumptions about the noninteracting exogenous variables $\underline{x}_j^n$ and the stochastic characteristics of the subsystem disturbance term $\underline{v}_j$.

ALGORITHM    Step 1: Each subsystem mails to the coordinator $f_j^i$, the interaction functions of the $j$th subsystem (equation 5).

Step 2: The coordinator specifies

$g$, the equation system of the coordination system 2b,

$\underline{w}$, the stochastic characteristics of the corresponding disturbance terms, and

$\underline{x}^c$, the (stochastic) assumptions about the exogenous variables of the coordination system.

Step 3: The coordinator uses the (stochastic) equation system $\{f_1^i, \ldots, f_n^i, g\}$ to calculate the forecast for $\hat{y}^i$, the interacting endogenous variables, and $\hat{x}^i$, the interacting exogenous variables.

Step 4: Each subsystem receives from the coordinator the forecast for its interacting exogenous variables $\hat{x}_j^i$ to calculate a complete subsystem forecast $\hat{y}_j$.

REMARKS    The big advantage of this forecasting method is the reduced information exchange between coordinator and subsystems. Instead of the whole subsystem equation system, only interaction functions for usually a few interacting endogenous variables have to be mailed. The interaction functions contain in compact form all subsystem information necessary for the coordinator to obtain a forecast that meets all system constraints.

The coordinator has to administer much less information. Information exchange should be quicker and easier with extremely reduced error potentials. The computational work is shared between the coordinator and the subsystems. The subsystems play an active role in the forecasting process. Advantage is taken of the hierarchical system structure to formulate a decentralized forecasting procedure.

The coordinator needs not even know all the subsystem equations (2a) explicitly, but may know them implicitly via their interaction functions. This may be important in cases where proprietors of subsystem models for some reason do not want to reveal all the details of their model and their assumptions about noninteracting exogenous variables.

This forecasting procedure is recommended even if the coordinator receives the complete subsystem information as indicated in step 1 of procedure 1, because the computational savings are considerable.

**Procedure 3 (Extraneous Information System)**

A completely different situation arises if the proprietors of the subsystem models have some extraneous information about the interacting variables $x_j^i$, expressed by some probabilistic statement. This information may stem from time-series analysis or institutional details. The question arises of how to process this information.

A first check of uncoordinated subsystem forecasts that are based on assumptions about their noninteracting and their interacting exogenous variables typically will reveal incompatibilities with some overall system constraints as formulated in the coordination system. One way to overcome this problem is to "believe" either the subsystem or the coordination system and to choose one of these models. The choice is obvious if there is reason to assume that one model is absolutely correct.

More realistic is the point of view that we are dealing with systems of limited accuracy because of the presence of error terms and the imprecise knowledge about exogenous variables. As a consequence, for decentralized forecasting procedures in hierarchical systems we have to evaluate two competing sources of information between two subsequent hierarchical levels. One source is the subsystems, the other is the coordination system. Both sources are usually imprecise. Statistical theory suggests that instead of choosing between sources of information it is desirable to combine them by a weighting scheme that takes into account the relative precision of the information channels.[4]

COMBINING IMPRECISE INFORMATION    The statistical instruments for combining imprecise information can easily be derived from Kalman filter theory (Kalman 1960). Assume that we want to obtain an estimate $\hat{s}$ of a directly unobservable (multivariate) random variable $s$. One source of information (the *state model*) tells us that the distribution of $s$ is described by mean $\bar{s}$ and variance $V$:

$$s \sim (\bar{s}, V). \tag{6}$$

With no other information available, statistical estimation theory suggests that for symmetrical loss functions the optimal estimate without additional information, denoted by $\hat{s}_-$, is given by the expectation

$$\hat{s}_- = \bar{s}, \tag{7a}$$

with estimation error

$$S_- = V. \tag{7b}$$

Assume that an observable (multivariate) random variable $m$ represents an additional source of information for the directly unobservable random variable $s$. Furthermore, assume that $m$ is related to $s$ via the following equation (the *measurement model*), assumed for convenience to be linear:

$$m = Hs + w \tag{8}$$

where $w$ is a disturbance term with known variance $W$ indicating the precision of the measurement $m$ with respect to $s$:

$$w \sim (0, W). \tag{9}$$

Then the optimal estimate for the same class of loss functions that makes use of both information channels, denoted by $\hat{s}$, is

$$\hat{s} = \bar{s} + c \tag{10}$$

where $c$ represents an additive correction term that is proportional to the information discrepancy:

$$c = K(m - H\bar{s}). \tag{11}$$

The factor of proportionality $K$ is determined by the relative precision of the two sources of information:

$$K = VH'(HVH' + W)^{-1}. \tag{12}$$

The reduction in estimation error from the additional information can be judged by comparing equation 7b with the estimation error of the combined estimate,

$$S = (I - KH)V. \tag{13}$$

For the detailed proofs see, for example, Anderson and Moore 1979. These results will be used to specify a decentralized forecasting procedure where the subsystems have extraneous information about the interacting exogenous system variables.

ALGORITHM    Step 1: Each subsystem mails to the coordinator

$f_j^i$, the interaction functions of the $j$th subsystem (equation 5),

$\underline{x}_j^i$, the stochastic control solution assumption about the interacting exogenous variables of the $j$th subsystem, described by expectation $\bar{x}_j^i$ and variance $\underline{X}_j^i$, where $\underline{x}_j^i \sim (\bar{x}_j^i, \underline{X}_j^i)$, and

$\underline{y}_j^i$, the uncoordinated subsystem forecast of the interacting endogenous variables of the $j$th subsystem, based on the assumptions about non-interacting and interacting exogenous subsystem variables $x_j^n$ and $x_j^i$, respectively, again described by expectation $\bar{y}_j^i$ and variance $\underline{Y}_j^i$, where $\underline{y}_j^i \sim (\bar{y}_j^i, \underline{Y}_j^i)$.

Step 2: The coordinator specifies

$g$, the equation system of the coordination system (equation 2b),

$\underline{w}$, the stochastic characteristics of its cooresponding disturbance terms, and

$\underline{x}^c$, the (stochastic) assumptions about exogenous variables of the co-ordination system.

Step 3: The coordinator combines the subsystem control solution (state model)

$$s \sim (\bar{s}, V),$$

where

$$s - \begin{bmatrix} \underline{y}^i \\ \underline{x}^i \end{bmatrix}, \quad \bar{s} - \begin{bmatrix} \bar{y}^i \\ \bar{x}^i \end{bmatrix}, \quad V = \begin{bmatrix} \underline{Y}^i & 0 \\ 0 & \underline{X}^i \end{bmatrix},$$

with the coordinator model (measurement model)

$$m = Hs + w, \quad w \sim (0, W)$$

which is composed of a linearized version of the condensed system specified in step 2 of procedure 2. Thus, $m$, $H$, and $W$ follow from the information collected in steps 1 and 2 and therefore are known. Using the Kalman filter equations 10–13, the forecast for $\hat{y}^i$ the interacting endogenous variables and $\hat{x}^i$ the interacting exogenous variables is calculated with mean

$$\hat{s} = \bar{s} + K(m - H\bar{s})$$

where

$$K = VH'(HVH' + W)^{-1}$$

and the estimation error covariance matrix is

$$S = (I - KH)V.$$

Step 4: Each subsystem receives from the coordinator the forecast for its interacting exogenous variables $\hat{x}^i_j$ to calculate a complete subsystem forecast $\hat{y}_j$.

REMARKS   This procedure stresses the stochastic character of a forecast. Each source of information entering the system is evaluated for accuracy by specifying its mean and variance.

Whenever the managers of the subsystems are able to make an informative probabilistic statement about their interacting exogenous variables, the relative precision of information provided by subsystem and the coordination system should be taken into account. A gain in forecasting precision in comparison with procedures 1 and 2 results from the fact that, in addition, extraneous information about the interacting exogenous variables is processed.

This forecasting procedure evaluates not only the relative precision between subsystem models and the coordination model, but also the relative precision between various subsystem models. Thus, a comparatively imprecise subsystem model will be given less weight in the calculation of the overall system forecast. If on the other hand a subsystem submits a forecast with comparatively low error variance, only slight modifications will be made by the coordinator.

Intuitively, the basic principle of this forecasting procedure can be explained as follows: Discrepancies between the uncoordinated subsystem forecasts and the overall system constraints expressed by the coordination system stem from errors in the subsystem models and errors in the coordination model. Instead of allocating the discrepancy only to the subsystems (which means overriding the uncoordinated subsystem forecasts) or only to the coordination system (which means neglecting the validity of the overall system constraints), the discrepancies are split among subsystems and the coordination system according to the relative precision of the two information sources.

This forecasting method may very well describe the administrative procedures in a forecasting exercise of a large organization: Forecast proposals submitted by a division are evaluated at the next hierarchical level and combined with any other available information; then the relevant portions of the corrected forecasts are mailed back to the division.

All the other advantages of procedure 2, such as reduced information exchange between coordinator and subsystems, active participation of the subsystems in the computational work, and reduced computational burden for the coordinator, are retained also in procedure 3.

## Application to a Model of International Trade

### Model Structure

In this section I discuss the application of the proposed forecasting procedures for hierarchical systems to a multicountry model of international trade. Such a model is composed of a number of country or regional models,

$$f_j(y_j^n, m_j, x_j^n, e_j, v_j) = 0, \quad j = 1, \ldots, n, \tag{14}$$

which are connected via a trade matrix model showing the international dependencies via trade flows:

$$e = Am + w_e. \tag{15}$$

For simplicity, let us only consider imports $m' = (m'_1, \ldots, m'_n)$ as interacting endogenous variables and exports $e' = (e'_1, \ldots, e'_n)$ as interacting exogenous variables. We denote by $A$ the trade share matrix, with $y_j^n$ the noninteracting endogenous variables and with $x_j^n$ the noninteracting exogenous variables. The stochastic characteristics of the disturbance terms are

$$v_j \sim (0, V_j), \quad j = 1, \ldots, n, \tag{16}$$

and

$$w_e \sim (0, W_e). \tag{17}$$

The formal structure of these trade-linkage models is discussed in Hickman 1973.

## Use of Extraneous Information in Country Models

Having made a stochastic specification of the assumptions about exogenous variables and disturbances, we can calculate the probability distribution of a forecast for all endogenous variables for the $j$th country or region by equation 14. In most cases, however, the model proprietor will not be content with this result. The forecaster's intuition and experience may lead him to make adjustments, usually by changing the values of some exogenous variables or by varying the constant terms in the stochastic equations. The *ad hoc* character of such adjustments has led to the criticism of excessive subjectivity in forecasting with econometric models (C. F. Christ 1975).

Constant term adjustments obviously reflect some extraneous information of the forecaster about some endogenous variables; otherwise he could not evaluate a particular model forecast. This information may originate from different sources. An analysis of recent residuals may indicate the need for an adjustment to offset a bias or trend in the single-equation prediction errors. Time-series analysis of monthly reported data such as industrial production, trade balance, and consumer prices may provide useful information about the corresponding model variables, at least for the subsequent quarters. Consumer and investment survey data may, after correction for reporting biases, shed some light on the actual level of private consumption and investment expenditures. It is intuitively plausible and confirmed by statistical methodology that the introduction of such extraneous information will increase the precision of the forecast.

Procedure 3's proposal of combining imprecise information allows us to make systematic and efficient use of extraneous information about endogenous variables in a forecasting exercise. Assume that for a country model a forecast was calculated by equation 14 on the basis of assumptions about all model inputs. For convenience we omit the country subscript $j$ and denote this forecast by

$$y \sim (\bar{y}, V) \tag{18}$$

where $V$ indicates the estimated forecasting-error variance. Assume further that $y^a$ describes extraneous information about some endogenous model variables which is related to the endogenous model variables $y$ via the linear stochastic relationship

$$y^a = Gy + w_a \tag{19}$$

where the disturbance term

$$w_a \sim (0, W_a) \tag{20}$$

indicates the precision of this extraneous information. Then procedure 3 suggests combining the model forecast with the extraneous information in the following way: The expectation of the combined forecast is

$$\hat{y} = \bar{y} + c \tag{21}$$

with

$$c = K(y^a - G\bar{y}) \tag{22}$$

and

$$K = VG'(GVG' + W_a)^{-1}. \tag{23}$$

The error covariance matrix of the combined forecast is

$$S = (I - KG)V. \tag{24}$$

The interpretation of this result seems to be very appealing. According to equation 21, the optimal forecast, which makes use of the structural econometric model, its input assumptions, and all available extraneous information about endogenous variables, is based on the model projection $\bar{y}$ plus an additive correction term. This result may be considered as a justification of the constant-term adjustment practice that is widespread among model proprietors. Instead of *ad hoc* adjustments, equations 22 and 23 yield corrections that meet statistical optimality properties and make the forecasting process more transparent as the model proprietor is induced to specify explicitly all the information used to produce a forecast.

Two conclusions are suggested: First, whenever a model proprietor uses constant adjustments in a forecasting exercise this indicates the presence of explicitly or implicitly used extraneous information. Second, there are methodologically sound procedures for including extraneous information in a forecast produced with a structural econometric model.

### Forecasting with a Model of International Trade

Forecasting procedures for a multicountry model of international trade need not be different from prediction analyses with any other econometric model. Procedure 1 indicates the information exchange between country-model proprietors and a project coordinator and the calculations that must be made. To employ this procedure, the project coordinator collects all subsystem models (country or regional models) and the assumptions about noninteracting exogenous variables. Together with the coordination system (trade model), the overall system is formed and solved to calculate forecasts for all system outputs. However, taking into account the pronounced hierarchical structure of the overall system, forecasting procedures can be developed, that are more efficient in terms of numerical effort and in terms of the amount of information exchange between the subsystem-model proprietors and a project coordinator.

### Forecasting with a Condensed System

Considerable computational savings can be achieved by switching to procedure 2. In the case of a multicountry model of international trade, the condensed system to be solved by the coordinator becomes extremely simple. Neglecting stochastic inputs, the following information has to be exchanged: Each regional or country model proprietor mails to the coordinator

$B_j$, the impact multiplier matrix of country exports on country imports,

$\underline{e}_j$, the control-solution assumption about country exports, and

$\underline{m}_j$, the control solution of country imports.

This information is sufficient to put together the interaction functions of the system,

$$m = \underline{m} + B(e - \underline{e}) \tag{25}$$

where

$$B = \begin{bmatrix} B_1 & \cdots & 0 \\ \cdot & \cdot & \cdot \\ 0 & \cdots & B_n \end{bmatrix}. \tag{26}$$

These interaction functions form, together with the trade model

$$e = Am, \tag{27}$$

the condensed version of the model of international trade. Substituting equation 25 into equation 27 and defining

$$d = ABe - Am, \tag{28}$$

$$D = AB, \tag{29}$$

$$F = D - I, \tag{30}$$

the coordinator only has to solve

$$d = Fe \tag{31}$$

in terms of exports $e$ to obtain an export vector compatible with all system constraints. The export solution then is mailed to the country-model proprietors to enable them to calculate a complete country solution that takes care of all system constraints.

This solution procedure for a forecasting exercise is recommended even if the coordinator has access to the complete country models and all their inputs, as it avoids iterating back and forth between country models and the trade model. The only additional computations required are the impact-multiplier calculations. Then equation 31 is solved for $e$ and subsequently all country models (equation 14) are solved for the non-interacting endogenous variables $y_j^n$.

In equation 25 I proposed a linear interaction function, which of course can only be regarded as a first-order Taylor-series approximation in the case of a nonlinear model. As the approximation is made around the control solution, the approximation error can be considered negligible. An extension of this procedure for multiperiod forecasts by enlarging the vector of interacting variables and the interaction functions is obvious.

**Forecasting with Extraneous Information**

Whenever the country-model or regional-model proprietors are able to make a probabilistic statement about their interacting exogenous variables (in our simplified trade model the country exports), then a control solution submitted by the subsystem proprietors carries valuable information that explicitly should be processed by the forecasting procedure. Then procedure 3 should be applied.

The regional- or country-model proprietors mail to the coordinator

$B_j$, the impact-multiplier matrix of country exports and country imports,

$\underline{e}_j$, the stochastic control solution assumptions about country exports, described by expectation $\bar{e}_j$ and variance $\underline{E}_j$ where $\underline{e}_j \sim (\bar{e}_j, \underline{E}_j)$, and

$\underline{m}_j$, the stochastic control solution of the country imports, described by expectation $\bar{m}_j$ and variance $\underline{M}_j$ so that $\underline{m}_j \sim (\bar{m}_j, \underline{M}_j)$.

The coordinator uses this information to put together the stochastic interaction functions

$$m = \bar{m} + B(e - \bar{e}) + w_m, \quad w_m \sim (0, M) \tag{32}$$

where

$$M = \begin{bmatrix} \underline{M}_1 & \cdots & 0 \\ \cdot & \cdot & \cdot \\ 0 & \cdots & \underline{M}_n \end{bmatrix} \tag{33}$$

and $B$ was defined in equation 26. Equations 32, together with the stochastic trade model

$$e = Am + w_e, \quad w_e \sim (0, W_e), \tag{34}$$

form the stochastic version of the condensed system. This system can be further reduced by substituting equation 32 into equation 34, which yields

$$f = Fe + w, \tag{35a}$$

$$w \sim (0, W), \quad W = W_e + AMA', \tag{35b}$$

where $F$ is as defined in equation 30 and $f$ is defined as

$$f = AB\bar{e} - A\bar{m}. \tag{35c}$$

Then the coordinator combines the country control solution assumption about country exports

$$\underline{e} \sim (\bar{e}, E) \tag{36}$$

where

$$E = \begin{bmatrix} \underline{E}_1 & \cdots & 0 \\ \cdot & \cdot & \cdot \\ 0 & \cdots & \underline{E}_n \end{bmatrix} \tag{37}$$

with the information contained in the trade model (equations 35) by means of the statistical technique outlined in procedure 3. Thus, we get as a mean for the combined forecast

$$\hat{e} = \bar{e} + K(f - F\bar{e}) \tag{38a}$$

where

$$K = EF'(FEF' + W)^{-1} \tag{38b}$$

with error covariance matrix

$$S = (I - KF)E. \tag{38c}$$

This forecasting method, which is based on an informative country control solution, can be given an intuitively plausible interpretation. Equation 38a states that the expectation for the overall system export forecast $\hat{e}$ is based on the expectation of the export assumptions made by the country proprietors $\bar{e}$ and an additive correction term. This correction term is basically proportional to the discrepancies of country-model and trade-model projections. The extent to which this discrepancy is allocated to the country model is determined by the weighting matrix $K$, which reflects the relative accuracy of the two information sources expressed by the error covariance matrix of the trade model $W$ and the error covariance matrix of the country export estimates $E$. The calculations in equations 38 are very simple. The maximal dimension of all matrices and vectors is equal to the number of countries times the number of commodity categories.

## Conclusions

In this chapter I have developed elements of a statistical forecasting theory for hierarchical systems that takes into account the specific system structure and indicates the organization of information exchange between subsystems and a central coordinator if a forecasting task is considered to be a decentralized decision process. The following main results were obtained:

• Decentralized forecasting procedures can be designed for hierarchical systems that take into account the administrative structure of such a system and divide the computational work of a forecasting task between a coordinator and the subsystems managers without violating overall system constraints.

• The adoption of a decentralized forecasting procedure leads to a considerable reduction of information exchange between subsystems and a central coordinator, and thus reduces the potential for transmission errors.

• In the case of a hierarchical system structure, computational advantages suggest the use of the proposed decentralized forecasting procedures even if all subsystem information is available to the central coordinator.

• Extraneous information of the subsystems about interacting variables can be included in the forecasting procedure by evaluating its relative precision with respect to the information available to the coordinator.

## Acknowledgments

This paper benefited markedly from my experience with Project LINK. Comments by Bert G. Hickman led to significant improvements of the exposition and are gratefully acknowledged.

## Notes

1. Documentation of Project LINK can be found in Ball 1973, Sawyer 1979, and Waelbroeck 1976.

2. A survey of optimal control methods for hierarchical systems is given in Athans 1975.

3. Besides the original work of Kalman (1960), this statistical model is presented, e.g., in Anderson and Moore 1979, McGarty 1974, and Mariano and Schleicher 1972.

4. This procedure generalizes the combination of forecasts as proposed by Granger and Newbold 1977.

## Bibliography

Anderson, B. D. O., and J. B. Moore. 1979. *Optimal Filtering*. Englewood Cliffs, N. J. : Prentice-Hall.

Athans, M. 1975. Theory and applications survey of decentralized control methods. *Annals of Economic and Social Measurement* 4: 343–355.

Ball, R. J., ed. 1973 *The International Linkage of National Economic Models*. Amsterdam: North-Holland.

Christ, C. F. 1975. Judging the performance of econometric models of the U.S. economy. *International Economic Review* 16: 54–74.

Granger, C. W. J., and P. Newbold. 1977. *Forecasting Economic Time Series*. New York: Academic.

Hickman, B. G. 1973. A general linear model of world trade. In Ball 1973.

Kalman, R. E. 1960. A new approach to linear filtering and prediction problems. *Journal of Basic Engineering* 82: 35–45.

Mariano, R. S., and Schleicher, S. 1972. On the Use of Kalman Filters in Economic Forecasting. Department of Economics Discussion Paper 247, University of Pennsylvania,

McGarty, T. P. 1974. *Stochastic Systems and State Estimation*. New York: McGraw-Hill.

Sawyer, J. A., ed. 1979. *Modelling the International Transmission Mechanism*. Amsterdam: North-Holland.

Waelbroeck, J. L., ed. 1976. *The Models of Project LINK*. Amsterdam: North-Holland.

# III APPLIED MICROECONOMICS

# 9 The Aggregate Production Function and the Representative Firm

W. Krelle

Economic theory must be based on the behavior of the economic agents, but to be operational it must be transformed to macroeconomics. This transition constitutes the aggregation problem. Lawrence Klein was one of the first to recognize this problem in the econometric context. He treated the problem theoretically (Klein 1946, 1952–53) as well as econometrically (Klein 1953). Thus, it may be fitting to dedicate to his sixtieth birthday a contribution on this problem, in gratitude for long years of friendship, cooperation, and inspiration.

There are many different aggregation problems in economics. First, there is the problem of aggregation over commodities. Under which conditions is it possible to represent different commodities by one composite commodity? This is the problem of index numbers. Fisher (1967) was the first to deal with it from a statistical point of view. Eichhorn (1976, 1978) continued along these lines. Starting with Frisch (1936), functional indices based upon economic theory have been developed as an alternative approach; see Samuelson and Swamy 1974 and Hasenkamp 1978. Sondermann (1973) developed a theory of optimal aggregation (optimal in the sense of minimizing the errors induced by aggregation). This first type of aggregation is not our subject here.

The second type of aggregation deals with aggregation over economic agents—households or firms. The problem is to state conditions under which it is possible to treat a set of $n$ different households or firms as if it were composed of $n$ identical "average" units, called representative households or firms. Marshall (1969) coined the term *representative firm*, but the idea was much older. As a matter of fact, large parts of economic theory rely on it, explicitly or implicitly. It does not matter whether one considers the representative firm or the representative household; the problem is basically the same, only utility functions are replaced by production functions. Thus, the whole literature on the representative household is relevant to the problem of the representative firm as well. Gorman (1953) was the first to show that aggregation over households is possible only under very restrictive assumptions on the individual household's utility function (linear Engel curves). Meanwhile, many economists have tried to relax the Gorman conditions by changing the approach (for examples, see Lau 1977a, 1977b; Muellbauer 1976; Chipman 1974, following Eisenberg 1961). But always, in one form or another, Gorman-type limitations of aggregation showed up again. Coming back to aggregation in production, it is evident that only very restrictive separability and linearity assumptions are suitable to guarantee the global existence of an aggregate production function. Let

$$f^i(y_1^i, \ldots, y_n^i, x_1^i, \ldots, x_m^i) = 0$$

be the implicit production function of firm $i$ ($i = 1, \ldots, H$), where $y =$ output and $x =$ input. An aggregate production function

$$F(\varphi_1(y_1), \ldots, \varphi_n(y_n), \psi_1(x_1), \ldots, \psi_m(x_m)) = 0$$

where $y_v = (y_v^1, \ldots, y_v^H)$ and $x_\mu = (x_\mu^1, \ldots, x_\mu^H)$ ($v = 1, \ldots, n; \mu = 1, \ldots, m$) exists globally, if the production functions $f^i$ are linearly separable:

$$f^i(\cdot) = \sum_v g_v^i(y_v^i) + \sum_\mu h_\mu^i(x_\mu^i).$$

If, in addition, we want the aggregate production function to be a function of the sum $\bar{y}_v = \sum_i y_v^i$, and $\bar{x}_\mu = \sum_i x_\mu^i$ of all outputs and inputs of the individual firms, respectively, the functions $f^i$ must be linear in the $y_v^i$ and $x^i$ with coefficients that are equal over firms for each $v$ and $\mu$—that is, the marginal rates of substitution must be equal for all firms:

$$f^i = \sum_v a_v y_v^i + \sum_\mu b_\mu x_\mu^i.$$

These conditions are surely not satisfied in reality. Must we therefore give up all hopes for macroeconomics? I will show that this is not the case. If we give up the false objective of an exact global aggregation and are content with an arbitrarily close local approximation, we arrive at quite positive results.

## An Approximation to All Factor Demand Systems: The Representative Firm

### One Firm

Consider a one-product firm that, for a given output $y$, wants to minimize cost $C$ under the constraint of a production function $f(x_1, \ldots, x_n)$ under given factor prices $p_1, \ldots, p_n$. The problem

$$C := \sum_i p_i x_i = \min! \text{ s.t. } y - f(x_1, \ldots, x_n) = 0$$

yields, after elimination of the Lagrangian multiplier, the relation

$$\frac{x_i p_i}{C} = \frac{x_i \partial f / \partial x_i}{\sum_i x_i \partial f / \partial x_i}, \quad i = 1, \ldots, n. \tag{1}$$

This implicit demand system has the basic properties of any admissible demand system, especially that the adding-up property $\sum_i x_i p_i = C$ is fulfilled by definition. Now we approximate the right-hand side of equation 1 in the following way:

$$\frac{x_i \partial f / \partial x_i}{\sum_i \partial f / \partial x_i} = a_{i0} + \sum_{j=1}^{n} a_{ij} x_j + \tfrac{1}{2} \sum_{k,j=1}^{n} a_{ijk} x_j x_k, \quad i = 1, \ldots, n, \tag{2}$$

where

$$\sum_{i=1}^{n} a_{i0} = 1$$

and where, for all $j, k \in \{1, \ldots, n\}$,

$$\sum_{i=1}^{n} a_{ij} = \sum_{i=1}^{n} (a_{ijk} + a_{ikj}) = 0.$$

We call equation 2 a quadratic approximation of the implicit demand system 1. The linear approximation is given by setting $a_{ijk} = 0$ in equation 2. System 1 and the linear approximation of 2 may be rewritten in matrix notation as follows:

$$[I - C \cdot \text{diag}(1/p) \cdot A] x = C \cdot \text{diag}(1/p) \cdot a_0, \tag{3}$$

where $x$, $a_0$, and $b$ are vectors with the components $x_1, \ldots, x_n$ and $a_{10}, \ldots, a_{n0}$, respectively; $\text{diag}(1/p)$ is a diagonal matrix with $1/p_1, \ldots, 1/p_n$ on the main diagonal; and $A$ is the matrix $(a_{ij})$ where $i, j = 1, \ldots, n$.

We assume that the matrix in brackets on the left-hand side of equation 3 is nonsingular. This is always true if the components of $A$ are small enough in absolute value. In this case we get a first approximation of the explicit demand system:

$$x = [I - C \cdot \text{diag}(1/p) \cdot A]^{-1} \cdot C \cdot \text{diag}(1/p) \cdot a_0. \tag{4}$$

This approximation is nonlinear in prices and costs. Thus, it admits inhomogeneity of the production function and cross-price elasticities of different signs. It applies to every firm independent of the special form of the production function.

The quadratic approximation of the implicit demand system may also be written in matrix notation:

$$x = C \cdot \mathrm{diag}(1/p)[a_0 + Ax + \tfrac{1}{2}X\bar{A}x] \tag{5}$$

where

$$X = \begin{pmatrix} x' & & & \\ & x' & & \\ & & \ddots & \\ & & & x' \end{pmatrix}$$

is an $n \times n^2$ matrix of vectors $x$ and

$$\bar{A} = \begin{pmatrix} \bar{A}_1 \\ \vdots \\ \bar{A}_n \end{pmatrix}$$

is an $n^2 \times n$ matrix with

$$\bar{A}_i = \begin{pmatrix} a_{i11} & \cdots & a_{in1} \\ \vdots & & \\ a_{i1n} & \cdots & a_{inn} \end{pmatrix}.$$

The general solution of the system 5 is

$$x_i = F_i(p_1, \ldots, p_n, C), \quad i = 1, \ldots, n \tag{6}$$

where

$$\sum_{i=1}^{n} p_i F_i(\cdot) = C.$$

The quadratic approximation of the explicit demand system can only be written in this form. Equation 6 cannot be solved explicitly, in general. Judging from empirical results to be presented below, the linear approximation 4 seems to fit the observations reasonably well.

## Many Firms, Approximate Aggregation

The linear and quadratic approximations 4 and 5 of the implicit demand system allow for aggregation over firms if certain distributions remain constant. Let

$$X_i = \sum_{h=1}^{H} x_i^h,$$

be the aggregate demand of commodity $i$, let

$$C = \sum_{h=1}^{H} C^h$$

be the total expenditure, let

$$\beta^h = C^h/C,$$

be the proportion of expenditure of firm $h$ in the total expenditure of all firms, let

$$\gamma_j^h = x_j^h/X_j,$$

be the proportion of demand of firm $h$ for commodity $j$ in total demand for commodity $j$, and let

$$\delta_{jk}^h = \frac{x_j^h \cdot x_k^h}{X_j \cdot X_k} = \gamma_j^h \cdot \gamma_k^h, \quad h = 1, \dots, H; \, i, j, k = 1, \dots, n \tag{7}$$

be the product of two such proportions. There are $H$ firms in the economy. Summing up the individual demand equations

$$x_i^h = \frac{C^h}{p_i} \left( a_{i0}^h + \sum_{j=1}^{n} a_{ij}^h x_j + \tfrac{1}{2} \sum_{j,k} a_{ijk}^h x_j^h x_k^h \right) \tag{8}$$

over all households yields the aggregate implicit demand system:

$$X_i = \frac{C}{p_i} \left( \bar{a}_{i0} + \sum_{j=1}^{n} \bar{a}_{ij} X_j + \tfrac{1}{2} \sum_{j=1}^{n} \sum_{k=1}^{n} \bar{a}_{ijk} \cdot X_j X_k \right), \quad i = 1, \dots, n \tag{9}$$

where

$$\bar{a}_{i0} = \sum_{h=1}^{H} a_{i0}^h \cdot \beta^h,$$

$$\bar{a}_{ij} = \sum_{h=1}^{H} a_{ij}^h \cdot \beta^h \cdot \gamma_j^h,$$

and

$$\bar{a}_{ijk} = \sum_{h=1}^{H} a_{ijk}^h \cdot \beta^h \cdot \delta_{ik}^h, \quad i, j, k = 1, \dots, n.$$

The constraints on equation 2 are preserved:

$$\sum_{i=1}^{n} \bar{a}_{i0} = 1, \quad \sum_{i=1}^{n} \bar{a}_{ij} = \sum_{i=1}^{n} (\bar{a}_{ijk} + \bar{a}_{ikj}) = 0,$$

for all $j, k \in \{1, \ldots, n\}$. If the mean expenditure (measured by $\bar{a}_{i0}$, $i = 1, \ldots, n$) and the mean demand (measured by $\bar{a}_{ij}$ and $\bar{a}_{ijk}$) stay constant, the aggregate demand system has the same analytic form as the individual firm. Since, as a rule, expenditure and demand distributions do not change drastically in a short time, we may approximate the aggregate demand system

$$X_i = \frac{1}{p_i} \sum_{h=1}^{H} C^h \left( a_{i0}^h + \sum_{j=1}^{n} a_{ij}^h x_j^h + \frac{1}{2} \sum_{j,k} a_{ijk}^h x_j^h x_k^h \right) \tag{10}$$

by the associated system given by equation 9, where $\bar{a}_{i0}$, $\bar{a}_{ij}$, and $\bar{a}_{ijk}$ are constants. We call equation 9 the quadratic approximation of the implicit demand system of the representative firm. It will be shown that the constants $\bar{a}_{i0}$, $\bar{a}_{ij}$, and $\bar{a}_{ijk}$ may be chosen in such a way that total demand derived from equation 9 as well as the changes of demand if prices change are arbitrarily close to the true total demand and its changes at a predetermined point and its environment.

## Integrability Conditions for Linear and Quadratic Approximations of the Implicit Demand System

If we are content with a linear or a quadratic approximation to an individual or aggregate implicit demand system, we may estimate the parameters $a_{i0}$ and $a_{ij}$ of equations 1 and 2 from empirical data. (For the linear case this will be done in the last section.) But in order that this demand system be derivable from a cost-maximizing behavior of a real or representative firm, the parameters $a_{i0}$, $a_{ij}$, and $a_{ijk}$ have to fulfill integrability conditions. These conditions are given in this section for the quadratic approximation. The conditions for the linear approximation follow as a special case. The proofs may be found in Krelle and Pallaschke 1980.

We rewrite the quadratic approximation of the implicit demand system (equation 2) in the following form:

$$\frac{x_i p_i}{C} = \frac{x_i \partial f / \partial x_i}{\sum_{j=1}^{n} x_j \partial f / \partial x_j}$$

$$= a_{i0} + \sum_{j=1}^{n} a_{ij}x_j + \sum_{j=1}^{n} b_{ij}x_j^2 + \sum_{r<s} c_{irs}x_r x_s, \quad i = 1, \ldots, n. \tag{11}$$

The necessary and sufficient integrability conditions for this system of partial differential equations are that

$$\sum_{i=1}^{n} a_{i0} = 1, \tag{11a}$$

that for all $i \in \{1, \ldots, n\}$ there exists a scalar $c_i$ such that

$$\frac{a_{ii}}{\displaystyle\sum_{\substack{j=1 \\ j \neq i}}^{n} a_{j0}} = -\frac{a_{ki}}{a_{k0}} = c_i, \tag{11b}$$

and that there exist scalars $\alpha_1, \ldots, \alpha_n$ such that, for all $i, j, k \in \{1, \ldots, n\}$,

$$b_{ij} = \alpha_j a_{ij} \quad \text{and} \quad c_{ijk} = \alpha_j a_{ik} + \alpha_k a_{ij}. \tag{11c}$$

Condition 11a is identical with a general constraint of any demand system and poses no problem (see equation 2). Unfortunately, conditions 11b and 11c are much more restrictive than the rest of the conditions any demand system must fulfill—namely that, for all $j, k \in \{1, \ldots, n\}$,

$$\sum_{i=1}^{n} a_{ij} = \sum_{i=1}^{n} (a_{ijk} + a_{ikj}) = 0. \tag{12}$$

Only in the linear case for $n = 2$ do the two sets of conditions coincide. For $\alpha_1 = \alpha_2 = 0$, condition 11b becomes $a_{11} + a_{21} = a_{12} + a_{22} = 0$, which is identical with equation 12. Thus, in the case of two commodities and a linear approximation, a representative firm always exists.

The integrability conditions 11a–11c may be stated in the following equivalent form: The system of partial differential equations of the second equation in 11 is locally solvable if and only if it can be written in the form

$$x_i \frac{\partial f}{\partial x_i} = \left( \sum_{j=1}^{n} x_j \frac{\partial f}{\partial x_j} \right) \left[ a_{i0} + (1 + H) \sum_{j=1}^{n} a_{ij}x_j \right]$$

where

$$H(x_1, \ldots, x_n) = \sum_{i=1}^{n} \alpha_i x_i, \quad \alpha_i \in \mathbb{R},$$

$$\sum_{i=1}^{n} a_{i0} = 1,$$

and where for all $i \in \{1, \ldots, n\}$ and for all $k \in \{1, \ldots, n\}\setminus\{i\}$,

$$\frac{a_{ii}}{1 - a_{i0}} = -\frac{a_{ki}}{a_{k0}} =: c_i.$$

For the linear approximation ($b_{ij} = c_{irs} = 0$ in equation 10) or for $\alpha_i = 0$ in 11c we may integrate the system of partial differential equations 11 explicitly. If we disregard the boundary cases and assume that

$$a_{i0} \notin \{0, 1\},$$

the system 11 has the solution

$$f(x_1, \ldots, x_n) = \prod_{i=1}^{n} (x_i)^{a_{i0}} - \sum_{j=1}^{n} c_j \left[ \prod_{\substack{i=1 \\ i \neq j}}^{n} \left(\frac{x_j}{x_i}\right)^{a_{i0}} \right]. \tag{13}$$

This may be considered as a production function of the approximate representative firm in the linear approximation case, if it is supposed that such a firm exists (that is, that the integrability conditions are fulfilled). In the special case $c_j = 0$ ($j = 1, \ldots, n$), the production function is simply the Cobb-Douglas function. Unfortunately, we cannot offer an explicit solution in the quadratic case.

## The Representative Firm as an Arbitrarily Close Approximation

Any system of continuous demand functions

$$F = (F_1, \ldots, F_n),$$

where

$$x_i = F_i(p_1, \ldots, p_n, C), \quad i = 1, \ldots, n$$

and

$$\sum_{i=1}^{n} p_i F_i = C,$$

may be approximated by a demand system derived from a linear or quadratic approximation (equation 2) of the implicit demand system.

This approximation is arbitrarily close with respect to the absolute level of demand ($= C_0$ approximation) in an environment of a predetermined point in the price space. This is true even in the linear case. In the quadratic case the approximation is also arbitrarily close with respect to all partial derivatives ($= C_1$ approximation). The proves may be found in Krelle and Pallaschke 1980.

## Some Empirical Results

Some preliminary results as to the degree of accuracy in aggregation may be given. I have used firm data from the "Bonn sample" of German firms, derived from the published balance accounts of incorporated firms and from official price data. Thus we arrive at figures on value added $Y$, wages $L$, value $V$ of fixed assets, and employment $A$ for the five largest chemical firms and the five largest automobile producers in Germany. Using the price index $p_1$ of investment goods, the invested real capital $K = V/p_1$ was estimated. The average wage rate $w$ is defined by $w = L/A$, and the average rate $r$ of capital cost by $r = (Y - L)/K$. Thus we have, by definition, $Y = wA + rK$. Assume that there exist production functions $Y_i = f_i(A_i, K_i)$ for all firms $i$ taken from the sample. How large is the error in estimating the labor demand (for example) by using the concept of a representative firm as compared with the summed-up individual-firm demands?

I will give only the results for the linear case. From equation 11 we get the system

$$\frac{wA}{Y} = a_1 A + a_2 K + a_3, \tag{14a}$$

$$\frac{rK}{Y} = \bar{a}_1 A + \bar{a}_2 K + \bar{a}_3 \tag{14b}$$

where

$$a_3 + \bar{a}_3 = 1, \quad a_1 + \bar{a}_1 = a_2 + \bar{a}_2 = 0, \quad 0 < a_3 < 1. \tag{14c}$$

Moreover, we have the definitional relation

$$K = (Y - wA)/r. \tag{14d}$$

The parameters of the system 14a, 14b have been estimated by the ordinary least-squares method. It turned out that the adding-up constraints in

equations 14c have been fulfilled automatically (almost precisely). We
also estimated the parameters by the full-information maximum-likelihood method, using the system 14a, 14d and by using a reduced form

$$A = \frac{a_3 + a_2 Y/r}{-a_1 + w(1/Y + a_2/r)}$$

(arrived at by substituting 14d into 14a). The parameters did not turn out
too differently. Thus, we only reproduce the simple ordinary-least-squares
estimates for the firms and for the two sectors as a whole. The sector data
are constructed by simply adding up the individual-firm data.[1]

From these estimations the following production function for the firms
and for the sectors emerges (see equation 13):

$$Y = f(A, K) = A^{a_3} K^{1-a_3} - c_1 (A/K)^{1-a_3} - c_2 (K/L)^{a_3}$$

where

$$c_1 = \frac{a_1}{1 - a_3}, \quad c_2 = -\frac{a_2}{a_3}.$$

We see from table 1 that, with the exception of one firm (BASF), all
parameters lie in the admissible region given by the last inequality in 14c.
The estimates for the sectors as a whole are reasonable as well. The
reference period is 1961–1974. Thus, we could use the years 1975–1977
for *ex ante* forecasts.

Table 2 shows the percentage deviations of the total demand for labor
and capital due to aggregation for the automobile industry. (The results
for the chemical industry are similar.) The errors of the FIML estimations are smaller, but all deviations (with the exception of the OLS
forecasts of capital for 1977) lie within 5% and most are much smaller.
Thus, we need not have a bad conscience about using aggregate data and
assuming a representative firm if we are content with arbitrarily close
local $C_0$ and $C_1$ approximations. But, as the estimates above show, the
"local" approximation may be good enough for quite substantial changes
as they occurred during the years 1961–1977.

## Acknowledgments

I wish to thank Dipl. Math. Weihs of the Sonderforschungsbereich 21 at
Bonn University for doing the computations in the last section.

**Table 1**
Ordinary-least-squares estimates of the parameters of equation 14a.

| Firm file no. | Name of firm | Parameter $a_1$ | $a_2$ | $a_3$ | DW | $R^2C$ |
|---|---|---|---|---|---|---|
| **Chemical firms** | | | | | | |
| 7 | BASF | $0.2149 \times 10^{-4}$ (7.79) | $-0.4802 \times 10^{-4}$ (2.77) | $-0.3382$ (3.03) | 1.33 | 0.876 |
| 32 | Bayer | $0.5173 \times 10^{-5}$ (2.41) | $0.4137 \times 10^{-4}$ (3.80) | $0.2343$ (2.00) | 0.81 | 0.750 |
| 33 | Höchst | $0.6611 \times 10^{-5}$ (3.05) | $-0.7547 \times 10^{-4}$ (2.13) | $0.4686$ (13.53) | 0.97 | 0.573 |
| 80 | Rütgers | $0.4313 \times 10^{-5}$ (0.17) | $0.6216 \times 10^{-3}$ (0.92) | $0.6736$ (7.47) | 0.39 | 0.165 |
| 84 | Schering | $-0.1136 \times 10^{-4}$ (0.40) | $0.1174 \times 10^{-2}$ (1.38) | $0.5401$ (9.02) | 0.64 | 0.673 |
| **Automobile firms** | | | | | | |
| 12 | BMW | $-0.2247 \times 10^{-4}$ (1.45) | $0.5769 \times 10^{-3}$ (1.20) | $0.9641$ (9.25) | 1.16 | 0.399 |
| 23 | Daimler-Benz | $0.1491 \times 10^{-5}$ (4.09) | $0.4448 \times 10^{-4}$ (2.49) | $0.5354$ (31.04) | 1.72 | 0.976 |
| 36 | Ford | $-0.5485 \times 10^{-5}$ (3.96) | $-0.1069 \times 10^{-4}$ (0.22) | $0.5107$ (10.66) | 1.14 | 0.673 |
| 68 | Audi-NSU | $0.5392 \times 10^{-6}$ (0.25) | $0.8432 \times 10^{-4}$ (0.85) | $0.8798$ (75.7) | 1.24 | 0.849 |
| 98 | VW | $-0.1078 \times 10^{-4}$ (2.56) | $0.8139 \times 10^{-3}$ (4.13) | $0.1501$ (2.21) | 0.76 | 0.897 |
| **Aggregation by sectors** | | | | | | |
| Chemical firms 7, 32, 33, 80, 84 | | $0.3132 \times 10^{-5}$ (4.66) | $-0.1450 \times 10^{-4}$ (2.08) | $0.1934$ (2.65) | 1.11 | 0.797 |
| Automobile firms 12, 23, 36, 68, 98 | | $0.1473 \times 10^{-5}$ (4.08) | $-0.1135 \times 10^{-4}$ (0.70) | $0.3925$ (14.23) | 1.08 | 0.949 |

Note: $t$ values are shown in parentheses.

**Table 2**

Percentage deviations of forecasts for automobile industry, using the concept of a representative firm, from the sum of the forecasts for the individual firms [$= 100 \times$ (Sector forecasts—Sum of individual-firm forecasts)/Sector forecast].

| Forecast no. | Estimation procedure | Forecast for[a] | Ex post forecasts | | | | | | | | | | | | | | Ex ante forecasts | | |
|---|---|---|---|---|---|---|---|---|---|---|---|---|---|---|---|---|---|---|---|
| | | | 1961 | 1962 | 1963 | 1964 | 1965 | 1966 | 1967 | 1968 | 1969 | 1970 | 1971 | 1972 | 1973 | 1974 | 1975 | 1976 | 1977 |
| 1 | OLS | L | -3.46 | -0.96 | 1.95 | 0.57 | -0.43 | -1.16 | 0.83 | 2.14 | 2.03 | 0.60 | -0.23 | -0.87 | -0.50 | -1.10 | -2.10 | -1.30 | 1.86 |
| 2 | OLS | C | 5.52 | 2.34 | -3.82 | -0.81 | 2.40 | 3.75 | -5.14 | -11.05 | -8.40 | -1.76 | 0.93 | 3.04 | 2.63 | 4.60 | 3.06 | -5.33 | -15.66 |
| 3 | Reduced form | L | -2.93 | -1.44 | -0.80 | -1.23 | -1.30 | -0.11 | 1.07 | 1.04 | 0.46 | -0.00 | -0.39 | -1.16 | -0.65 | -0.59 | -1.83 | -3.67 | -4.19 |
| 4 | FIML | L | -1.85 | -0.51 | 0.45 | -0.21 | -0.24 | 0.20 | 1.20 | 1.07 | 0.53 | 0.22 | -0.04 | -0.55 | -0.47 | -0.69 | -2.00 | -3.50 | -3.80 |

a. L indicates labor demand. C capital demand.

# Note

1. Actually, we used three years' moving averages for value added, labor, and capital figures in order to eliminate erratic movements which cannot be reproduced by the long-term concept of a production function as used above.

# Bibliography

Chipman, J. S. 1974. Homothetic preferences and aggregation. *Journal of Economic Theory* 8: 26–38.

Eichhorn, W., and J. Voeller. 1976. Theory of the Price Index. *Lecture Notes in Economics and Mathematical Systems*, vol. 140. Berlin: Springer.

Eichhorn, W. 1978. What is an economic index? An attempt of an answer. In W. Eichhorn et al., eds., *Theory and Applications of Economic Indices*. Würzburg: Physica.

Eisenberg, E. 1961. Aggregation of utility functions. *Management Science* 7: 337–350.

Fisher, I. 1967. *The Making of Index Numbers*, 3rd edition. New York: Kelly.

Frisch, R. 1936. Annual survey of general economic theory: The problem of index numbers. *Econometrica* 4: 1–38.

Gorman, W. M. 1953. Community preference fields. *Econometrica* 21: 63–80.

Hasenkamp, G. 1978. Economic and atomistic index numbers: Contrasts and similarities. In W. Eichhorn et al., eds., *Theory and Applications of Economic Indices*. Würzburg: Physica.

Klein, L. R. 1946. Macroeconomics and the theory of rational behavior. *Econometrica* 14: 93–108.

Klein. L. R. 1953. *A Textbook of Econometrics*. Evanston and New York: Row, Peterson and Lomp.

Klein, L. R. 1952–53. On the interpretation of *Professor* Leontief's System. *Review of Economic Studies* 20: 131–136.

Krelle, W., and D. Pallaschke. 1980. The Approximate Representative Household Does Exist. Discussion paper 103, Institut für Gesellschafts- und Wirtschaftswissenschaften, Universität Bonn, Wirtschaftstheoretische Abteilung.

Lau, L. J. 1977a. Existence Conditions for Aggregate Demand Functions: The Case of a Single Index. Technical report 248, Economics Series, Institute for Mathematical Studies in the Social Sciences, Stanford, California.

Lau, L. J. 1977b. Existence Conditions for Aggregate Demand Functions: The Case of Multiple Indexes. Technical report 249 (R), Economics Series, Institute for Mathematical Studies in the Social Sciences, Stanford, California.

Marshall, A. 1969. *Principles of Economics*, 8th edition. London: Macmillan.

Muellbauer, J. 1976. Community preferences and the representative consumer. *Econometrica* 44: 979–999.

Samuelson, P. A., and S. Swamy. 1974. Invariant economic index numbers and canonical duality: Survey and synthesis. *American Economic Review* 64: 566–593.

Sondermann, D. 1973. Optimale Aggregation von grossen linearen Gleichungssystemen. *Zeitschrift für Nationalökonomie* 33: 235 ff.

# 10 The Share of Services in Economic Growth

Irving B. Kravis
Alan W. Heston
Robert Summers

The positive association between economic growth and the share of services in the industrial distribution of the labor force has been noted and documented by a number of investigators, including Fisher (1935), Clark (1941), Kuznets (1957), Chenery (1979), and Fuchs (1980). Clark traced the observation of this relationship back to Sir William Petty and proposed that the shift of the working population from agriculture to manufactures and from manufactures to services in the course of economic growth be called Petty's Law. Kuznets, Fuchs, and others have suggested that the relative expansion of service employment could be due either to high income elasticities of demand for final-product services or to slower growth in productivity in the service industries.

In the literature cited, the statistical association between service employment and income growth, and the productivity explanation for the relationship, are both cast mainly in terms of the relative expansion of employment and output in the service industries—that is, industries that produce intermediate or final products other than commodities. (Commodities are defined as storable physical objects.) Kuznets, for example, pointed to a number of structural changes that would shift employment to service industries. These included the effect of economies of plant scale in concentrating production in a limited number of localities and thus increasing the need for distributive services, the increase in financial services with growing personal wealth, the expansion of government services (police, sanitation, education) necessitated by the shift away from family and rural production to production by units employing wage earners concentrated in urban areas, and the increase in military expenditures (Kuznets 1966, p. 150.)

The elasticity explanation, on the other hand, is based on the concept of final-product services—that is, goods other than commodities, purchased for ultimate use rather than as inputs to further production. There is a great deal of overlap between the output of service industries and final-product services, but the former includes purely intermediate activities (such as wholesale trade) as well as activities that count as intermediate when performed for a business purchaser and as final when performed for a household (for example, repair of an electrical outlet).

This chapter examines the elasticity explanation in both interspatial and intertemporal terms, and offers some insights on the productivity explanation as well. In isolating the pure income effect, account is taken of a systematic tendency for the price of services to be affected by changes in income. The interspatial data are drawn largely from the international comparisons of prices and real outputs produced by the United Nations International Comparison Project (ICP). The ICP data refer to 151 final expenditure categories of gross domestic product (GDP) for 34 countries for the year 1975 (Kravis, Heston, and Summers 1982).

## The Nature of Final-Product Services

Final-product services constitute a heterogeneous collection of goods. They are alike in that the production of each is necessarily simultaneous with its consumption, and consequently none of them can be stocked. In few other respects, however, do all final-product services share common characteristics.[1]

Although services tend to be labor-intensive, some, such as air travel and electricity, are produced using extensive capital. Indeed, the industries producing commodities are clearly more concerned with the transformation of physical objects into other physical objects than are the industries usually classified in the service sector.[2] The differences emerge in the data from U.S. input-output tables for 1963 and 1972 presented in table 1.

Table 1
Relative importance of service and commodity inputs in the output of U.S. service and commodity industries, as shown by percentage of total output.

|  | 1963 | | 1972 | |
| --- | --- | --- | --- | --- |
|  | Service industries | Commodity industries | Service industries | Commodity industries |
| **Intermediate inputs** | | | | |
| Services | 23.5 | 12.8 | 19.2 | 16.0 |
| Commodities | 12.5 | 48.7 | 8.6 | 43.7 |
| **Value added** | 64.0 | 38.5 | 72.2 | 40.3 |
|  | 100.0 | 100.0 | 100.0 | 100.0 |

Sources: Derived from data in *Survey of Current Business*, November 1969 (pp. 30–35) and April 1979 (pp. 62–67). In the latter source, commodities numbers 1–64, 80, 81, 83, and 85 have been treated as commodities and the rest as services.

Commodity inputs accounted for only around 10 percent of the output of service industries, while they accounted for around 45 percent of the output of commodity industries. Also, value added is much larger relative to output in the service industries than in the commodity sector.

Final-product services also may vary in the degree of unambiguity with which they can be differentiated from commodity production. Major final-product services such as health, education, and government have closely associated commodity flows, which may be regarded either as inputs (the doctor's stethoscope) or as supplementary or concomitant expenditures (drugs, textbooks). In the empirical analysis below, goods of detailed ICP categories that reach the hands of consumers in commodity form, such as drugs and textbooks, are treated as commodities even though they might in terms of their broader purpose be subsumed under a heading that is primarily a service, such as health care or education. Consistently, government purchases of goods and services are treated as commodities here, though they could logically be included as part of the total services provided by government.[3] After all, commodities purchased by governments are for the most part not passed on to the population *qua* commodities. In what follows, however, government services consist of only the compensation of government employees. It appears that including government purchases as a service would not alter the conclusions reached in this paper.

Nothing that has been said here provides any basis for expecting a high or a low income elasticity of demand for most final-product services.

## Comparisons of Service Shares in Current and Constant Prices

### Interspatial

The role of final-product services in final expenditures on GDP is shown in table 2 for groups for countries classified by real income level.[4] In lines 4–6 the per-capita expenditures on GDP and on the commodity and service components of final expenditures on GDP are presented. These data, based on exchange-rate conversions, suggest that poor-country per-capita spending on services is smaller relative to rich-country spending than is poor-country spending on commodities.[5] (Compare lines 5 and 6.) The lowest-income countries, for example, spent only 2.0 percent as much as the United States on services, but 5.0 percent as much on commodities. The impression is given that final-product services are indeed highly income-elastic (under the implicit assumption that price is unchanging). The same inference can be drawn from line 7, where the shares of services in final expenditures on GDP are given. The lowest-income countries (group I) spent only about 22 percent of their GDP on services, the middle-income countries (groups II, and III, and IV) from 25 to 30 percent, and the highest-income countries (groups V and VI) from 35 to 45 percent. (The only country in group VI is the United States.)

In real terms—that is, in terms of the actual physical flows of commodities and services—matters are very different. This can be seen when purchasing-power parities (PPPs) rather than exchange rates are used to

**Table 2**
Nominal and real per-capita absorption of GDP in the form of services and commodities, and price indexes, by real per-capita GDP group, 1975.

| | Income group | | | | | |
|---|---|---|---|---|---|---|
| | I | II | III | IV | V | VI |
| **Real GDP per capita (U.S. = 100)** | | | | | | |
| 1. Number of countries | 8 | 6 | 6 | 4 | 9 | 1 |
| 2. Range | 0–14.9 | 15–29.9 | 30–44.9 | 45–59.9 | 60–89.9 | ≥90 |
| 3. Mean | 9.01 | 23.1 | 37.3 | 52.4 | 76.0 | 100.0 |
| **Per-capita expenditures converted at exchange rate** | | | | | | |
| 4. GDP (U.S. = 100) | 3.7 | 12.1 | 24.2 | 38.7 | 82.3 | 100.0 |
| 5. Commodities (U.S. = 100) | 5.0 | 15.2 | 31.1 | 50.6 | 92.7 | 100.0 |
| 6. Services (U.S. = 100) | 2.0 | 8.1 | 15.5 | 23.4 | 69.1 | 100.0 |
| 7. Share of services | 22.2 | 28.4 | 27.4 | 25.6 | 36.8 | 43.9 |
| **Per-capita quantity indices (based on PPP conversion of expenditures)** | | | | | | |
| 8. Commodities (U.S. = 100) | 8.8 | 23.4 | 37.5 | 53.8 | 77.4 | 100.0 |
| 9. Services (U.S. = 100) | 9.4 | 22.7 | 37.0 | 49.2 | 73.0 | 100.0 |
| 10. Share of services | 33.8 | 31.7 | 31.8 | 30.3 | 31.2 | 32.3 |
| **Price indices** | | | | | | |
| 11. GDP (U.S. = 100) | 40.6 | 51.7 | 64.7 | 73.5 | 107.5 | 100.0 |
| 12. Commodities (U.S. = 100) | 57.2 | 65.9 | 83.1 | 94.0 | 119.0 | 100.0 |
| 13. Services (U.S. = 100) | 20.7 | 34.1 | 41.2˙ | 46.3 | 94.6 | 100.0 |

Source: Kravis, Heston, and Summers 1982.
The entries in lines 3–13 are unweighted averages of the values for the countries within each income group.

$$\text{Line 2: } \frac{(\text{GDP in domestic currency/Population})/\text{PPP}}{\text{GDP in U.S./U.S. population}} \times 100$$

$$\text{Line 4: } \frac{(\text{GDP in domestic currency/Population})/\text{Exchange rate}}{\text{GDP in U.S./U.S. population}} \times 100$$

Lines 11–13: (PPP/Exchange rate) × 100

convert expenditures to a common currency, U.S. dollars. Before we examine the impact of PPP conversions on services and commodities, we should note the effect of the use of PPPs on overall GDP. When PPPs are used to convert national-currency GDPs, the dispersion of per-capita incomes across the countries is much smaller than the dispersion for exchange-rate-converted GDPs. The average index of real GDP per capita for the eight lowest-income countries is 2.4 times the nominal index. (Group I: line 3 divided by line 4.) Differences for the succeeding income classes are smaller and smaller, but the ratio of the real to the nominal per-capita GDP of the countries in income class IV (real per-capita GDPs 45–60 percent of the United States') is still nearly 1.4. This relationship can also be described in terms of price levels in different countries.[6] Price levels tend to be low in the poor countries; the price level of GDP for the group I countries is about 40 percent of that for the United States (line 11).

This tendency for real quantities to be larger than nominal ones extends to both the commodity and service components of final expenditures on GDP for the four lowest income classes in the table (compare lines 8 and 5, and lines 9 and 6.[7]) Correspondingly, for each of the four lowest groups, prices are lower than U.S. prices for both sets of categories (lines 12 and 13).

It is noteworthy that the margin by which the real-quantity indices exceed the nominal indices is greater for services than for commodities. Furthermore, this margin of difference is greater the lower the income group. (For example, the ratio of line 9 to line 6 exceeds the ratio of line 8 to line 5 to a greater degree for group I countries than for group II countries.) The underlying cause is that services are much cheaper in the relative price structure of a typical poor country than in that of a rich country. Some illustrative ratios of the price indexes for the different income classes (table 3) show this. A quadrupling of real per-capita

**Table 3**
Ratio of real per-capita incomes and price indices for commodities and services, selected country groups.

|  | Ratio of real per-capita incomes | Ratio of price indices for | |
| --- | --- | --- | --- |
|  |  | Commodities | Services |
| Group III to group I | 4.1 | 1.45 | 1.99 |
| Group V to group III | 2.0 | 1.43 | 2.30 |

income (group III relative to group I) is associated with a doubling of service prices, while commodity prices increase by less than half. Doubling income again (group V relative to group III) leads to a more than doubling of service prices, but again to only an increase of less than one-half in commodity prices.

The upshot is that, in real terms, the low-income countries tend to consume services in at least the same proportions as the high-income countries — indeed, in the case of the lowest-income countries, in a higher proportion (table 2, line 10). In real terms, the differences between the quantity indices for commodities and services (lines 8 and 9) tend to be smaller for each income class than the exchange-rate-converted expenditure indexes (columns 5 and 6). The gross impression of a high income elasticity for services conveyed by the use of the exchange rate as a conversion factor disappears when the PPP is used, but again this ignores the rise in service prices as income rises. Obviously, the income elasticity of services cannot be evaluated without simultaneously taking account of price and income effects.

In table 4, similar comparisons between exchange-rate-converted expenditures relative to the United States and PPP-converted quantity indexes are presented for consumption rather than for GDP. (The ICP definition of *consumption* is used here; it includes public expenditures for health care, education, and recreational services. The services in consumption include all the services in GDP less all those of government; the commodities in consumption include all the commodities in GDP except government purchases and capital formation.) Almost everything said about the behavior of commodities and services in GDP applies here with little modification. There is, however, one notable change: The share of services in real spending (that is, in international dollars) does rise. The increase in real terms, from 33 percent for group I to 40 percent for groups IV–VI (line 8) is, however, much lower than the rise from 24 to 53 percent found when exchange-rate conversions are used (line 4). The consumption data seem more hospitable to the hypothesis of high income elasticity for services than the more inclusive GDP data, particularly since relative service prices appear to rise with income.

### Intertemporal

Changes in the relative importance of services over time are summarized for three countries—France, the United Kingdom, and the United States

**Table 4**
Nominal and real per-capita consumption in the form of services and commodities, and price indexes, by real per-capita GDP group, 1975.

| | Income group | | | | | |
|---|---|---|---|---|---|---|
| | I | II | III | IV | V | VI |
| | 192 | 612 | 1,130 | 1,830 | 3,825 | 5,183 |
| **Per-capita consumption converted at exchange rate** | | | | | | |
| 1. Consumption (U.S. = 100) | 3.7 | 11.8 | 21.8 | 35.3 | 73.8 | 100.0 |
| 2. Commodities (U.S. = 100) | 5.8 | 16.8 | 30.0 | 49.1 | 87.1 | 100.0 |
| 3. Services (U.S. = 100) | 1.8 | 7.3 | 14.4 | 23.0 | 61.9 | 100.0 |
| 4. Share of services | 23.9 | 31.7 | 33.9 | 33.3 | 44.3 | 52.7 |
| **Per-capita quantity indices (based on PPP conversion of expenditures)** | | | | | | |
| 5. Consumption (U.S. = 100) | 9.4 | 23.5 | 36.2 | 50.7 | 71.3 | 100.0 |
| 6. Commodities (U.S. = 100) | 10.5 | 25.0 | 37.2 | 51.2 | 72.3 | 100.0 |
| 7. Services (U.S. = 100) | 7.7 | 21.3 | 34.6 | 49.9 | 69.7 | 100.0 |
| 8. Share of services | 33.3 | 36.8 | 38.9 | 40.1 | 39.7 | 100.0 |
| **Price indices** | | | | | | |
| 9. Consumption (U.S. = 100) | 39.9 | 50.1 | 59.5 | 69.1 | 102.9 | 100.0 |
| 10. Commodities (U.S. = 100) | 56.6 | 68.6 | 81.2 | 95.8 | 119.5 | 100.0 |
| 11. Services (U.S. = 100) | 23.6 | 33.2 | 40.1 | 45.4 | 88.7 | 100.0 |

Source: Kravis, Heston, and Summers 1982.
See notes to table 2.

**Table 5**
Changes in Service Shares Over Time, France, United Kingdom, and United States.

| | Index of real per-capita GDP | Shares of | | | |
| --- | --- | --- | --- | --- | --- |
| | | Private household services in private consumption | | Services in GDP[a] | |
| | | Current prices | Constant prices | Current prices | Constant prices |
| **France** | | | | | |
| 1959–60 | 49.1 | 28.9 | 36.3 | 31.3 | 38.0 |
| 1977–78 | 100.0 | 37.5 | 37.7 | 37.9 | 36.5 |
| **United Kingdom[b]** | | | | | |
| 1957–58 | 65.0 | 22.8 | 35.2 | 39.5 | 51.6 |
| 1967–68 | 81.1 | 29.4 | 33.6 | 43.8 | 50.5 |
| 1977–78 | 100.0 | 31.6 | 33.2 | 47.6 | 49.7 |
| **United States** | | | | | |
| 1947–48 | 52.3 | 31.4 | 39.6 | 33.2 | 42.4 |
| 1957–58 | 62.6 | 38.4 | 41.5 | 44.9 | 49.6 |
| 1967–68 | 82.0 | 42.2 | 43.6 | 48.8 | 50.8 |
| 1977–78 | 100.0 | 45.6 | 45.5 | 49.7 | 49.0 |

U.K. shares of

| | Private household services in private consumption | | Services in GDP | |
| --- | --- | --- | --- | --- |
| | Current prices | Constant prices | Current prices | Constant prices |
| 1968–69 | 29.5 | 33.8 | 42.9 | 49.8 |
| 1977–78 | 31.6 | 33.2 | 47.6 | 49.7 |

Sources: France: Institute National de la Statistique et des Etudes Economiques, *La Consommation des Menages*, October 1979; OECD, *National Accounts of OECD Countries, 1950–1979*, vol. 1 (Paris, 1981). United Kingdom:: *National Income and Expenditure*, 1962, 1972, 1979; Central Statistical Office. United States: *Survey of Current Business*, January 1980, pp. 36, 38.
a. Includes all final expenditures of government. GNP is used for the U.S. instead of GDP.
b. The shares in current and constant prices were linked in the years 1961 and 1968 to cope with revisions in the series and the changes in the base year for constant prices. Since in each of these years the constant-price service shares were higher at the new prices than at the old, the use of the unlinked shares would produce rising service shares rather than the generally declining ones shown in the table. However, if the comparisons are made less equivocal by confining them to the most recent series, starting in 1968, the same attenuation of the upward movement of shares in current prices appears when a shift is made to constant-price shares, including a reversal of the trend in both concepts of service shares:

—in table 5. In each of the countries the share of expenditures on services rises quite sharply over time as its income rises when shares are calculated in the current prices of each period. This is true whether the service share is defined as privately purchased services in household consumption or as the share of all services, including government, in GDP. When service shares are measured in constant prices, however, the secular rise in shares disappears completely in the cases of France and the United Kingdom and is sharply reduced in the case of the United States.[8] In the United States there was a moderate shift toward services, which was confined in the case of GDP to the 1950s.

The obvious inference is that, as the incomes of the countries rose, service prices must have been rising relative to commodity prices.[9] The ratios of terminal to initial implicit deflators for the three countries confirm this (table 6).

## The Income Elasticity of Final-Product Services

The common view that services are characterized by relatively high income elasticities is based on the idea that commodities fill one set of human wants (the basic necessities) and services another (the desire for luxuries) (Fisher 1935, p. 31). The fact is, however, that changing times bring different forms through which age-old wants are satisfied, and it is easy to go astray by identifying luxuries with services.

The income elasticity of demand is only one of three sets of factors that influence the changes over time in the division of consumers' expenditures between services and commodities. Some generalizations can probably be legitimately made about income elasticities for broad categories of wants —for example, that the demand for recreation tends to be highly elastic

**Table 6**
Ratios of terminal to initial implicit deflators: France, United Kingdom, and United States.

|                            | Services | Commodities | GDP  |
| -------------------------- | -------- | ----------- | ---- |
| France,<br>1977–78/1959–60 | 3.77     | 2.64        | 2.99 |
| United Kingdom,<br>1977–78/1957–58 | 5.45 | 3.67    | 4.35 |
| United States,<br>1977–78/1950–51  | 3.24 | 2.29    | 2.65 |

with respect to income—but such generalizations do not lead to a clear conclusion about shifts in the relative importance of services and commodities in consumer expenditures. Even a broad category of wants can be satisfied in a variety of ways, some involving a service and others involving a commodity. Higher incomes, for example, may lead to the substitution of a commodity for a commodity (meat for bread), or of a service for a service (an expensive restaurant meal for a cheap one), or of a service for a commodity (restaurant food for home-cooked food), or of a commodity for a service (ready-to-serve food for household help).

Another set of factors that determine whether the expansion path goes toward services or toward commodities are technological. Consider, for example, the possible ways for an individual to satisfy an income-elastic desire for entertainment in the form of a musical experience. The most direct physical sensation associated with the musical experience involves movements of molecules in the air and their impact on the ear (though clearly a variety of other sensations—e.g., visual—play a role too). The alternative ways by which an individual can arrange to have the molecules move in order to receive his entertainment depends upon the molecule-moving technological possibilities available. In the nineteenth century, the options were limited to direct contact between the performer and the listeners. In the twentieth century, various disembodied sources of music are available (phonograph records and live and recorded performances transmitted by radio and television), but access to these sources requires the purchase of commodities (records and record players, radios, television sets) instead of the purchase of a service in the form of a concert ticket. At some points in the evolution of music technology a stimulus was given to expenditures on services (radio broadcasting and later TV broadcasting) and at other points to expenditures on commodities (records and record players, radios, TV sets, and recording equipment).

The remaining factors with which the income elasticities and the technological factors interact, sometimes in a causative way, are relative prices. The existing structure of relative prices at a given moment may influence the relative size of income elasticities for different means of satisfying a broad want. For example, whether a high income elasticity of demand for recreation leads with an increase of income to a relative expansion of spending on services or on commodities is likely to depend on which ways of providing the desired form of recreation are the cheapest.

The influence that price may exercise on the income elasticities of close substitutes may vary with the level of income.

Relative prices will in turn be influenced by technological changes. If (as seems plausible) the cost-reducing aspects of technological change affect commodities more often than services, commodity prices will tend to fall relative to services prices. This behavior of relative prices is made more likely by the facts that services tend to be produced in a more labor-intensive way than commodities and that wage rates rise relative to the rent of capital with development.

The powerful influence of the relative prices of commodities and services may help to explain the predominance of commodity over service avenues of satisfying the demand for musical performances. Though the enjoyment of theatrical and musical performances is usually thought of as involving a service transaction, in the United States consumers spend much more on the commodities necessary to get access to such entertainment (in 1975, $14.6 billion on radios, TV sets, records, and musical instruments) than on direct payments for the services these involve ($2.5 billion on motion-picture admissions and $0.8 billion on theater, opera, and other performances). More broadly, over 70 percent of the U.S. consumption expenditures on "recreation" were for commodities.[10]

Recreation is not the only example of this phenomonon. Switches from the purchase of commercial laundry services to home washing machines and dryers and from the services of washers of dishes to dishwashers further illustrate the consequences of cost minimization even in the absence of changes in the state of technology.

The rise in service prices relative to commodity prices and their influence in tilting the balance in favor of shifts from the satisfaction of wants through services to their satisfaction through commodities may help explain the limited expansion of the share of services in final expenditures despite the fact that services often seem to contribute to income-elastic wants.

It seems clear, then, that there are no strong *a priori* grounds for expecting collections of final products classified as services to have higher income elasticities than those we classify as commodities, and that tables 2, 4, and 5 indicate that prices and income were both changing interspatially and intertemporally, so the separate effect of income change on service quantity has not been measured. The actual elasticities may be estimated in several ways.

**Table 7**
Price and income elasticities for services and commodities, based on cross-section data for
34 countries, 1975.

| | Elasticity estimates[a] | |
|---|---|---|
| | Price | Income |
| **ICP consumption[b]** | | |
| Services | −0.1940 | 1.1274 |
| | (0.1364) | (0.0412) |
| Commodities | −0.3064 | 0.9271 |
| | (0.1406) | (0.0202) |
| **ICP GDP** | | |
| Services | −0.1491 | 1.0015 |
| | (0.1488) | (0.0493) |
| Commodities | −0.2717 | 0.9900 |
| | (0.1853) | (0.0243) |

a. Elasticities were estimated using regression equations of the form $\ln q = \alpha \ln(p/P) + \beta \ln(y/y_{U.S.}) + u$ where $q$ and $p$ are the quantity and price of the sectors and $y$ represents income. In ICP consumption, $P$ refers to the price level for consumption and $y$ to real per-capita consumption. In ICP GDP, $P$ and income refer to GDP. Numbers in parentheses are standard errors.
b. Includes public expenditures on education and medical care.

### Cross-National Estimate of Income Elasticity

One approach, the results of which are set out in table 7, relies on cross-section data for the 34 ICP countries. The parameters of log-linear demand regressions were estimated for both commodities and services on the basis of two different income concepts.[11] When the service-commodity dichotomy in "ICP consumption" (the concept in which government expenditures on education and medical care are included) is analyzed, the income elasticity for services is distinctly above unity, and significantly so; correspondingly, that for commodities is below unity, and significantly so. However, when all final-product services (including those of government) are taken into account, the difference between the service and commodity elasticities virtually disappears. Since the purpose of this chapter is to describe the changes in the structure of the economy, the latter is the more relevant basis.

It may be of further interest to examine the pattern of the income elasticities that emerges from the estimation of individual demand equations for each service and commodity category. The results for ICP consumption categories are given in table 8. Although the service set

**Table 8**
Percentage distributions of income elasticities for commodity and service categories.

| Income elasticity | Percent distribution of categories | |
|---|---|---|
| | Commodities | Services[a] |
| <0.5 | 18.2 | 7.7 |
| 0.5–0.99 | 14.3 | 3.8 |
| 1.0–1.49 | 37.7 | 53.8 |
| ≥1.5 | 29.9 | 34.6 |
| | 100.0 | 100.0 |

*Note*: The income variable is total consumption inclusive of the public expenditures alluded to in text. The numbers of categories for which income-elasticity estimates were computed were 77 for commodities and 26 for services. Data from Kravis, Heston, and Summers 1982.
a. Includes both private and public expenditures on health, education, and recreation, but excludes general government.

clearly has a higher proportion of elasticities over unity, the margin by which it exceeds the commodity set in the very high elasticity category (1.5 and over) is modest and the difference between the median elasticities for service categories (1.36) for commodity categories (1.23) is not very great. When the significance of the difference between the two distributions is assessed (albeit with limited power) by a $\chi^2$ contingency table test, the null hypothesis that the distributions are the same is accepted at the 0.10 level. There is no very strong basis here for predicting an income elasticity on the basis of the classification of a final-product category as a commodity or a service.

**Intertemporal Elasticies**

Another approach to the estimation of income elasticities is through time-series data. Price and income elasticities based on annual data for periods of 10 to nearly 30 years for France, the United Kingdom, and the United States are shown in table 9. As might be expected from the dampened expansion of service shares over time when data were expressed in constant prices in table 5, the evidence on the difference between services and commodities is mixed in these regressions. While the French data indicate higher income elasticities for services than for commodities, the U.K. and U.S. data definitely do not. The quite possible endogeneity of prices and the almost certain oversimplification of the "model" limit the weight that can be placed on these results. (This is particularly true in view of some positive and significant price elasticities.)

**Table 9**
Price and income elasticities for services and commodities, France, United Kingdom, and United States.

| | Elasticity estimates[a] | |
| --- | --- | --- |
| | Price | Income |
| **France, 1959–78** | | |
| Private consumption | | |
| 1. Services[b] | −0.6029 | 1.0383 |
| | (0.1831) | (0.0472) |
| 2. Commodities[b] | −0.5146 | 0.7465 |
| | (0.1168) | (0.0155) |
| GDP | | |
| 3. Services[b] | −0.7869 | 1.2300 |
| | (0.3436) | (0.1151) |
| 4. Commodities[b] | −0.7836 | 0.8745 |
| | (0.3964) | (0.0681) |
| **U.K., 1968–78** | | |
| Private consumption | | |
| 5. Services | +0.0142 | 0.5704 |
| | (0.0079) | (0.0975) |
| 6. Commodities | −0.1463 | 1.0913 |
| | (0.2933) | (0.0965) |
| GDP | | |
| 7. Services | +0.4696 | 0.6838 |
| | (0.1533) | (0.1155) |
| 8. Commodities | +0.5416 | 1.3040 |
| | (0.1913) | (0.1206) |
| **U.S., 1950–77** | | |
| Private Consumption | | |
| 9. Services[b] | −0.3862 | 0.6665 |
| | (0.1540) | (0.0701) |
| 10. Commodities[b] | −0.4555 | 1.2254 |
| | (0.1809) | (0.0558) |
| GDP | | |
| 11. Services[b] | +0.4598 | 0.8703 |
| | (0.3521) | (0.1033) |
| 12. Commodities[b] | −0.0982 | 0.9887 |
| | (0.4757) | (0.1204) |

a. Elasticities were estimated using regression equations of the form $\ln q = \alpha \ln(p/P) + \beta \ln(y/y_{U.S.}) + u$ where $q$ and $p$ are the quantity and price of the sector and $y$ represents income. In lines 1, 2, 5, 6, 9, and 10, $P$ refers to the price level for consumption and $y$ to real per-capita consumption. In lines 3, 4, 7, 8, 11, and 12, $P$ refers to the price of all GDP and $y$ to real per-capita GDP. Numbers in parentheses are standard errors.
b. The Durbin-Watson test rejected non-autocorrelated disturbances at the 0.05 level of significance. Reported elasticities are based upon Cochrane-Orcutt transformed data.

**Service Shares and Petty's Law**

From the reconciliation of the cross-section analysis of shares in table 2 and demand regressions in table 7 emerges a story of economic development involving Petty's Law about shifts in manufacturing industry and service industry employment over time. For GDP, table 2 shows sharply rising service expenditure shares associated with rising nominal incomes but constant shares when both services and incomes are expressed in real terms. The price and income elasticity coefficients of table 7 suggest the reason for the difference: Neither the quantity of services nor that of commodities is very responsive to changes in relative prices, but both expand in equal proportions as income rises. Thus, service shares remain constant in real terms from group I to group VI. They are altered neither by changes in prices nor by changes in incomes. Though relative service-commodity prices change and income rises as development proceeds, the real shares remain the same. The nominal shares (which are the same as the exchange-rate-converted shares) reflect the change in relative prices, and on that account would rise with rising income. Rising service prices, as will be argued in the next section, reflect a lower rate of productivity improvement than is experienced in commodities. The inference, then, is that equal rates of expansion in the absorption of the two forms of final product require a more rapid expansion of employment in services.

A similar analysis applies if attention is confined to the consumption component of GDP. The main difference is that the real service share rises from group I to group IV (though not as much as the nominal service share). This behavior is reflected in the higher income elasticity of consumption services relative to that for consumption commodities shown in table 7 (lines 1 and 2). However, similar inferences can be made about the reasons for the difference between real and nominal shares and about Petty's Law.

## Why Services Are Low in Price in Low-Income Countries

The most striking characteristic of services that has emerged from this review is the behavior of their prices relative to those of commodities as real per-capita income rises. As table 2 shows, in 1975 at the lowest income level (group I countries) this association involved service prices that were one-fifth of the U.S. level and average real per-capita GDPs that were less than 10 percent of the U.S. level. Commodity prices are also positively correlated with real incomes, but the gradient is much smaller, and prices in the lowest-income countries were slightly over 60 percent of the U.S. level.

These differences were explained in earlier work in terms of the productivity-differential model (Kravis, Heston, and Summers 1978). As a first approximation it may assumed for purposes of explaining the model that the prices of traded goods (mainly commodities) are the same in different countries. With similar prices for traded goods in all countries, wages in the industries producing traded goods will differ from country to country according to differences in productivity—a standard conclusion of Ricardian trade theory. In each country the wage level established in the traded-goods industries will determine wages in the industries producing nontraded goods (mainly services). Because international productivity differences are smaller for such industries, the low wages established in poor countries in the low-productivity traded-goods industries will apply also to the not-so-low-productivity service-and-other-nontraded-goods industries. The consequences will be low prices in low-income countries for services and other nontraded goods. (An algebraic treatment of this productivity-differential model is presented in the appendix.)

Here, a more extensive effort is made to seek empirical verification of the model than was undertaken before. This involves probing into the question of the capital and labor intensities of services and commodities.

In the first place, the data of the ICP, as has just been mentioned, show that although commodity prices are far from uniform in countries at different income levels, they are much more similar than service prices (see table 2). Logically, the next proposition of the model that should be investigated is the behavior of wages in service- and commodity-producing industries, but we move directly to the penultimate propositions of the model dealing with relative productivity in services and commodities. (The final proposition is that prices reflect these productivity differences.) For this purpose we find it necessary to shift from the concept of commodities and services as final products to a consideration of the industries that produce both final and intermediate services. Direct evidence on the relative behavior of productivity may be found in Kuznets-type sectoral productivity ratios (sectoral shares in output divided by sectoral shares in employment).[12] Kuznets's own work relating first to 1950 and later to 1960 and the independent work of Chenery and Syrquin (1975) summarizing the period 1950–1970 show clearly that the productivity of the service sector relative to the commodity sector tends to be inversely related to the income level of the country. This finding is confirmed when sectoral productivity indices, circa 1975,[13] are regressed against real per-capita GDP for the 20 ICP phase III countries for which data for such indices were available. In the following regression, productivity in the service industries (SP) relative to productivity in the commodity industries (CP) of each country is taken as the dependent variable and the ICP estimate of 1975 real per capita GDP (r) is the independent variable (standard errors are shown in parenthesis):

$$\ln(\text{SP/CP}) = 7.3988 - 0.3100 \ln r$$
$$\quad\quad\quad\quad (0.4349) \quad (0.0550)$$

(1)

where $\bar{R}^2 = 0.618$, S.E.E. $= 0.198$, and $n = 20$. The coefficient of $r$ is negative and highly significant. The higher the country's per-capita income, the lower its service-sector productivity relative to its commodity-sector productivity.

An alternate assessment of the relative productivity in the service- and commodity-producing industries, using a completely different body of data and also offering insights into the relative factor intensities of the two sets of industries, can be obtained by using input-output data for countries at various income levels. Fortunately, the formidable task of assembling input-output studies for different countries and reconciling differences in the industrial classification can be avoided by relying upon a World Bank study by Stern and Lewis (1980) which gives capital and labor requirements for 30 sectors for eight income levels of countries based on a sample of input-output tables.[14] It was relatively easy to adapt this grouping to the six ICP income groups used in table 2. Three of the sectors represented services (transportation, communication, and a catch-all category that combined all other services, including those of barbers, restaurants, physicians, and educational institutions); the others involved commodity production. For each of the six income groups of countries, we computed weighted average direct capital and labor requirements. The weights were based on the relative importance of each sector in contributing to GDP within individual countries. The percentages indicating relative importance were averaged for the countries in each income group.[15] The resulting coefficients for services and for commodity-

**Table 10**
Average direct capital and labor requirements by ICP income groups for commodities and services, in 1970 dollars.

| Income group | Capital[a] ($K/$ output) | | | Labor[b] | | |
|---|---|---|---|---|---|---|
| | Commodity | Service | GDP | Commodity | Service | GDP |
| | (1) | (2) | (3) | (4) | (5) | (6) |
| 1 | 0.755 | 0.401 | 0.622 | 0.172 | 0.162 | 0.200 |
| 2 | 1.081 | 0.816 | 1.008 | 0.117 | 0.158 | 0.158 |
| 3 | 1.015 | 0.590 | 0.834 | 0.180 | 0.095 | 0.140 |
| 4 | 1.085 | 0.613 | 0.872 | 0.157 | 0.097 | 0.132 |
| 5 | 1.009 | 0.850 | 0.931 | 0.062 | 0.090 | 0.080 |
| 6 | 1.075 | 0.855 | 0.937 | 0.049 | 0.078 | 0.067 |

Derived from Stern and Lewis 1980. See text.
a. Thousands of dollars per dollar of output.
b. Man-years per $1,000 of output.

**Table 11**
Inputs of capital and labor per unit of output in group I countries relative to group VI.

| | Group I/Group VI | |
|---|---|---|
| | Capital | Labor |
| Service | 0.47 | 2.08 |
| Commodity | 0.70 | 3.51 |

producing industries, presented in table 10, are expressed as dollars of capital required per dollar of output and as man-years of labor per thousand dollars of output in 1970 prices.

What are the implications of these data for relative productivity in service and commodity industries for countries at different levels of income? The relationships can be seen by concentrating on the two extreme groups, I and VI. The ratio of the inputs of capital and labor per unit of output in group I to the inputs in "group VI" (the United States) is given in table 11. For example, from columns 1 and 2 of table 10, 0.401/0.855 = 0.47 and 0.755/1.075 = 0.70.

The quantity of each factor used by the lowest-income countries is relatively smaller for services than for commodities.[16] The lowest-income countries use only 2 times as much labor as the United States to produce $1,000 worth of services, as compared with 3.5 times as much for commodities. The relatively small amounts of capital used by the low-income

**Table 12**
Capital/labor ratios for commodities and services, country groups I–VI.

| Income group | Capital/labor ratio[a] | |
| --- | --- | --- |
| | Commodities | Services |
| I | 4.39 | 2.48 |
| II | 9.24 | 5.16 |
| III | 5.64 | 6.21 |
| IV | 6.91 | 6.32 |
| V | 16.27 | 9.44 |
| VI | 21.94 | 10.96 |

Source: Table 10.
a. Thousands of dollars' worth of capital per man-year. For a thoughtful assessment of various measures of capital intensity, including the capital-labor ratio, see Stern 1977, pp. 10 ff.

countries probably reflect their much less extensive substitution of capital for labor.

Table 10 also presents significant insights into the factor intensities of service and commodity production at different levels of income. Capital requirements in the services are lower than those in commodities for all groups. The use of labor per unit of output declines with rising incomes, reflecting the higher labor productivity of higher-income countries. The association of capital requirements with per-capita income is less clear-cut, owing to the offsetting effects of greater productivity and of substitution of capital for labor in the higher-income countries.

When the two inputs are put together to form capital-labor ratios, the results are those given in table 12. Services are generally more labor-intensive than commodities (in the sense of low capital-labor ratios). It is difficult to know whether the lack of a more regular progression in the capital-labor ratios for commodities—the ratio for group II is out of line—reflects statistical noise or represents a genuine economic phenomenon.

Sometimes the ICP ratios of relative per-capita GDP are interpreted as a rough estimate of relative labor productivity. The problem with this interpretation is that it uses total population as a proxy for total labor input. It may be of interest, then, to compare the total factor-productivity levels implied by the data in table 10 with the labor-oriented estimates directly derived from the ICP. For example, the implied weighted average productivity for GDP as a whole for group I countries is 38 percent of the U.S. value, whereas the ICP estimate is a little under 10 percent.[17] This large difference (and the somewhat smaller differences for the other income groups) might be accounted for by difference in quantities of capital as well as labor inputs, but may also reflect data problems.

Attention must be called to two caveats about the input-output data. One is that the original task of distilling the input-output matrices of different countries into a consistent set of industrial categories for eight different groups of countries required a broad-brush approach. In particular, the work of correcting exchange-rate-converted values for capital and output to a basis that took into account differences in the purchasing power of the currencies could only be done very roughly, as those who carried out the task clearly realized. Further possibilities for substantial errors arise in the considerable liberties we have taken in further pressing the data into a form suitable for the present analysis.[18] The second caveat concerns the heterogeneity of both sets of goods. This means that averages relating to them may not be typical of all of their components. This lack of intragroup similarity marks the capital-labor ratios as well. For example, table 13 gives the diversity in capital-labor ratios that can be found for income groups I and VI. Transportation (a service industry) is more capital-intensive than textiles (a commodity industry). Textiles, wearing apparel (a commodity industry) is not always more capital-intensive than services, N.E.S. Nevertheless, as table 10 indicates, the amount of capital per person is, on average, higher in commodity than in service industries.

**Table 13**
Capital-labor ratios of services and commodities, country groups I and VI.

| | Direct capital-labor ratio[a] | |
| | I | VI |
|---|---|---|
| **Services** | | |
| Transportation | 4.17 | 40.43 |
| Services, N.E.S.[b] | 0.98 | 7.75 |
| **Commodities** | | |
| Textiles, Wearing Apparel | 2.00 | 4.75 |
| Electrical Machinery | 10.40 | 6.60 |

a. Excludes the labor and capital content of inputs purchased from other industries.
b. N.E.S. = not elsewhere specified.

**Reasons for the Differences in Sectoral Productivity**

The intersectoral productivity indexes can be decomposed as follows:

$$\frac{P_s}{P_c} = \frac{[(W_s + O_s)Q_s]/N_s}{[(W_c + O_c)Q_c]/N_c}$$

where s indicates services, c indicates commodities, $P$ = output per worker in own-currency prices, $W$ = labor compensation per unit of output, $O$ = non-labor costs per unit of output, $Q$ = units of output, and $N$ = number of workers. The decline in relative productivity found in the service industries as we move from low- to high-income countries and in the course of time as individual countries move from lower to higher income levels could be due to any of the terms on the right. One possibility is that the variation may be due not to differences in physical output per worker ($Q_s/N_s$ and $Q_c/N_c$) but to differences in the relative compensation of labor in the two sectors ($W_s$ and $W_c$). Alternatively, the intersectoral differences in labor productivity may be attributed to differences in nonlabor costs, mainly capital costs ($O_s$ and $O_c$); that is, in either the quantity of capital per person or the rate of return on capital or both. A third explanation is that the intersectoral differences do indeed reflect differences in physical output per worker (the $Q$s in relation to the $N$s).

It seems rather doubtful that high relative wages in services can explain the high sectoral productivity of services in poor countries. There is, indeed, some evidence that education and skill differentials tend to be higher in poor countries (Phelps Brown 1977, chapter 3), and some services are intensive in their use of educated and skilled personnel (e.g., medical services). On the other side, there is a clear tendency for service wages to rise with rising per-capita incomes. This tendency is revealed when ICP data on compensation of particular types of service workers are related to per-capita income. For example, exchange-rate-converted compensation of first- and second-level teachers ($W_T/XR$) is related to real per-capita GDP ($r$) across the countries as follows:

$$\ln W_T/XR = -2.8489 + 0.8528 \ln r$$
$$(1.0589)\ \ (0.1349) \tag{2}$$

where $\bar{R}^2 = 0.600$, S.E.E. $= 0.629$, and $n = 27$. Price levels of commodities and services ($PPP_c/XR$ and $PPP_s/XR$) generally tend to be correlated

**Table 14**
Estimates of coefficients of $\ln r$ and standard errors for five occupational groupings.

|  | Estimated coefficient[a] | Standard error |
|---|---|---|
| Unskilled government employees | 0.79 | 0.07 |
| Skilled government employees | 0.64 | 0.07 |
| White-collar government employees | 0.56 | 0.07 |
| First- and second-level teachers | 0.44 | 0.11 |
| Professional government employees | 0.36 | 0.09 |

a. $\hat{\alpha}_1$ of $\ln(W_T/\text{PPP}_{GDP}) = \alpha_0 + \alpha_1 \ln r$

with income levels, so it is more relevant to consider compensation relative to the purchasing-power parity for GDP as a whole ($\text{PPP}_{GDP}$):

$$\ln(W_T/\text{PPP}_{GDP}) = 0.7730 + 0.4361 \ln r$$
$$(0.8755) \quad (0.1115) \tag{3}$$

where $\bar{R}^2 = 0.355$, S.E.E. $= 0.520$, and $n = 27$.

Similar relationships indicating rising absolute and relative compensation are found for each of the four ICP categories of government employees. There is some indication, however, that among these groups, those with the most education tend to have relatively higher compensation in poor countries compared with their relative compensation in rich countries. The coefficients of $\ln r$ in equations like 3 for five groups, arrayed in what may be guessed to be an ascending order of educational qualifications, are given in table 14. Salaries of all groups rise with rising incomes, but those of the more educated groups tend to rise less.[19] Thus, these occupational data provide some support for the hypotheses of higher income differentials for educated people in low-income countries. However, relative incomes in the whole set of service occupations are positively correlated with incomes and hence are lower rather than higher in poor countries. We do not know the extent of the education and skill intensities of workers in the service industries relative to commodity industries, but it seems unlikely that the differences in the intensities in conjunction with the differences in the labor market shown in table 14 are sufficient to produce such marked differences in sector productivity.

It is even less plausible to think that higher labor productivity in services relative to commodities in poor countries is attributable to larger amounts of capital. Table 10 and 11 clearly show less physical capital per dollar of output in services than in commodities in very-low-income countries. Conceivably, the smaller amount of capital could be more richly rewarded than capital employed in commodity production, but it is not at all apparent why this should be the case, and it is highly implausible that the differential in the rate of return could be large enough to inflate the product of the service sector in low-income countries sufficiently to produce the substantial differences in sectoral productivity that are observed.

We are left with the hypothesis that the poor country-rich country physical productivity ratios in the service industries, though well below unity, are higher than in commodity industries. There are two circumstances that point to this as the probable explanation. One is the ICP finding of low final-product prices in the services, an outcome that would be less likely if there were high factor rewards. (In assessing this result, however, it must be recognized that the sectoral-productivity indices pertain to an industrial classification while the price comparisons relate to categories of final product.) The second circumstance is the apparent tendency for the dispersion of country-to-country ratios of outputs per person to be greater across industries than the dispersions in the corresponding country-to-country wages per person (Kravis 1956). This tendency, though observed across manufacturing industries, suggests that the low service prices are more apt to be attributable to productivity differences than to wage differences.

Finally, in the area of the relative behavior of service and commodity prices over time, too, it may be surmised that the underlying explanation for the rise in service prices relative to commodity prices is to be found in productivity trends. One may speculate that technological advance in its innovative aspects may affect both commodity and service industries (especially transportation, communication, and health care among the latter), but that in its cost-reducing aspect it has borne most heavily on the commodity-producing industries. If so, the higher wages this made possible in such industries may have pushed service wages and thus service prices up in relation to commodity prices.

## Conclusion

The analysis suggests that the driving force behind the expansion of service employment associated with higher per-capita incomes in both cross-national and intertemporal data is the evolution of technology rather than the change in wants associated with rising income. This inference rests on the absence of any clear evidence that the income elasticity of demand is consistently (or even on the average) higher for final-product services than for final-product commodities, and the tendency for service prices to rise relative to commodity prices as incomes rise (a tendency observed in both cross-national and intertemporal data). We ascribe this tendency to differential productivity ratios. Across countries, productivity is, of course, lower in poor countries relative to rich countries in both services and commodity-producing sectors, but it is lower by a larger margin in commodities. (The possibility that these differences may reflect mainly superior renumeration of the factors of production in service industries is rejected.)

It seems plausible that, in the creation of new ways of satisfying wants, technological changes are as important in service sectors (such as health care) as in commodity sectors, but that when it comes to cost reduction for existing products or services technological change is more frequent and more powerful in its effects in the commodity sector.

## Acknowledgments

Chad Leechor and Martin Shanin helped in the statistical work and Kathleen Conway prepared the manuscript. The work was supported by grant SES-7913980 from the National Science Foundation.

## Appendix

### Glossary

Lower case refers to a poor country, upper case to a rich country.

| | |
|---|---|
| $q^T, Q^T$ | Output of traded goods |
| $q^{NT}, Q^{NT}$ | Output of nontraded goods |
| gdp, GDP | Gross domestic product |
| pop, POP | Population |
| $s^{NT}, S^{NT}$ | Share of nontraded goods in gross national product |
| $l^T, L^1$ | Labor input in producing traded goods |
| $l^{NT}, l^{NT}$ | Labor input in producing nontraded goods |
| $p^T, P^T$ | Price of traded goods |
| $p^{NT}, P^{NT}$ | Price of nontraded goods |

$k^T, K^T$      Productivity per worker in traded-goods industry
$k^{NT}, K^{NT}$   Productivity per worker in nontraded-goods industry
$w, W$      Wages in both industries (equal because of labor mobility within each country)
XR        Exchange rate
$\mu$       Markup in both industries in both countries (assumed equal for simplicity.)
$\bar{p}, \bar{w}$     Poor country's prices or wages expressed in rich country's currency by conversion at the exchange rate
$C^{NT}$      Poor country's labor productivity in nontraded-goods industry divided by the corresponding rich-country labor productivity
$C^T$       Poor country's labor productivity in traded-goods industry divided by the corresponding rich-country labor productivity
$C$        Ratio of $C^T$ to $C^{NT}$
$I^{XR}$      Income comparison between the poor and rich countries obtained through exchange-rate conversion
$I^{PPP}$      Income comparison between the poor and rich countries obtained through purchasing-power-parity conversion

**Algebraic Treatment**

The production functions (where output depends on quantity and productivity of labor) are, for the poor country,

$$q^T = f_1(l^T, k^T)$$

and

$$q^{NT} = f_2(l^{NT}, k^{NT}),$$

and, for the rich country,

$$Q^T = F_1(L^T, K^T)$$

and

$$Q^{NT} = F_2(L^{NT}, K^{NT}).$$

The wage-price equations are, for the poor country,

$$p^T = \frac{l^T w}{q^T}(1 + \mu)$$

and

$$p^{NT} = \frac{l^{NT}w}{q^{NT}}(1 + \mu),$$

and, for the rich country,

$$P^T = \frac{L^T W}{Q^T}(1 + \mu)$$

and

$$P^{NT} = \frac{L^{NT} W}{Q^{NT}}(1 + \mu).$$

The assumptions are (a) that $\bar{p}^T = P^T$ (that is, the prices of traded goods are the same everywhere), and therefore $p^T/P^T = XR$, (b) that

$$C^T < 1,$$

$$C^{NT} < 1,$$

and

$$C^T < C^{NT} \quad \text{so } C < 1$$

(that is, labor productivity is greater in rich countries than in poor but the differential is smaller in the nontraded-goods sector), and that

$$p^T = \frac{l^T w}{k^T l^T}(1 + \mu) = \frac{w}{k^T}(1 + \mu)$$

and

$$p^{NT} = \frac{l^{NT} w}{k^{NT} l^{NT}}(1 + \mu) = \frac{w}{k^{NT}}(1 + \mu)$$

for the poor country and

$$P^T = \frac{L^T W}{K^T L^T}(1 + \mu) = \frac{W}{K^T}(1 + \mu)$$

and

$$P^{NT} - \frac{L^{NT} W}{K^{NT} L^{NT}}(1 + \mu) = \frac{W}{K^{NT}}(1 + \mu)$$

for the rich country.

The exchange-rate conversions are

$$\bar{p}^{\mathrm{T}} \equiv \frac{p^{\mathrm{T}}}{\mathrm{XR}}, \quad \bar{p}^{\mathrm{NT}} \equiv \frac{p^{\mathrm{NT}}}{\mathrm{XR}}, \quad \bar{w} \equiv \frac{w}{\mathrm{XR}}.$$

Therefore,

$$\bar{p}^{\mathrm{T}} = \frac{w}{k^{\mathrm{T}}} \frac{(1 + \mu)}{\mathrm{XR}}, \quad \bar{p}^{\mathrm{NT}} = \frac{w}{k^{\mathrm{NT}}} \frac{1 + \mu}{\mathrm{XR}}, \tag{A1}$$

$$\frac{\bar{p}^{\mathrm{T}}}{P^{\mathrm{T}}} = \left(\frac{w}{k^{\mathrm{T}}} \frac{1 + \mu}{\mathrm{XR}}\right) \Big/ \left[\frac{W}{K^{\mathrm{T}}}(1 + \mu)\right] = \frac{\bar{w}}{W} \Big/ \frac{k^{\mathrm{T}}}{K^{\mathrm{T}}} = \frac{\bar{w}}{W} \Big/ C^{\mathrm{T}}, \tag{A2}$$

$$\frac{\bar{p}^{\mathrm{NT}}}{P^{\mathrm{NT}}} = \left(\frac{w}{k^{\mathrm{NT}}} \frac{1 + \mu}{\mathrm{XR}}\right) \Big/ \left[\frac{W}{K^{\mathrm{NT}}}(1 + \mu)\right] = \frac{\bar{w}}{W} \Big/ \frac{k^{\mathrm{NT}}}{K^{\mathrm{NT}}} = \frac{\bar{w}}{W} \Big/ C^{\mathrm{NT}}. \tag{A3}$$

Under assumption a,

$$\frac{\bar{w}}{W} = C^{\mathrm{T}}.$$

It follows then from equation A3 that

$$\frac{\bar{p}^{\mathrm{NT}}}{P^{\mathrm{NT}}} = \frac{(\bar{w}/W)/C^{\mathrm{NT}}}{(\bar{w}/W)/C^{\mathrm{T}}} = \frac{C^{\mathrm{T}}}{C^{\mathrm{NT}}}$$

and

$$\frac{\bar{p}^{\mathrm{NT}}}{P^{\mathrm{NT}}} = C.$$

Under assumption b,

$$\frac{\bar{p}^{\mathrm{NT}}}{P^{\mathrm{NT}}} < 1.$$

For the poor country,

$$\mathrm{gdp} = q^{\mathrm{T}} p^{\mathrm{T}} + q^{\mathrm{NT}} p^{\mathrm{NT}},$$

$$I^{\mathrm{XR}} = \frac{\mathrm{gdp/pop}}{\mathrm{XR}} \Big/ \frac{\mathrm{GDP}}{\mathrm{POP}},$$

$$I^{\mathrm{PPP}} = \frac{\mathrm{gdp/pop}}{\mathrm{PPP}} \Big/ \frac{\mathrm{GDP}}{\mathrm{POP}},$$

$$\frac{I^{\mathrm{XR}}}{I^{\mathrm{PPP:P}}} = \frac{\mathrm{PPP}^{\mathrm{(Paasche)}}}{\mathrm{XR}},$$

$$\mathrm{PPP}^{(\mathrm{Paasche})} = \frac{q^T p^T + q^{NT} p^{NT}}{q^T P^T + q^{NT} P^{NT}} = \frac{q^T P^T \mathrm{XR} + q^{NT} \bar{p}^{NT} \mathrm{XR}}{q^T P^T + q^{NT} P^{NT}}$$

$$= \frac{q^T P^T + q^{NT} P^{NT} C}{q^T P^T + q^{NT} P^{NT}} \mathrm{XR},$$

$$\frac{I^{\mathrm{XR}}}{I^{\mathrm{PPP:P}}} = \frac{q^T P^T + q^{NT} P^{NT} C}{q^T P^T + q^{NT} P^{NT}} = 1 + S^{NT}(C-1) < 1;$$

for the rich country,

$$\mathrm{GDP} = Q^T P^T + Q^{NT} P^{NT}$$

and

$$\frac{I^{\mathrm{XR}}}{I^{\mathrm{PPP:L}}} = \frac{\mathrm{PPP}^{(\mathrm{Laspeyres})}}{\mathrm{XR}}.$$

Similar algebra leads to $I^{\mathrm{XR}}/I^{\mathrm{PPP:L}} < 1$. Furthermore, relaxing assumption a to allow the price level of tradables to be lower in the poor country than in the rich, $\bar{p}^T < P^T$, leads to $I^{\mathrm{PPP}}$ exceeding $I^{\mathrm{XR}}$ by even more.

## Notes

1. See chapter 5 of Kravis, Heston, and Summers 1982 for a discussion of the characteristics of services. See also Hill 1977.

2. To make this comparison it is necessary to shift from final-product definitions to an industrial classification.

3. For the ICP classification see Kravis, Heston, and Summers 1982, chapter 2 appendix.

4. The classification is by real per-capita GDP—i.e., own-currency GDP converted to a common currency via purchasing-power parities rather than through exchange rates. See Kravis, Heston, and Summers 1982, table 1.2.

5. Exchange-rate-converted shares are the same as shares calculated from expenditures in own currency.

6. The price level is the PPP divided by the exchange rate, both taken relative to the U.S. dollar. The ratio of the real to the nominal per-capita GDP, referred to as the exchange-rate deviation index, is the reciprocal of the price level.

7. These figures are based on the treatment of government purchases of goods and services as commodities. Neither these figures nor the others in table 2 are altered very much if these purchases are classified with services.

8. There are at least two sources of possible error in these constant-price comparisons: there may be errors in the deflators for both goods and services, and there are probably incomparabilities in deflation procedure between the countries. It would be a major task to investigate these possible errors, and this task has not been attempted. In any case, there does not appear to be any obvious direction in these possible errors.

9. Clark (1979, pp. 147–155) reports similar results for Australia, Belgium, France, Japan, and the United States. However, Clark makes the point for Japan that from 1926 to 1960 service productivity apparently rose as rapidly as commodities, as only after 1960 did service prices rise substantially relative to commodities.

10. 1975 data from *Survey of Current Business*, July 1977, p. 29. Expenditures on admissions to spectator sports were $1.6 billion. If the $3.7 billion spent in producing and broadcasting TV entertainment were included, the service expenditure would still be only 33 percent of the enlarged recreation total. The TV expenditure estimate was kindly provided by John E. Cremeans of the U.S. Department of Commerce. For the methods underlying this estimate see Cremeans 1979.

11. The log-linear functional form for the demand functions must be regarded as only an approximation to the true functional form. Postulating that the income elasticity of each good is the same at all levels of income cannot be right unless the elasticities are equal to unity. This is because the weighted average of the elasticities, with the shares of total expenditure devoted to each good as the weights, must be equal to unity. The income elasticities reported in table 7 meet this condition (using the average share for all 34 countries as weights), suggesting that perhaps the approximation is acceptable. However, such income elasticities estimated from the time-series data underlying table 5 (reported in table 9) do not average out to unity.

12. The original source is Kuznets 1957; see p. 41 for the data and p. 53 for Kuznets's discussion of the meaning of sectoral productivity measures. See also the revision reaching the same conclusions on the basis of later data: Kuznets 1971, pp. 208–248. The latter part of that section (pp. 236ff.) considers the possible explanations for the observed intersectoral differences.

13. The labor force employed in agriculture, mining, manufacturing, and construction was regarded as engaged in commodity production, while that employed in electricity, gas and water, transportation and communication, trade, finance, and real estate, and community and social services was regarded as engaged in service production. The percentage shares were calculated on the basis of the labor force, excluding those whose industrial affiliation was unknown. Labor-force data were from International Labor Organization 1979. For production, a similar division was used. The categories treated as services were electricity, gas and water, transportation and communication, trade and finance, public administration and defense, and others (including ownership of dwellings, private services, and any statistical discrepancy from the use of alternative methods of estimating GDP). Data were from International Bank for Reconstruction and Development 1980.

14. Stern and Lewis 1980. This set of coefficients did not include labor coefficients for agriculture for low-income countries. These coefficients were approximated on the basis of the relations within the 1973–74 input-output table for India. The labor-requirement coefficients for India were kindly supplied by R. G. Nambiar.

15. The weights were based on data for 29 of the 34 countries in phase III of the ICP. The relative importance of broad sectors (agriculture, manufacturing, etc.) was based on data in United Nations 1979, and the breakdown within manufacturing, which contained the large preponderance of the Stern-Lewis sectors, was based on data in United Nations 1975.

16. This is true of any weighted combination of the inputs.

17. $(0.15 \times 0.622/0.937) + (0.85 \times 0.200/0.067) = 2.64$, where the weights 0.15 and 0.85 are from Kravis, Heston, and Summers 1982 and the ratios are the ratios respectively of capital and labor requirements for a dollar's worth of GDP of group I to group VI taken from table 10. The weighted average use of labor and capital per dollar of output in the group I countries is 2.64 times that of group VI. The reciprocal of 2.64, 0.38, may be taken as the productivity ratio.

18. The difficulty of treating the agricultural sector in group I countries, noted above, may be an important factor. Another possibility is that the more extensive unemployment and underemployment in low-income countries pull down relative real per-capita incomes below the level implied by labor requirements per unit of output.

19. Elliot 1975, chapters 7 and 8 and particularly pp. 189–190. Elliot attributes some of these differences to the heritage of colonial salary structures, and reports that although they have been reduced in some countries they still tend to exceed those in higher-income countries.

## Bibliography

Chenery, H. 1979. *Structural Change and Development Policy.* Washington, D.C.: Oxford University Press, for the World Bank.

Chenery, H., and M. Syrquin. 1975. *Patterns of Development.* Oxford University Press.

Clark, C. 1941. *The Conditions of Economic Progress.* London: Macmillan.

Clark, C. 1979. Productivity in the service industries. In C. H. Hanumantha Rao and P. C. Joshi, eds., *Reflections of Economic Development and Social Change: Essays in Honar of Professor V.K.R.V. Rao.* New Delhi: Allied Publishers Private Ltd.

Cremeans, J. E. 1979. Consumer Services Provided by Business Through Advertising Supported Media in the U.S. Presented at Sixteenth General Conference of the International Association for Research in Income and Wealth.

Elliot, C. 1975. *Patterns of Poverty in the Third World.* New York: Praeger.

Fisher, A. G. B. 1935. *The Clash of Progress and Security.* New York: Augustus M. Kelley.

Fuchs, V. 1968. *The Service Economy.* New York: National Bureau of Economic Research.

Fuchs, V. 1980. Economic Growth and the Rise of Service Employment. Prepared for conference "Towards Explaining Economic Growth," Institute of World Economics, Kiel, Federal Republic of Germany.

Hill, T. P. 1977. On goods and services. *Review of Income and Wealth* series 23, no. 4: 315–338.

International Bank for Reconstruction and Development. 1980. *World Tables.* Baltimore: Johns Hopkins University Press.

International Labor Organization. 1979. *Yearbook of Labor Statistics.*

Kravis, I. B. 1956. "Availability" and other influences on the commodity composition of trade. *Journal of Political Economy* VXIV, no. 2: 143–155.

Kravis, I. B., A. Heston, and R. Summers. 1978. *International Comparisons of Real Product and Purchasing Power.* Baltimore: Johns Hopkins University Press.

Kravis, I. B., A. Heston, and R. Summers. 1982. *World Product and Income: International Comparisons of Real GDP.* Baltimore: Johns Hopkins University Press.

Kuznets, S. 1957. Quantitative aspects of the economic growth of nations. II. Industrial distribution of national product and labor forces. *Economic Development and Cultural Change,* supplement to vol. V, no. 4.

Kuznets, S. 1971. *Economic Growth of Nations.* Cambridge, Mass.: Harvard University Press.

Kuznets, S. 1966. *Modern Economic Growth: Rate, Structure, and Spread.* New Haven: Yale University Press.

Phelps Brown, H. 1977. *The Inequality of Pay*. Oxford University Press.

Stern, J. J. 1977. The Employment Impact of Industrial Investment: A Preliminary Report. World Bank Staff Working Paper 255.

Stern, J. J., and J. D. Lewis. 1980. Employment Patterns and Growth. World Bank Staff Working Paper 419.

United Nations. 1975. *Growth of World Industry, 1973 Edition*. New York: United Nations.

United Nations. 1979. *Yearbook of National Account Statistics, 1978*. New York: United Nations.

# 11 Some Hard Economics of Soft Energy: Optimal Electricity Generation in Pulp and Paper Mills with Seasonal Steam Requirements

John F. Helliwell
Michael Margolick

The quadrupling of world oil prices in 1973–74, and their further doubling in 1979, have led to substantial improvements in the economic attractiveness of a large variety of techniques designed to capture the full energy potential in the harnessing of primary energy to useful tasks. Two of the most attractive possibilities are the burning of industrial wastes and the cogeneration of electricity and process steam. Pulp and paper mills, with their easy access to wood wastes and their large heat requirements, offer both these possibilities.

The burning of industrial wastes is attractive because it offers the possibility of obtaining an energy material at a cost of next to nothing, or possibly less than nothing if the energy project can get credit for the avoided costs of waste disposal. Cogeneration is attractive because it combines effective use of the high-pressure steam for generating electricity and the low-pressure steam for an industrial process. If the industrial process bears the full cost of the steam required at low pressure, then the thermal efficiency of industrial cogeneration of electricity can reach 80 percent in small installations. This is in contrast with thermal efficiencies of 35–40 percent in the most efficient thermal generation plants operated by electric utilities and less than 20 percent in smaller, lower-pressure installations.

British Columbia's pulp and paper industry is estimated to have used 28 percent of all the primary energy used in the province in 1978. Although 17 percent of this energy was supplied from the burning of wood wastes and a further 49 percent from the burning of "black liquor" (a residue produced in the preparation of kraft pulp), the industry was still by far the province's largest purchaser of electricity, natural gas, and heavy fuel oil.[1] In addition, the production of wood wastes in the province's sawmills and pulp mills is almost three times as large as the amount currently used.[2]

British Columbia thus offers a substantial potential for generation of electricity and process heat from wood wastes. A careful economic analysis of these possibilities is required for forest planners and energy planners as well as for the individual forest firms making long-term investment decisions. An additional and crucial policy element is injected by the large divergence between world energy prices and those paid by B.C. industrial users, especially for electricity and natural gas. In October 1980 the export price for B.C. natural gas was about 5.25 Canadian dollars (4.47 U.S. dollars) per thousand cubic feet (mcf), while the domestic wholesale price was $1.17/mcf and had been unchanged for three years. Electricity is being sold by B.C. Hydro, the Crown-owned utility serving most of British Columbia, to pulp and paper mills at an average price of 1.78¢/kWh— less than 65 percent of the cost of electricity from B.C. Hydro's new generation projects. A careful economic analysis of the economics of wood waste is necessary to learn whether the current energy-pricing policies are foreclosing or delaying a substantial amount of investment in the energy use of wood wastes.

These issues have been the subject of three years of modeling efforts in the University of British Columbia's Programme in Natural Resource Economics. Earlier papers have shown that, even before the 1979 doubling of world oil prices and natural gas export prices, the use of wood wastes to replace fossil fuels was highly profitable to society, although less attractive to the pulp and paper firms buying natural gas at B.C. industrial rates. The economics of electricity generation are more complicated, as they depend on boiler pressure, seasonal variation in the requirements for process steam, the costs of wood wastes (known as "hog fuel" from the "hogger" used to shred the wood wastes to the right size for burning), and the costs of fossil fuels used to improve the burning characteristics of the hog fuel.

Our initial models, applied to all the pulp and paper mills in the province, suggested that if the mills were not constrained by their existing stock of burners and boilers, if hog fuel were freely available, and if electricity were bought and sold at B.C. Hydro's cost of new projects, the mills could profitably install 1,250-psi boilers with almost 900 megawatts of capacity, with annual electricity production equal to almost 90 percent of B.C. Hydro's 1977–78 sales to all its industrial customers in British Columbia (Helliwell and Cox 1979, p. 59). That paper also showed the considerable impact of electricity pricing on the profitability of electricity generation by pulp and paper mills, and showed how the scope for profitable electricity generation projects was constrained, at least in the short run, by the existing stocks of fossil-fuel burners and low-pressure boilers. Cox and Helliwell 1980 contained a preliminary analysis of the resulting supply and demand conditions for hog fuel showing the likely incentives to transport hog fuel into the lower coast and Vancouver Island zones and a continuing surplus of hog fuel in the interior zones. Updated data have largely validated the results of Cox and Helliwell 1980 in that, of the 324 MW of unrecovered economic potential predicted, 277 MW will have been installed by 1983. (The 324 MW figure assumed generation from new power boilers at 1,250 psi, but only 600-psi boilers have been built. This makes the 324 MW figure slightly higher than would be expected. However, the 277 MW that will have been installed by 1983 also includes some potential realized from production expansions not previously accounted for.)

This chapter reports on a number of recent extensions and refinements of the model designed to analyze the economics of generating still more electricity (by the use of balance condensers and condensing generators) in areas of ample hog-fuel supply and/or seasonal heat requirements, and to permit the optimal allocation of hog fuel among competing uses, taking account of the regional distribution of the source material and the relatively high costs of transport.

## The Technological Options for Electricity Generation

Figure 1 shows the alternative ways of using steam raised in a power boiler operating at 1,250 psi. Steam at 1,250 psi containing 29,400 Btu of energy is sufficient to generate 1 kWh of electricity by a noncondensing generator. This uses 3,555 Btu of energy (and thus, since there are 3,412 Btu in a kilowatt-hour, has a thermal efficiency of $3,412/3,555 = 96\%$) (Canada 1979, p. 3-14) and leaves 25,845 Btu of energy in the steam, which is now at a temperature and a pressure (160 psi) suitable for use in the pulp-and-paper-making process and for subsequent return to the boiler. The number of kilowatt-hours of electricity per million Btu of steam delivered to process decreases as the exhaust pressure of the turbine increases. At an exhaust pressure of 60 psi, 55 kWh can be generated per million Btu delivered to process. At an exhaust pressure of 160 psi, only 40 kWh are available. Pulp and paper mills in British Columbia usually require process steam at one of these two pressures. For this chapter we have modeled the 160-psi case. Part b of figure 1 is analogous to part a and describes the 60-psi case. Clearly the 60-psi case requires less total fuel input per kWh produced. (Canada 1979, figure 3-1). If the steam is not required for process use, it can be put through a balance condenser and then returned to the boiler, as shown by option 2 in figure 1. Since there is no additional electricity generated by the balance condenser (and no productive use made of steam), the electricity generated by

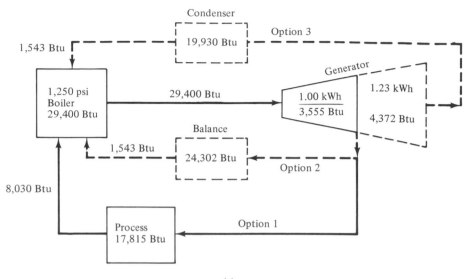

(a)

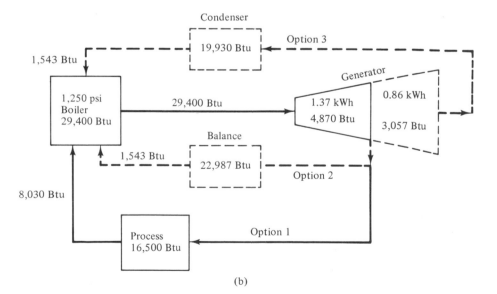

(b)

**Figure 1**
Energy balances for three electricity-generation schemes in prototype pulp mill. (a) 160-psi exhaust/extraction, (b) 60-psi exhaust/extraction.

steam that subsequently goes through the balance condenser has a thermal efficiency of only 12 percent ($= 3,412/27,857$).

Alternatively, it is possible to install a condensing turbine that offers the possibility of generating more electricity from steam that is not required for process purposes. As shown in figure 1, the additional electricity generated by the lower-pressure steam has a relatively low efficiency ($1.23 \times 3,412/24,302 = 17\%$). The combined efficiency of the high- and low-pressure segments of the condensing generator is higher ($2.23 \times 3,412/27,857 = 27\%$) than that of the noncondensing generator plus balance condenser in the handling of all steam that is not required for the pulp and paper process. If the pulp-and-paper-making process requires all the steam that is available at 160 psi, then all three generation options produce the same amount of electricity and all at the same high ($96\%$) thermal efficiency. Under these circumstances, the balance condenser (in option 2) and the lower-pressure portion of the condensing generator (in option 3) would never be used. Thus, one would expect to find option 1 to be preferred whenever the process heat requirements were seasonally stable, unless the price of electricity were high enough and the cost of fuels low enough to attract the firm to option 3.

In regions with big seasonal swings in the outside air and water temperatures, such as in the interior of British Columbia, the process heat requirements may have a substantial seasonal variation, as shown by the graph of the function $H(t)$ in figure 2. If the mill installs sufficient noncondensing generator capacity to utilize fully the noncondensing potential, the amount of additional steam required will be 3,555 Btu for each 25,845 Btu of process steam, and the total steam requirements would follow the path marked by the dotted cosine function noted as $H_1(t)$. The amount of electricity generated, $J(t)$, in megawatt-hours, is thus[3]

$$J(t) = [H_1(t) - H(t)]/3,555. \tag{1}$$

The seasonal heat requirements of the mill, coupled with the proportional relationship between cogeneration potential and heat requirements, mean that burner, boiler, and generator capital invested to take advantage of peak midwinter cogeneration potential would be to some extent underutilized throughout the rest of the year. We have modeled two of the techniques open to the firm in dealing with this investment choice. One, which we embodied in our earlier modeling, was to have the firm exogenously choose to take advantage of only a certain percentage

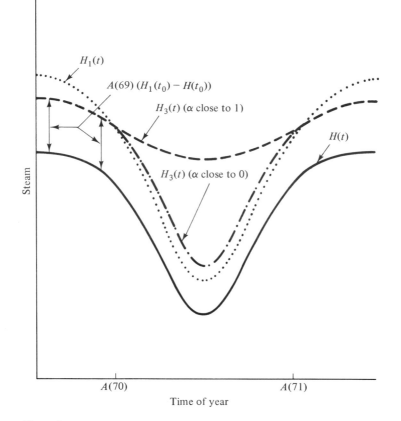

**Figure 2**
Steam-production profiles.

of the peak winter cogeneration potential. If this proportion is denoted by $A(69)$, this means that the generator would be fully utilized during all times of the year where process heat requirements exceeded a critical amount. With $H(t_0)$ representing peak seasonal process steam requirements, the generator would be fully utilized at all times when

$$H_1(t) > A(69)[H_1(t_0) - H(t_0)] + H(t). \tag{2}$$

Figure 2 shows, for an arbitrarily chosen $A(69)$ with a value of about 0.7, the dates $A(70)$ and $A(71)$ marking the inner boundaries of the periods of full utilization of the noncondensing generator. The burners and boilers do not have an equivalent period of full utilization, however, as is shown by the function $H_2(t)$, which has the following values:

$$H_2(t) = H_1(t) \qquad\qquad \text{if } A(70) < t < A(71)$$

$$= H(t) + A(69)[H_1(t_0) - H(t_0)] \text{ if } t < A(70) \text{ or } t > A(71). \tag{3}$$

Thus, the generator is fully utilized for part of the year, but the burners and boiler are still only fully utilized on the few days of peak seasonal steam requirements. The second investment option is designed to deal with this problem, as well as to obtain a still higher average utilization of the noncondensing generator. This option involves installing a balance condenser, thus permitting the generator to be run as fully as desired, with the balance condenser used to condense the excess low-pressure steam and return it to the boiler. We define a parameter $\alpha$ which measures the extent to which the generator is kept fully utilized between the dates $A(70)$ and $A(71)$. If $\alpha = 0$, then no balance condenser is installed, and the amount of electricity generated is the same as in the previous case. If $\alpha = 1$, then the generator is run at full capacity between $A(70)$ and $A(71)$, and hence all throughout the year. In general, the amount of electricity generated is determined as follows:

$$J(\alpha, t) = \frac{H_2(t) - H(t)}{3,555} + B(t) \tag{4}$$

where

$$B(t) = \alpha[H_2(A(70)) - H_2(t)]/27,857 \text{ if } A(70) < t < A(71)$$

$$= 0 \qquad\qquad\qquad \text{if } t < A(70) \text{ or } t > A(71).$$

The corresponding steam requirements, including requirements for process heat, are given by the function $H_3(t)$:

$$H_3(t) = H_2(t) + \alpha[H_2(A(70)) - H_2(t)] \text{ if } A(70) \leq t \leq A(71)$$

$$= H_2(t) \qquad\qquad\qquad \text{if } t < A(70) \text{ or } t > A(71). \qquad (5)$$

The function $H_3(t)$ is drawn in figure 2 for two example values of $\alpha$. If $\alpha$ were set equal to 1.0, the quantity of steam generated and the quantity of electricity produced would be a constant between $A(70)$ and $A(71)$. If $A(69)$ and $\alpha$ were both set equal to 1.0, the boiler and the generator would both be fully utilized throughout the year. For any value of $\alpha$ greater than zero, the amount of low-pressure steam passed through the balance condenser follows a seasonal pattern between $A(70)$ and $A(71)$ (being zero during the rest of the year) and is greatest in midsummer, when the seasonal heat requirements are least.

The third technological option is the condensing generator, which we have modeled to run all year at the full capacity of the burner and the boiler, which themselves can be set at any scale equal to or greater than the scale required to meet fully the seasonal process steam requirements with the efficient high-pressure section of the generator fully utilized and the lower pressure section not utilized at all. The amount of electricity generated is

$$J(t) = \frac{[H_1(t) - H(t)] \times 1.0}{3{,}555} + \frac{[H_1(t_0) - H_1(t)] \times 2.33}{27{,}857}$$

$$+ \frac{[H_4 - H_1(t_0)] \times 2.33}{27{,}857} \qquad\qquad\qquad (6)$$

where $H_4$ is the chosen constant level of steam produced with year-round full utilization of the burner and boiler facilities. $H_1(t)$ is, as defined in equation 2, the amount of steam required to utilize fully the potential for noncondensing generation, and $H_1(t_0)$ is the midwinter value of $H_1(t)$. The condensing generation project can therefore be thought of as three component projects: the full utilization of noncondensing potential, the use of seasonal excesses of process steam in both pressure sections of the generator, and additional use of both sections of the generator for all quantities of steam above $H_1(t_0)$.

## Economic Choice of Optimal Cogeneration

With the three cogeneration options outlined in the preceding section, the firm's investment decision involves choosing the optimal intensity of each of the options and then a preference among the three. In the next section we will show how these decisions, when considered simultaneously, can be used to define an electricity supply function for each firm. In this section we set the stage by showing how the price and cost conditions for fossil fuel, electricity, hog fuel, and capital influence the firm's decision about the optimal values for $\alpha$, $A(69)$, and the scale of condensing generation.

In the preceding section we emphasized the seasonal variations within a representative year. In this section we extend the time variation to cover the entire lifetime ($= L$ years) of the generation project. The financial analysis will be presented in terms of annual flows of income and expenditure, and the appendix to Helliwell and Margolick 1980 gives the expressions required to obtain the yearly total of inputs and outputs derived from the continuous $H(t)$ and $J(t)$ functions used in the preceding section. The present value of the project, as seen from the viewpoint of the investing firm, is given by the total present value of the electricity produced minus the cost of the additional fossil fuel, hog fuel, capital and operating expenditures, and corporation income taxes. There are four types of capital required: burners and boilers (considered together, as they are strict complements for any given steam capacity and fuel mix), noncondensing generators, balance condensers, and condensing generators. Thus, we have

$$V = \frac{\displaystyle\sum_{t=1}^{t=L}\left(Q_{Et}P_{Et} - Q_{Ht}P_{Ht} - Q_{Ft}P_{Ft} - CO_t - T_{Ct} - \sum_{j=1}^{4} P_t(r + \delta_t)K_{jt}\right)}{(1 + \rho)^t} \tag{7}$$

where the subscripts $E$, $H$, and $F$ stand for electricity, hog fuel, and fossil fuels, respectively; the $Q$s and $P$s represent quantities and prices, respectively; $T_{Ct}$ is corporation income tax paid in year $t$; $CO_t$ is operating costs in year $t$; $K_{jt}$ is the undepreciated stock of capital type $j$ in year $t$ ($j = B$ for burners and boilers, $NC$ for noncondensing generators, $BL$ for balance condensers, and $C$ for condensing generators); $\delta_t$ [$= 1/(1 + L - t)$] is the proportionate rate of depreciation in year $t$; $r$ is the after-tax cost of funds; $\rho$ is the nominal discount rate, where $1 + \rho = (1 + \dot{P}_t)$

$(1 + r)$; $\dot{P}_t$ is the proportionate rate of general inflation in year $t$; and $P_t$ is the general price level in year $t$, with value 1.0 at time $t = 0$. Equation 7 yields the private present value of an electricity-generation project. To calculate the social value, we use the social costs or opportunity values for the prices of electricity, fossil fuel, and hog fuel. $T_C$ is set equal to zero, but the rental price $r + \delta$ is augmented by $r_T = 0.03$, an estimate of the average corporation tax collected from capital invested in Canada.

The choice of optimal values for $\alpha$ and $A(69)$, which between them imply the choice of noncondensing generators and balance condensers, is done by constructing present-value equivalents (denoted by a tilde) of the main elements of equation 7. If we ignore the dynamic complexities posed by the nonindexing of the corporation income tax, it is possible to define present values for the equal annual flows of electricity and fuels and present-value-weighted prices for any prices that grow at constant rates. With operating costs and taxes ignored, the project can be evaluated in present-value terms as follows:

$$V = \tilde{Q}_E \tilde{P}_E - \tilde{Q}_H \tilde{P}_H - \tilde{Q}_F \tilde{P}_F - K_j. \tag{8}$$

The optimization proceeds with a choice of the optimal value of $\alpha$ for any given value of $A(69)$, and choosing the optimal value of $A(69)$. Because increasing the value of $\alpha$ for any given value of $A(69)$ involves adding only one type of capital (the balance condenser), the effects on the present value for any given pattern of prices can be expressed as follows:

$$\frac{\partial V}{\partial \alpha} = \frac{\partial \tilde{Q}_E}{\partial \alpha} \tilde{P}_E - \frac{\partial \tilde{Q}_H}{\partial \alpha} \tilde{P}_H - \frac{\partial \tilde{Q}_F}{\partial \alpha} \tilde{P}_F - \frac{\partial K_{BL}}{\partial \alpha}. \tag{9}$$

As shown in the appendix to Helliwell and Margolick 1980, $\partial \tilde{Q}_E/\partial \alpha$ is a constant. The same is true of $\partial \tilde{Q}_H/\partial \alpha$ and $\partial \tilde{Q}_F/\partial \alpha$, since each unit of extra electricity produced has the same extra steam requirement and hence implies the same additional amount of fuels. $\partial K_{BL}/\partial \alpha$ decreases as $\alpha$ increases, because the capital cost function for the balance condenser implies that the cost of the condenser increases by 0.6 percent for each 1 percent increase in capacity.

In the absence of any induced changes in the prices of wood waste and other energy, equation 9 can be expressed more simply as

$$\frac{\partial V}{\partial \alpha} = a - b\alpha^{-0.4} \tag{10}$$

where $a$ and $b$ are constants. This shows that $\partial V/\partial \alpha$ increases as $\alpha$ increases, which means that for any given values of $A(69)$ and energy prices it is necessary to calculate $V$ only for $\alpha = 0$ and $\alpha = 1.0$ and choose whichever of the two $\alpha$ values gives the higher $V$. We assume throughout this chapter that the prices of electricity and fossil fuel are independent of the scale of the electricity project, but the same may not be true of the price of hog fuel. If the cost of acquiring hog fuel increases with the quantity, the possibility arises that $V$ may have a peak value for $\alpha$ with some value between 0 and 1.0. This is not very likely, since the amount of hog fuel required is not large, but there is a simple way of finding out. Since (as shown below) $P_H$ rises uniformly with $\sqrt{Q_H}$, we can infer that if any $\alpha$ arbitrarily close to 1.0 has a lower $V$ than $\alpha = 1.0$, and if

$$V\big|_{\alpha=1.0} > V\big|_{\alpha=0},$$

then $\alpha = 1.0$ has a higher $V$ than any value of $\alpha$ below 1.0. We use $\alpha = 0.97$ for our test, and if it produces a lower $V$ than $\alpha = 1.0$ we can choose $\alpha = 1.0$ or $\alpha = 0$ without further concern. If $\alpha = 0.97$ produces a higher $V$ than either $\alpha = 1.0$ or $\alpha = 0$, then a search must be undertaken for the optimal $\alpha$.

Solving for the optimal $A(69)$ is more complex. The first-order conditions for optimal $A(69)$ require

$$\frac{\partial V}{\partial A(69)} = \frac{\partial \tilde{Q}_E}{\partial A(69)} \tilde{P}_E - \frac{\partial \tilde{Q}_H}{\partial A(69)} \tilde{P}_H - \frac{\partial \tilde{P}_H}{\partial A(69)} \tilde{Q}_H - \frac{\partial \tilde{Q}_F}{\partial A(69)} \tilde{P}_F - \frac{\partial K_j}{\partial A(69)}. \tag{11}$$

In this expression we have made explicit the induced variation in $\tilde{P}_H$, in recognition of the greater probability that it might be materially altered by changes in $A(69)$. There are either two or three types of capital required for changing $A(69)$: burners and boilers, noncondensing generators, and balance condensers (if the optimal $\alpha$ is greater than zero). The empirically based cost functions for burners and boilers and for noncondensing generators involve regions of both increasing and decreasing returns to scale, so there is a real possibility of multiple local maxima for the $V$ function for values of $A(69)$ between 0 and 1.0. For $\alpha = 1$, $\partial \tilde{Q}_E/\partial A(69)$, $\partial \tilde{Q}_H/\partial A(69)$, and $\partial \tilde{Q}_F/A(69)$ are all constants, whereas for $\alpha = 0$ they are complex expressions that decrease as $A(69)$ increases. We therefore compute $V$ using equation 8 for all values of $A(69)$ between 0 and 1.0.

In solving for the optimal scale of condenser generation, $A(55)$, we have an expression analogous to equation 9 to determine the variation in $V$ with changes in capacity:

$$\frac{\partial V}{\partial A(55)} = \frac{\partial \tilde{Q}_E}{\partial A(55)} \tilde{P}_E - \frac{\partial \tilde{Q}_H}{\partial A(55)} \tilde{P}_H - \frac{\partial \tilde{P}_H}{\partial A(55)} \tilde{Q}_H - \frac{\partial \tilde{Q}_F}{\partial A(55)} \tilde{P}_F - \frac{\partial K_C}{\partial A(55)}. \tag{12}$$

In this case $\partial \tilde{Q}_E/\partial A(55)$, $\partial \tilde{Q}_H/\partial A(55)$, and $\partial \tilde{Q}_F/\partial A(55)$ are all constants, while $\partial K_C/\partial A(55)$ declines as $A(55)$ rises because the costs of condensing generators are taken to be subject to increasing returns throughout. Thus, for $A(55)$ great enough to let the costs for burners and boilers enter their final increasing-returns phase, $\partial V/\partial A(55)$ increases with $A(55)$ in the absence of induced increases in the cost of hog fuel, $\tilde{P}_H$. Our modeling of the hog-fuel supply assumes that the hog fuel required for electricity generation is incremental to that required for process steam. However, there is assumed to be a quantity of wood wastes generated on site, so there may actually be a net surplus of wood waste on site even after we allow for fossil-fuel replacement in the generation of process steam. The quantity of hog fuel needed for generation thus comprises a (possible) constant amount available locally plus an amount that must be transported from elsewhere. For simplicity, we assume that the timber and the sawmill sites are distributed evenly (with density $D$) in the area surrounding the pulp mill and can be transported to the mill at a cost of $A(149)$ dollars per mile per unit ($= 200$ cubic feet) of hog fuel.

If each unit of hog fuel has an opportunity cost of $A(151)$ dollars per unit and a direct cost of handling (unless it is available on site) of $A(155)$ dollars per unit, the marginal costs of hog fuel are

$$\frac{\partial (P_H Q_H)}{\partial Q_H} = A(149) \left(\frac{Q_H}{\pi D}\right)^{1/2} + A(155) + A(151). \tag{13}$$

Thus, the marginal costs rise continuously with the square root of the quantity used. Since hog-fuel costs rise at an increasing rate, while capital costs decline at a decreasing rate (since they are bounded by zero), we are assured of finding a determinate solution to the firm's optimal electricity investment decision even in the presence of economies of scale in capital costs.

## Deriving Supply Functions for Electricity

The optimization model we have developed can be applied in several different ways. In this chapter we emphasize the impact of average electricity prices and hog-fuel prices on the firm's optimal decision as seen from the viewpoint of society as a whole, rather than the impacts of alternative electricity rate structures and corporation income taxes. Our main emphasis is on how the nature and scale of optimal electricity generation varies with the value of the electricity generated and the value of hog fuel in alternative uses.

Our results are based on a fairly typical interior mill with 600 tons per day of kraft pulp capacity and a winter process heat requirement 1.35 times the summer requirement. This means that the mill has a peak winter noncondensing potential of 23 MW, sufficient to produce 190 GWh (gigawatt-hours) per year with $A(69)$ and $\alpha$ both equal to 1.0.

Figure 3 shows the supply curves based on optimal project selection with three different values for $A(151)$, the opportunity cost of hog fuel. The electricity prices shown on the vertical axis are average prices that use a load factor of 84 percent and estimates of marginal capacity and energy costs in the B.C. Hydro system. The rate structure is unimportant in our current experiments because we alter the average price of electricity by means of equiproportionate changes in capacity and energy charges.

In the curve closest to the horizontal axis in figure 3, there are assumed to be no profitable alternative uses for hog fuel (fossil-fuel replacement to the assumed maximum extent has been given a prior claim on the hog-fuel supplies). The costs of transport and handling amount to only $1.15/unit in the smallest noncondensing project. In the largest condensing project assessed (560 GWh of total electricity production) the marginal cost of hog fuel is $3.41/unit and the average cost $2.37/unit. These modest increases in cost are based on estimated trucking costs and an assumed density of hog fuel equal to the average density in the interior regions of the province. Because the hog-fuel costs do not rise rapidly, the economies of scale in capital dominate the rising marginal cost of hog fuel over the range of project sizes depicted in figure 3. As a consequence of this, the supply curves tend to be very elastic at electricity prices high enough to make the value of a condensing project exceed the value of the best noncondensing projects.

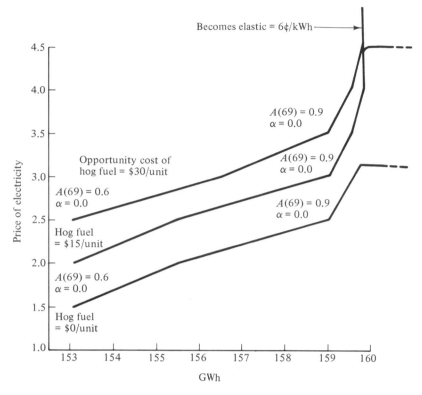

**Figure 3**
Optimal electricity supply curves.

The middle supply curve shows results based on a $15/unit opportunity value for hog fuel, while the curve farthest from the horizontal axis is based on a competing use with a value of $30/unit. The elastic portions of these curves occur at higher electricity prices, because the energy-efficient noncondensing projects dominate the condenser projects for longer when there is a higher opportunity cost for hog fuel.

At our estimated value of the marginal cost of electricity to B.C. Hydro (about 2.8¢/kWh), the optimal project (with a zero opportunity value for hog fuel) involves $A(69) = 0.9$ and $\alpha = 0$. The project has a net present value of $23.0 million. At lower prices the optimal $A(69)$ drops and the optimal $\alpha$ remains at zero. At higher prices the optimal $A(69)$ approaches 1.0 and the condensing generation takes over without optimal $\alpha$ ever being greater than zero. This same pattern reappears in the supply curves that assume higher opportunity values for hog fuel. It is to be expected that the energy-inefficient but capital-efficient balance condenser option would be ruled out when hog fuel has valuable alternative uses. Why does this also happen when hog fuel is very cheap? For the optimization reported in figure 3, the firm is making the socially optimal choices and is thus taking into account the export price rather than the domestic price for natural gas. The 15 percent natural-gas proportion in the burning mix means that the total expenditure on natural gas is three times the expenditure on hog fuel. When $\alpha$ is raised from 0 to 1.0 in the 2.8¢/kWh case mentioned above, with $A(69) = 0.90$, the total present value of electricity produced rises by \$5.8 million (an increase of about 14 percent) but the total present value of natural gas used rises by over \$8 million. The cost of hog fuel rises, in this case, from \$0.7 to \$1.6 million, while the cost of capital rises only from \$6.8 to \$6.9 million. Thus, if the firm paid less than the export price of natural gas, or if the burning mix could be adjusted to reduce the use of natural gas, then optimal $\alpha$ could well become 1.0 rather than 0.0. Indeed we find this to be the case when we undertake the private optimization, where we find optimal $\alpha$ sometimes to be 1.0 and sometimes to be less.

## Summary and New Directions

In this chapter we have developed and applied techniques for choosing optimally the scale and nature of electricity generation in pulp and paper mills with seasonal heat requirements. By using explicit modeling of three alternative technologies and their related cost functions, we are able to prepare electricity supply functions based on optimal project selection for any given pattern of prices for electricity, fossil fuels, and hog fuel.

One of the most interesting issues in investment analysis is how to model the optimal investment decision for the price-taking firm facing technological options with increasing returns to scale. This phenomenon arose in the case of balancing condensers and condensing generators, although not for the degree of utilization of noncondensing potential. In the case of balance condensers the increasing returns to scale raise no basic problems, because the feasible scale of the investment is in any case limited by the noncondensing potential and the degree of seasonality in the heat requirements.

In the case of condensing generators, however, the presence of increasing returns would have led to an infinite desired scale of investment for electricity prices higher than some critical value. We dealt with this issue by introducing an explicit hog-fuel cost function that embodies higher marginal transport costs as the volume of hog fuel used increases. This guarantees a determinate optimal scale for condensing generation, although our preliminary estimates of hog-fuel density and transport costs imply a fairly high elasticity of optimal scale with respect to electricity prices.

By introducing a spatial element into the optimal choice of scale, we have made the necessary first steps toward an integrated regional analysis of the various competing uses for wood wastes. Our list of promising directions for further development includes the following:

electricity supply functions based on alternative investment decision rules,

integration of the firm-specific optimization models in a spatial model including geographically dispersed point sources of wood waste (e.g., sawmills), competing point uses of wood waste (e.g., particle-board production), and the potential for gathering increasing quantities of wood waste during logging and clearing operations,

the analysis of alternative burning technologies, especially those (such as fluidized-bed combustion and the predrying of hog fuel) that permit reduction in the amount of fossil fuels included in the burning mixture,

extending the regional optimization model to include the optimal choice of the output mix and location for new mills,[4]

closer analysis of the economics of alternative boiler pressures,[5] and

extending the analysis to choose the optimal scrapping and change over dates in cases where the existing boiler pressures, generator sizes, and burner mixes are suboptimal.

## Acknowledgments

The authors are grateful for comments, especially from Don Dewees and Michael Davies, on an earlier version presented to the Canadian Economics Association in May 1980. A longer version of the paper, with appendix material, is available as Helliwell and Margolick 1980. The research was financed by the Social Science and Humanities Research Council of Canada through its support of the Programme in Natural Resource Economics at the University of British Columbia.

# Notes

1. The pulp and paper industry buys 17% of the province's purchased electricity, 16% of natural gas, and 10% of refined petroleum products, based on tables 4.28 and 9.3 of Province of British Columbia 1980.

2. According to Province of British Columbia 1980, the 1978 wood wastes supply was 192 petajoules (p. 4-42) and the amount used for energy was 69 petajoules (p. 4-67).

3. In this chapter the units for $H(t)$ are taken to be thousands of Btu. This simple exposition ignores the complications posed by the nonseasonal steam production from the recovery boilers, which usually are operated at 650 psi and sometimes have noncondensing generators attached. In the model, this entails appropriate adjustments to all the functions determining steam requirements and cogeneration potential.

4. This is important because the output mix has a large impact on the electricity and heat requirements, and hence on the cogeneration potential, while the location affects the amount of chips and hog fuel available with minimum transportation costs.

5. This will require better information about the costs, safety, and operating characteristics of boilers with pressures above 1,250 psi.

# Bibliography

Canada Department of Energy, Mines, and Resources. 1979. Study of Potential for Co-generation in Canada. Industry Series, report 1.

Cox, A. J., and J. F. Helliwell. 1980. Economic modelling of energy supply from burning wood wastes at B.C. pulp and paper mills. In W. T. Ziemba et al., eds., *Energy Policy Modeling: U.S. and Canadian Experiences.* Hingham, Mass.: Martinus Nijhoff, 1980.

Helliwell, J. F., and A. J. Cox. 1979. Electricity pricing and electricity supply: The influence of utility pricing on electricity production by pulp and paper mills. *Resources and Energy* 2: 51–74.

Helliwell, J. F., and M. Margolick. 1980. Some Hard Economics Of Soft Energy: Optimal Electricity Generation In Pulp And Paper Mills with Seasonal Steam Requirements. Resources Paper 56, Department of Economics, University of British Columbia.

Province of British Columbia. 1980. British Columbia Energy Supply and Requirements Forecast, 1979–1990. Technical report of Ministry of Energy, Mines, and Petroleum Resources.

# IV APPLIED MACROECONOMICS: NATIONAL

# 12 Economic Management and Aggregate Supply

R. J. Ball

Thirty years divides the publication of Lawrence Klein's *The Keynesian Revolution* (1947) and his 1977 presidential address to the American Economic Association (Klein 1978). The first exemplifies Keynesian economics in a way that was to become standard in the literature, emphasising the importance of effective demand and the guide to economic policy making that the general theoretical apparatus appeared to provide. The second sounded new notes of caution. Despite the belief that over this period we have come a long way professionally,

The economic problems of today seem to be intractable when studied through the medium of simplified macro models. The new system should combine the Keynesian model of final demand and income determination with Leontief model of interindustrial flows. This is the motivation for ... focusing attention on the supply side of the economy. (Klein 1978, p. 1)

The focus of attention shifts from effective demand to considerations of supply.

The above quotation suggests that the problem is one of adding more detailed modeling of the individual sectors of the economy to what we know about the behavior of effective demand. It is clear that this is of importance in its own right in generating additional information and in attempting to impose consistency and feasibility on the behavior of the economic aggregates. Moreover, it is arguable that specific problems have arisen, such as that of energy, which require explicit treatment if the limits to stabilization policy are to be defined.

However, even within more traditional frameworks of thought, there remains disagreement about the interaction of aggregate demand and supply as opposed to problems of consistency at the industrial level, particularly in the United Kingdom. Characteristically, aggregate supply has been thought of largely in physical rather than economic terms, and what has appeared as measured unemployment and spare physical capacity has been seen as a signal for the active expansion of monetary demand. The labor market has received little or no attention, and there has been a general presumption that the achievement of a rate of unemployment desired by government is not inhibited by the behavior of real wages. Concurrently, until recently, little or no importance had been assigned to the behavior of the monetary aggregates and monetary policy generally.

In the United States, on the other hand, aggregate supply phenomena and the significance of monetary policy in relation to inflation, as well as to output and employment, have long been recognized. There the debate shifted some years ago to the general desirability and feasibility of discretionary stabilization policy (see, for example, Modigliani 1977 and Sargent and Wallace 1976).

This chapter addresses these problems, essentially in a British context. I begin with some discussion of the labor market and then go on to examine the limits to demand-management policies aimed at the level of output and employment. Finally, I make some observations on the role of aggregate supply as it affects the interpretation of current controversies relating to the problem of the underlying rate of economic growth in the United Kingdom.

## The Labor Market

The neoclassical theory of output and employment, both in the closed and in the open economy, has been much discussed, recently at length by Beenstock (1980). In the long run the levels of output and employment are determined by the supply and demand for labor. Labor markets are efficient, and exogenous shifts in demand that alter the balance of supply and demand in the labor market will be equilibrated by variations in real wages. If aggregate demand is stabilized, then neoclassical models of this kind will have the property that, in the long run, for a given capital stock and technology, the aggregate supply schedule in the sense of Keynes, relating the level of output to the aggregate price level, will become perfectly inelastic. Full employment is thus in principle defined as the level of employment that clears the market, which will be influenced by underlying changes affecting both the demand and the supply of labor.

The criticisms of neoclassical labor-market theory have been many and varied. At the outset it is important to distinguish the arguments that concern primarily the speed of adjustment in the labor market from those that are more fundamental. Moreover, the prime concerns of the critical parties may vary. In the majority of cases the concern is essentially with the delineation of the limits of and possibilities for discretionary stabilization policy, but in some there is a concern to discredit the efficient operation of the labor market in either the short run or the long run as part of a general theory of market failure in the capitalist economy.

It is not difficult to produce plausible reasons why, in the general framework of the neoclassical model, real wage adjustments to an imbalance in the labor market might be expected to be slow in relation to the political horizons of the economic authorities. Nominal wages are likely to be sticky, at least downward, in part because of the contractual nature of agreements and in part for reasons embedded in social behavior or enforced by trade-union monopoly. In the face of recession, workers may be unwilling to attempt to undercut existing employed workers, maintaining some form of social solidarity, while employers may be unwilling to employ such labor at lower rates for fear of longer-run consequences for labor relations. In any case, the general power of trade unions and the existence of the closed shop could prevent any willingness to work at reduced wages without trade-union compliance. The existence of substantial unemployment compensation and associated benefits would in general be expected to slow down the process of real wage adjustment for those employed. After periods of persistent labor shortage, such as existed for much of the postwar period, employers may have been more prepared to absorb temporary setbacks through reduced profits rather than intensive pressure on the level of wage settlements. Moreover, the behavior of wages and the speed of adjustment will be markedly affected by the state of expectations of both management and the employed. If the disturbance to demand is thought to be temporary in a significant sense, either because of expected action by government to promptly offset it or for some other reason, real wage adjustment will not be thought appropriate by either side. For all these and perhaps for other reasons, one should hardly be surprised to observe substantial stickiness in the behavior of real wages since the war, given the size of the disturbances observed for much of the period. This has led to a belief in a relatively long period of adjustment in the labor market relative to the political time horizon.

In itself, this conclusion neither validates nor invalidates the exercise of discretionary stabilization policy. Even if in the long run the labor market clears and the effects of monetary expansion are neutral, it has been argued that the time scale of the adjustment is such as to provide scope for the authorities to beneficially offset demand shocks (see, for example, Modigliani 1977). If, on the other hand, expectations are formed rationally, then it is argued that the fact that the time scale of adjustment is perceived to be long is irrelevant (Beenstock 1980), for in this case the key question is whether the path of adjustment is optimal, not how long it takes. The fact that full employment is appropriately defined as the long-run equilibrium position to which the labor market will move does not in itself destroy the case for intervention, but neither do the facts that real wages are sticky and that there are considerable lags in the adjustment process constitute a *prima facie* case for intervention.

A more fundamental challenge to neoclassical labor-market theory stems from the literature examining the nature and possibility of non-Walrasian market equilibria (surveyed in Drazen 1980). The possible significance of wage and price rigidity in distinguishing between Keynesian and neoclassical theory has of course long been recognized (see, for example, Modigliani 1948). In more recent times, starting from the model of Barro and Grossman (1971), increasing attention has been paid to the argument that the Walrasian framework of market clearing and the competitive assumptions that underlie it may be inappropriate.

In this context it is important to note two things. The first is that we must distinguish between the argument just rehearsed (which suggests that there may be reasons for expecting wage and price stickiness coupled with delays in market clearing) and the notion that in some sense the market never clears at all. In the former case, involuntary unemployment and disequilibrium may persist for some time, but are in a significant sense temporary; the latter seeks to establish the existence of a permanent equilibrium in which quantity constraints exist and which, in the case of unemployment, can be eliminated by an increase in monetary demand. The second is that, following Barro and Grossman, it is of course easy to show that, if nominal prices and wages are fixed, virtually by definition equilibrium can only be established, if at all, through quantity adjustments. This simply stands the neoclassical argument on its head. In neoclassical analysis, output is effectively fixed in the long run, so that all that monetary expansion can do is to affect prices. If wages and prices are fixed, all it can do is affect quantity—a comparison reminiscent of Friedman's remarks concerning the missing equation (see Friedman 1970 and Ball 1977). But, as Drazen has pointed out, "The main question, however, is not what happens when prices don't move, but *why* prices don't move. The effects of exogenous price rigidity are clear." (Drazen 1980, p. 286) On this, the results to date, even at a purely theoretical level, are not wholly convincing.

The third view, as exemplified by the Cambridge Economic Policy

Group in the United Kingdom, not only dismisses the role of labor-market adjustment in a neoclassical sense but also explicitly eschews any attempt to rationalize real wage rigidity. Workers are assumed to attempt to adjust nominal wages to a target real wage. Cripps and Godley (1976, p. 342) have argued that "the factors determining the target real wage cannot be formulated with any precision. In particular, it has not been perceptibly influenced by the level of unemployment." Elsewhere, Godley (1977, p.467) has written "There is, in my opinion, no valid general theory—at least one applicable to the United Kingdom—that defines a set of forces governing wage inflation; there is no equilibrium rate of increase in wage rates .... My suggestion is that the rate of wage inflation will be changed quite simply, whenever there is widespread pressure to change it. The going rate has only a weak inertia that may be readily shoved from one position to another." The levels of both the nominal and the real wage are left hanging in midair, suspended by their own bootstraps.

But from a practical point of view, apart from other criticisms of the Cambridge position, it is hard to believe that the level of employment does not depend on the going level of real wages, at least at some point. If, for the sake of argument, the real wage is kept rigid by trade-union monopoly power, there will be a limit to the amount of employment that firms will be able to offer profitably at the given real wage level independent of the level of monetary demand. In such a model, as exemplified in Corden 1978, Keynesian unemployment (in the sense of a lack of monetary demand) and classical unemployment (in the sense of a real wage in excess of that required to elicit the employment level that government may seek to determine) may coexist. The Keynesian unemployment can of course be eliminated by demand management, and the classical unemployment cannot. Most Keynesian analyses beg the question and ignore the possibility of classical unemployment. Implicit in the Corden model is the familiar L-shaped aggregate supply curve, but the vertical part of the curve is not determined by physical constraints but by the level of real wages. From the viewpoint of practical demand management, the question whether the point of zero inelasticity of aggregate supply is determined in this way or by equilibrium in the labor market is of less significance than the general point that the attainable level of stable employment is not independent of the level of real wages. In an upward direction, it all comes to the same thing in practice—namely, where that point actually is. The accumulated evidence from demand management in the United Kingdom's economy suggests that the authorities have consistently underestimated the supply constraint imposed upon them.

Despite the obvious importance of the subject matter, it is perhaps remarkable that so many strong conclusions with regard to the working of the labor market and the role of demand management have been drawn on the basis of *a priori* reasoning rather than empirical evidence. Empirical work in the United Kingdom was originally directed at attempts to estimate the Phillips curve, which after the mid-1960s ran up against the formidable difficulty of accounting for inflationary expectations. The case for demand management, whether supplemented by incomes policies, import controls, or both, was related back to the behavior of the underlying rate of growth of productive potential, which was in large measure determined exogenously. Early work by Ball and St. Cyr (1966) popularized employment functions in which output and exogenously given technical progress substantially determined employment behavior such that variations around the underlying trend of employment were largely accounted for by the behavior of aggregate demand. These sorts of employment function appeared in a variety of econometric models. More recently, versions of this model have been combined with forecasts of aggregate output and extrapolations of the behavior of the supply of labor to yield unemployment projections into the 1980s, as exemplified in Cripps, Featherston, and Ward 1978 and Leicester 1977. On occasion these relatively mechanical projections have suggested massive and increasing unemployment in the United Kingdom through the 1980s and into the 1990s on the basis of unchanged policies. Such projections have been followed by demands for import controls and protection.

However, an attempt to estimate the structure of labor-market behavior derived essentially from a neoclassical labor-market theory has been reported in Beenstock 1979 and Beenstock and Warburton 1980. For the purposes of estimation, data for the period 1948–1977 were used. The basic approach was to derive equilibrium real wage and employment functions under the alternative assumptions of profit maximization and cost minimization, whose principle initial arguments were the level of output and the working population, representing arguments of the demand and supply equations respectively. To this was added a specification of disequilibrium behavior and additional variables tested, such as the female participation rate, a measure of unemployment benefit, other employment costs such as national insurance, and a measure of the real cost of capital. The statistical estimates suggested that the behavior of real wages and employment since World War II could reasonably be accounted for by a model of this type.

Simulations from the Beenstock-Warburton model suggest that predictions of unemployment made by other models, given what might be agreed forecasts for the behavior of output, are much exaggerated. It has been forecast that unemployment in the United Kingdom could top 4 million in the 1980s. A set of calculations based on the Beenstock-Warburton model is given in table 1. Figures for the rate of growth of the gross domestic product up to 1983 were taken from forecasts made at the time of writing by the London Business School. For 1984 onward, the consequences of a relatively modest 2 percent average rate of economic growth are considered. As the table shows, although the level of unemployment shows little change between 1981 and 1986, it falls rapidly in the following four years. Given the fixed rate of growth of output, the dominant influence in all this is clearly the rate of growth of the working population. On the basis of these tentative calculations,

**Table 1**
Unemployment simulation for Great Britain, 1980–1990.

|  | Gross domestic product, % change[a] | Population, % change[b] | Employment, % change[a] | Unemployment Great Britain, M[a] |
|---|---|---|---|---|
| 1979 | 1.7 | 0.46 | 0.7 | 1.33 |
| 1980 | −1.9 | 0.48 | −0.9 | 1.62 |
| 1981 | −0.1 | 0.56 | −0.7 | 1.90 |
| 1982 | 2.0 | 0.64 | −0.2 | 2.12 |
| 1983 | 2.1 | 0.69 | 0.7 | 2.15 |
| 1984 | 2.0 | 0.41 | 1.4 | 1.95 |
| 1985 | 2.0 | 0.22 | −0.3 | 2.06 |
| 1986 | 2.0 | 0.12 | 0.6 | 1.96 |
| 1987 | 2.0 | 0.08 | 1.6 | 1.59 |
| 1988 | 2.0 | −0.06 | 1.6 | 1.20 |
| 1989 | 2.0 | −0.07 | 1.1 | 0.92 |
| 1990 | 2.0 | −0.07 | −0.5 | 1.01 |

Sources:
a. Derived from equation in Beenstock and Warburton 1980.
b. Interpolation of official projections, *Annual Abstract*.

it is unfortunate that the fall in output in the early part of the period is followed by an acceleration in the rate of increase in the working population. The sharp fall in unemployment toward the end of the decade results almost entirely from the deceleration in the rate of growth of the working population. If the assumption for the growth of gross domestic product is reduced to 1 percent, it is estimated that the unemployment rate in 1990 would stand at about 1.75 million, having peaked at 2.3 million in 1986.

Some rough idea of the efficiency of the labor market, given the underlying specification of the Beenstock-Warburton model, can be gained from figure 1. This graph compares the actual behavior of employment against the steady-state level of employment implied at each moment of time for the level of output prevailing, and shows that, given the historical character of the output shocks, employment can depart for considerable periods of time from its equilibrium value. Other simulation results make it clear that this model, estimated from United Kingdom data, exemplifies the view that the adjustment period is long

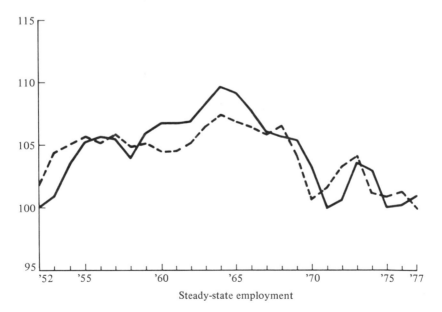

**Figure 1**
Actual unemployment (solid line) versus steady-state unemployment (broken line) implied at each moment of time for level of output prevailing. (1975 = 100.)

in relation to the political time horizon. For the period as a whole, Beenstock and Warburton (1980, p. 17) conclude that "although disequilibrium processes were undoubtedly at work, and institutional and legislative powers over agents in the United Kingdom labor market did increase, there still appears to be evidence of an active labor market."

As emphasised above, the fact that the adjustment process on this evidence has to be measured in years rather than months does not in itself mitigate in favor of or against discretionary demand management. However, it is at least consistent with the important general view I have emphasized: that the equilibrium level of employment is not independent of real wage behavior.

## Discretionary Stabilization Policy

The debate on the role of discretionary stabilization policy has turned on a number of central analytical questions, the first of which relates to the neutrality of either expansionary fiscal policy or expansionary monetary policy. As noted above, the existence of neutrality, at least in the medium term, when starting from a position of equilibrium in the labor market, does not in general rule out some form of intervention if the economy finds itself in disequilibrium. Its existence, however, when combined with some degree of optimism with regard to the stability of employment equilibrium once it has been established, suggests both caution in undertaking interventionary policies and the possibility of substantial economic limits to the power of such policies to determine arbitrarily chosen levels of output and employment. In some respects the debate, if taken to its logical conclusion, is likely to miss the point. The question at issue is not simply whether neutrality holds or not. As remarked on by Buiter (1980, p. 39), shifts in fiscal policy reflecting changes in tax policy or changes in government spending are unlikely ever to be completely neutral. Even in the neoclassical world, changes in tax rates may alter the tradeoff between work and leisure, while shifts in the level and pattern of public spending may have direct effects on the underlying rate of productive potential. The important questions are whether the real world is more or less like the models of neoclassical theory and whether, in practice, fiscal and monetary expansion is likely to feed relatively rapidly into prices and the balance of payments (an outcome that depends crucially on the elasticity of supply in the short and the medium term).

The debate between monetarists and Keynesians has also focused on the question as to the nature of pure fiscal policy effects given alterations in the fiscal stance coupled with no change in the supply of money. In empirical terms, the question has been whether the effects of changes in fiscal policy are small and relatively transitory compared with shifts in the real stock of money. This has of course led to the attempts to construct appropriate measures of the fiscal stance, as discussed for example by Blinder and Solow (1973) within a general Keynesian framework. It is, however, extremely doubtful that the debate cast in this form is really worthwhile once we recognize the important point that monetary and fiscal policy are inextricably linked through the portfolio behavior of those who are holders of government debt and nominal money. In general, fiscal policy is likely to have monetary effects. Given the constraints imposed by the portfolio behavior of wealth holders, there exists an underlying symmetry which could be expressed equally well by saying that deficit spending tends to lead to the creation of money or that increases in the supply of money will tend to require deficit spending.

In the case of the United Kingdom, it has been argued by Budd and Burns (1978) that, as an empirical matter, variations in the change in the money supply have been dominated by changes in the fiscal deficit in the medium term. The change in the money supply is identically equal to the government borrowing requirement plus additional net lending by the banks plus the sales of public-sector debt to the public. The net stocks of the last two items, it is argued, are empirically associated with the behavior of interest rates and income, although the flow behavior may be erratic in the short run (see Beenstock and Longbottom 1980). Moreover, over the cycle, the behavior of bank lending and debt purchases tend to be offsetting, with the result that the medium-term growth of the money supply has been substantially determined by the government's borrowing requirements. Over the cycle, of course, the relationship between the borrowing requirement and monetary growth shifts. As a result of the existence of the automatic stabilizers, the fiscal deficit in the recession would be expected to rise without inducing a corresponding increase in the rate of monetary growth. Budd and Burns apply their estimates to the adjustment of the observed fiscal deficit for the effects

**Table 2**
Adjusted financial surplus and growth of the real-money stock.

|      | Adjusted financial surplus (% of gross domestic product) | Growth of real-money stock (annual rate) |
|------|------|------|
| 1964 | −3.6 | 3.1 |
| 1965 | −2.5 | 1.7 |
| 1966 | −1.8 | 2.0 |
| 1967 | −2.8 | 3.1 |
| 1968 | −3.5 | 3.7 |
| 1969 | 0.7 | −1.5 |
| 1970 | 3.4 | 0 |
| 1971 | 2.6 | 2.4 |
| 1972 | −0.4 | 13.2 |
| 1973 | −3.4 | 15.5 |
| 1974 | −1.2 | −2.2 |
| 1975 | 0.5 | −12.9 |
| 1976 | −1.9 | −8.5 |
| 1977 | 0.3 | −4.6 |

Source: Budd and Burns 1978.

of inflation and output to obtain the equivalent effect on demand corresponding to zero inflation and the trend level of output. As shown in table 2, this produces the result that change in the monetary aggregate constitutes a relatively efficient measure of the overall fiscal stance, since the output and inflation effects are automatically contained in the monetary measure. In practice, therefore, the dispute as to whether it is fiscal or monetary policy that is in some sense effective is not particularly meaningful in the medium term. Moreover, recognition of the portfolio effects of the fiscal deficit imposes limits on the behavior of the fiscal deficit under equilibrium conditions. In the stationary state, a stable ratio of wealth to income and an equilibrium asset distribution, consistent with zero inflation and zero output growth, would require the fiscal deficit to be zero. In the case of zero inflation and a steady rate of growth of output, the optimal fiscal deficit is unlikely to be zero since there will be a growing demand for new money and government securities along the growth path consistent with zero inflation and stable nominal interest rates.

Though this debate may be less important than it sometimes appears, discretionary fiscal and monetary policy has been challenged on the assumption that expectations are formed rationally. Under certain specifications, the combination of the natural rate hypothesis and Muth-rational expectations produces the result of superneutrality where, even in the short run, no output effects follow a monetary expansion (Sargent and Wallace 1976). However, it is easy to show (see, for example, Shiller 1978 and Beenstock 1980) that the conclusion about superneutrality is not robust with regard to the specification. It must be regarded as something of a curiosum. More generally, risk aversion combined with some degree of market imperfection can—even if labor-market adjustment is of a neoclassical type—result in considerable lags. In this case, the argument against discretionary fiscal and monetary policy turns on the optimality of the adjustment path. If expectations are formed rationally, then, it is argued, the attempt by the authorities to guide the economy back to equilibrium still requires the existence of market failure to be demonstrated in the sense that the path secured by intervention is more optimal than that which the market finds for itself, irrespective of the length of the adjustment period.

The key issues relating to rational expectations concern the nature of market failure and the actual process by which market expectations are formed. Market imperfections and their possible effects on the limits to discretionary stabilization policy have already been discussed in the last section. If the relevant economic model is as a result of market failure strictly non-neutral in character, the existence of rational expectations loses much of its significance in a macroeconomic context. If rational expectations are narrowly defined in the sense of Muth 1961 to mean the predictions from the relevant economic model, there arises the obvious question of how economic agents know what this is. In some cases where the hypothesis has proved useful, as in the case of speculative markets, the models used are often limited and all information is easily available to participants in the market. It is, however, open to question how far economic agents can make structured sense of the economy as a whole. The intuitive counterargument seems to turn on the question of why one should believe that the predictions of the market are likely to be systematically inferior to those of the economic authorities. As matters stand, a certain amount of agnosticism all round would not seem inappropriate. There is little or no direct evidence that economic agents form their expectations rationally, and it may be the case that governments do have some information advantage, although it follows from neither of these propositions that discretionary intervention is justified. There is a further problem of specifying how agents learn the consequences of changes in government policy rules and converge to rational expectations about them (see, for example, Shiller 1978). A tentative conclusion at this stage is that, although the rational-expectations hypothesis has presented us with some significant problems to consider in the process of model building and the prediction of policy consequences (see, for example, Lucas 1976), it is not yet clear that, on the basis of the existence of rational expectations alone, discretionary fiscal and monetary policy should be eschewed.

Fiscal and monetary policy in the United Kingdom since World War II has, for the most part, been bedeviled by excessive optimism with regard to the capacity of supply to respond to changes in monetary demand in the short and the medium term, and by a misunderstanding of the consequences of the exchange-rate regime that has been in force. There has been no presumption that the efficiency of fiscal and monetary policy to achieve permanent increases in output and employment has been limited by the elasticity of supply, which in turn has had consequences for the interpretation of the behavior of the balance of payments.

From the devaluation of 1949 to the mid-1960s, the scope for discretionary monetary and fiscal policy in determining the level of output and employment was limited by the policy objective of pegging sterling to the U.S. dollar. The misunderstanding of this limitation is reflected in the widespread belief that government was operating under what might be described as Keynesian rules, which provided the economic consensus of the middle ground. In practice, however, the commitment to the dollar set limits to the extent that domestic fiscal and monetary policy could be independent of the standard set by the United States. Attempts to pursue unilateral expansion were followed by balance-of-payments crises in the periods of "stop-go." However, the fact that the results of monetary expansion were reflected in the behavior of the balance of payments, and not primarily and immediately in changes in prices, led to the belief that monetary control was largely irrelevant to the behavior of inflation. The misperception was the failure to see that under a pegged exchange rate, given the limitations on supply, the balance-of-payments behavior—whether supported by declining reserves or overseas loans—reflected (at least for a while) a supply failing and so in effect a form of disguised inflation. It is true that many did see the commitment to parity with the dollar as a limitation of freedom of action; indeed, by 1967 there was wide support among economists for devaluation. But the failure to understand the relation between monetary behavior and what has been described as disguised inflation had near-catastrophic results in the early 1970s when the pound was floated on top of a massive monetary expansion, on which was imposed the rise in the real price of oil. The floating exchange rate provided the transmission channel through which excessive monetary expansion relative to the rest of the world was rapidly fed, not into output and employment other than during the initial burst in 1972–73, but into prices and subsequently money wages. Clearly, in itself, criticism of the behavior of the monetary authorities during this episode does not provide a general case for nondiscretionary intervention and stabilization, although it certainly provokes caution. Nor does it imply, as the subsequent behavior of the sterling exchange rate makes clear, that monetary behavior is the sole cause of changes in the nominal exchange rate (see Burns, Lobban, and Warburton 1977). Nonetheless, the belief that floating the exchange rate in some sense allowed the authorities to regain control over the behavior of output and employment once the commitment to the dollar was terminated was an egregious error. Given the existence of free collective bargaining, the authorities had not gained control over the level of output and employment, but had gained substantial influence over the behavior of the price level. Part of the problem, of course, stemmed from the supply shock resulting from the rise in the real price of energy. But, as Modigliani (a supporter of discretionary policy) has argued in this case, " . . . there is no way of returning to the initial equilibrium except after a painful period of both above-equilibrium unemployment and inflation" (Modigliani 1977, p. 15). An attempt to avoid that by expansionary monetary and fiscal policies can be disastrous. In general terms, there is no case for believing that, through the exercise of discretionary monetary and fiscal policy, even in the absence of rational expectations, government can determine an arbitrarily chosen level of employment.

A way out of this difficulty has been sought by those who have advocated general protection and/or incomes policy of some kind. Apart from the obvious costs of incomes policies and the political difficulties surrounding them, the debates on this issue in the United Kingdom have been confused by a failure to distinguish between the problems of controlling nominal wages on the one hand and real wages on the other. This is associated with the confusion as to whether, in a direct sense, incomes policy is directed at the rate of inflation or whether it is a device used to permit a higher long-term level of employment. In the former case, something like a wage freeze may have its place, under exceptional circumstances, as part of the process of breaking inflationary expectations. But if the economy is experiencing a relatively low elasticity of supply, in the medium term a permanently higher level of employment brought about by monetary expansion will require not simply control over the nominal wage but also control over the real wage in order to eliminate what has been described as classical unemployment. The notion of permanent central direction of real wages is one that even American supporters of discretionary monetary and fiscal policy would find hard to swallow. In a world of powerful trade unions, it hardly looks feasible.

Thus, there is a clear problem of identifying the limits of aggregate supply in the economy, and little evidence that since the war autonomous demand shocks other than those instituted by government have played much of a role in creating disequilibrium. The shocks administered by government have had the familiar unfortunate side effects without permanent effects on employment resulting from a failure to take into account the economic limits to supply, with the further result that there has been a failure to see that inflation is a central cause of the behavior of the level of unemployment rather than simply its result. Moreover, as we have seen under a floating exchange rate, for a given level of real efficiency, a further channel is opened through which monetary changes are transmitted into price increases, leaving on one side the direct effects of monetary expansion on other domestic prices. Even if the power of rational expectations is somewhat discounted, there remains both theoretically and on the basis of historical experience a strong case for what might be described as practical monetarism.

The case for practical monetarism rests on a number of propositions. The first is the belief that, in the medium term, the behavior of the monetary aggregates is closely related to the overall stance of fiscal policy, and that as one of the components of that stance the control of public expenditure and its method of financing has important monetary consequences. The second is that, in the medium term, there is a stable if not precise relationship between the growth of the supply of money and the growth of nominal income, although this relationship may vary taking one year with another because of the substantial lags that exist in the economic system. Third, in the medium term, the main influence of monetary changes is on nominal rather than real magnitudes, and this period of adjustment is short enough to be relevant to current economic policy making. If to this is added some belief in the power of rational expectations, the word *relevant* should perhaps be replaced by *highly relevant*. Fourth, although there is a presumption that in the medium term the behavior of the money supply is relevant to the behavior of the inflation rate, in the short run prices may change for other reasons. The practical monetarist does not seek to replace one spurious target, (the level of employment) with another (the price level). Fine-tuning the price level is not the name of the game. Rather, the general thesis is that a stable and (by recent standards) historically low rate of growth of the money supply are necessary conditions for the control of inflation and for steady growth in real output and a stable level of employment.

As suggested above, these propositions cast considerable doubt on the ability of the economic authorities to ensure desired levels of output and employment in the medium term through discretionary fiscal and monetary policy in any significantly general sense. They also emphasize the importance of conducting fiscal and monetary policy in an essentially medium-term framework, with the belief that the consequences of policy changes must not simply be looked at on a year-to-year basis in view of the nature of the relevant economic relationships and the lags involved. Finally, as far as discretionary monetary policy is concerned, the practical monetarist does not subscribe to any particular monetary rule, nor does he rule out on principle the need for monetary targets as objects of policy to be changed as circumstances alter. He would, however, believe that past intervention has been largely for the worse, and that changes in the monetary and fiscal stance should be the exception rather than the rule. The capacity of governments to do better than the market is strictly limited, and the emphasis of macroeconomic policy should rest on providing a stable financial environment rather than resting on a spurious belief in governments' power to manipulate the economy.

### Economic Growth

Practical monetarism (or even conventional monetarism) has little or nothing to say about the underlying rate of economic growth, beyond a belief in the necessary importance of a stable monetary environment. In the United Kingdom the cry has gone up that "monetarism is not enough," which in its strictest form is precisely what monetarism implies. Monetarism as such says nothing of how the tax structure should be determined or what share of national resources should accrue to the public rather than the private sector. Nonetheless, for one reason or another, the notion that real public spending has been excessive in the United Kingdom has become associated with monetarism, and the view has been taken that the size of public spending in itself has been associated with relatively slow economic growth and the behavior of aggregate supply.

This thesis first found its expression in Bacon and Eltis 1978 under the banner of "too few producers." The simplest version of this thesis suggested that the growth of the public sector (specifically the nonmarket public sector) had preempted resources of labor and capital that might otherwise have been utilized in manufacturing. Initially, the phenomenon of deindustrialization was noted in terms of the change in the pattern of employment since the late 1960s, with something like 1.5 million jobs disappearing in manufacturing and about 1.2 million jobs being created in the nonmarket public sector. In one sense there was presumed to be crowding out of employment in industry as well as possibly crowding out of investment.

Stated in this form, the thesis is hardly plausible. As shown by Thatcher (1979), a careful and detailed analysis of employment changes suggests that, although the decline in industrial jobs was substantially attributable to a decline in male employment, the major part of the increase in the public sector was in female employment. (The United Kingdom has virtually the highest female participation rate in Europe.) Moreover, since (rightly or wrongly) overmanning was reckoned to be commonplace in industry, the notion of industrial expansion being limited by a labor shortage was somewhat dubious. As far as capital was concerned, repeated industrial surveys seemed to show that the industrial problem was not so much a shortage of funds as a low expected rate of return. On both counts the crude idea of an industry being physically deprived of resources by the preemption of the public sector does not really stand up.

The more subtle version of the Bacon-Eltis story relates supply behavior to the consequences of excessive taxation that was taken to result from the excessive growth in real public spending. The argument was that, in order to pay for the increase in public-sector jobs, the burden of taxation on the "productive" or "wealth-producing" sector of the economy had to be increased. This in turn led to increased wage demands to offset the increased taxation, with the presumption (never clearly explained) that organized labor had the power to shift the burden of direct taxation forward. However, firms operating in an international market were deemed to be price takers, and so the result was a squeeze on profits and a reduction in the rate of return on industrial capital, reducing the underlying rate of economic growth. The investable surplus of the private industrial sector was thus held to have been dissipated in public consumption, which, since the underlying growth rate was so slow, spilled over into the balance of payments.

There are no doubt elements of truth in this analysis, although it is not easy to determine where the main emphasis should be placed. It is of course theoretically possible, although difficult to establish, that the disincentive effects of taxation in a direct sense were of major significance in affecting supply. It is clear that rapidly increasing public spending may be distorting and disruptive, insofar as it has deleterious financial consequences resulting in monetary instability and inflation; it is not difficult to characterize the 1970s in these terms. However, it is not easy to relate this to the Bacon-Eltis argument, since, like some of their critics, they do not seem to provide an integrated theory of the inflationary process or of exchange-rate behavior. In addition, even if their arguments are taken at face value, it is not easy to see how they adequately explain the slow growth performance of the United Kingdom in the 1950s and the 1960s, when the rate of growth of the OECD countries was at its peak. The control of public spending may have been a problem in the 1970s, and an important one, but it lacks plausibility as a general explanation of the failure of the United Kingdom to exploit the postwar industrial boom when, by 1970s standards, there was a relatively low rate of inflation and relative monetary stability. This has led to the search for a more unified explanation of the United Kingdom's growth performance, which has been found by many in the constraint imposed by the behavior of the balance of payments (see, for example, Singh 1979).

Whereas Bacon and Eltis focused initially on the behavior of employment as a symptom of deindustrialization, the balance-of-payments approach argues that the key statistic is the United Kingdom's share of

**Table 3**
Export growth and output growth for selected countries, 1953–1976.

|  | Growth in output (annual average) | Growth in exports (annual average) |
|---|---|---|
| United States | 3.23 | 5.88 |
| Federal Republic of Germany | 4.96 | 9.99 |
| Netherlands | 4.99 | 9.38 |
| France | 4.95 | 8.78 |
| Italy | 4.96 | 12.09 |
| Belgium | 4.07 | 9.24 |
| Japan | 8.55 | 16.18 |
| United Kingdom | 2.71 | 4.46 |

Source: D. Kern, *National Westminster Bank Review*, May 1978.

world trade. Poor export performance combined with a "high" marginal propensity to import has prevented expansionary demand management from providing the required impetus to the growth rate. Balance-of-payments crises have prevented monetary demand from growing at the rate required by the underlying growth of productive potential. In a further version of the story emphasized by Thirlwall (1979), the sustainable rate of economic growth of the industrial countries has been determined by their export performance. Thus it is concluded that growth performance has been limited in the deficit countries by the state of their balance of payments. (Balance-of-payments behavior is invariably measured in terms of the behavior of the current account.)

The correlation between export growth and output growth is illustrated in table 3. It is important to distinguish between the proposition that if a country's rate of export growth had been faster so would its rate of growth and the proposition that the balance of payments as such acted as a constraint on the growth of domestic monetary demand. The interpretation turns crucially on the behavior of supply. From the viewpoint of an international monetarist, with a pegged exchange rate the emergence of an overall balance-of-payments deficit would be seen as a reflection of excess monetary demand relative to supply. With a floating exchange rate the overall balance of payments should be kept broadly in equilibrium. Insofar as a balance-of-payments problem emerges with a pegged exchange rate, and inflation with a floating rate, the crucial question is the extent to which both originate from the constraints imposed by domestic supply. If this is the case, it is a curious and misleading use of language by definition to describe the economy as being constrained by the balance of payments. It is by no means clear that the direction of causation flows from exports to output rather than the other way around. Moreover, it may be equally incorrect to assign the behavior of imports solely or even substantially to the behavior of demand independent of the conditions of competitive supply. To the extent that imports are determined by supply rather than by demand, protectionism would (other things being equal; e.g., in the absence of an incomes policy) lead to excess demand and domestic inflation rather than a permanent increase in output and employment.

The data on output and export behavior does not in itself support the conclusion that the balance of payments is the major factor that accounts for differences in growth rates among the industrial countries. Taken across the board, they do reflect two phenomena. The first is the rapid growth over the period in traded relative to nontraded goods in the industrial world. In all the countries in table 3 the rate of export growth exceeded that of output, and in this respect the relationship for the period as a whole between export growth and output growth for the United Kingdom is not usual. Second, obviously and not surprisingly, the fast-growing countries have been those that have most successfully exploited the fast-growing sector—that is, those with rapid export growth. As far as the United Kingdom is concerned, the conclusion that must be drawn is not that growth has been constrained by the balance of payments, but quite simply that it has been unable to sustain its share of an expanding world demand. In the broadest sense, the United Kingdom has been uncompetitive. The reasons for this must be found in the supply side of the economy. To this extent, economists such as Singh must be right in focusing on the decline in Britain's share of world trade as the key indicator of performance. But from there it is important not to make the jump to identifying the behavior of the balance of payments as a cause of slow growth, which focuses attention on demand rather than supply and leads to calls for protection, which would only at best treat the symptoms rather than the underlying lack of competitiveness.

The concept of export-led growth can be dangerously misleading. As Thirlwall points out, it implies that variations in growth rates are to be explained in the long run principally by variations in rates of growth of monetary demand. It assumes elasticities of supply that are highly questionable. To demonstrate that the balance of payments is a real constraint on economic growth, it is necessary to demonstrate how it prevents exogeneous shifts in productivity and real competitiveness on the supply side of the economy. So far no one has explained how and why it may do so.

## Concluding Remarks

The aggregate elasticity of supply in the very short run and in the medium term is crucial to the determination of the response of the economy to monetary and fiscal expansion. This is fundamentally an empirical question that cannot be settled by *a priori* reasoning. In the case of the United Kingdom's economy since the war, a "high" elasticity of supply (in an economic as opposed to a physical sense) has, for the most part, been taken for granted. Demand, it has been presumed, will create its own supply up to "full" employment, although with expansionary demand policies there might be unfortunate side effects reflected in both inflation and the balance of payments, which have therefore been treated as constraints on economic policy. However, the fact that both inflation and balance of payments behavior over the period as a whole are themselves reflections of supply constraints has been widely misunderstood and has promoted the repeated calls for incomes policies, and latterly for protection.

The case for what has been described as practical monetarism is not rooted in *a priori* theory. On the contrary, it is derived from the historical record of the United Kingdom over the postwar period. It does not imply that discretionary monetary and fiscal policy is impossible (as in the case of some extreme version of the rational-expectations story) or always undesirable. However, those who have advocated active discretionary policies as a matter of course have spent little time in positively justifying their approach, and more in seeking to discredit the unnecessarily extreme position taken up by their opponents. Alternatively, they have sought to show that discretionary intervention is possible under certain assumptions about market clearing and the formation of expectations. None of this in itself provides a case for any general confidence in the power of governments to exert a major and positive influence on the determination of output and employment of a permanent kind through fiscal and monetary policy, whether accompanied by incomes policies, protection, or both. Both the history of the United Kingdom's economy and the current state of economic theory point to the need for fiscal and monetary policies that are robust with respect to time and that focus on objectives that governments may reasonably expect to achieve.

## Acknowledgments

I am grateful to Alan Budd and Heather Morley for comments on an earlier draft.

## Bibliography

Bacon, R., and W. Eltis. 1978. *Britain's Economic Problem: Too Few Producers.* Second edition. New York: Macmillan.

Ball, R. J. 1977. The theory of employment revisited. In Horst Albach et al., eds., *Quantitative Wirtschaftsforschung: Wilhelm Krelle zum 60 Geburtstag.* Tübingen: J. C. B. Mohr.

Ball, R. J., and E. B. A. St. Cyr. 1966. Short-term employment functions in British manufacturing industry. *Review of Economic Studies* 33, no. 3: 179–207.

Barro, R. J., and H. I. Grossman. 1971. A general disequilibrium model of income and employment. *American Economic Review* 61 (March): 82–93.

Beenstock, M. 1979. Do U.K. labour markets work? In Economic Outlook 1978–1982. London Business School Centre for Economic Forecasting. Volume 3, pp. 21–31.

Beenstock, M. 1980. *A Neoclassical Analysis of Macroeconomic Policy.* Cambridge University Press.

Beenstock, M., and A. Longbottom. 1980. The statistical relationship between the money supply and the public sector borrowing requirement. In Economic Outlook 1979–1983. Volume 4, pp. 27–31.

Beenstock, M., and P. Warburton. 1980. An Aggregative Model of the U.K. Labour Market. Discussion Paper 75, Econometric Forecasting Unit, London Business School.

Blinder, A. S., and R. M. Solow. 1974. Analytical foundations of fiscal policy. In *The Economics of Public Finance: Essays.* Washington, D. C.: Brookings Institution.

Budd, A. P., and T. Burns. 1978. The Relationship between Fiscal and Monetary Policy in the LBS Model. Discussion Paper 51, Econometric Forecasting Unit, London Business School.

Buiter, W. H., 1980. The macroeconomics of Dr. Pangloss: A critical survey of the new classical macroeconomics. *Economic Journal* 90 (March): 34–50.

Burns, T., P. W. M. Lobban, and P. Warburton. 1977. Forecasting the real exchange rate. In Economic Outlook 1977–1981. Volume 2, pp. 13–20.

Corden, W. M., 1978. Keynes and the others: Wage and price rigidities in macro-economic models. *Oxford Economic Papers* 30 (July): 159–180.

Cripps, F., and W. Godley. 1976. A formal analysis of the Cambridge Economic Policy Group model. *Economica* 43 (November): 335–348.

Cripps, F., M. Fetherston, and T. Ward. 1978. The effects of different strategies for the U.K. economy. In Economic Policy Review no. 4. Department of Applied Economics, Cambridge University.

Drazen, A. 1980. Recent developments in macroeconomic disequilibrium theory. *Econometrica* 48 (March):283–306.

Friedman, M. 1970. A theoretical framework for monetary analysis. *Journal of Political Economics* 78: 193–238.

Godley, W. 1977. Inflation in the United Kingdom. In *Worldwide Inflation*, L. B. Krause and W. S. Stallart, eds. Washington, D. C.: Brookings Institution.

Klein, L. R. 1947. *The Keynesian Revolution*. Second edition 1966. New York: Macmillan.

Klein, L. R. 1978. The supply side. *American Economic Review* 68 (March): 1–7.

Leicester, C. 1977. Unemployment 2001 A.D.. Institute of Manpower Studies, University of Sussex.

Lucas, R. E., Jr. 1976. Econometric policy evaluation: A critique. *Journal of Monetary Economics* Suppl. 1: 19–46.

Modigliani, F. 1948. Liquidity preference and the theory of interest and money. *Econometrica* 12 (January): 543–564.

Modigliani, F. 1977. The monetarist controversy, or, Should we forsake stabilization policies? *American Economic Review* 67 (March): 1–19.

Muth, J. F. 1961. Rational expectations and the theory of price movements. *Econometrica* 29 (July): 315–335.

Sargent, T. J., and N. Wallace. 1976. Rational expectations and the theory of economic policy. *Journal of Monetary Economics* 84 (April): 207–237.

Shiller, R. J. 1978. Rational expectations and the dynamic structure of macroeconomic models: A Critical Review. *Journal of Monetary Economics* 4 (January): 1–44.

Singh, A. 1978. North Sea oil and the reconstruction of U.K. industry. In F. T. Blackaby, ed., *De-industrialisation*. London: Heinemann, for National Institute of Economic and Social Research.

Thatcher, A. R. 1978. Labour supply and employment trends. In F. T. Blackaby, ed., *De-industrialisation*. London: Heinemann, for National Institute of Economic and Social Research.

Thirlwall, A. P. 1979. The balance of payments constraint as an explanation of international growth rate differences. *Banca Nazionale del Lavoro* 128 (March): 45–54.

# 13 Redistribution of Earnings by Unemployment and Inflation

Jere R. Behrman
Paul Taubman

Does the distribution of income change over the business cycle? Many economists believe so. It is often argued, for example, that a major social cost of inflation is the arbitrary way in which it redistributes income. Cyclical unemployment variations also may be associated with cyclical shifts in the income distribution if unemployment is concentrated in particular groups. Different economic policies, or the lack thereof, affect various groups differentially. Thus, it is important to gauge these impacts.

There have been several previous attempts to estimate the separate and joint effects of unemployment and inflation on the distribution of income. Bhageri 1978 provides a useful survey. The studies most comparable to ours are Schultz 1969, Metcalf 1972, Beach 1976, Thurow 1970, Gramlich 1974, and Bhageri 1978. In all of these studies a measure of inequality, such as the variance in the logarithm of earnings or the ratio of the $n$th decile to the median income is obtained from a series of annual surveys. The inequality measure is then regressed on inflation, unemployment, a time trend, and other variables.

Our study differs from these earlier attempts in that we have a new source of data with several important advantages. We have a large sample with data on individuals. With this we can standardize better for individual differences in earnings ability at a point of time and over time. We are also able to calculate the effects of inflation and unemployment across and within various age, education, and other groups, which previous studies have not been able to examine. In principle, similar disaggregated data could be generated from each of the annual or biannual Current Population Survey samples, but the CPS information on individuals has been retained only from the mid-1960s. Our data cover the period 1951–1976. We also have the advantage over earlier studies of including the data from the 1970s, which contain the high level of unemployment in 1975 and the steep (by those days' standard) inflation in the mid-1970s.

It is also possible to study these issues with longitudinal samples, such as the National Longitudinal Survey and the Michigan Panel of Income Dynamics. For the problem which we wish to study, a real advantage of our data in comparison with these two valuable surveys is that we have available annual earnings for the period 1951 through 1976. During our longer time interval there have been more substantial variations in unemployment and inflation than in the 1966–present period covered by these longitudinal surveys and analyzed in (for example) Hanushek and Quigley 1978 and Plantes 1978. Moreover, the CPS-SSA[1] sample is 20 times as large as these other two samples, so it is feasible to divide our sample into various homogenous cells and yet be able to study characteristics of the distributions other than the means. We examine, for example, the variance of the logarithm of earnings and the percentage of people in a group whose earnings are below the poverty line. We also can study redistribution among various demographic groups. We pay for these benefits by having to restrict our attention to earnings rather than to total income and by having to deal with a severe truncation problem.

## Theoretical Considerations

### Inflation and Distribution

Inflation can change the distribution of earnings for several different reasons, which reflect different mechanisms.

First, it is often argued that in many occupations money wages are not flexible enough to equate supply and demand instantaneously. The inflexibility occurs because of explicit contracts with unions or because of implicit contracts that maximize utility and profits, conditional on expectations of inflation. People whose wages are relatively rigid may be concentrated at various parts of the distribution. Such people suffer relative income losses if actual inflation exceeds expected levels. Of course, many contracts have cost-of-living protection, but often the protection is less than 100 percent. The type of model used below to explain cyclical variations in inequality in earnings implies that many of the flexible-wage occupations have relatively low wages. This suggests that unanticipated inflation may reduce inequality.

Another mechanism that may be important derives from the search theory often used to explain the short-run Phillips curve. According to this theory, people's inflationary expectations initially lag behind reality. People stop searching too soon because they receive a nominal wage offer that meets their reservation wages, which incorrect expectations caused them to set too low. Although this model is usually invoked to discuss unemployment, it also would apply to labor-force participation decisions in which the decision maker either searches directly or obtains wage quotations from friends. Because prime-age males have smaller turnover rates and less elastic labor-supply curves than others, this mechanism may yield differential effects for them in comparison with younger and older males and women. It may also affect the differentials between low- and high-skill workers. (This effect, incidentally, operates via labor supply rather than through wage rates.)

This particular mechanism has a somewhat ambiguous impact on the distribution of annual earnings. The usual search-theory model concludes that the reservation wage is set so that the rate of return derived from finding a better job to be held over a particular time period just equals the interest rate. If the person takes a wage less than the optimal reservation wage and if most searchers are relatively low-paid, then people in the bottom part of the distribution are losing earnings, which increases inequality. But during the year in which the unemployment occurs, average annual earnings on the misselected job may exceed the average of zero earnings during the search and subsequent earnings from employment at the optimal reservation wage.

A third mechanism that is important for our considerations of earnings relative to gross national product relates to nonearnings income sources. Some of these, such as rents and interest payments, change relatively slowly in response to inflation. Because of these phenomena, earnings' share of the GNP per worker can rise with inflation unless still other non-earnings-income components, such as profits, rise sufficiently to offset the inertia in these income sources.

### Unemployment and Distribution

Unemployment has an obvious negative effect on the mean of earnings, which might be obscured in our estimates because people with zero annual earnings are not included in our calculations. Similar considerations apply to the percentage with earnings below the poverty line.

What happens to the variance of the logarithm of earnings is more ambiguous. If all people were unemployed for the same percentage of time, the variance of the log of earnings would be unchanged. We think, however, that Wachter's (1970) characterization of the cyclical movements in the coefficient of variation is likely to be correct.

A way to think of Wachter's model is that there are two types of firms that hire labor of a given quality. One type of firm is typified by the steel industry, which is unionized and oligopolistic and competes on the basis of services rather than prices. The other type of firm is represented by laundries, which are nonunionized and are competitive in product markets on a price basis. The firms in the steel industry pay higher wages for a given skill to be guaranteed that they always have a sufficient labor force and that they do not have to forgo orders another steel firm can fill. The laundry industry sets wages to equilibrate its current supply and demand curves.

Usually some people who would like to receive the wage premiums in the steel industry are rationed out and have to settle for laundry jobs. When aggregate demand rises, workers shift into the higher-paid steel industry, which does not adjust wages immediately. The laundry industry continues to set wage rates by equating supply and demand, and as a result raises them. Therefore, the overall reduction in unemployment is associated with reduced variance in earnings and in inequality.

Unemployment also affects the distributions of earnings by changing the hours worked. If no new participants are added to a particular distribution, a fall in unemployment and an associated increase in hours worked almost undoubtedly increases mean earnings and reduces the percentage of earners below the poverty line. At the lower end of the distributions, many workers' earnings rise because of increased hours. Higher in the distributions, such a tendency is reinforced by the often high premiums for overtime pay. The net impact on the variance of the logarithm of earnings therefore may be ambiguous, depending upon the relative effects of those formerly low in the distribution and on those higher in the distribution.

If the possibility of new participants with low earnings due in part to part-time work is allowed for, the impact on the dispersion becomes more ambiguous and that on the means and on the proportion in the left-hand tail becomes somewhat ambiguous. It is conceivable that there are enough low-earning new participants to offset the higher earnings of previous participants and to reduce the average earnings for all participants and increase the proportion below the poverty line; however, this seems unlikely.

### Relation of Our Interests to the Phillips Curve

There are many empirical studies of the Phillips wage curve or the relationship between the percentage changes of wages and of variables such as unemployment and proxies for inflationary expectations. Since we are studying various moments or aspects of earnings, not wages, we are not estimating Phillips curves. Yet the literature on wage changes does contain several important lessons. The first is that unemployment need not enter the analysis linearly; however, tests performed with our data indicate that the linear relationship is as good as other common specifications. The second is that unemployment and actual price changes can be related causally, and thus for some purposes it may be inappropriate to use as the estimate of the effect of unemployment on earnings the coefficient of unemployment in an equation that controls for inflation. The third is that the relationships might be unstable, especially if people adjust their inflationary expectations more quickly or learn to include cost-of-living clauses in their contracts.

## Data

The earnings data we use are drawn from the 1973 CPS-SSA Exact Match file, of which Rosen and Taubman (1979) provide the following description:

The March 1973 Current Population Survey was a stratified multistage cluster sample of about 45,000 interviewed households containing some 136,000 persons. To be eligible for the CPS, an individual had to be living in one of the 50 States or the District of Columbia. The institutional population was excluded as were all Armed Forces members except those living off-post or on-post with their families.

As part of the 1973 Exact Match Study, an attempt was made by the Census Bureau to obtain the social security numbers of the 101,000 sampled persons 14 years or older. In about 80,000 cases, potentially usable numbers were recorded by the interviewers. An additional 10,000 adults were matched to SSA files using CPS data on name, age, sex, and race. Available evidence suggests that the matching was done accurately, and that inability to match everyone has not caused the matched subset to differ greatly from the whole CPS.

There are, however, two major difficulties with the CPS-SSA sample. The first is that SSA records only contain information on earnings paid in industries covered by the Social Security Act.[2] The second problem is that Social Security records for an employee only contain earnings received up to the taxable limit per year per employer.[3]

Noncovered employees are found at all wage and education levels;

for example, the federal government is not covered. We assume that any biases introduced into the various moments of the earnings series because of noncoverage are uncorrelated with inflation and unemployment. Since we use cell means and variances, this may not be too strong an assumption.

The truncation problem is potentially more important. Although the ceiling currently is well above mean family income and thus well above mean individual earnings, there have been periods when the ceiling on taxable earnings was below the mean of earnings of individuals. As is well known, such truncation causes estimated means and variances to be biased. We attempt to solve this problem by assuming that the distribution of earnings in every cell is log-normal (see Klein 1962) and using standard formulas to estimate the true mean for each cell. In most cases, this method yields results that are reasonable in the following senses: The cells used are defined in terms of race, sex, education, and years of work experience. As a whole, the data indicate that white males have more earnings than white females or blacks, that age earnings profiles rise until close to retirement age except in recessionary years, and that average earnings increase with education.

There are, however, some obvious instances in which the results are unreasonable—for example, estimated average earnings in the mid-1960s of \$50,000 or even \$300,000 for a few cells. We excluded all estimates in which average estimated earnings at various education levels exceeded average estimated earnings in the least educated group of that year by $X$, with $X$ varying by education level. Instead we use estimates based on the assumption that in the year in question, within a race or sex grouping, earnings of all people in the same age group can be represented by a log-normal distribution. We use this overall estimated variance of the cell in question. To obtain the estimated mean of a particular education cell, we adjust the estimated mean of the overall distribution by $0.07 (S_j - \bar{S})$ where $S_j$ is the average education level of the group whose previous estimated mean was unacceptable.[4]

We have used the resulting modified data to obtain the following dependent variables: $\ln(\bar{Y}_{jt}/P_t)$, $\ln[\bar{Y}_{jt}/(\text{GNP}_t/L_t)]$, $\sigma_{\ln Y_{jt}}^2$, and the proportion in a distribution below the poverty level for a family with two children. $\ln \bar{Y}_{jt}$ refers to the log mean earnings of the $j$th schooling group in year $t$. At times we divide $\bar{Y}$ by the level of GNP per worker in year $t$. The resulting variable differs from the share of GNP only in that both the numerator and the denominator are defined on a per-worker basis, which adjustment is required to pool the various-sized cells. This variable permits us to study shifts between earnings and nonearnings. At other times we divide by the consumer price index, $P_t$, to examine effects on mean real earnings and to facilitate a within- and between-variance decomposition. The variance of the log of earnings within each cell $(\sigma_{\ln Y_{jt}}^2)$ is a measure of inequality. It is an incomplete measure, since it ignores between-cell variation $(\sigma_{\ln Y_{jt}}^2)$. The percent below the poverty line is an alternative measure of inequality that focuses on the left-hand tail of the distributions. This measure is unaffected by the truncation problem in our sample.

We have used the cell means, variances, etc. to estimate weighted regressions where the weights are the square root of the number of observations in each cell. The regressions have been estimated separately for males and females, whites and blacks, and those who in year $t$ fell into the age groups $17 \leq 24$, $25 \leq 49$, and $50 < 65$.[5] Such a disaggregation can help determine who is hurt most by inflation or unemployment.

Although we are interested in studying the effects of unemployment and inflation, we must control for other determinants of earnings to minimize omitted-variable bias. Prior research suggests that it is important to control for schooling and work experience. We measure the latter in two different ways: Age — Years of school — 6 (Mincer 1974) and the number of quarters a person has had at least \$50 of earnings in employment covered by Social Security. The latter is a measure of long-term unemployment and nonparticipation contaminated by noncovered employment, and for this variable we assume that the effect of noncovered employment remains proportional over time. We also have included a time trend to control for systematic secular shifts.

## Results

We include these variables and the unemployment and inflation variables in weighted least-squares regressions,[6] which are presented in detail in the appendix below. The appendix also includes a discussion of the coefficients of the variables other than unemployment and inflation. Because the SSA data had to be manipulated to overcome the truncation problem and because there is a small SSA-noncovered sector, there is a question of whether the means, the variances, and the poverty-percentage data are useful for our purpose. The appendix provides some comfort in this respect. It concludes that the results for the coefficient estimates for schooling, experience, etc. are comparable to those obtained from other studies. We think, therefore, that the equations are useful for analyzing the effects of inflation and unemployment.

The five dependent variables that we analyze yield different information about redistribution. The cell means deflated by the CPI, $\ln(\bar{Y}/P)$, indicate how real earnings vary. The logarithm of the ratio of the cell mean to the GNP per worker, $\ln[\bar{Y}/(GNP/L)]$, indicates how the average earnings share of average GNP per worker varies. The percentage below the poverty line conveys information on the left-hand portion of the distribution. The variance of earnings within the cell, $\operatorname{var}\ln Y_j$, conveys information about the dispersion in the full distribution. Though we could combine the results for each dependent variable to see if a coherent explanation is possible, we begin our analysis by examining the patterns for one variable for various age, race, and sex groups. We present in tables 1–4 the coefficients on the overall unemployment rate and inflation rate in the equations in the appendix in which the other variables listed therein are held constant. We also have estimated equations containing the specific unemployment rate for various age, race, and sex groups. The specific unemployment rate usually has a larger $t$ statistic and yields a higher $R^2$ than the overall rate, though the sign and significance of unemployment are not much affected.[7] To study the differential impact of business cycles, we would have to link the specific rate to the overall rate. To limit confusion and to save space, we focus here on the results with the overall unemployment rate.

**Share of GNP Per Worker**

Table 1 contains eleven coefficients on the unemployment and inflation variables in the equations for $\ln[\bar{Y}/(GNP/L)]$.[8] For unemployment, seven of these eleven coefficients are significant and negative, and two are positive and significant.[9] The significant positive coefficients are found in the equations for prime-age women, who may be forced to work more when their husbands are laid off. It is not surprising that unemployment most often leads to lower earnings (though we exclude those with zero earnings in a calendar year). It is of interest and perhaps a surprise that average earnings in all these groups fall faster than does GNP per worker as overall unemployment rises. Apparently the difference between average earnings and average GNP (primarily profits, rents, and

**Table 1**
Effects of unemployment and inflation on $\ln[\bar{Y}/(\text{GNP}/L)]$.

|               | Age |       |        | Age |       |        |
|---------------|-----|-------|--------|-----|-------|--------|
|               | 17–25 | 25–50 | 50–64 | 17–25 | 25–50 | 50–64 |
|               | **Unemployment rate** | | | **Inflation rate** | | |
| White males   | −0.030 | −0.048 | −0.17 | 0.64[a] | −1.77 | −0.74[a] |
| White females | −0.010[a] | −0.0040[a] | −0.0016[a] | 0.91[a] | −1.15 | −0.90 |
| Black males   | −0.068 | −0.040 | b | 0.74[a] | −1.21 | b |
| Black females | −0.026[a] | −0.015[a] | 0.0031[a] | 2.80 | 0.63[a] | 1.31[a] |

Source: tables A1–A4.
a. Not significantly different from zero at the 5% level.
b. Too few observations to use.

interest) is more stable than earnings. The coefficients in table 1 indicate that the biggest impact for a unit change in the unemployment rate occurs for black males 17–25 years old and 25–50 years old. "Last hired, first fired" comes to mind. The results in table 1 suggest that young people and males are strongly affected by business-cycle conditions. The strong effects for prime-age males may occur because they are subject to layoffs, during which they may not look for work if they expect to be recalled (see Feldstein 1976).

The inflation rate also has some important effects. Of the eleven coefficients, seven are significant at the 5 percent level. All the insignificant coefficients are in the equations for the young people. All but two of the significant coefficients are negative. Thus, generally, when there is inflation, the nonearnings part of GNP before taxes rises faster than earnings. The data suggest that prime-age white and black males have the biggest reduction in their share of GNP when inflation occurs. The groups with positive or insignificant coefficients are the young and black females. Perhaps these groups with weaker labor-force attachment are those who are fooled by inflation, as in Phelps's (1970) model.

**Effects on $\ln(Y/P)$**

The effects of unemployment and inflation on $\ln(Y/P)$ are given in table 2. Of the eleven coefficients on the unemployment variable, nine are significantly negative. Though inflation lowers average real earnings, we cannot say to what extent this reflects fewer hours worked or lower wages. The insignificant coefficients are for the two older groups of black females. The largest reductions are for the males and for the young

**Table 2**
Effects of unemployment and inflation on $\ln(Y/P)$.

| | Age | | | Age | | |
|---|---|---|---|---|---|---|
| | 17–25 | 25–50 | 50–64 | 17–25 | 25–50 | 50–64 |
| | **Unemployment rate** | | | **Inflation rate** | | |
| White males | −0.059 | −0.052 | −0.038 | −0.24[a] | −3.20 | −0.21[a] |
| White females | −0.039 | 0.00081 | −0.028 | 0.0040[a] | −1.65 | −1.32 |
| Black males | −0.098 | −0.061 | b | −0.20[a] | −0.76[a] | b |
| Black females | 0.054 | 0.0042[a] | 0.022[a] | 1.92 | 0.70[a] | 0.94[a] |

Source: table A1–A4.
a. Not significantly different from zero at the 5% level.
b. Too few observations to use.

**Table 3**
Effects of unemployment and inflation on var $\ln Y$.

| | Age | | | Age | | |
|---|---|---|---|---|---|---|
| | 17–25 | 25–50 | 50–64 | 17–25 | 25–50 | 50–64 |
| | **Unemployment rate** | | | **Inflation rate** | | |
| White males | 0.025[a] | −0.025[a] | 0.034[a] | 2.08[a] | −2.89[a] | 3.82[a] |
| White females | 0.027[a] | 0.027 | 0.025[a] | −2.80 | −3.22 | −2.00[a] |
| Black males | 0.10 | 0.089 | b | 2.41[a] | −5.22 | b |
| Black females | 0.086 | 0.023[a] | −0.071[a] | −0.77[a] | −1.37[a] | −4.01[a] |

Source: tables A1–A4.
a. Not significantly different from zero at the 5% level.
b. Too few observations to use.

of both sexes, the two largest for young blacks. Again we suspect that we are observing the effects of long periods of unemployment for youths, but temporary layoffs for men.

For real mean earnings the inflation rate has seven significantly negative coefficients. The biggest impact is for the prime-age groups, who are likely to have long-term contracts. By far the biggest coefficient in absolute value is for prime-age white males, who apparently have lost most, at least in the short run, in periods of unexpected inflation.

**Effects on the Within-Cell Variance of** $\ln Y$

The unemployment rate in table 3 has positive significant coefficients for the four young groups and for prime age black males. This result is consistent with the hypothesis that skilled workers are less likely to be laid off than less skilled ones. However, the coefficient for prime-age white males, among whom there are many skilled and unskilled workers, is an insignificant −0.048. This suggests that some laid-off "steel" workers remain at home rather than becoming "laundry" workers and increasing the variance by lowering the laundry wage rate.

The inflation rate is significantly negative in five cases, including three of the four prime age groups and all three age groups of white females. The Phelps (1970) phenomenon may be at work, leading job searchers to accept wages that are below their real reservation wages because of lagged recognition of inflationary increases, but the large impacts for prime age groups suggests the Wachter (1970) "laundry-steel" model.

### Effects on Percentage Below Poverty Level

We have measured the poverty level only for a family of four. When data on the poverty level were not available, we extrapolated on the basis of the CPI. These considerations suggest that we are really measuring the share of the left-hand portion of the distribution and that inflationary effects may be understated because of the extrapolation method using the CPI. Still the results are interesting. Of the eleven unemployment coefficients in table 4, ten are significantly positive. Thus, more unemployment causes more people to be in the left-hand tail. The estimates are fairly uniform for all age, race, and sex groups except for the much larger effect for black prime-age males, the much smaller effect for prime-age white females, and the lack of a significant effect for prime-age black females.

The coefficients on the inflation variables are significant in only five cases, of which two are negative. The three significantly positive estimates

**Table 4**
Effects of unemployment and inflation on percentage below poverty line.

|  | Age | | | Age | | |
|---|---|---|---|---|---|---|
|  | 17–25 | 25–50 | 50–64 | 17–25 | 25–50 | 50–64 |
|  | **Unemployment rate** | | | **Inflation rate** | | |
| White males | 0.013 | 0.017 | 0.013 | −0.32 | −0.090[a] | 0.17 |
| White females | 0.0074 | 0.015 | 0.014 | 0.28 | 0.66 | 0.70 |
| Black males | 0.016 | 0.027 | b | −0.59 | 0.081[a] | b |
| Black females | 0.0054[a] | 0.015 | 0.019 | −0.57 | −0.25[a] | 0.19[a] |

Source: tables A1–A4.
a. Not significantly different from zero at the 5% level.
b. Too few observations to use.

are for white females; this suggests that the reductions in ln variance in table 3 for these groups are accompanied by increased concentration in the left-hand tail. The two significantly negative estimates are for blacks (young males and prime-age females), perhaps because of relatively rapid adjustments due to the presence of few explicit or implicit fixed contracts.

### Comparison Across Tables by Race and Sex

It is also of interest to examine the effects on the various aspects of the distribution for each race and sex group. First, consider prime-age white males. An increase in the unemployment rate is associated with significant reductions in $\ln[\bar{Y}/\text{GNP}/L)]$, $\ln(\bar{Y}/P)$, and the percentage above the poverty line. This pattern is consistent with the distribution of earnings shifting to the left proportionately and falling more than nonwage income as unemployment rises.

For the younger and older white males, the pattern is very similar to that of the above group, though coefficients are generally smaller for the non-prime-age groups. Also, the variance of log earnings increases significantly for young white males, so the shift is not proportional for this group.

The results for prime-age white females are more varied than those for their male counterparts. An increase in the unemployment lowers mean earnings and the percentage above the poverty level. Both these effects are small relative to those for white males, so it is not surprising that unemployment also significantly raises the share of GNP accruing to prime-age females. The lack of significance in the variance log earnings relations suggests that the overall distribution shifts fairly uniformly to the left.

The results for younger and older white women are very similar to those for their male counterparts, with the single exception that the share of GNP accruing to older white females is not altered significantly.

The results for prime-age and young black males are similar to those for white males of comparable age, except that as unemployment increases both the within-cell variance and the percentage below the poverty line increase greatly.

For black women, half the coefficients are insignificant. For young black women, however, all four characteristics of the distribution are affected as unemployment increases, with a leftward shift absolutely and relative to overall GNP and with increased dispersion. In contrast, for prime-age black women the only significant effect is a positive one on the relative share of GNP accruing, and for older black women the only significant estimates implies an increase in the proportion in the left-hand tail.

Let us now turn to the effects of inflation. For prime-age white males, inflation significantly lowers real earnings, share of GNP, and variance. Those in the left-hand tail fare better, as suggested by the "laundry-steel" example. Mean earnings are reduced significantly for the young and the old white males (although relatively to GNP only for the old), but the shapes of the distributions are unaffected.

For prime-age white females, inflation lowers share of GNP, mean earnings, variance, and percentage above poverty level. This suggests a leftward but not proportional displacement, with more people above the mean affected. The coefficients generally differ in size from those for prime-age white males. Similar results hold for older and younger white females.

The results for black males are similar to those for their white counterparts, except that for younger blacks the inverse response in the left-hand tail is significant and the response in log average real earnings is not. For black females few coefficients are significant, and the signs of the two significant estimates are opposite from those of their white counterparts.

## Conclusion

The estimates obtained in this paper suggest that inflation and unemployment significantly alter the distributions of earnings. In general, unemployment causes the mean earnings levels, the shares of GNP, and the percentages above the poverty level to fall. Unemployment, however, tends to increase within-cell variance.

Inflation tends to redistribute before-tax GNP from earnings. The effects on the mean of real earnings are generally negative. There also is an indication that workers in the prime age groups, who might be expected to be in occupations with longer contracts, are hurt most by inflation.

The impacts of inflation and unemployment are not distributed uniformally across subgroups. Inflation tends to have the biggest effects on the distributions for prime-age people, whereas unemployment tends to affect the young and the black males more strongly.

The results also suggest that unemployment and inflation alter the shapes of the distributions, though the results vary enough by age, race, and sex to preclude identifying some "standard" effects.

## Appendix

Tables A1–A4 contain weighted least-squares regressions for black and white males and females. In these tables we have excluded people over 64 years old in any year because relatively few of the elderly are working and much of their income is not obtained from earnings.

Although the major focus of our work is on the effects of unemployment and inflation, here we summarize briefly the effects of the other variables. Human-capital theory suggests that education leads to more earnings and probably to an increase in the variance of earnings (Mincer 1974). The first effect also suggests that education leads to a decrease in the incidence of absolute (but maybe not relative) poverty. On the whole, these expectations are borne out, with years of education and its square having significant coefficients. There are, however, two anomalies. The first is that for several groups (but not white males) the poverty incidence rises until about twelfth grade or later and then falls. We have no good explanation for this result, though for women it may reflect patterns of part-time work.[10] The second point, which is related, is that for the groups other than white males we often estimate increasing returns to school. Freeman has shown that, for blacks, it was the most educated whose earnings rose most in the 1960s and the 1970s. The same may be true for white women once we control for actual work experience. This spurt in earnings may show up as increasing returns in our estimates.

We have used two sets of variables to control for labor-market experience. One is Mincer's Age (Years of schooling − 6. The second is based on the Social Security Administration's calculation of the number of quarters per year an individual has received $50 or more of pay in covered industries. This variable is cumulated over time and averaged over individuals. It would be a good measure of long-term unemployment and nonparticipation except that about 5–10 percent of the labor force has worked in noncovered employment during the sample period. We

**Table A1**

| | $\ln[Y(GNP/L)]$ | | | | |
|---|---|---|---|---|---|
| | White males | | | White females | |
| | 17–24 | 25–49 | 50–64 | 17–24 | 25–49 |
| Inflation rate | −0.35[a] | −2.48 | −1.10 | 0.053[a] | −0.59 |
| Unemployment | −0.026 | −0.38 | −0.020 | −0.014[a] | 0.016 |
| 1/4 | 0.15 | 0.028 | 0.013 | 0.25 | 0.015 |
| $(1/4)^2$ | −0.0029 | −0.00015 | −0.000012[a] | 0.0063 | −0.00013 |
| exp | 0.12 | 0.054 | −0.030[a] | 0.045 | 0.0061 |
| $(exp)^2$ | −0.36 | −0.11 | −0.026[a] | −1.03 | 0.034 |
| $S$ | 0.28 | 0.16 | −0.033[a] | 0.014[a] | −0.032 |
| $S^2$ | −0.0090 | −0.00096[a] | 0.0048 | 0.00034[a] | 0.0069 |
| $T$ | −0.013 | −0.027 | −0.042 | −0.015 | −0.012 |
| Constant | −4.74 | −2.3 | 1.20 | −3.57 | −2.55 |
| $\bar{R}^2$ | 0.93 | 0.74 | 0.77 | 0.87 | 0.77 |
| Standard error | 0.19 | 0.27 | 2.6 | 0.23 | 0.16 |
| Degrees of freedom | 631 | 1734 | 773 | 597 | 1682 |

a. Not statistically significant at the 5% level.

**Table A2**

| | $\ln(Y/P)$ | | | | |
|---|---|---|---|---|---|
| | White males | | | White females | |
| | 17–24 | 25–49 | 50–64 | 17–24 | 25–49 |
| Inflation rate | −1.30 | −3.30 | −1.82 | −0.90 | −1.53 |
| Unemployment | −0.056 | −0.067 | −0.049 | −0.043 | −0.015 |
| 1/4 | 0.15 | 0.031 | 0.017 | 0.24 | 0.016 |
| $(1/4)^2$ | −0.0030 | −0.00017 | −0.000032[a] | −0.0062 | −0.00015 |
| exp | 0.12 | 0.049 | −0.027[a] | 0.051 | 0.0065 |
| $(exp)^2$ | −0.36 | −0.099 | −0.029[a] | −1.03 | 0.034 |
| $S$ | 0.27 | 0.15 | −0.043[a] | 0.028[a] | −0.032 |
| $S^2$ | −0.0088 | −0.00060 | 0.0053 | 0.000041[a] | 0.0069 |
| $T$ | 0.011 | −0.0045[a] | −0.022 | 0.0099 | 0.012 |
| Constant | −0.30[a] | 2.08 | 5.4 | 0.67[a] | 1.78 |
| $\bar{R}^2$ | 0.93 | 0.76 | 0.79 | 0.87 | 0.81 |
| Standard error | 0.19 | 0.27 | 0.26 | 0.23 | 0.16 |
| Degrees of freedom | 631 | 1734 | 773 | 597 | 1682 |

a. Not statistically significant at the 5% level.

| | Black males | | Black females | | |
|---|---|---|---|---|---|
| 50–64 | 17–24 | 25–50 | 17–24 | 25–49 | 50–64 |
| −0.74 | 0.80[a] | −1.56 | −0.24[a] | 1.29 | 1.48[a] |
| −0.000099[a] | −0.059 | −0.042 | −0.044 | 0.022 | 0.012[a] |
| 0.028 | 0.15 | 0.0035[a] | 0.33 | 0.012 | 0.051 |
| −0.00016 | −0.0036 | −0.000003[a] | −0.0071 | −0.00017 | −0.00028 |
| 0.081 | 0.14 | 0.087 | −0.10 | 0.053 | 0.19 |
| −0.13 | −0.63 | −0.19 | −0.21[a] | −0.072 | −0.28 |
| −0.21 | −0.54 | −0.93 | −0.026[a] | −0.054 | −0.31 |
| 0.014 | 0.030 | 0.051 | −0.0016[a] | 0.0097 | 0.019 |
| −0.024 | 0.0086 | 0.022 | −0.0043[a] | 0.0099 | −0.029 |
| −2.37 | −1.28[a] | 1.76 | −3.28 | −3.60 | −5.03 |
| | | | | | |
| 0.81 | 0.96 | 0.79 | 0.91 | 0.86 | 0.85 |
| 0.17 | 0.11 | 0.15 | 0.16 | 0.15 | 0.17 |
| 835 | 85 | 180 | 131 | 274 | 58 |

| | Black males | | Black females | | |
|---|---|---|---|---|---|
| 50–64 | 17–24 | 25 50 | 17–24 | 25–49 | 50–64 |
| −1.59 | −0.15[a] | −2.37 | −1.15[a] | 0.31[a] | 0.89[a] |
| −0.031 | −0.089 | −0.072 | −0.072 | −0.0091[a] | −0.016[a] |
| 0.031 | 0.15 | 0.0079[a] | 0.32 | 0.013 | 0.054 |
| −0.00019 | −0.0035 | −0.000038[a] | −0.0070 | −0.00018 | −0.00029 |
| 0.081 | 0.15 | 0.083 | −0.094 | 0.053 | 0.19 |
| −0.13 | −0.63 | −0.18 | −0.21[a] | −0.071 | −0.28 |
| −0.21 | −0.53 | −0.89 | −0.0051[a] | −0.052 | 0.32 |
| 0.014 | 0.031 | 0.049 | −0.0021[a] | 0.0096 | 0.019 |
| −0.0012[a] | 0.033 | 0.044 | 0.021 | 0.034 | −0.011[a] |
| 1.94 | 3.00 | 5.9 | 0.89[a] | 0.74 | −0.58[a] |
| | | | | | |
| 0.83 | 0.97 | 0.86 | 0.93 | 0.91 | 0.86 |
| 0.17 | 0.11 | 0.15 | 0.16 | 0.15 | 0.17 |
| 835 | 85 | 180 | 131 | 274 | 58 |

**Table A3**

| | $\sigma^2 \ln Y$ | | | | |
|---|---|---|---|---|---|
| | White males | | | White females | |
| | 17–24 | 25–49 | 50–64 | 17–24 | 25–49 |
| Inflation rate | 1.33[a] | −3.90 | −0.92[a] | −2.37 | −4.12 |
| Unemployment | 0.039 | −0.048[a] | 0.012[a] | 0.044 | 0.0076[a] |
| 1/4 | −0.31 | 0.018[a] | 0.019[a] | −0.18 | 0.022 |
| $(1/4)^2$ | 0.0052 | −0.000002 | 0.000049[a] | 0.0039 | −0.00024 |
| exp | 0.57 | 0.11 | −0.50 | 0.29 | 0.051 |
| $(\exp)^2$ | −0.81 | −0.27 | 0.55 | −0.62 | −0.16 |
| S | 0.41 | −0.68 | −0.86 | 0.12[a] | −0.54 |
| $S^2$ | 0.0026[a] | 0.043 | 0.047 | 0.0029[a] | 0.030 |
| T | −0.020 | −0.049 | −0.085 | −0.0041[a] | −0.0080[a] |
| Constant | −2.59 | 3.79 | 16.0 | 0.21[a] | 3.86 |
| $\bar{R}^2$ | 0.47 | 0.34 | 0.31 | 0.34 | 0.39 |
| Standard error | 0.44 | 1.41 | 1.27 | 0.31 | 0.60 |
| Degrees of Freedom | 631 | 1734 | 773 | 597 | 1682 |

a. Not statistically significant at the 5% level.

**Table A4**

| | Percentage below poverty level | | | | |
|---|---|---|---|---|---|
| | White males | | | White females | |
| | 17–24 | 25–49 | 50–64 | 17–24 | 25–49 |
| Inflation rate | −0.11[a] | 0.038[a] | 0.016[a] | 0.58 | 0.44 |
| Unemployment | 0.012 | 0.014 | 0.013 | 0.012 | 0.0066 |
| 1/4 | −0.030 | −0.0092 | −0.0035 | −0.039 | −0.0031 |
| $(1/4)^2$ | 0.000094[a] | 0.000063 | 0.000011 | 0.00036 | 0.000020 |
| exp | −0.018 | −0.0038 | −0.023 | 0.0024[a] | 0.0018 |
| $(\exp)^2$ | 0.084 | 0.0065 | 0.041 | 0.28 | −0.013 |
| S | −0.072 | −0.047 | −0.015 | 0.070 | −0.021 |
| $S^2$ | 0.0027 | 0.0012 | 0.00023 | −0.0029 | −0.00083 |
| T | −0.0019 | −0.0021 | −0.0012[a] | −0.0068 | −0.0075 |
| Constant | 1.47 | 0.82 | 0.75 | 0.70 | 1.14 |
| $\bar{R}^2$ | 0.91 | 0.83 | 0.86 | 0.85 | 0.86 |
| Standard error | 0.067 | 0.039 | 0.043 | 0.064 | 0.050 |
| Degrees of freedom | 631 | 1734 | 773 | 597 | 1682 |

a. Not statistically significant at the 5% level.

| 50–64 | Black males | | Black females | | |
| --- | --- | --- | --- | --- | --- |
| | 17–24 | 25–50 | 17–24 | 25–49 | 50–64 |
| −2.48 | 1.97[a] | −5.14 | 1.32[a] | −1.022[a] | −3.09[a] |
| 0.021[a] | 0.091 | 0.088 | 0.067 | 0.0064[a] | −0.081[a] |
| 0.0064[a] | −0.14[a] | −0.023[a] | −0.12[a] | −0.040 | −0.053[a] |
| 0.000082[a] | 0.0032[a] | 0.000065[a] | 0.00082[a] | 0.00043 | 0.00029[a] |
| 0.0094[a] | 0.14[a] | 0.12 | 0.24 | 0.026[a] | −0.24[a] |
| −0.036[a] | −0.74[a] | −0.16[a] | −1.00 | −0.082 | 0.30[a] |
| −0.65 | −0.42[a] | −0.23[a] | −0.27[a] | −0.16 | −0.078[a] |
| 0.035 | 0.025[a] | 0.021[a] | 0.019 | 0.011 | 0.0091[a] |
| −0.029 | −0.015[a] | 0.0058[a] | 0.0055[a] | 0.016 | 0.11 |
| 4.43 | 3.34[a] | 0.92[a] | 2.12[a] | 2.05 | 6.03[a] |
| 0.32 | 0.096 | 0.27 | 0.065 | 0.19 | 0.25 |
| 0.58 | 0.45 | 0.65 | 0.42 | 0.39 | 0.41 |
| 835 | 85 | 180 | 131 | 274 | 58 |

| 50–64 | Black males | | Black females | | |
| --- | --- | --- | --- | --- | --- |
| | 17–24 | 25–50 | 17–24 | 25–49 | 50–64 |
| 0.55 | −0.63 | 0.0011[a] | 0.033[a] | −0.46 | 0.15[a] |
| 0.014 | 0.019 | 0.026 | 0.014 | 0.0036[a] | −0.015 |
| −0.0087 | −0.030 | −0.0037[a] | −0.044 | −0.0020[a] | −0.011 |
| 0.000039 | 0.00014[a] | 0.000033 | 0.000073[a] | 0.000015[a] | 0.000052[a] |
| −0.012 | −0.0065[a] | −0.022 | 0.027 | −0.012 | −0.051 |
| 0.025 | 0.22 | 0.041 | 0.22 | 0.023 | 0.08 |
| 0.041 | 0.22 | 0.19 | 0.12 | 0.057 | 0.13 |
| −0.0034 | −0.010 | −0.011 | −0.0038 | −0.0049 | −0.0081 |
| −0.0028 | −0.0089 | −0.018 | −0.0028 | −0.012 | −0.0097[a] |
| 0.86 | 0.089[a] | 0.13[a] | 0.25 | 1.09 | 1.56 |
| 0.89 | 0.91 | 0.90 | 0.91 | 0.90 | 0.94 |
| 0.054 | 0.049 | 0.046 | 0.035 | 0.054 | 0.043 |
| 835 | 85 | 180 | 131 | 274 | 58 |

assume that noncovered employment is a constant proportion of the population across cells, with any secular shifts over time controlled by the included time trend.

Previous research suggests that average earnings and the percentage below the poverty level are concave from below functions of experience. The relationship of experience with the variance log income is not clear. For example, the models of Mincer 1974 can generate practically any pattern. For the most part, the coefficient of experience meets our expectations. However, the percentage below the poverty line increases with experience calculated in the Mincer sense for the two youngest groups of white females and for prime-age black females. This may indicate that affirmative action and antidiscrimination programs were not effective for the young.

The time trend is generally significant. It has negative coefficients in the equations for the incidence of poverty despite some positive trend in the real value of the poverty cutoff. The coefficients for the within-cell variance are generally negative for whites, but are positive for blacks. There has been a trend toward blacks receiving a higher covered share of the GNP and whites a lower one. Real covered earnings are growing at a much faster rate for blacks than for whites.

## Notes

1. SSA: Social Security Administration.

2. Since 1956 about 90 percent of workers are covered.

3. Beginning in 1978, the SSA has recorded earnings reported to the IRS above the Social Security limits. They apparently do not record earnings in noncovered occupations.

4. The 0.07 is consistent with much of the research and with earnings functions. (See, e.g., the survey in Behrman et al. 1980.) We do not change the variance, since the method used assumes a constant expected variance for all observations.

5. We do not study earnings for those over 64, because the labor supply is highly variable.

6. The weights are $\sqrt{N_i}$ where $N_i$ is the number of people in the cell.

7. The exceptions occur in the equations for $\ln[Y/(GNP/L)]$ for females.

8. Black males aged 50–65 have too few observations for the results to be robust, so we have excluded them.

9. The two insignificant coefficients are for older women, for whom this same phenomena may approximately cancel out the negative impact, which dominates in most cases.

10. The SSA has no information on hours worked.

# Bibliography

Beach, C. 1976. Cyclical impacts on the personal distribution of income. *Annals of Economic and Social Measurement* (winter): 29–52.

Behrman, J. R., et al. 1980. *Socioeconomic Success: A Study of the Effects of Genetic Endowments, Family Environment and Schooling* (with Z. Hrubec, P. Taubman, and T. Wales). Amsterdam: North-Holland.

Bhageri, F. 1978. Distributional Impacts of Macroeconomic Fluctuations on the Structure of Earnings: A Longitudinal Approach. Ph.D. diss., University of Pennsylvania.

Feldstein, M. 1976. Temporary layoffs in the theory of unemployment. *Journal of Political Economy* 84: 937–958.

Gramlich, G. M. 1974. The Distributional Effects of Higher Unemployment. Brookings Papers on Economic Activity, no. 2.

Hanushek, E., and J. Quigley. 1978. Implicit investment profiles and intertemporal adjustment of relative Wages. *American Economic Review* 68.

Klein, L. R. 1962. *An Introduction to Econometrics.* Englewood Cliffs, N. J.: Prentice-Hall.

Metcalf, C. 1972. *An Econometric Model of the Income Distribution.* Chicago: Markham.

Mincer, J. 1974. *Schooling, Experience, and Earnings,* New York: NBER.

Phelps, E. 1970. *Microeconomic Foundations of Employment and Inflation Theory.* New York: Norton.

Plantes, M. 1978. An Intercoherent Analysis of Lifetime Earnings: The Role of Cyclical Fluctuations in Labor Demand and Labor Supply Conditions. Mimeograph, University of Wisconsin.

Schultz, T. P. 1969. Secular trends and cyclical behavior of income distribution in the United States: 1944–1965. In L. Sottow, ed., *Six Papers on the Size Distribution of Income and Wealth.* New York: NBER.

Rosen, S., and P. Taubman. 1979. Changes in the impact of education and income on mortality in the U.S. In Statistical Uses of Administrative Records with Emphasis on Mortality and Disability Research, U.S. Department of Health, Education, and Welfare.

Thurow, L. C. 1970. Analyzing the American income distribution. *American Economic Review* 60 (May): 261–270.

Wachter, M. 1970. Cyclical variation in inter-industry wage structure. *American Economic Review* 60 (March): 75–84.

# 14 Japan's Macroeconomic Policies During the 1970s

Chikashi Moriguchi

In its experiences in macroeconomic policy management during the 1970s, Japan shared some problems with many other industrial countries during the same period: high inflation, unemployment, and industrial adjustment prompted by high energy prices and import liberalization at an unprecedented pace. At the same time, Japan managed to cope with most difficulties in a manner characteristic of the Japanese economic system.

The decade of trial and error in macroeeonomic policy management can be divided into four periods. The first period was 1971–1973, during which the economy was given some shocks by the United States' New Economic Policies announced on August 14, 1971, and then by worldwide inflation. The policy response, overexpansion of the money supply and public spending, resulted partly from an overestimation of the deflationary effect of yen appreciation. Inflation had been going on when the first oil shock hit the economy in late 1973.

The second period was characterized by a policy reversal toward controlling high inflation. Some public-works projects were suspended, and a tight money policy quickly materialized in the effective credit-control scheme of the central bank. The result was a sharp drop in production, consumption, and corporate profit, while employment was curtailed at a gradual pace.

The third period was characterized by stagnant domestic activity and a sharp increase in net exports. Employment adjustment became a top-priority problem for business firms; latent unemployment within firms was estimated to be larger than the actual unemployment level shown by official statistics. A macroeconomic requirement for public policy was to maintain the level of aggregate economic activity so that the adjustment of employment and industrial structure might proceed without much difficulty. Undervaluation of the yen rate became obvious with the rising trade surplus. A basic policy issue in this period was whether the deficit spending was insufficient and whether its timing was right. There were some complicating factors in relation to the above question: the "J-curve effect" of exchange-rate change and the fiscal authority's attitude toward massive deficit financing in fear of mounting difficulties in fiscal management.

The fourth and last period of the decade saw a recovery of domestic demand in the private sector, the eventual effect of exchange-rate appreci-

**Table 1**
Key indicators, at average annual rate of exchange.

|  | 1965–70 | 1971–73 | 1974–75 | 1976–78 | 1979–80[a] |
|---|---|---|---|---|---|
| Money supply | 16.4 | 24.5 | 14.0 | 10.0 | 9.5 |
| Read GDP | 11.1 | 8.6 | 0.6 | 5.7 | 5.0 |
| CPI | 5.8 | 7.4 | 17.9 | 7.0 | 5.8 |
| GDP deflator |  |  |  |  |  |
| Imported material | 0 | 36.0 | 0 | −2.0 | 37.8 |
| Yen/dollar (rate of appreciation) | 0 | 10.0 | −4.0 | 14.0 | −4.0 |

a. Estimated

ation on the balance of payments, and an absolute halt in inflation. Employment adjustment was almost complete. The economy succeeded in getting rid of both internal and external imbalances in early 1979. Even though the economy was again hit by a wave of doubling oil prices and a subsequent depreciation of the yen rate, domestic inflation was put successfully under control this time by a cautionary monetary policy. However, the generally accepted outlook of the economy in the medium-term future was accompanied by a continuation of a large deficit in the current fiscal balance. It is highly likely that more than 30 percent of the current revenue of the central government's General Account will have to be financed by bond issuance. The current deficit in fiscal 1979 was 9.7 trillion yen, or 32 percent of total household savings. There is a national consensus on the necessity of reducing the size of current deficit, but the problem is how. This is a basic issue for the first half of the 1980s.

The purpose of this chapter is to look into some of the above-mentioned policy issues, partly on the basis of econometric model analysis and partly with recourse to more casual but broader observations. I will be concerned mainly with a change in the magnitude of the fiscal multiplier, the manner of expectation formation, and the role of the Phillips curve in a non-key-currency open economy.

## Causes of Monetary Expansion During 1971–1973

Money supply M2 increased by 55 percent during the two-year period starting from April 1971. This appears to be a very high expansion rate in retrospect, but as of early 1971 the generally accepted view on the long-run equilibrium rate of monetary expansion was somewhat around 16

**Table 2**
Stylized modes of macroeconomic policies.

| | 1971–73 | 1974–75 | 1976–78 | 1979–80 |
|---|---|---|---|---|
| **Monetary policy** | | | | |
| Rediscount rate | 4.25% | 9% | 3.5% | 9% |
| Credit control | None | Strict | None | Somewhat strict |
| Money-supply target | None | None | 10–12% | 9–10% |
| **Fiscal policy** | | | | |
| Spending | Expansionary | Neutral | Expansionary | Suppressed |
| Tax | Small cut for TP | Raise TC, large cut for TP | Small cut for TP | No change |
| Public fund for housing | Expansionary | Expansionary to 78 | | Neutral |
| Transfer to households | Increase throughout to 78 | | | Neutral |
| **Wage-price control** | None | Price control on oil products, suasion for wage restraint | Suasion continues | None |

**Table 3**
Various Phillips curves with unemployment rate.

| | $\sum_{0}^{3} w_i \dot{C}PI_{-i}$ | $\sum_{0}^{3} w_i(RU/5\%)^{-1}_{-i}$ | $\sum_{0}^{3} w_i \dot{\gamma} C_{-i}$ | $\bar{R}^2$ | S.C. | DW |
|---|---|---|---|---|---|---|
| $\dot{W}$T, 1966.4–1978.4 | 0.7030 | 2.694 | — | 0.834 | 1.90 | 0.74 |
| | (13.7) | (8.34) | | | | |
| $\dot{W}$T, 1970.1–1978.4 | 0.6137 | 3.314 | — | 0.872 | 1.86 | 1.04 |
| | (11.0) | (9.20) | | | | |
| $\dot{W}$S, 1966.4–1978.4 | 0.8030 | 3.338 | 0.0347 | 0.789 | 2.6 | 1.96 |
| | (11.0) | (7.38) | (2.65) | | | |
| $\dot{W}$S, 1970.1–1978.4 | 0.7138 | 3.760 | 0.0400 | 0.817 | 2.7 | 2.38 |
| | (8.47) | (6.81) | (2.61) | | | |

Notes: WT is "regular" wage payment index for all industries but service. WS is total wage payments index for all industries but service. Weights of distributed lags are $w_0 = 0.4$, $w_1 = 0.3$, $w_2 = 0.2$, and $w_3 = 0$.

percent. In fact the Japanese economy had maintained a high monetary growth of 16–18 percent in the previous five years without accelerating inflation. Thus, a key question to macroeconomic policy makers during this period ought to have been "What added 8 percent to the long-run rate?"

Of two potential factors that contribute to an increase in reserve money—namely, net purchase of public bonds and of foreign assets in the form of changes in foreign-exchange reserves—the former showed a decrease in the period in question, while the latter increased by 3.8 trillion yen. The total increase in the central bank's assets was 2.6 trillion yen, an average annual rate of 18.6 percent. It is clear that the increase in high-powered money was solely realized through the government's intensive purchase of dollars when the undervaluation of the yen was so obvious in the world foreign-exchange market.

Even though the fiscal balance was a little contractionary in this period, owing to an increase in personal and corporate tax revenue, the scale of public spending was highly expansionary. It reached a tremendous momentum when Kakuei Tanaka came to power in 1972, announcing his plan of "Restructuring the Japanese Archipelago." Under a historical money ease, this brought about nationwide speculation in stocks and the commodity market and in real estate. The Marshallian $k$ rose sharply in this period.

The whole process originally started from a fear of the great deflationary impact of yen rate upvaluation on the economy. Government and business sectors as well as all opposition party leaders and most economists tended to overestimate the magnitude of the deflationary impact.[1] There was, therefore, nationwide agreement on the necessity of a drastic expansionary policy in order to maintain the aggregate demand level. Some extreme opinion had it that the government needed to raise the inflation rate by deliberate policy in order to "evade" yen rate appreciation. It is not certain whether the government actually pursued this extreme policy, but the actual development of the economy was as if it did so.

The first period of the 1970s started with a misguided policy in relation to the impact of the fluctuating exchange rate. Expectation of a high long-run growth rate was deep-rooted. When the Bank of Japan switched to a tight money policy in early 1973, the business sector was stepping up its investment plans. Even though the government suspended some scheduled public works in the 1973 budget, it was not quite consistent with the change in monetary policy. A public housing-loan bank was expanding its funding to private housing investment, and consumer expenditures were stimulated by a new large-scale social security program starting in 1973.

## 1974–75: Inconsistent Policy Mix?

By the time the first oil shock hit the economy, two-digit inflation was already being recorded, and the threat of an oil embargo by the Organization of Petroleum Exporting Countries in combination with tripled oil prices gave the final push. Throughout 1973, the Bank of Japan kept raising the official discount rate and tried hard to reinforce its "window operation" by which the credit expansion of private banks' was controlled. The credit expansion rate dropped from 25.5 percent to 16.8 percent at the year's end compared with the previous year. Together with 2.5 trillion yen worth of selling operations on the foreign exchange, the rate of monetary expansion dropped similarly to 15.5 percent.

On the other hand, fiscal policy was not really anti-inflationary in this period. Although public spending was suppressed significantly, overall public spending showed an increase of 28 percent over the preceding fiscal year even in 1974, owing to a more than 30 percent rise in public employees' wages. There is a remarkable downward rigidity in current government spending, in which more than 70 percent is for personnel expenses. Wage rates are linked to those of the private sector under an arbitration system, and the level of public employment is virtually fixed under Japan's permanent-employment system. Further, government funds for housing-investment loans were given additional resources in order to make up for higher construction costs, and social security benefits and other government transfers continued to increase under the newly expanded program.

In addition, the Tanaka government implemented income-tax cuts on a massive scale (2 trillion yen, or 28 percent of the personal-tax revenue expected without the tax cut). The main reason was to adjust the progressive tax scheme to the latest inflation rate. Because of the tax cuts, revenue from the national personal income tax for 1974 remained at the 1973 level. This brought back the average national personal-tax rate from 6.3 percent in 1973 to 5.0 percent—the 1971 level. Thus, all in all, the current fiscal balance of the central government ended in a deficit in fiscal 1974.

The 1974 tax cut is remembered now for its massive scale and for its effect on the "deficit muddle" that will be continuing for some time in the future. Was a tax cut that large really necessary? If not, then why did it happen?

The answer to the first part of the question is no, but of course it is based on some wisdom of hindsight. Perhaps the Tanaka government, knowing the necessity of a certain level of tax cuts, made a political calculation on the basis of the high long-run real rate of a growth.[2] If 10 percent real growth or 15 percent nominal growth in the GNP resumed, tax revenue from a modified scheme would flow in at a rate of 18 percent and the economy would reach the stage of full employment surplus again.[3]

However, by the end of 1974 the real impact of high energy prices and a reaction to the investment boom in 1972–73 began to take effect. The new large plants in the steel and petrochemical industries turned out to be excessive. Household saving rates jumped to a historical high. The generally accepted anticipation for high growth had to be revised downward. The whole economy was moving to a period of exploring a new long-run potential growth path and adjusting itself to it. The basic assumption for the massive income-tax cut of 1974 was just not right. The same argument can be used to explain why the 1974 Spring Labor Offensive won a 33 percent wage increase. A gain of 6–7 percent in real wages was only compatible with a 10 percent real growth anticipation by business management.

During this period, the overly expanded money supply had to be contracted and credit control was pursued singlemindedly. Fiscal policy, on the other hand, disclosed its inherent inflexibility as a policy instrument. Spending for public works had shown some flexibility, but it was almost offset by a rigidity in current spending. Throughout 1975, the above-stated characteristics revealed themselves. Overall public expenditures showed an increase of 29 percent, and, owing to a drop in corporate income, the deficit in the central government's current balance jumped from 1.5 to 5.6 trillion yen.

## Effectiveness of Fiscal Policy, Phillips Curve, and J Curve: 1976–1978

After a fast cooloff, the economy fell into stagnation. Major factors were the high personal savings ratio, low business investment resulting from excess capacity and low profit, inactive housing investment because of squeezed loans and high construction costs, and slow export growth because of worldwide recession. The Bank of Japan had already started to ease the monetary situation, but by early 1976 it was clear that a stimulative fiscal policy was needed to maintain the economic activity level.[4]

However, public spending was not expanded on a large scale until 1978. Besides the modest fiscal spending program, there was the great political confusion of 1976: Tanaka stepped down amidst the Lockheed scandal and the 1976 budget plan was damaged by a delay in Diet procedure. Investment plans by some public corporations had to be cut when the Diet shelved some bills for price adjustment and rationalization. If it had not been for a 20 percent increase in commodity exports in 1976 (mainly supported by the recovery of the U.S. economy), the growth rate of real GDP would have been 4 percent or so instead of the actual 5.8 percent.

Despite the increased current deficit of central government for 1976, total public expenditures showed a 1.3 percent growth in real terms, and throughout 1977 the economy was virtually back in recession.[5] Individual firms were preoccupied with curtailing employment by various means, and the macroeconomic impact was becoming clear in unemployment statistics. "Surplus employees" were estimated at 2 million. The economic slump brought down the rate of import growth, widening the balance-of-payments surplus to a historic high. Thus, it became apparent that the economy had moved to a new stage of internal and external imbalance.

Even though this situation was not a dilemma for policy assignment, the existence of certain complicating factors could not be denied. One was a fairly long time lag in the effect of yen rate appreciation on the trade balance, and the other was the declining multiplier effect of public spending.

The long time lag in the effect of yen rate change on trade balance was quite remarkable. There are some factors contributing to the prolonged part of the J-curve which could be explained in association with certain characteristics of the Japanese economy. Yen rate upvaluation first brings down the cost of imported material inputs and hence brings down the cost of exported goods. Second, keen competition among Japanese exporters made it rather difficult to pass the upvalued yen rate on to export prices in terms of, say, U.S. dollars. Yen-denominated export prices showed a significant decline, and this further encouraged exporters efforts to cut costs. Third, Japan's import market did not respond to the rising profitability so readily; the market was not sufficiently competitive or open to new entries by potential competitors, domestic or overseas.

Besides, the whole process that generated the prolonged part of the J-curve was strengthened by existing wage flexibility. During the process of fast cooloff and the economic slump that followed, the short-run Phillips curve kept shifting downward. Moreover, stabilization of the inflation rate was reinforced by yen rate appreciation. In Japan's case, contractionary policy can bring down the rate of wage increases by rising unemployment rates and by downward price movements through a slack domestic market and a higher yen rate (see figure 1 and table 3). Inflationary expectations played an important role in the great inflation period, but those nonwage factors that affect price changes played a much greater role afterward in resisting price increases and thus suppressing inflationary expectations. This brought the whole inflation process to a complete halt.[6]

The second complicating factor was that the magnitude of the fiscal multiplier effect had been reduced, for the following reasons. First, the personal savings ratio became higher; the marginal saving ratio in the 1970s was somewhere around 30 percent, as compared to 20–25 percent in the 1960s. Second, with the long-run growth rate expected to be around 5–6 percent and with a low capacity utilization ratio, fixed business

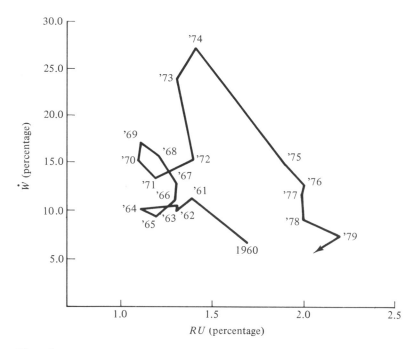

**Figure 1**
Wage-rate change and unemployment.

investment became much less responsive to increased demand. Third, because of the high prices of imported oil and other materials, the marginal rate of leakage of income from the multiplier process through payments abroad was raised. Finally, with enforced codes of safety and environmental protection, and other public regulations, a larger proportion of spending on public works was allocated to preliminary research and design and other "software." The direct impact on industrial production was therefore significantly reduced.[7] All in all, the multiplier effect of government investment on GDP decreased from 2.5 to 3.0 in 1970 and to 1.5–1.8 in 1977.[8]

In addition, there was the question of the possible relationship between public spending and employment change. In an economy with a "permanent employment" system, only a sustained increase in demand can bring about a significant increase in employment. Employment on a permanent basis is a long-term matter for employers, perhaps with equal weight given to fixed investment decisions. Temporary increases in public works might produce some increases in construction workers, but the latter are supplied mainly from the agricultural sector as "seasonal migrants." They might have nothing to do with reducing the unemployment of those who are in the core labor population with family dependents. Employers tend to respond to temporary demand increases by extending overtime or hiring short-term workers.

The effect of public spending on employment levels is further inhibited by labor productivity increases, the existence of surplus employees within firms, and the classical link between wage rates and demand for labor. The last factor in particular is not negligible when a contractionary policy can work on a downward shift along the Phillips curve through labor-market conditions and through yen rate appreciation.

A key question arises: Was the 1978 fiscal expansion effective? If it was, should it not have taken place earlier? With respect to the effectiveness of Keynesian policy, I am certain not that it contributed significantly to employment levels, but that it contributed to maintaining the aggregate demand at a 5–6 percent growth rate, thus avoiding a further recession in the economy in late 1977. Admittedly, the "cost" of the deficit required to obtain a given policy target has increased owing to the lowered multiplier effect.[9] Nevertheless, this was a justifiable policy in view of the situation of Japan's economy.

With regard to the appropriate timing for the expansionary policy, the policy authority could have performed better. The stagnant domestic demand that led to virtually zero growth in imports could have been avoided by a stepped-up stimulus policy. However, how much it would have affected imports remains a question. Without a more open import market, Japan's import demand would not have responded. Earlier efforts to open up Japan's market to imports of manufactured goods and to make it more competitive seem to have been more appropriate. Some argue that a certain time span is needed to destroy high inflationary expectations and that the process of low growth from 1975 to 1977 was necessary. However, the rate of inflation as of late 1977 was more stable than in early 1970 or in the 1960s. It is rather doubtful that the 1977 slump was actually needed for that purpose.

There seems to be a more positive reason that a stepped-up stimulus package was more desirable. It would have brought about a recovery in private-sector demand earlier and contributed to an early improvement in the balance of payments, thus bringing about a more stable path of yen appreciation. In view of the development of the economy in late 1978, high public spending and a strong recovery in domestic demand produced a 7 percent annual real growth rate. As a result of this and the long-awaited positive effect of yen appreciation on trade, the balance of payments started to show marked improvement. The yen rate, after recording a historic high in November 1978, started to fall, and this time it showed a large margin of depreciation. This was readily reflected in wholesale price increases. The entire process could have been made much smoother by a stepped-up policy.

## Conclusion

Throughout the 1970s Japan's policy management had to respond to "new situations" emerging one after another, without clear views of the potential outcomes. Policy reaction tended to be late and, partly as a result, over-reactive. Overresponse had to be dealt with by further overresponse. This description of policy behavior seems particularly applicable to the man-agement of fiscal policy, where decision making and the execution of policy change had to go through political processes in the Diet.

The monetary authority, after learning a few lessons from the 1971–1973 overexpansion and its consequences, became highly concerned with the rate of monetary growth and seemed to be badly in need of an adequate independence of the central bank from the government in its relevant policy decisions. After 1976 the Bank of Japan seemed to have established leadership as far as monetary policy was concerned. It was responsible for successful management of stable monetary growth. When a series of strong inflationary pressures came from abroad in early 1979 and the wholesale price index showed a sharp rise, the whole situation was somewhat reminiscent of the 1973–74 inflation, except for one thing. This time, the monetary situation was entirely different: The Bank of Japan responded readily by switching to a tigher monetary policy from its already cautionary one. Further, the fiscal authority, which had been strongly concerned with the cumulative growth of public bonds, was quick to reduce and suspend some of the scheduled public spending. Thus, the domestic inflation rate as measured by the GDP deflator was not affected much by the imported inflationary factor.

Social security programs should not be considered as an instrument of stabilization policy, yet it cannot be denied that introducing new transfer schemes or raising the social security contributions of employees has some aspects of an anticyclical policy. Large-scale expansion of social security programs in 1973–74 was originally planned as part of the government's economic plan to help the Japanese economy shift from industrial-production-oriented high growth to a moderate growth path, with much emphasis put on welfare. An increase in social security benefits was considered to offset the economic efforts of a misconceived "slump" caused by yen appreciation.

By 1976 the fiscal authority was aiming at an appropriate balance in social security benefits and contributions as a part of its campaign for suppressing deficit accumulation. Social security contributions—particularly contributions to medical insurance—were raised considerably in 1977.[10] It was apparently carried out with most inappropriate timing, and the rate of increase in personal real consumption expenditure was affected, which was one of the factors that explained the mini-recession.

It is rather easy to criticize the inadequate performance of Japan's fiscal policy throughout the 1970s. However, the reality was that the whole fiscal system was just not organized for the purpose of countercyclical policy measures. Public investment played the role of stabilization policy,[11] while the government's final consumption was barely responsive. Central government and local government do not cooperate particularly well in implementing stabilization policy in Japan. Even though local government undertakes more than half the total general government capital formation, the actual spending behavior of some local governments is not consistent with that of the central government. An additional complicating factor here is the difference in the time-lag structure of national and local personal income taxes. Local personal income tax is collected on the basis of income earned in the preceding year. Current income tax withdrawn from one's income has a significant portion that is associated with the previous year's income. This is likely to cause inconsistent spending behavior between central and local governments. In 1974, when the central government was tightening its spending, local governments were still maintaining a fairly expansionary policy, thanks to their growing tax revenue based on the inflationary income of 1973. When the central government turned quickly to a tighter budget in 1979, some local governments tried to step up their planned public works in order to get them started before the central government might intervene and halt them.

Despite the above-mentioned problems, demand management with recourse to fiscal measures was necessary to support the economy against the potential macroeconomic consequences of individual business effort adjusting itself to the new situation by employment curtailment or "weight reduction." There seem to be many incidences in which discretionary policies could have performed better if there had been better prediction of the actual development of the economy. More realistic evaluation of the impact of yen rate appreciation and of the lowering of the anticipated long-run growth rate of the economy would have led to more successful policy management.

Judging from the fact that the economic fluctuations during the first half of the 1970s were hard to forecast as an "outside sample" prediction, it is not certain that Japan could have performed better in macroeconomic policy management. However, extensive research on the macroeconomic behavior of an open economy under a floating exchange-rate system seems to have built a more solid ground for stabilization policy in late 1970s. Regression back into a simple economic model in which only random disturbances are given overstressed treatment does not seem to offer a solution.

## Notes

1. One reason for the overestimation of the deflationary effect was that the price elasticity of the Japanese export equation, as estimated in early 1970, was rather high (ranging from 3 to 5). Another was the overestimation of possible rises in export prices (in terms of foreign currencies).

2. Evidence supporting this conjecture can be found in the first five-year economic plan drawn up by the Tanaka government at this time.

3. Personal-income-tax elasticity with respect to personal income is assumed to be about 1.2.

4. The Forum for Policy Innovation, a small group of economists and political scientists, appealed for a switch to a stimulative policy in April 1976. The group quickly became known as the "Keynesian hard core" in Japan.

5. In 1977 the official business-cycle indicator showed it for five consecutive months.

6. The wage-price relation as described in my model works as follows: 10 percent yen rate appreciation brings down the price of imported materials by the same margin, leading to a drop in wholesale price levels by about 3 percent and a drop in the CPI by 1.5 percent. In addition, the negative impact on the volume of exports, on domestic production, and on profits leads to a further drop in wholesale prices and to a rise in unemployment.

7. A survey showed that, as of 1978, the hardware content of public-works spending was reduced by 30 percent from 1970.

8. This is based on simulation results from the Kyoto University Macroeconomic Model, using macroeconomic parameters estimated from observations of the 1960's and the 1970's, respectively. Long-run accumulated effects are taken.

9. To exemplify this point, the following case is helpful. With wages twice as high as in early 1970, and with a fiscal multiplier half the 1970 magnitude, the fiscal deficit needed to create wage-income increases worth 10,000 regular jobs could be four times as large as in 1970.

10. In this year, social security contributions increased by a larger rate than social security benefits, and net transfers from the government sector to households as a proportion of total national income were reduced for the first time since 1973.

11. It is interesting to see that the reaction pattern of public investment, as described by following policy-response function, retains a considerably strong aspect of stabilization policy:

$$\dot{IG} = 5.2 - 2.40\dot{p} - 1.39\,\dot{Y}_{priv} - 0.13D75$$
$$\quad\;\;(7.1)\;\;(6.4)\quad\;(3.8)\qquad\;\;(3.6)$$

where $\bar{R}^2 = 0.758$, S.E. $= 0.042$, D.W. $= 2.07$, the dot indicates rate of change, $IG$ is aggregate public capital formation, $P$ is the GDP inflator, $Y_{priv} = \text{GDP} + M - G$, and $D75$ is a dummy variable that corresponds to a shift of intercept after (and in) 1975. $IG$ and $Y_{priv}$ are in real terms. See C. Moriguchi et al., *Nihon Keizai to Zaisei no Keiryo Bunseki* (An Econometric Analysis of Japan's Economy and Public Finance) (Osaka: Kansai Keizai Kenkyu Center, 1980).

# 15 Finance and Economic Growth: The Japanese Experience

## Mitsuo Saito

This chapter evaluates the contributions of monetary factors to Japanese economic growth in the 1960s. In a large-scale econometric model, I simulate a hypothetical growth path in which the saving ratio is approximately 5 percent lower than the actual level and compare it with the actual saving growth path of the Japanese economy. The comparison between these two growth paths indicates that in the period 1959–1965 a 5 percent reduction in the saving ratio would have resulted in a 1.2 percent decline in the average GNP growth rate together with a 1.2 percent increase in the average inflation rate.

## General Features of the Model

The accounting framework of the time-series data on which the model is based is the SNA (System of National Accounts) format (United Nations 1968), which was introduced in Japan in 1978. The main feature of this scheme is its unified approach to social accounting; the national income accounts, flow-of-funds table, input-output table, national balance sheets, and balance-of-payments account are all included and are consistent with one another.

Economic agents in the model consist of five groups: households, nonfinancial firms, financial firms (banks), the central bank, and the government. Nonfinancial firms are further disaggregated into 27 industries in the interindustry transactions table.[1]

All transactions of goods, services, assets, and liabilities and all tax and transfer payments of each group are recorded in (1) the production account, (2) the income-outlay account, (3) the capital finance account of real assets, (4) the capital finance account of financial assets and liabilities, (5) the closing balance sheet of real assets, and (6) the closing balance sheet of financial assets and liabilities. An example of the items recorded under 2–6 above for households are shown in table 1; similar accounts under 1–6 are given for other groups. The various accounts of a more conventional format can easily be obtained by appropriate combinations of these accounts. The consolidation of accounts 2 and 3 of all the agents gives us the national income accounts. Similarly, the flow-of-funds table of the national economy can be produced by collecting

**Table 1**
The accounts of households.

| **2. Income-outlay account** | |
|---|---|
| Consumption expenditures | Compensation of employees |
| Direct taxes | Proprietors' income |
| Transfer payments | Property income (interests, dividends, rents) |
| Savings | Transfer payments |
| Total payments | Total receipts |

| **3. Capital finance account of real assets** | |
|---|---|
| Purchases of equipment and change in inventories | Savings |
| | Capital consumption allowances |
| Purchases of houses | Total capital financing |
| Net change in financial assets | |
| Total accumulation | |

| **4. Capital finance account of financial assets** | |
|---|---|
| Currency | Net change in financial assets |
| Demand deposits | Loans by financial institutions |
| Time deposits | Other liabilities |
| Trusts and insurance | Total liabilities |
| Bonds | |
| Stocks | |
| Other financial assets | |
| Total financial assets | |

| **5. Balance-sheet account of real assets** | |
|---|---|
| Stock of equipment and inventories | Net worth |
| Stock of residential structures | Year-end net worth |
| Difference between financial assets and liabilities | |
| Year-end assets | |

| **6. Balance-sheet account of financial assets and liabilities** | |
|---|---|
| Currency | Loans by financial institutions |
| Demand deposits | Other liabilities |
| Time deposits | Difference between financial assets and liabilities |
| Trusts and insurance | |
| Bonds | Year-end liabilities |
| Stocks | |
| Other financial assets | |
| Year-end financial assets | |

accounts 4 and 6 of all the agents, while accounts 5 of all the agents constitute the national balance sheet. Finally, disaggregating account 1 for firms into a number of industries yields the input-output table.

My former econometric model of the Japanese economy (1972) was a statistical model combining input-output analysis with standard econometric methods of inference which utilized national income accounts and the input-output table as basic data. It was a version of the so-called Keynes-Leontief model; the economic theory underlying it was a combination of general-equilibrium theory of the Walras-Hicks type with Keynsian income-determination theory. The present model extends the former model to encompass the monetary sector; its basic data therefore include the flow-of-funds accounts as well as the national income accounts and the input-output table. Given the purpose of the model, it is clear that the behavioral equations of each economic group require the inclusion of portfolio decisions concerning the individual assets and liabilities in the balance sheet. In addition, banks should be treated as an independent economic group. Because of these considerations, the model is based on a general-equilibrium theory of the Tobin type (Tobin 1969; Brainard and Tobin 1968), in which the interaction of portfolio behaviors among firms, households, banks, and the government serve to determine asset prices and interest rates.

**The Household Sector**

In principle the model is composed of the behavioral equations explaining the individual items in all the accounts for each group of agents and the market equations describing the adjustment processes in the markets for goods, services, assets, and liabilities. In the following summary of the way in which household behavior is modeled, the household sector is elucidated in more detail than other sectors in order that the general features of the model may be better understood. Household behavior may be viewed as composed of three basic types of decision making: the allocation of income among total consumption, housing investment, and the net change in financial assets; the allocation of net total holdings of financial assets among individual financial assets and liabilities; and the division of total consumption into expenditures for individual consumption items.

Consolidation of accounts 2 and 3 for households in table 1 yields the budget restraint

$$YGh = Sh + IRh + IOh + Ch, \tag{1}$$

where $YGh$ is gross disposable income (including capital consumption allowances), $Sh$ is net increase in financial assets (including capital consumption allowances), $IRh$ is housing investment, $IOh$ is other investment (business investment by unincorporated enterprises), and $Ch$ is total consumption expenditure. Each variable is deflated and defined in per-household terms.

The equations concerning household allocation of income among total consumption, housing investment, and net change in financial assets are

$$YH = a \cdot XH,$$

$$\begin{array}{ccc} YH = [YH_i], & XH = [XH_i], & a = [a_{ij}] \\ (4 \times 1) & (10 \times 1) & (4 \times 10) \end{array} \tag{2}$$

where $YH_1 = Sh/YGh$, $YH_2 = IRh/YGh$, $YH_3 = IOh/YGh$, $YH_4 = Ch/YGh$, and $XH$ is the vector of the ten explanatory variables listed in table 2. Estimates of the elements of the coefficient matrix, $a$, are shown in table 2. Equations 2 must satisfy equation 1; that is, they must satisfy the following constraints:

$$\sum_{i=1}^{4} a_{ij} = 0, \quad i = 1, 2, 3, 5, \ldots, 10,$$

$$\sum_{i=1}^{4} a_{i4} = 1. \tag{3}$$

The fourth explanatory variable is unity; thus, $a_{i4}$ measures the marginal propensity to save or to consume, adding up to unity. If the explanatory variables are common in all four equations, the least-squares estimates meet the above conditions, as seen in the estimates in table 2.

Given the large number of explanatory variables in equations 2, it is very likely that direct application of the ordinary regression method to them will yield unstable coefficient estimates due to multicollinearity. In order to avoid this difficulty, the method (Klein 1974) of pooling cross-section and time-series data was adopted for the estimation. The coefficients of holdings of financial assets $(a_{i1})$, lagged consumption $(a_{i2})$, number of persons in household $(a_{i3})$, and marginal propensity to save or consume $(a_{i4})$ were estimated from individual responses of the Family Savings Surveys in 1970–1974. These estimates and the annual time series

**Table 2**
Estimates of the saving and consumption functions of households.

|          | (1) $XH_1$      | (2) $XH_2$     | (3) $XH_3$      | (4) $XH_4$     | (5) $XH_5$     |
|----------|-----------------|----------------|-----------------|----------------|----------------|
| $Sh/YGh$ | $-0.095$        | $-0.129$       | $-0.017$        | $0.361$        | $-51.5$        |
|          | (14.8)          | (6.4)          | (2.9)           | (11.2)         | (3.1)          |
| $IRh/YGh$| $0.019$         | $0.016$        | $0.004$         | $0.038$        | $-30.7$        |
|          | (4.5)           | (1.1)          | (0.9)           | (1.7)          | (5.5)          |
| $IOh/YGh$| $0.015$         | $0.013$        | $-0.007$        | $0.052$        | $20.3$         |
|          | (4.7)           | (1.3)          | (2.5)           | (3.3)          | (3.5)          |
| $Ch/YGh$ | $0.061$         | $0.101$        | $0.020$         | $0.550$        | $61.8$         |
|          | (14.4)          | (7.6)          | (5.2)           | (25.8)         | (4.1)          |

Note: $XH_1 = $ (Deflated, year-beginning holdings of financial assets)$/YGh$; $XH_2 = $ (Deflated, lagged consumption)$/YGh$; $XH_3 = $ Number of persons in household; $XH_4 = 1$ (constant term in the cross-section regression); $XH_5 = 1/YGh$; $XH_6 = $ Gini coefficient; $XH_7 = $ (New housing loans)/(Year-beginning outstanding housing loans), commercial

of 1954–1974 were used to estimate the coefficients of the other variables. The number in parentheses below each coefficient in table 2 indicates its $t$ value; $\bar{R}$, S.E., and D.W. (Durbin-Watson statistics) were obtained from the time-series regression.

Next, let us turn to the allocation of net total holdings. Denote the year-end holdings of asset (or liability) $i$ by $A$ih and the net total of year-end holdings of financial assets and liabilities by $WFh$; then the identity in account 6 of table 1 is represented by

$$\sum_{i=1}^{9} A\text{ih} = WF\text{h}. \qquad (4)$$

Note that holdings of liabilities are defined as negative values. Also, an accounting identity between accounts 3 and 6, that is,

$$WF\text{h}_{t-1} + S\text{h}_t = WF\text{h}_t, \qquad (5)$$

must hold.[2] The behavioral equations for the decision pertaining to the allocation of the net total of financial assets among individual financial assets and liabilities are written as

$$AH = c \cdot BH,$$

$$\begin{array}{lll} AH = [AH_i], & BH = [BH_j], & c = [c_{ij}] \\ (9 \times 1) & (18 \times 1) & (9 \times 18) \end{array} \qquad (6)$$

where $AH$ represents the vector of the explained variables, whose $i$th element is $A$ih$/WF$h (each variable is deflated and defined in per house-

| (6) $XH_6$ | (7) $XH_7$ | (8) $XH_8$ | (9) $XH_9$ | (10) $XH_{10}$ | (11) $\bar{R}^2$/S.E. | (12) D.W. |
|---|---|---|---|---|---|---|
| 1.098 | -0.252 | -0.056 | -0.022 | -0.139 | 0.736 | 1.54 |
| (3.7) | (3.3) | (4.1) | (0.3) | (2.3) | (0.013) | |
| -0.531 | 0.032 | 0.012 | 0.072 | 0.111 | 0.966 | 2.06 |
| (2.8) | (1.2) | (2.6) | (2.8) | (5.6) | (0.004) | |
| -0.201 | 0.010 | 0.008 | 0.029 | 0.022 | 0.419 | 2.51 |
| (1.9) | (0.4) | (1.6) | (1.1) | (1.1) | (0.004) | |
| -0.366 | 0.210 | 0.036 | -0.078 | 0.006 | 0.902 | 1.42 |
| (1.4) | (3.1) | (2.9) | (1.1) | (0.1) | (0.011) | |

banks; $XH_8$ = (New housing loans)/(Year-beginning outstanding loans), Housing Loan Corporation; $XH_9$ = rate of change in general consumer prices; $XH_{10}$ = 1 (constant term in time-series regression).

hold terms), and $BH$ is the vector of the explanatory variables, listed in table 3. The primary three determinants of asset holdings are net total of financial assets, income, and a spectrum of rates of returns. Lagged $Aih$ values are added in order to allow for adjustments in the stock portfolio.

As regards the coefficients of the $c$ matrix, the following adding-up constraints must hold by identity 4:

$$\sum_{i=1}^{9} c_{i1} = 1,$$

$$\sum_{i=1}^{9} c_{ij} = 0, \quad j = 2, \dots, 18. \tag{7}$$

The least-squares estimates, as noted above, satisfy the constraints. As with the estimation of equations 2, cross-section and time-series data are pooled because of the possible presence of multicollinearity. The coefficients of net total of assets ($c_{i1}$), income ($c_{i2}$), and lagged $Aih$ ($c_{i3}, \dots, c_{i11}$) were first estimated from individual responses of the 1970–1974 Family Savings Survey; then, the coefficients of the rates of returns ($c_{i13}, \dots, c_{i16}$), the rate of price change ($c_{i17}$), and $1/WFh$ ($c_{i12}$) were estimated by use of these estimates and the time-series data of 1954–1974. The estimated results are shown in table 3. Lagged $Aih$ coefficients are not shown in the table to save the space. The coefficients of the own lagged $Aih$ range between 0.40 and 0.78; those of other lagged $Aih$ values are in general small and negative.

**Table 3**
Estimates of the portfolio equations of households.

|  | (1) $BH_1$ | (2) $BH_2$ | (3) $BH_{12}$ | (4) $BH_{13}$ | (5) $BH_{14}$ |
|---|---|---|---|---|---|
| $A1h/WFh$: Currency | 0.032 | 0.024 | 2.3 (1.1) | −0.11 (0.4) | 0.56 (2.1) |
| $A2h/WFh$: Demand deposits | 0.061 | 0.047 | −6.8 (1.6) | −0.25 (0.4) | −0.36 (0.7) |
| $A3h/WFh$: Time deposits | 0.209 | 0.082 | −16.5 (1.7) | 5.95 (4.3) | 3.93 (3.1) |
| $A4h/WFh$: Trust and insurance | 0.045 | 0.063 | −39.9 (7.3) | 1.20 (1.6) | 0.84 (1.2) |
| $A5h/WFh$: Bonds | 0.053 | 0.023 | −23.1 (4.3) | 0.08 (0.1) | 2.59 (3.8) |
| $A6h/WFh$: Stocks | 0.111 | 0.013 | −31.4 (1.3) | −10.4 (3.1) | −4.26 (1.4) |
| $A7h/WFh$: Other assets | 0.021 | 0.018 | 12.0 (0.8) | −0.51 (0.2) | −0.69 (0.34) |
| $A8h/WFh$: Bank loans | 0.338 | −0.192 | 87.0 (7.0) | −0.57 (0.3) | −2.15 (1.4) |
| $A9h/WFh$: Other liabilities | 0.131 | −0.078 | 16.2 (1.5) | 4.58 (2.9) | −0.47 (0.3) |

Notes: $BH_1 = 1$ (constant term of the cross-section regression); $BH_2 = $ income$/WFh$; $BH_3 \sim BH_{11} = A$ih$_{-1}/WFh$ (i = 1 $\sim$ 9); $BH_{12} = 1/WFh$; $BH_{13} = $ the interest rate of time deposits; $BH_{14} = $ the bond yield; $BH_{15} = $ the rate of returns of stocks; $BH_{16} = $ the bank loan rate; $BH_{17} = $ the rate of change of the general consumer price; $BH_{18} = 1$ (constant term of the time series regression).

For the allocation of total consumption expenditures among expenditures for the 23 individual consumption items,

$$\ln Ci = d_{i1} + d_{i2} \ln Ch + d_{i3}(\ln Ch)^2 + d_{i4} \ln(P_i^c/P^c), \quad i = 1, 2, \ldots, 22$$

$$\text{(8)}$$

$$C23 = Ch - \sum_{i=1}^{22} Ci \qquad (9)$$

where $Ci$ is expenditure for consumption item $i$, $P_i^c$ is price of consumption item $i$, and $P^c$ is general consumer price. The income effect (or total consumption effect) is given by the log-quadratic terms of $Ch$, and the price effect by a log-linear term of the own price relative to the general consumer price. Income effects were, as before, estimated from the Family Expenditure Surveys (cross-section data) of 1953–1975, while price effects were calculated from these estimates and the time-series data of 1958–

| (6)<br>$BH_{15}$ | (7)<br>$BH_{16}$ | (8)<br>$BH_{17}$ | (9)<br>$BH_{18}$ | (10)<br>$\bar{R}^2$/S.E. | (11)<br>D.W. |
|---|---|---|---|---|---|
| −0.00<br>(0.1) | −0.71<br>(2.0) | −0.24<br>(1.0) | 0.018<br>(1.1) | 0.764<br>(0.002) | 2.12 |
| −0.01<br>(0.7) | −0.53<br>(0.7) | −1.10<br>(2.5) | 0.098<br>(2.9) | 0.768<br>(0.004) | 2.83 |
| −0.08<br>(1.1) | −10.7<br>(6.4) | −0.89<br>(0.8) | 0.324<br>(4.1) | 0.958<br>(0.010) | 1.57 |
| −0.03<br>(3.0) | −2.18<br>(2.4) | −0.28<br>(0.5) | 0.079<br>(1.8) | 0.971<br>(0.005) | 1.98 |
| −0.02<br>(2.5) | −2.99<br>(3.3) | −0.40<br>(0.7) | 0.074<br>(1.7) | 0.936<br>(0.005) | 1.67 |
| 0.21<br>(4.8) | 15.2<br>(3.8) | 0.98<br>(0.4) | −0.270<br>(1.4) | 0.679<br>(0.023) | 1.97 |
| −0.04<br>(1.5) | 0.27<br>(0.1) | −0.94<br>(0.6) | 0.040<br>(0.3) | 0.008<br>(0.016) | 3.20 |
| −0.02<br>(0.9) | 1.25<br>(0.6) | −1.47<br>(1.1) | −0.042<br>(0.4) | 0.969<br>(0.012) | 2.76 |
| −0.00<br>(0.2) | 0.38<br>(0.2) | 4.33<br>(3.7) | −0.320<br>(3.6) | 0.873<br>(0.011) | 2.48 |

The *t*-values of the coefficients for $BH_1$ and $BH_2$ are not shown, since these coefficients are computed as a weighted average of the estimates for workers' households and those for nonworkers' households.

The coefficients for $BH_3 \sim BH_{11}$ are not shown.

1975. The last consumption item is determined as a residual, and thus the adding-up restraint is satisfied.

## The Nonfinancial-Firm Sector

The economic behavior of nonfinancial firms involves decisions on the current account (accounts 1 and 2 above) and on the capital account (accounts 3–6 above). The former decision, governed by the profit-maximization principle under given technology and given equipment, determines the output levels, employment, and required amounts of material inputs. The production accounts of nonfinancial firms are disaggregated into 27 industries, yielding a table of interindustry transactions. Within the framework of this input-output structure it is assumed that each industry is confronted with the Cobb-Douglas-type production function

$$\ln X_i = \ln A_i + \gamma_i t + \sum_{j=1}^{27} \alpha_{ji} \ln X_{ji} + \sum_{k=1}^{7} \zeta_{ki} \ln Z_{ki} + \lambda_i \ln L_i + \kappa_i \ln K_i,$$

$$\sum_{j=1}^{27} \alpha_{ji} + \sum_{k=1}^{7} \zeta_{ki} + \lambda_i + \kappa_i = 1$$

(10)

where $i = 1, 2, \ldots, 27$, $X_i$ is the output of industry $i$, $X_{ji}$ is the portion of the output of industry $j$ used in industry $i$, $Z_{ki}$ is the amount of the non-competitive import $k$ used in industry $i$, $L_i$ is the labor input of industry $i$, $K_i$ is the stock of capital of industry $i$, and $t$ is the time trend.

Suppose that Klein's nonsubstitution theorem (1952) holds. Then estimates for the exponents of the Cobb-Douglas function, $\hat{\alpha}_{ji}$, $\hat{\zeta}_{ki}$, $\hat{\lambda}_i$, and $\hat{\kappa}_i$, can be obtained from the value input coefficients of the input-output table.[3] From the marginal productivity conditions, we have

$$X_{ji} = \hat{\alpha}_{ji} \{ P_i (1 - t_i) X_i / P_j \},$$

$$Z_{ki} = \hat{\zeta}_{ki} \{ P_i (1 - t_i) X_i / P_k^z \}$$

(11)

where $i, j = 1, 2, \ldots, 27$, $k = 1, 2, \ldots, 7$, and where $P_j$, $P_k^z$, and $t_i$ are the prices of output $j$, noncompetitive import $k$, and the indirect tax ratio of industry $i$, respectively. By using these relationships together with the estimates, $\hat{\alpha}_{ji}$, $\hat{\zeta}_{ki}$, $\hat{\lambda}_i$, $\hat{\kappa}_i$, and the time series for $X_i$, $L_i$, $K_i$, $P_j$, $P_k^z$, and $t_i$, we can obtain estimates for $\gamma_i$ and $\ln A_i$.

When Klein's theorem prevails, the output level of each industry can be determined from the demand side by the equations

$$X = \hat{P}^{-1} [I - A(I - \hat{T})]^{-1} \hat{P} \cdot H \cdot FC$$

(12)

where $X$, $A$, $FC$, and $H$ are respectively the vector of outputs, the matrix of value input coefficients, the vector of final demands, and the matrix converting final demands into industrial demands and where $\hat{P}$ and $\hat{T}$ are the diagonal matrices of prices and the indirect tax ratios, respectively.

The markup price in each industry is given by

$$P = B' \cdot P + \hat{S} \cdot P + \hat{T} \cdot P + \hat{Z} \cdot PZ + \hat{n} \cdot WR + \hat{d} \cdot PI,$$

or by

$$P = (I - B' - \hat{S} - \hat{T})^{-1} (\hat{Z} \cdot PZ + \hat{n} \cdot WR + \hat{d} \cdot PI)$$

(13)

where $P$, $PZ$, and $WR$ are the vectors of output prices, noncompetitive import prices, and wage rates, respectively; $PI$ is a deflator for fixed investment; $B$ represents the matrix of quantity input coefficients; and $\hat{S}$, $\hat{Z}$, $\hat{n}$, and $\hat{d}$ are the diagonal matrices whose diagonal elements are respectively surpluses, noncompetitive imports, labor inputs, and capital consumption allowances per unit output. We assume that there is a first-order serial correlation in the errors of equations 12 and 13. The deflators for final demands are determined by a weighted average of industry prices.

The notional employment of each industry may be obtained by solving the production function 10 for $L_i$. It is assumed that there exists an adaptive expectation relationship between actual and notional employment for each industry.

The second type of decision making by firms, decisions on the capital account, is represented by a set of portfolio equations relating to financial assets, liabilities, capital stock, and inventory stock:

$$(A\text{ic}/W\text{c}) - (A\text{ic}/W\text{c})_{-1} = d_{i1} + d_{i2}[(A\text{ic}^*/W\text{c}) - (A\text{ic}/W\text{c})_{-1}] + \sum_j m_{ij} R_j \tag{14}$$

where $A$ic is the deflated, year-end holdings of asset $i$; $A$ic$^*$ is the desired, deflated, year-end holdings of asset $i$; $W$c is the deflated, year-end net worth $(= \sum_i A\text{ic})$; and $R_j$ is the nominal rate of returns of asset $j$. $A$ic$^*$ is the volume of asset $i$ desired for carrying out current production acitivity, and is assumed to be proportional to the current output level. The coefficient of proportion was estimated by a time trend of the asset-output ratio of each asset; for example, in the case of demand deposits, $A$ic$^*$ is the desired holding of demand deposits for transaction purposes, while, with respect to the capital stock, it represents the desired holding of capital stock when the acceleration principle is taken into account. Owing to the limited availability of data, the portfolio equations for each asset were estimated from the time-series data on the whole industry. The financial assets and liabilities held by firms are in the form of currency, demand deposits, time deposits, bonds, stocks, trade credit, other financial assets, trade debt, bank loans, and other liabilities (including bonds).

As regards fixed investment, the increase in the capital stock of the whole industry determined by equations 14 is further allocated among individual industries according to

$$IG_i = e_{i1} + e_{i2}(K_i^* - K_{i,-1}) + e_{i3}(LN_i/PI) \tag{15}$$

where $IG_i$ is gross fixed investment, $K_i^*$ is the desired, year-end stock of capital, $LN_i$ is the supply of new bank loans to industry $i$, and $K_i^*$ is obtained by evaluating

$$\frac{\kappa_i(P_i X_i)}{PI(1 - R8 - RD_i)}$$

where $R8$ is the interest rate of bank loans, $RD_i$ is the depreciation ratio of industry $i$, and $\kappa_i$ is the capital exponent of the production function (equation 10) of industry $i$. The preceding formula is derived from the marginal productivity relationship with respect to capital. $LN_i$ is determined from the behavioral equations representing banking-sector activity.

## The Banking Sector

Banks are assumed to accept as given and beyond their control the quantities of demand and time deposits, and to allocate their available funds among various assets on the basis of interest rates and the balance-sheet constraint. Their available funds are represented by

Demand deposits + Time deposits − Required reserves

+ Bank debentures + Bank equities.

It follows that their portfolio equations may be written as

$$Aib/WFb = f_{i1} + f_{i2}(DE/WFb) + f_{i3}(Aib_{-1}/WFb) + f_{i4}(1/WFb)$$

$$+ \sum_j f_{ij}Rj \tag{16}$$

where $Aib$ is the deflated, year-end holdings of asset (or liability) $i$; $DE$ is the deflated, year-end holdings of deposits less required reserves; $WFb$ is the deflated, year-end net worth, or $DE$ plus bank debentures plus bank equities; and $Rj$ is the rate of return of asset $j$. As with the procedure employed in the estimates of coefficients relating to household behavior, $f_{i1}$, $f_{i2}$, and $f_{i3}$ were estimated from cross-section data (the 1975 balance sheets of banks). The other coefficients were estimated by use of these estimates and the 1954–1974 time-series data.

A greater part of bank loans in Japan have been appropriated for the purchase of industrial equipment. New loans specifically for equipment are allocated among industries by the equations

$$LN_i/LN = g_{i1} + g_{i2}RP_i + g_{i3}t \tag{17}$$

where $i = 1, 2, \ldots, 27$, $LN_i$ is the new loans for equipment in industry $i$, $LN$ is $\Sigma_i\, LN_i$, $RP_i$ is the rate of profits, or (Profits plus capital consumption allowances)/(Capital stock), and $t$ is the time trend. $LN$ is related to increases in bank loans, $\Delta A8$b, by a statistical equation. The variable $RP_i$ is included to indicate that banks prefer to lend more funds to more profitable industries. The time trend, on the other hand, is introduced to reflect the difference in growth rates among industries, the industrial policy of the government, and other exogenous factors.

## Market Adjustment Equations

The output levels of each industry are given by the equation set 12, which implies that the demand factor plays a major role in output determination. On the other hand, price equations 13 represent the markup pricing principle, emphasizing supply factors in price determination. The employment level in each individual industry, as explained above, is determined chiefly by the labor demand of firms. Total employment affects the determination of the average wage in the whole economy through a Phillips curve. Exports and most imports are treated as exogenous.

In general, for each economic group we have the flow-of-funds equations for each asset and each liability. Collecting them asset by asset yields the market demand and supply of each asset. The bank-loan rate is determined so as to equate the demand and the supply of bank loans; however, in the dynamic simulation it is assumed that there is a band around the rate of the previous year beyond which the loan rate cannot move. If excess demand should prevail in the loan market at the rate of the upper limit of the band, the rate is fixed at this upper limit; the quantity of loan supply is realized, while the quantity of loan demand is curtailed. If the loan market is found to be in excess supply at the rate of the lower limit of the band, the rate is fixed at this lower limit and the quantity of demand is realized. The rate of return of bonds is decided similarly; that of stocks is considered exogenous. As noted above, the quantities of demand deposits and time deposits are given by the demand-for-deposits equations of households and firms, and their interest rates are treated as exogenous; trust and insurance are considered similarly. Finally, the bank of Japan determines the discount rate.

The model as a whole was tested by the so-called final method of *ex post* forecasting within the sample period 1959–1973. The results indicated that the general trend of the macrovariables, such as GNP, consumption, fixed investment, and demand and time deposits were traced by the model. However, it was found that relatively large errors existed in some of the variables relating to individual industries and individual asset categories, and that most of these errors tended to be serially correlated. Thus, the control solution, used as a base solution in the simulation study below, was calculated by adding constant adjustment terms in several of the equations for output prices, industry employments, and fixed investment.

## The Effect of Saving on Economic Growth

Recently, attention has been drawn to the favorable effects that a relatively high saving rate has on productivity and price in the process of economic growth. As explained above, the present model is contructed so as to trace out in detail the possible consequences of a change in the saving rate and its repercussions for the whole economy. An increase in personal savings[4] will lead to an increase in funds available to banks, which will bring about an increase in the supply of bank loans and a decrease in the loan rate, thereby expanding investment. The increase in investment will, in turn, result in an increase in productivity through the accumulation of capital, thereby lessening inflationary pressure.

It is important to note, however, that an increase in savings *per se* does not necessarily contribute to higher economic growth. By the budget restraint, an increase in savings will be accompanied by a curtailment of consumption of the same amount, and, as Keynes emphasized, the latter will lead to a fall in effective demand and a decline in national income. In the present model an increase in the propensity to save is represented by a set of simultaneous shifts in both the saving and consumption functions which keep the budget restraint met as before (for example, a shift of 0.02 in the constant term $a_{14}$ and of $-0.02$ in the constant term $a_{44}$ in equations 2). In fact, a ten-year simulation based on this shift in the two functions revealed that the level of GNP on the growth path with the higher saving ratio was always short of that with the lower saving ratio; that is to say, the fall in effective demand due to the consumption decrease was larger than the increase in effective demand occasioned by the investment expansion brought about by the increase in savings.

One may indeed argue that saving is a virtue, since with a higher saving ratio there exists the possibility of realizing a more rapid accumulation of capital and a faster rate of productivity increase at a given employment level than the economy with a lower saving ratio. In a country with a higher consumption ratio it is difficult to raise significantly the share of investment and simultaneously maintain a given level of effective demand. Conversely, in a country with a higher saving ratio the share of investment can be increased only if the policy succeeds in stimulating investment demand. It must be emphasized that a difference of long-run economic performance arises because of the difference in the composition of effective demand, even if both countries maintain the same level of employment.[5]

As is well known, the saving ratio of Japanese households has been very high; the personal gross saving ratio averaged 21.8 percent in 1959–1971.[6] In addition, investment demand was very strong throughout this period; among other things, the importing of technology supplied Japanese firms with opportunities for profitable investment. These factors made it possible for the Japanese economy to grow with a high ratio of investment to GNP.

Taking account of all the above considerations, I performed a simulation in order to numerically estimate the contribution of the high saving ratio in Japan to her economic performance in the seven-year period 1959–1965. The following procedures were used:

1. Throughout the period, the consumption function was shifted up by 5.5 percent. The saving function for the net change in financial assets was shifted down by the same amount.

2. The investment function was shifted down so as to maintain practically the same level of employment as in the control solution.

3. Corresponding to procedure 2, the bank-loan demand function of firms was shifted down.

4. Both the bank-loan supply function and the demand function for Bank of Japan loans were shifted down by 2 percent in the banks' equations.

The measure of item 4 was added to absorb excess liquidity in the banking sector brought about by the decline in investment.

The results are given in table 4. The performance of each economy is measured by the average ratio or average rate of growth of the variable

**Table 4**
Comparative performance among different saving ratios, 1959–1965.

|  | (1) Control solution | (2) Low-saving economy[d] | (3) Difference, columns 2 and 1 | (4) Low-saving economy[e] | (5) Difference, columns 4 and 1 |
|---|---|---|---|---|---|
| Consumption ratio[a] | 0.788 (0.792) | 0.844 (0.850) | 0.056 (0.058) | 0.842 (0.848) | 0.054 (0.056) |
| Saving ratio[a] | 0.115 (0.118) | 0.061 (0.060) | −0.054 (−0.058) | 0.064 (0.062) | 0.051 (0.056) |
| Real GNP[b] | 10.9 (11.6) | 9.7 (9.7) | −1.2 (−1.9) | 10.9 (11.3) | 0.0 (−0.3) |
| Real consumption[b] | 9.1 (8.9) | 8.8 (8.8) | −0.3 (−0.1) | 9.7 (10.0) | 0.6 (1.1) |
| Employment[b] | 2.3 (2.4) | 2.5 (2.3) | 0.2 (−0.1) | 3.0 (2.9) | 0.7 (0.5) |
| GNP deflator[b] | 4.8 (4.8) | 6.0 (5.7) | 1.2 (0.9) | 6.1 (5.4) | 1.3 (0.6) |
| CPI[b] | 4.6 (4.3) | 6.0 (5.8) | 1.4 (1.5) | 6.0 (5.2) | 1.4 (0.9) |
| Industry price, all manufacturing[b] | −0.5 (0.0) | 0.9 (1.3) | 1.4 (1.3) | 1.0 (0.9) | 1.5 (0.9) |
| Industry price, light industries[b] | 0.7 (1.0) | 1.6 (2.0) | 0.9 (1.0) | 1.8 (1.6) | 1.1 (0.6) |
| Industry price, heavy and chemical industries[b] | −1.5 (−0.3) | 0.7 (1.1) | 2.2 (1.4) | 0.8 (0.7) | 2.3 (1.0) |
| Loan rate[c] | 8.8 (9.0) | 8.6 (9.1) | −0.2 (0.1) | 9.5 (9.5) | 0.7 (0.5) |

Numbers in brackets are averages for 1959–1962.
a. Average ratio.
b. Average rate of growth or average rate of change (percent).
c. Average rate (percent).
d. First simulation.
e. Second simulation.

for the whole seven years, 1959–1965, and for the first four years, 1959–1963 (the values in parentheses).

Let us first examine the seven-year average figures. The saving ratio of the low-saving economy is 5.4 percent lower than that of the control solution, while the consumption ratio of the low-saving economy is 5.6 percent higher. The growth rates of employment in both solutions are practically the same. The growth rate of GNP is 1.2 percent higher in the control solution than in the low-saving economy. The growth rate of consumption is slightly smaller in the low-saving economy, in spite of the upward shift in the consumption function. Although the consumption level of the control solution is lower in the first three years than that of the low-saving economy, the former catches up with the latter after the fourth year. In the low-saving economy the rate of price change is 1.2 percent higher for the GNP deflator and 1.4 percent higher for the general consumer price. In the 1960s the wholesale prices of manufacturing industries, particularly the heavy and chemical industries, were very stable. The simulation revealed that the downward shift in the saving ratio would have led to a 2.2 percent increase in the average inflation rate in these industries. The average rate or average rate of growth of the first four years is generally fairly close to that of seven years of the table.

In the next simulation, item 2 of the first simulation was replaced by the following: The investment function was shifted down so as to maintain practically the same level of GNP as in the control solution. The results are shown in column 4 of table 4. Except for the fact that the growth rate of employment is higher and the rate of price change is a little more inflationary, the results are close to those of the first simulation.

## Concluding Remarks

The followers of the production-function approach to economic growth maintain that the high rate of technical progress was one of the major causes of the phenomenal growth of the Japanese economy in the 1960s. Measurement of the production function at the aggregative and individual-industry levels has provided evidence that the rate of technical progress was remarkably high, particularly in the heavy and chemical industries, which experienced the highest growth rates during that period (see, for example, Saito 1972).

There is no doubt that the high rate of technical progress owed much to the favorable conditions pertaining in the period, such as the availability of the high technology of the Western countries and an ample labor force with good discipline and education. But the study also revealed the fact that, even if a country is provided with these favorable conditions and even if her production possibilities are represented by a production function having the same high rate of technical progress as Japan's, her economy will experience a 1.2 percent fall in the GNP growth rate and a 1.2 percent rise in the rate of change of the GNP deflator should there be a 5 percent decline in the saving ratio.[7]

### Acknowledgments

I am greatly indebted to T. Oshika, Y. Matsuo, and F. Anai for their valuable research assistance at an earlier stage of this study.

### Notes

1. In principle, the accounting framework of this model is in line with the SNA; however, the classifications of industry and consumption are much more disaggregated in the model than in the published data.

2. The flow quantities of financial assets and liabilities in account 4 are determined as the difference between $A\mathrm{ih}_t$ and $A\mathrm{ih}_{t-1}$.

3. For empirical testing of the validity of this procedure, see Saito 1972 and Sarma 1972.

4. In what follows, saving is defined as the net change in holdings of financial assets, but does not include residential investment and investment by unincorporated enterprises.

5. For an econometric study of the effects of consumption restraint on U.S. growth see Saito and Caton 1969. In that study, which was based on the Wharton model, the source of investment funds was not traced.

6. This is the gross saving ratio, $(S\mathrm{h} + IR\mathrm{h} + IO\mathrm{h})/YG\mathrm{h}$ in the above notation. The average of the net saving ratio, excluding capital consumption allowances, was 18.3 percent.

7. It is likely that the effects of a high saving ratio have been underestimated, since the rate of technical progress will be accelerated by the increase in new investment brought about by the high saving ratio.

### Bibliography

Brainard, W. C., and J. Tobin. 1980. Pitfalls in financial model building. *American Economic Review* 58 (May): 99–122.

Klein, L. R. 1952–53. On the interpretation of Professor Leontief's system. *Review of Economic Studies* 20: 131–136.

Klein, L. R. 1974. *A Textbook of Econometrics*, second edition. Englewood Cliffs, N.J.: Prentice-Hall.

Saito, M. 1972. A general equilibrium analysis of prices and outputs in Japan, 1953–65. In M. Morishima et al., *The Working of Econometric Models*. Cambridge University Press.

Saito, M., and C. Caton. 1969. Consumption Restraint and Price Stability. Discussion Paper 132, University of Pennsylvania Department of Economics.

Sarma, K. S. 1972. Comparative Performance of Input-Output Models with Alternative Production Functions. Ph.D. diss., University of Pennsylvania.

Tobin, J. 1969. A general equilibrium approach to monetary theory. *Journal of Money, Credit*, and *Banking* 1 (February): 15–29.

United Nations. 1968. *A System of National Accounts*. New York.

# V Applied Macroeconomics: International

# 16 A Global Model of Oil-Price Impacts

F. Gerard Adams
Jaime R. Marquez

After the two oil "shocks" in the 1970s, there can be little disagreement that sharp increases in the price of petroleum have major effects on the economies of the developed industrial countries (DCs) and the non-oil-producing "less developed" countries (LDCs). The direct impact of higher oil prices is readily apparent, but the more complex feedbacks must be seen in a comprehensive model system. Questions like the following are posed:

What is the global impact on economic activity in the industrial and developing economies, and how does the feedback affect oil consumption?

To what extent does the recycling of oil revenues offset the impact of higher oil prices?

What is the impact on the growth rate of the non-oil-producing LDCs, and what are the consequent feedbacks on the industrial economies?

What is the effect on prices of manufactures, and how does the cost of manufactures feed back to affect the economies of the oil-producing countries and the LDCs?

What are the impacts of responses such as restrictive fiscal policy in the DCs, higher recycling by the oil countries, and extension of credit to the LDCs?

These questions are not only important in themselves; the quantitative dimensions of feedbacks must be considered by the oil-producing economies in determining the optimum price of oil, by the developed countries in determining a response to higher petroleum prices, and by the LDCs in seeking assistance for economic development.

There have been a number of studies of impacts in large, complex world model systems,[1] such as Project LINK. Although these provide a disaggregated view, their magnitude and their heterogeneous complexity often obscure the channels of interactions. There is some advantage in simplicity and transparency. In this chapter we consider the phenomenon of oil-price increases with a small global model of the developed economies, the less-developed economies, and the Organization of Petroleum Exporting Countries (OPEC).

## Description of the Model

The model considers three blocks of countries:

the industrial economies (denoted by a superscript d), whose GDP is determined in a demand-dominated Keynesian-type model,

the non-oil-producing less-developed countries (superscript l), whose output is determined from the supply side in a production-function framework, and

the OPEC countries (superscript o), for whom we show only the recycling of revenues earned from the sale of oil to purchase manufactures.[2]

The model includes four prices:

the price of oil,[3] exogenously determined,

the export price of manufactures of the developed countries, endogenously determined,

the raw materials export price, given exogenously, and

the export price of manufactures by the LDCs, given exogenously.

The principal trade flows considered are the following:

Oil is sold by OPEC to both DCs and LDCs.

Raw materials are purchased only by the DCs from the LDCs.

The DCs export manufactures to OPEC and the LDCs.[4]

The LDCs export manufactures to the DCs.

Appendix A presents the estimated equations.

### Developed Economies

Real GDP in the developed economies, $Y^d$ (equation 1 in appendix A) is determined from the demand side, by a Keynesian approach, as the sum of private consumption ($C^d$), private investment ($I^d$), government expenditures ($G^d$), and trade account ($X^d - M^d$). Private consumption, $C^d$ (equation 2), is a function of a welfare notion of income ($W^d$). This variable measures income adjusted for the direct impact of a change in the terms of trade; that is, the amount of goods and services available in the economy (Adams 1979; Woodland 1980). Accordingly, an increase in the price of oil would affect consumption through changes in both income generated from domestic real output and changes in the trade account. In equation 2, the short-run elasticity (at the means) of consumption with respect to $W^d$ is 0.86. The short-run marginal propensity to consume (mpc) appears to be low (0.5236), but this is because this mpc is estimated in relation to GDP (adjusted for the trade account) rather than to its personal-disposable-income component. The long-run income elasticity is 1.06, not significantly different from unity.

Private investment in the DCs, $I^d$ (equation 3), is estimated as a function of real GDP. Because of the obvious lags in planning, delivery of equipment, and construction of plants, we use lagged real GDP. The form of investment equation that worked best contains real GDP lagged one period. The short-run marginal propensity to invest (mpi) is 0.20 and the long-run income elasticity is 0.98 (not significantly different from unity).

Imports of oil by developed economies, $M_o^d$ (equation 6), are a function of real GDP in the DCs and of the terms of trade between developed economies and OPEC, measured by the price of oil relative to the price of manufactures ($P_o/P_m^d$). The elasticity of petroleum imports with respect to GDP appears very high (2.02). This reflects the fact that imported petroleum is the marginal energy supply in many countries and petroleum accounts for only a share of total energy use.[5] An increase in the price of oil relative to the price of manufactures, which means that an extra amount of manufactures is needed to pay for the same quantity of oil, induces a reduction in oil imports. It is reasonable to expect delays in adjusting the level of oil imports to changes in the price of oil. The length of this lag and the size of the response coefficient has been the subject of considerable debate (Kennedy 1976; Anderson 1973; Houthakker and Taylor 1970). Several alternative lag distributions were tried, but in our data set the lag hypothesis that works best has the terms of trade ($P_o/P_m^d$) lagged just one year, capturing principally short-run effects. In this model, oil imports are price-inelastic (the price elasticity is $-0.23$).

Imports of raw materials by developed economies, $M_r^d$ (equation 7), are price-inelastic in the short run (elasticity $-0.14$) and in the long run (elasticity $-0.69$). These imports are also income-inelastic (elasticity 0.63). Such a low income elasticity has been used as an argument to explain the growing disparity of income between developed and less-developed economies.

The export price of manufactures of the DCs, $P_m^d$, is determined using equations 8–8‴. There are three relevant variables: the prices for oil and raw materials and a proxy for capacity utilization in the DCs. An estimated trend for real GDP of the DCs serves as a proxy for potential output, $Y^*$ (equation 8‴). Historically, this potential output has grown at an annual average rate of 4.2 percent, but its growth rate is likely to be sensitive to the oil price relative to the price of other inputs. The export price of manufactures, $P_m^d$, responds to changes in the price of raw materials in the same period with an elasticity of 0.38. This response is stronger than the reaction of $P_m^d$ to changes in the price of oil, which is lagged one period and equal to 0.13. This reflects the proportions these inputs represent in the value of production during the sample period (Vanek 1963).

## OPEC

For OPEC we have only one behavioral equation: imports of manufactures by OPEC from DCs, $M_m^o$ (equation 11). This equation captures the recycling of oil money by OPEC, essentially its spending of oil revenues to purchase manufactures from the DCs. The explanatory variable is a distributed lag (extending back three years) of OPEC's oil export revenues, deflated by the price of imported manufactures. Experience suggests that it takes some time for the OPEC countries to adjust their spending to their revenue potentials. These adjustments take the form of a first-year revenue elasticity of 0.30, a peak of 0.36 in the second year, 0.27 in the third year, and a fourth-year elasticity of 0.04. The sum of the recycling elasticities after four years is 0.98. This indicates that the relation of OPEC's imports to its revenues returns to the base level after four years.

### Non-OPEC Less-Developed Economies

The output of the non-OPEC LDCs is supply-determined. Here we began with a neoclassical production function, equation 12, with Hicks-neutral technological change. The production function used assumes that capital is the binding constraint in the production process, and labor is assumed to be an abundant resource in the LDCs. The output-capital elasticity is 0.212.

The investment equation for the LDCs, $I^1$ (equation 14), depends crucially on two variables: level of real activity $Y^1$ (which brings in the domestic savings constraint) and imports of manufactures by the LDCs (which are the effective external constraint arising out balance-of-payments considerations). We use real activity, lagged one period because of delays in plans and lags in delivery; the lagged income coefficient is 0.23. Imports of manufactures have a coefficient of 0.63, which is very close to what has been observed in "two-gap" models (Taylor 1979).

Imports of manufactures by LDCs, $M_m^1$ (equation 15), are estimated using the availability of foreign-exchange reserves as an argument, since these represent a constraint for such imports. Availability of foreign exchange is represented here by the level of international reserves,[6] which is deflated by the export price of manufactures of the DCs. The application of the Koyck distribution to the "real" foreign-exchange reserves $(R^1/P_m^d)$ resulted in a short-run elasticity of 0.23. This relatively low value captures the limited short-run absorption capacity of the LDCs. The long-run elasticity with respect to real international reserves is 0.99. This important point indicates that, in the long run, the LDCs spend a constant fraction of their foreign-exchange reserves or keep their foreign-exchange reserves at a constant ratio to imports.

Oil imports by the LDCs, $M_o^1$ (equation 16), depend on the terms of trade between OPEC and the LDCs $(P_o/P_r)$ and the real GDP of the LDCs $(Y^1)$. We find a very inelastic oil import demand in the short run (a price elasticity of $-0.08$). This persists even in the long run, where the price elasticity is $-0.22$. In view of their greater dependence on oil, the response of oil imports to price by LDCs is even less than in the DCs. The income elasticity of oil imports by the LDCs is 1.51, smaller than the income elasticity for the DCs (2.02). Traditionally, the underlying energy elasticity with respect to real GDP has been seen as higher in the LDCs undergoing industrialization than in the DCs (Zilberfarb and Adams 1981). This is true for energy use in general, but, as we have explained above, in the DCs the petroleum elasticity with respect to income is high because petroleum imports represent the marginal fuel supply.

Although exports of manufactures by the LDCs do not represent a large share of international trade in manufactures, their share has increased during recent years. This has been due to the export-promotion development strategy followed by some non-OPEC LDCs (Brazil, Korea). Exports of manufactures by LDCs to DCs, $X_m^1$ (equation 17), are explained by the real GDP of the DCs $(Y^d)$, the principal market for these exports, and the ratio of the export price of manufactures of DCs

**Table 1**
Performance of the global model as shown by percent error for selected variables.

| | Mean absolute Error (%) 1968–1977 | Error (%) | | |
|---|---|---|---|---|
| | | 1973 | 1974 | 1975 |
| $Y^d$ | 1.3 | $-4.5$ | $-0.5$ | 0.9 |
| $C^d$ | 1.7 | $-3.2$ | 0.5 | $-0.9$ |
| $M_r^d$ | 3.8 | $-5.5$ | 0.4 | $-2.8$ |
| $M_o^d$ | 3.8 | $-0.6$ | $-0.3$ | $-0.3$ |
| $P_m^d$ | 7.9 | $-8.4$ | $-9.0$ | $-8.5$ |
| $M_m^o$ | 3.9 | $-3.2$ | 4.7 | 2.0 |
| $Y^l$ | 1.3 | $-2.2$ | $-2.1$ | 0.5 |
| $M_m^l$ | 4.3 | 6.3 | 3.2 | 4.6 |
| $M_o^l$ | 4.0 | $-6.7$ | $-1.7$ | 1.6 |
| $X_m^l$ | 7.4 | $-8.6$ | $-19.7$ | $-1.6$ |

to the export price of manufactures of LDCs ($P_m^d/P_m^l$), reflecting "competitiveness" by the LDCs. We find these exports to be elastic with respect to foreign income ($Y^d$) (the coefficient is 2.67). The coefficient for the ratio of export prices of manufactures ($P_m^d/P_m^l$) is 0.70, reflecting the competition posed by the LDCs.

## Model Simulation

The model presented in appendix A was dynamically simulated (without adjustments) over the period 1968–1977. We present its performance in table 1 and plot this movement in figure 1. In view of the fact that the model was simulated over one of the most unstable periods in recent times, the errors seem satisfactory. Except for $P_m^d$ and $X_m^l$, the remaining variables have errors well below 5 percent. The relatively large error of exports of manufactures by LDCs ($X_m^l$) is due to the variability in the export price of manufactures of DCs, $P_m^d$ (see equation 17). The relatively large error in $P_m^d$ (which is in levels) is due to the compounding effects of errors in the inflation rate (see equation 8′).

Several conclusions emerge from the performance of the global model during 1973–1975. First, errors in 1973 are significant (above the corresponding MAPE for the simulation period). Second, the model underestimated, in general, the actual levels of the endogenous variables in

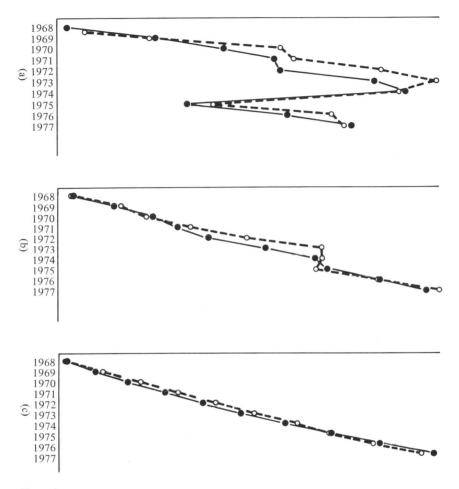

**Figure 1**
Dynamic simulations for selected variables. (a) Imports of oil, LDCs; (b) real GDP,
(c) real GDP, LDCs. Solid lines indicate predicted values; dotted lines indicate actual
values.

**Table 2**
Results of dynamic simulations for 1968–1972: selected variables under alternative scenarios (billions of 1970) dollars.

| | Simulation | 1968 | 1969 | 1970 | 1971 | 1972 | Average difference with respect to base solution |
|---|---|---|---|---|---|---|---|
| **Real GDP, DCs** $Y^d$ | | | | | | | |
| Base solution | | 1910.186 | 2007.218 | 2078.174 | 2127.018 | 2184.882 | 0 |
| High oil prices | 1 | 1911.174 | 2010.604 | 2081.635 | 2129.114 | 2185.545 | 2.118 |
| Lower prod. | 2 | 1911.174 | 2010.497 | 2081.092 | 2127.604 | 2182.257 | 1.029 |
| Rest. policy | 3 | 1911.174 | 1993.878 | 2053.178 | 2092.069 | 2141.879 | −23.060 |
| High capacity | 4 | 1933.347 | 2038.064 | 2114.442 | 2164.720 | 2220.778 | 32.774 |
| Capt. Trans. | 5 | 1914.578 | 2019.684 | 2096.394 | 2147.946 | 2205.510 | 15.326 |
| **Imports of Oil, DCs** $M_o^d$ | | | | | | | |
| Base solution | | 9.837 | 10.932 | 11.887 | 12.548 | 12.592 | 0 |
| High oil prices | 1 | 9.848 | 8.667 | 9.715 | 10.252 | 10.607 | −1.741 |
| Lower prod. | 2 | 9.848 | 8.666 | 9.726 | 10.289 | 10.684 | −1.716 |
| Rest. policy | 3 | 9.848 | 8.522 | 9.453 | 9.912 | 10.229 | −1.966 |
| High capacity | 4 | 10.081 | 8.923 | 10.081 | 10.719 | 11.166 | −1.365 |
| Capt. trans. | 5 | 9.883 | 8.749 | 9.881 | 10.511 | 10.955 | −1.563 |

**Imports of manufactures, OPEC**

| $M_m^o$ | | 1968 | 1969 | 1970 | 1971 | 1972 | Average Effect* |
|---|---|---|---|---|---|---|---|
| Base solution | | 5.515 | 5.919 | 6.287 | 7.106 | 8.111 | 0 |
| High oil prices | 1 | 7.494 | 10.381 | 12.860 | 13.307 | 14.291 | 5.079 |
| Lower prod. | 2 | 7.494 | 10.358 | 12.744 | 13.014 | 13.698 | 4.874 |
| Rest. ploicy | 3 | 7.494 | 10.331 | 12.668 | 12.917 | 13.639 | 4.822 |
| High capacity | 4 | 30.223 | 29.033 | 32.743 | 33.455 | 33.445 | 25.192 |
| Capt. trans. | 5 | 7.499 | 10.380 | 12.792 | 13.071 | 13.740 | 4.908 |

**Prices of manufactures, DCs**

| $P_m^d$ | | | | | | | |
|---|---|---|---|---|---|---|---|
| Base solution | | 92.98 | 97.647 | 100.998 | 101.877 | 108.894 | 0 |
| High oil prices | 1 | 93.008 | 111.991 | 116.029 | 117.090 | 122.901 | 11.724 |
| Lower proc. | 2 | 93.008 | 112.796 | 118.598 | 122.422 | 132.529 | 15.391 |
| Rest. policy | 3 | 93.008 | 112.219 | 116.980 | 119.434 | 127.692 | 13.387 |
| High capacity | 4 | 93.647 | 114.542 | 121.681 | 127.051 | 139.186 | 18.742 |
| Capt. trans. | 5 | 93.106 | 113.235 | 119.624 | 124.259 | 135.487 | 16.663 |

**Real GDP, LDCs**

| $Y^1$ | | | | | | | |
|---|---|---|---|---|---|---|---|
| Base solution | | 284.781 | 304.003 | 324.055 | 345.233 | 367.812 | 0 |
| High oil prices | 1 | 284.739 | 303.805 | 323.614 | 344.491 | 366.746 | −0.497 |
| Lower proc. | 2 | 284.739 | 303.802 | 323.599 | 344.448 | 366.648 | −0.529 |
| Rest. policy | 3 | 284.739 | 303.801 | 323.594 | 344.441 | 366.642 | −0.533 |
| High capacity | 4 | 284.741 | 303.806 | 323.606 | 344.456 | 366.650 | −0.525 |
| Capt. trans. | 5 | 284.892 | 304.320 | 324.668 | 346.188 | 369.094 | 0.655 |

**Capital stock, LDCs**

$K^1$

| | | 1968 | 1969 | 1970 | 1971 | 1972 | Average Effect* |
|---|---|---|---|---|---|---|---|
| Base solution | | 1024.566 | 1057.002 | 1095.138 | 1139.348 | 1190.605 | 0 |
| High oil prices | 1 | 1023.852 | 1053.770 | 1088.120 | 1127.842 | 1174.427 | −7.729 |
| Lower prod. | 2 | 1023.852 | 1053.718 | 1087.883 | 1127.181 | 1172.943 | −8.216 |
| Rest. policy | 3 | 1023.852 | 1053.699 | 1087.817 | 1127.072 | 1172.854 | −8.273 |
| High capacity | 4 | 1023.874 | 1053.780 | 1087.991 | 1127.300 | 1172.970 | −8.148 |
| Capt. trans. | 5 | 1026.437 | 1062.221 | 1104.938 | 1154.285 | 1210.306 | 10.305 |

**Imports of manufactures, LDCs**

$M_m^1$

| | | 1968 | 1969 | 1970 | 1971 | 1972 | Average Effect* |
|---|---|---|---|---|---|---|---|
| Base solution | | 22.997 | 23.850 | 26.790 | 29.073 | 32.398 | 0 |
| High oil prices | 1 | 22.032 | 21.466 | 21.742 | 23.148 | 26.309 | −4.082 |
| Lower prod. | 2 | 22.032 | 21.396 | 21.494 | 22.582 | 25.212 | −4.478 |
| Rest. policy | 3 | 22.032 | 21.370 | 21.432 | 22.523 | 25.241 | −4.502 |
| High capacity | 4 | 22.061 | 21.448 | 21.552 | 22.589 | 25.082 | −4.475 |
| Capt. trans. | 5 | 25.521 | 29.333 | 32.876 | 35.829 | 38.555 | 5.401 |

**Real International reserves, LDCs**

$\$R^1/P_m^d$

| | | 1968 | 1969 | 1970 | 1971 | 1972 | Average Effect* |
|---|---|---|---|---|---|---|---|
| Base solution | | 15.952 | 16.655 | 17.835 | 19.798 | 24.076 | 0 |
| High oil prices | 1 | 13.292 | 10.262 | 11.790 | 14.770 | 20.785 | −4.683 |
| Lower prod. | 2 | 13.292 | 10.120 | 11.348 | 13.796 | 18.790 | −5.394 |
| Rest. policy | 3 | 13.292 | 10.068 | 11.253 | 13.774 | 19.039 | −5.370 |
| High capacity | 4 | 13.368 | 10.181 | 11.388 | 13.696 | 18.360 | −5.464 |
| Capt. trans. | 5 | 24.852 | 24.067 | 24.896 | 24.803 | 25.638 | −5.988 |

**International Reserves, LDCs**
$R^1$

| | | | | | | |
|---|---|---|---|---|---|---|
| Base solution | | 14.832 | 16.263 | 18.010 | 20.169 | 26.218 | 0 |
| High oil prices | 1 | 12.363 | 11.493 | 13.680 | 17.294 | 25.545 | -3.023 |
| Lower prod. | 2 | 12.363 | 11.414 | 13.459 | 16.889 | 24.902 | -3.293 |
| Rest. policy | 3 | 12.363 | 11.298 | 13.163 | 16.451 | 24.312 | -3.581 |
| High capacity | 4 | 12.519 | 11.662 | 13.857 | 17.400 | 25.555 | -2.899 |
| Capt. trans. | 5 | 23.139 | 27.252 | 29.781 | 30.820 | 34.737 | 10.047 |

**Imports of oil, LDCs**
$M_o^1$

| | | | | | | |
|---|---|---|---|---|---|---|
| Base solution | | 2.167 | 2.400 | 2.671 | 2.893 | 3.070 | 0 |
| High oil prices | 1 | 2.000 | 1.908 | 2.120 | 2.319 | 2.519 | -0.467 |
| Lower prod. | 2 | 2.000 | 1.908 | 2.120 | 2.318 | 2.518 | -0.467 |
| Rest. policy | 3 | 2.000 | 1.908 | 2.120 | 2.318 | 2.518 | -0.467 |
| High capacity | 4 | 2.000 | 1.908 | 2.120 | 2.318 | 2.518 | -0.467 |
| Capt. trans. | 5 | 2.002 | 1.913 | 2.131 | 2.336 | 2.543 | -0.455 |

**Exports of manufactures, LDCs**
$X_m^1$

| | | | | | | |
|---|---|---|---|---|---|---|
| Base solution | | 7.149 | 8.288 | 9.201 | 9.602 | 10.604 | 0 |
| High oil prices | 1 | 7.159 | 8.327 | 10.168 | 10.605 | 11.693 | 0.621 |
| Lower prod. | 2 | 7.159 | 8.326 | 10.212 | 10.748 | 12.013 | 0.722 |
| Rest. policy | 3 | 7.159 | 8.143 | 9.815 | 10.176 | 11.232 | 0.336 |
| High capacity | 4 | 7.384 | 8.676 | 10.771 | 11.460 | 12.920 | 1.273 |
| Capt. trans. | 5 | 7.194 | 8.434 | 10.443 | 11.092 | 12.488 | 0.961 |

1973. The underestimation in real GDP of the DCs ($Y^d$) is due to a 14 percent underestimation of private investment ($I^d$), which is reinforced by the subsequent 3.2 percent underestimation in private consumption ($C^d$). The underestimation of $Y^d$ also induces an underestimation of the price of manufactures ($P_m^d$), and both, acting together, lead to an underestimation of import activities of the DCs. Such a result is not altogether surprising in view of the widespread problems with predicting the cyclical swing of inventories and investment by many forecasters in 1973–74. Finally, in general, the accuracy of the model improves substantially after 1973.

The results of alternative simulations to show the impact of higher oil prices are shown in table 2. The simulated increase of oil prices is combined with a decline in labor productivity and restrictive policy in the DCs. We also consider higher absorption capacity by OPEC and higher capital transfers to the LDCs. For these simulation exercises, we used the period 1968–1972 in order to deal with a time that was less tumultuous than the "oil shock" years.

**Effects of Higher Oil Prices (Simulation 1)**

An increase in the price of oil of 3 dollars per barrel—approximately a 100 percent increase at the time it was applied—causes oil imports in both DCs and LDCs to decline very little. Because of the price inelasticity of these imports, there is an increase in oil revenue to OPEC. Of this increase in export earnings, OPEC recycles only a fraction in the same year in the form of imports of manufactures. This increase in imports is $2.0 billion in 1968 and $6.2 billion in 1972, reaching an annual average increase of $5 billion. Simultaneously, the higher oil bill paid by the LDCs lowers the level of their international reserves, reducing their imports of manufactures by $0.9 billion in 1968 and $6.1 billion in 1972, an average of $4.1 billion. Lower imports of manufactures dampen capital accumulation, capital stock, and therefore real GDP of the LDCs ($Y^l$). The reduction in $Y^l$ goes from only $42 million in the first year (1968) to more than $1 billion in 1972.

The increase in imports of manufactures by OPEC is larger than the decrease in imports of manufactures by the LDCs. This results in a net increase in exports of the DCs, which, coupled with lower imports, raises real GDP in the DCs ($Y^d$) by $1.0 billion (1970 prices) in the first year and by an annual average of \$2 billion (1970 prices). This increase in $Y^d$ puts pressure on excess capacity, raising the export price of manufactures ($P_m^d$) only slightly in the first year. The big oil-price impact shows up the following years, with oil prices having a lagged effect on $P_m^d$. Thus, $P_m^d$ is an average of 11.7 percent higher than the base solution. This increase in $P_m^d$ partially offsets the deterioration in the terms of trade of the DCs, which in turn slows down the reduction in oil imports and raises imports of raw materials by the DCs. But higher prices for manufactures tend to reduce imports of manufactures by the LDCs ($M_m^1$) because of the reduction in the purchasing power of foreign-exchange reserves held by the LDCs. This reduction in $M_m^1$ dampens capital accumulation in the LDCs and reduces their real GDP. Therefore, an increase in the price of oil reduces the real income of the LDCs directly and indirectly—directly because of the reduction in foreign-exchange reserves due to the higher oil bill, and indirectly because the increase in the price of manufactures reduces the purchasing power of the already-reduced foreign-exchange reserves. An increase in the price of oil raises the real GDP of the DCs, however, because it improves their real trade account.

### Lower Labor Productivity as a Result of Higher Oil Prices (Simulation 2)

Recent studies (Baily 1981; Kendrick 1981; Norsworthy, Harper, and Kunze 1979; Nordhaus 1980) show that, as a result of the complementarity relation between energy and capital, an increase in the price of oil raises the combined price of capital and energy. This may make capital-intensive facilities uneconomical and may reduce potential output.

To make our simulation reflect the impact of higher oil prices, we lowered the growth rate of potential output from 4.2 percent to 3 percent for the years 1968–1972. Lower growth of labor productivity raises the price of the manufactures of the DCs ($P_m^d$) by an average of 4.6 percent as compared with simulation 1. This leads to larger imports by the DCs and also lowers their exports, resulting in a real GDP for the DCs ($Y^d$) below the higher-oil-price simulation (1) by \$0.1 billion in 1969 and \$3.3 billion in 1972. For the LDCs, higher values of $P_m^d$ reduce imports of manufactures and capital accumulation, and reduce their real GDP by only \$1.1 billion in 1972. The small impact on the real GDP of the LDCs is due to the relatively short simulation period, which does not show the compounding effect of lower capital accumulation.

### Restrictive Fiscal Policy to Combat Oil-Price Inflation (Simulation 3)

To offset the inflation produced by higher oil prices, governments have frequently imposed restrictionary policies. Here we assume a cutback in government expenditures, in addition to the assumptions of simulation 2. Given the delays in carrying out these policies and the lagged effect of the oil price on the price of manufactures, we assume a reduction of $8 billion (1970 prices) in government expenditures from 1969 (one year after the increase in the price of oil) to 1972.[7] In view of the unfavorable tradeoff between inflation and economic activity in the model, such an expenditure cut would not go very far toward offsetting the inflationary effect of the oil-price increase.

The initial impact of a decrease in government expenditures in the DCs is a reduction in their real GDP ($Y^d$) by $16.6 billion and $40.4 billion in 1972 as compared with simulation 2.[8] This decline in $Y^d$ lowers oil imports from OPEC and imports from the LDCs. Imports of the DCs are further dampened by a 0.5 percent reduction in the export price of their manufactures. This reduction in $P_m^d$ is due to the excess capacity generated by the decline in the real GDP of the DCs. There is also a reduction in exports of manufactures by the DCs ($M_m^1 + M_m^o$). This is a result of the transmission of lower real GDP in the DCs to both OPEC and the LDCs in the form of a lower import demand for their products. The reduction in import demand by the DCs results in a decline in the purchasing power of export earnings of both OPEC and the LDCs, which leads to a fall in their imports of manufactures from the DCs.

The reduction in exports of manufactures of the DCs is not offset by the fall in their imports from OPEC and the LDCs. This deterioration in the real trade account of the DCs is combined with the reduction in government expenditure ($G^d$), leading to a net average reduction of $23.1 billion in the real GDP of the DCs ($Y^d$) as compared with the base solution. The effectiveness of fiscal policy against inflation is limited. The reduction in $P_m^d$ is 0.5 percent in 1969 and 4.8 percent in 1972, reaching an average reduction of 2.5 percent as compared with simulation 2. Fiscal policy measures would need to be massive to make any significant dent in the inflation attributable to higher oil prices. For the LDCs there is an average reduction in real GDP of $4.75 million. This small decline is the result of two offsetting forces. On the one hand, the decline in $Y^d$ operates directly by lowering imports from the LDCs; this in turn reduces the availability of foreign exchange of the LDCs, dampening their imports of manufactures, their capital accumulation, and, therefore, their real GDP. On the other hand, lower real activity in the DCs operates indirectly via the export price of manufactures ($P_m^d$). A lower $P_m^d$ raises the purchasing power of the international reserves of the LDCs, stimulating imports of manufactures and real GDP ($Y^1$). The results show that the direct effect of a decline in real GDP of the DCs (lower imports from LDCs) offsets its indirect effect (lower price of manufactures), resulting in a small decline in the real GDP of the LDCs.

### Higher Absorption by OPEC (Simulation 4)

A remedial tool that has often been suggested is that the oil countries would spend a larger share of their oil earnings. In this scenario we examine the impact of an increase in the recycling of OPEC surpluses. We assume that the OPEC countries spend the difference between their export earnings and their imports from the DCs by importing more manufactures from the DCs.[9] The increase in imports of manufactures by OPEC raises the real GDP of the DCs ($Y^d$) by \$22.1 billion in 1969 and \$38.5 billion in 1972, an average increase of \$30.6 billion as compared with simulation 2. This increase in $Y^d$ has two effects. First, it raises imports of DCs from the LDCs, raising their international reserves. Second, it puts pressure on excess capacity, raising the price of manufactures ($P_m^d$). The net effect is a small increase in the purchasing power of the foreign-exchange reserves of the LDCs, allowing more imports of manufactures and faster capital accumulation and increasing their real GDP marginally.

### Higher Capital Transfers (Simulation 5)

Another way to offset the burden of high oil prices on the LDCs is an increase in capital transfer by OPEC. We assume an increase in capital transfers of \$14 billion from 1968 to 1972.[10] The first impact of higher reserves in the LDCs is to increase their imports of capital goods by \$3.5 billion in 1968, and consequently to increase their real GDP in 1968 by \$0.2 billion as compared with simulation 2. At the same time, the increase in exports of manufactures by the DCs also raises their real GDP by \$3.4 billion in 1968 as compared with simulation 2. This increase in $Y^d$ stimulates imports of the DCs from the LDCs, raising further the international reserves of the LDCs. On the other hand, the increase in $Y^d$ raises the price of manufactures ($P_m^d$) by 3 percent in 1972.

This dampening effect of $P_m^d$ is not strong enough to offset the large increase in international reserves, however, and the net result is an increase in the purchasing power of international reserves of the LDCs by an average of $10.6 billion as compared with simulation 2. As seen above, this increase leads to a higher real GDP in the LDCs. This increase reaches $2.4 billion in 1972 as compared with simulation 2, and $1.2 billion as compared with the base solution without the oil-price increase.

## Summary and Conclusion

Although a *ceteris paribus* increase in the price of oil does not necessarily reduce real GDP in the DCs, it does so when the impact on productivity and fiscal policy is taken into account. Higher oil prices reduce the GDP of the LDCs directly by reducing the available foreign exchange that finances imports of capital goods, and indirectly because of the higher prices for manufactures. Additionally, the effect of higher oil prices on the export price of manufactures leads to a deterioration in the trade account and a reduction in real GDP of the DCs.

The impact of a restrictive fiscal policy in the DC's, intended to control their inflation rate, has limited success in this regard. However, it causes sizable reductions in the real GDP of the DCs and of the LDCs.

An increase in absorption capacity in OPEC (because of a higher propensity to import) or in the LDCs (because of higher capital transfers) increases the real GDP of the DCs and of the LDCs. If OPEC has a higher absorption capacity, then the increase in $Y^d$ is transmitted to the LDCs as a small increase of their real GDP in spite of a higher price for manufactures. Capital transfers from OPEC to the LDCs raise the real GDP of the LDCs significantly. In addition, OPEC's capital transfers to the LDCs increase the real GDP of the DCs.

It goes without saying that many of the phenomena described by the model simulations had their counterparts in real-world experience during the 1970s.

## Acknowledgments

We acknowledge helpful suggestions from Albert Ando, Lawrence R. Klein, Wilfred Ethier Michael McCarthy and Peter Urban and partial financial support from CONICIT.

## Appendix A: Equations for the Global Model

(Estimation period: 1960–1977 except where indicated.)

### Developed Economies

1. $Y^d = C^d + I^d + G^d + X^d - M^d$

2. $C^d = -63.258 + 0.5296(W^d - W^d_{-1}) + 0.6529 W^d_{-1}$
$\quad\quad\ (-1.61)\ \ (6.78) \quad\quad\quad\quad\quad\quad (33.25)$

2'. $W^d = Y^d + M^d - X^d$
$\quad R^2 = 0.987,$
$\quad \rho = 0.6174$

3. $I^d = 22.0275 + 0.2048\, Y^d_{-1}$
$\quad\quad\ (0.512) \quad\ (9.38)$
$\quad R^2 = 0.853,$
$\quad \rho = 0.5783$

4. $X^d = M^o_m + M^l_m + X^d_{exo}$

5. $M^d = M^d_o + M^d_r + X^l_m + M^d_{exo}$

6. $M^d_o = \exp[0.0321 - 0.2319 \ln(P_o/P^d_m)_{-1} + 2.0284 \ln Y^d]$
$\quad\quad\quad\quad (0.14) \quad\ (-10.5) \quad\quad\quad\quad\quad (39.6)$
$\quad R^2 = 0.9924,$
$\quad \text{D.W.} = 1.913$

7. $M^d_r = \exp\left( \sum\limits_{i=0}^{3} \hat{\phi}_i \ln(P_r/P^d_m)_{t-i} + 0.6306 \ln Y^d - 0.078 \right)$
$\quad\quad\quad\quad\quad\quad\quad\quad\quad\quad\quad\quad (9.41) \quad\quad\quad\quad\quad (-0.24)$
$\quad R^2 = 0.923,$
$\quad \text{D.W.} = 2.35$
$\quad \hat{\phi}_0 = -0.1384\ (-3.08)$
$\quad \hat{\phi}_1 = -0.2076\ (-3.62)$
$\quad \hat{\phi}_2 = -0.2076\ (-2.24)$
$\quad \hat{\phi}_3 = \underline{-0.1384}\ (-0.24)$
$\quad\quad\ \ \, -0.692$

8. $P^d_m = (1 + \Delta\% P^d_m) P^d_{m_{-1}}$

8'.  $\Delta\% P_m^d = 0.0114 + 0.3771\Delta\% P_r + 0.1336\Delta\% P_{o_{-1}}$
$\qquad$ (1.55) $\qquad$ (7.24) $\qquad\qquad$ (5.82)

$\qquad\qquad + (3.088 \times 10^{-4})CU$
$\qquad\qquad$ (2.74)

$\quad R^2 = 0.881,$

$\quad$ D.W. $= 2.33$

8".  $CU = Y^d - \exp(\ln Y^*)$

8"'.  $\ln Y^* = 4.675 + 0.042t$
$\qquad\qquad$ (52.98) (32.7)

$\quad R^2 = 0.985$

OPEC

9.  $X^o = M_o^d + M_o^1 + X_{exo}^o$

10.  $M^o = M_m^o + M_{exo}^o$

11.  $M_m^o = \exp\left( \sum_{i=0}^{3} \hat{\psi}_i \ln[(P_o/P_m^d)(M_o^d + M_o^1)]_{t-i} - 2.986 \right)$
$\qquad\qquad\qquad\qquad\qquad\qquad\qquad\qquad\qquad$ $(-29.7)$

$\quad R^2 = 0.998,$

$\quad$ D.W. $= 2.467,$

$\quad$ Sample period: 1965–1977

$\quad \hat{\psi}_0 = 0.3058 \ (8.91)$

$\quad \hat{\psi}_1 = 0.3613 \ (11.63)$

$\quad \hat{\psi}_2 = 0.2732 \ (10.42)$

$\quad \underline{\hat{\psi}_3 = 0.0416} \ (1.07)$
$\qquad\quad 0.982$

**Non-OPEC Less-Developed Economies**

12.  $Y^1 = \exp(0.6233 + 0.2121 \ln K^1 + 0.0525t)$
$\qquad\qquad$ (1.05) $\qquad$ (1.76) $\qquad\qquad$ (13.44)

$\quad R^2 = 0.994,$

$\quad \rho = 0.618$

13.  $K^1 = K_{-1}^1 + I^1$

14.  $I^1 = -48.2515 + 0.2279 Y_{-1}^1 + 0.6392 M_m^1$
$\qquad$ $(-7.29)$ $\qquad$ (4.154) $\qquad$ (1.23)

$\quad R^2 = 0.947,$

$\quad \rho = 0.67131$

15. $M_m^l = \exp(0.16304 + 0.2349 \ln(\$R^l/P_m^d) + 0.7619 \ln M_{m_{-1}}^l)$
$\qquad\qquad$ (1.3) $\qquad$ (2.69) $\qquad\qquad$ (7.69)
$\quad R^2 = 0.983,$
$\quad$ D.W. $= 2.24$

16. $M_o^l = \exp[-7.799 - 0.0785 \ln(P_o/P_r)$
$\qquad\qquad$ (−6.08) $\quad$ (−0.965)

$\qquad\quad - 0.1459 \ln(P_o/P_r)_{-1} + 1.5196 \ln Y^l]$
$\qquad\qquad$ (−2.02) $\qquad\qquad$ (6.83)
$\quad R^2 = 0.948,$
$\quad$ D.W. $= 3.01$

17. $X_m^l = \exp[-18.2776 + 2.6796 \ln Y^d + 0.6966 \ln(P_m^d/P_m^l)]$
$\qquad\qquad$ (−20.82) $\quad$ (23.47) $\qquad\quad$ (2.45)
$\quad R^2 = 0.984,$
$\quad$ D.W. $= 1.28$

18. $X^l = M_r^d + X_m^l + X_{exo}^l$

19. $M^l = X^d + X^o + X^l - M^o - M^d$

20. $\$R^l = \$R_{-1}^l + \$X^l - \$M^l + \$F$

**Glossary**

Notes:
a. Billions of U.S. dollars.
b. At 1970 prices and exchange rate.

VARIABLES
$\$F$ $\quad$ Net capital flows to LDCs[a]
$C$ $\quad$ Private consumption[a,b]
$G$ $\quad$ Government expenditures[a,b]
$I$ $\quad$ Investment[a,b]
$M$ $\quad$ Imports[a,b]
$P$ $\quad$ Price index (1970 = 100)
$\$R$ $\quad$ International reserves[a]
$X$ $\quad$ Exports[a,b]
$Y$ $\quad$ Gross domestic product[a,b]
$Y^*$ $\quad$ Potential gross domestic product[a,b]

Superscripts

d    Developed economies (OECD)

o    OPEC

l    Less-developed economies (excluding OPEC and centrally planned economies)

Subscripts

m    Manufactures, categories 5–9 of SITC.

r    Raw materials, categories 0–1 and 2 plus 4 of SITC

o    Oil, category 3 of SITC

exo    Exports or imports not included in categories described above

$    Indicates that the variable is in nominal terms, U.S. dollars

## Appendix B: Data Construction

### Developed Economies (OECD Countries)

| | |
|---|---|
| $Y^d$ | Real gross domestic product in 1970 U.S. dollars at 1970 exchange rates (IMF *Yearbook*, 1980) |
| $Y_t^d$ | $= \Sigma\, Y_t^{d,i} E_{70}^i / P_{t,70}^i$ |
| $Y_t^{d,i}$ | GDP of country i in domestic currency |
| $E_{70}^i$ | exchange rate, domestic currency per U.S. dollar in 1970 |
| $P_{t,70}^i$ | GDP deflator, domestic currency (1970 = 100) |
| $C^d, I^d, G^d$ | Real consumption, Real investment, and real government expenditures (annual OECD *National Accounts*, adjusted the same way as GDP, Paris 1976, 1980) |
| $M_o^d, M_r^d, X_m^l$ | Imports of oil from OPEC (SITC 3), imports of raw materials (SITC 0–1 plus 2 and 4) from LDCs excluding OPEC, and imports of manufactures from LDCs excluding OPEC (SITC 5–9) (U.N. *Trade Statistics*) |
| $P_m^d$ | Export price of manufactures of developed economies (U.N. *Trade Statistics*) |
| $P_r$ | Import price of raw materials as a weighted average of the import price of SITC 0–1 and 2 plus 4. The weights are trade value shares (U.N. *Trade Statistics*) |
| $P_o$ | Price of oil as a chained price index of three oil prices: Ras Tanura (Saudi Arabia), Es Sidra (Libya), and Tia Juana (Venezuela) (IMF *Yearbook*, 1980). Levels of production used in the weighting: *Commodity Yearbook*, 1980. |
| $X_{exo}^d, M_{exo}^d$ | See note 4 |

**OPEC (Algeria, Ecuador, Gabon, Indonesia, Iraq, Iran, Kuwait, Libya, Nigeria, Qatar, Saudi Arabia, United Arab Emirates, Venezuela)**

$M_m^o$  Imports of Manufactures from developed economies (U.N. *Trade Statistics*)

$X_{exo}^o$  See note 4

**Non-OPEC Less-Developed Economies (all less-developed economies except OPEC members)**

$Y^1, K^1$     Real GDP and capital stock (Bijou Yeh, A Global Economic Model of a Three Region World, Ph.D. diss., University of Pennsylvania, 1981). Here, GDP for non-OPEC LDCs is estimated in the same way we estimate GDP for the developed economies. Capital stock by accumulation of net investment. For this, an initial capital output ratio of 3.38 and a 3% depreciation rate are assumed. (Main sources: World Bank, United Nations, International Monetary Fund.)

$M_m^1$     Imports of manufactures (SITC 5–9) from developed economies (U.N. *Trade Statistics*)

$R^1$     International reserves (IMF *Yearbook*, 1980)

$P_m^1$     Index of export unit value of manufactures (U.N. *Trade Statistics*)

$\$M^1, \$X^1$  Nominal value of total imports and exports of LDCs (U.N. *Trade Statistics*)

$M_o^1$     Imports of oil from OPEC (SITC 3) (U.N. *Trade Statistics*)

$X_{exo}^1$  See note 4

## Notes

1. Some of the publications in this area are Nordhaus 1977 and 1980; Pindyck 1979; Klein, Fardoust, and Filatov 1981; Schmid 1976; Committee for Economic Development 1975; Findlay and Rodriguez 1977.

2. The centrally planned economies are excluded, since they have had only marginal impact on the petroleum supplies of the "market" economies.

3. The price of oil used here is a chained price index of three countries' oil prices: Venezuela, Saudi Arabia, and Libya.

4. However, for the remaining trade flows, there is a residual category called "other." Each region (d, o, l) has two "other" categories: other imports and other exports. These residual groups contain intraregional trade (which cancels out) as well as interregional trade flows. OPEC's other exports to DCs in categories 0–2 and 4–9 represent an average

of 5.4 percent of total exports. OPEC's "other" imports from DCs 0–4 represent an average of 14 percent of total OPEC imports. "Other" exports of LDCs to DCs (category 3) represent 8 percent on average. "Other" imports of LDCs from DCs (categories 0–4) are 19 percent.

5. An alternative approach could have been to estimate total energy needs first with an elasticity near unity (Adams and Miovic 1968) and to then compute petroleum imports as a residual after allowing for available supplies of energy from domestic sources.

6. Another measure of foreign-exchange availability would be total export revenues minus the oil bill. This presumes that the oil bill is paid first to keep the economy functioning, and that a fraction of what is left over is used to finance imports of manufactures. This approach to estimating foreign exchange is quite sensitive to simulation errors in its components, which results in poor simulation performance.

7. This $8 billion is 2.2 percent of the average of the real government expenditures for 1968–1972.

8. This relatively large impact of a decrease in $G^d$ on $Y^d$ is due to the absence of automatic stabilizers that would boost consumption in a cyclical downturn.

9. Therefore the level of international reserves of OPEC, in real terms, is kept constant at its 1968 level.

10. This is the average capital transfer to the LDCs during the period 1968–1972. Thus, in fact, we are doubling the average capital transfer to LDCs. This increase represents about half of the increase in OPEC reserves as a result of the $3 per barrel price increase.

# Bibliography

Adams, F. G. 1979. Must high commodity prices depress the world economy? An application of a world model system. *Journal of Policy Modeling* 1 (no. 2): 201–215.

Adams, F. G., and J. R. Marquez. 1982. The impact of petroleum and commodity prices in a model of the world economy. In *Global International Economic Models*, B. Hickman, ed. Laxenberg, Austria: International Institute for Applied Systems Analysis.

Adams, F. G., and P. Miovic. 1968. On relative fuel efficiency and the output elasticity of energy consumption in Western Europe. *Journal of Industrial Economics* XVII (no. 1): 41–56.

Anderson, K. P. 1973. Residential Energy Use: An Econometric Analysis. Rand Corporation report R-1297-NSF.

Baily, M. 1981. Productivity and the Services of Capital and Labor. *Brookings Papers on Economic Activity* no. 1: 1–50.

Bradley, A., and J. Kraft. 1976. *Econometric Dimensions of Energy Demand and Supply*. Lexington, Mass.: Lexington.

Committee for Economic Development. 1975. *International Economic Consequences of High Priced Energy*. New York.

Findlay, R., and C. A. Rodriguez. 1977. Intermediate imports and macroeconomic policy under flexible exchange rates. *Canadian Journal of Economics* X (no. 2): 208–217.

Griffin, J., and H. Steele. 1980. *Energy Economics and Policy*. New York: Academic.

Houthakker, H. S., and L. D. Taylor. 1970. *Consumer Demand in the United States, Analysis and Projections*. Cambridge, Mass.: Harvard University Press.

Hudson, E., and D. Jorgenson. 1976. Tax policy and energy conservation. In *Econometric Studies of U.S. Energy Policy*, Dale Jorgenson, ed. North-Holland, American Elsevier.

Kendrick, J. 1981. International comparisons of recent productivity trends. In *Essays in Contemporary Economic Problems: Demand, Productivity, and Population*. Washington, D.C.: American Enterprise Institute for Public Policy Research.

Kennedy, M. 1976. A world oil model. In *Econometric Studies of U.S. Energy Policy*, Dale Jorgenson, ed. North-Holland, American Elsevier.

Klein, L. R., S. Fardoust, and V. Filatov. 1981. Long Term Projection of World Trade, Output and Prices when Oil Prices are Indexed: LINK System Simulations for 1981–1990. Paper presented at CEME Seminar on Comparative Simulations of Global Interrelational Economic Models, Stanford University.

Landsberg, H. ed. 1979. *Energy: The Next Twenty Years*. Cambridge, Mass.: Ballinger.

Nordhaus, W. 1977. *International Studies of the Demand for Energy*. New York: North-Holland.

Nordhaus, W. 1980. Oil and Economic Performance in Industrial Economies. *Brookings Papers on Economic Activity* no. 2: 341–401.

Norsworthy, J. R., M. J. Harper, and K. Kunze. 1979. The slowdown in productivity growth: Analysis of some contributing factors. *Brookings Papers on Economic Activity* no. 2; 387–421.

Pindyck, R. 1979. *The Structure of World Energy Demand*. Cambridge, Mass.: MIT Press.

Powelson, J. 1977. The oil price increase: Impact on industrialized and less developed countries. *Journal of Energy and Development* no. 1 (autumn): 10–26.

Schmid, M. 1976. A model of trade in money, goods and factors. *Journal of International Economics* 6: 347–361.

Taylor, L. 1979. *Macro Models for Developing Countries*. New York: McGraw-Hill.

Vanek, J. 1963. *The National Resource Content of United States Foreign Trade 1870–1955*. Cambridge, Mass.: MIT Press.

Woodland, A. 1980. Direct and indirect trade utility functions. *Review of Economic Studies* XLVIII: 907–926.

Zilberfarb, B., and F. G. Adams. 1981. The energy-GDP relationship in developing countries, empirical evidence and stability tests. *Energy Economics* 3, no. 4: 244–248.

# 17 A Decomposition of International Income Multipliers

Bert G. Hickman
Victor Filatov

In this chapter we introduce an analytical decomposition of international income multipliers as a method of summarizing key parameters of the international transmission mechanism and apply the new method to multipliers calculated for unsynchronized expenditure shocks from six large countries in the Project LINK world model.

It is appropriate that a volume honoring Lawrence Klein include a chapter concerning Project LINK,[1] which he has served as a founding member and as Project Coordinator since its inception. The project is a cooperative international research activity in which independently constructed structural econometric models of various nations and regions are linked into a world model through trading relationships, exchange rates, and capital flows.

## A Multiplier Decomposition in a Simplified Two-Country Model

Although the numerical multipliers reported below are derived from the highly complex econometric models of the LINK system, their interpretation can be clarified by reference to the simplest two-country multiplier model of income determination. Each country $i (= 1, 2)$ is assumed to have an expenditure function $E_i = e_i Y_i$, where $e_i$ is the marginal propensity to spend on investment and consumption goods, and an import function $M_i = m_i Y_i$, with marginal propensity to import $m_i$. Income is $Y_i = G_i + E_i + X_i - M_i$, where $G_i$ is government expenditures and $X_i$ is exports. Then, since $X_1 = M_2$ and vice versa, we have semireduced forms for each country's income in terms of its own exogenous demand component $G$ and the other country's income:

$$Y_1 = \frac{G_1 + X_1}{1 - e_1 + m_1} = \frac{G_1 + m_2 Y_2}{1 - e_1 + m_1}, \tag{1}$$

$$Y_2 = \frac{G_2 + X_2}{1 - e_2 + m_2} = \frac{G_2 + m_1 Y_1}{1 - e_2 + m_2}. \tag{2}$$

Substituting equation 2 into equation 1 yields the reduced-form equation for income in country 1:

$$Y_1 = \frac{(1 - e_2 + m_2)G_1 + m_2 G_2}{(1 - e_1 + m_1)(1 - e_2 + m_2) - m_1 m_2}. \tag{3}$$

The comparable expression for $Y_2$ is

$$Y_2 = \frac{(1 - e_1 + m_1)G_2 + m_1 G_1}{(1 - e_1 + m_1)(1 - e_2 + m_2) - m_1 m_2}. \tag{4}$$

In an unlinked model neglecting the induced expansion of own exports following an increase in own autonomous expenditure, the own-income multiplier for country 1, as obtained from the first equality in equation 1, would be

$$\left. \frac{\partial Y_1}{\partial G_1} \right|_{X_1 = \bar{X}_1} = \frac{1}{1 - e_1 + m_1}. \tag{5}$$

In a linked system recognizing the trading interdependence between the economies, however, the own multiplier, as derived from equation 3, is larger:

$$\frac{\partial Y_1}{\partial G_1} = \frac{1 - e_2 + m_2}{(1 - e_1 + m_1)(1 - e_2 + m_2) - m_1 m_2}$$

$$= \frac{1}{(1 - e_1 + m_1) - m_1 m_2 / (1 - e_2 + m_2)} \tag{6}$$

where the second term in the denominator allows for the favorable feedback effects of the induced income and import expansion in country 2 on the exports of country 1.

The cross-multiplier for country 2 is obtained from equation 4 as

$$\frac{\partial Y_2}{\partial G_1} = \frac{m_1}{(1 - e_1 + m_1)(1 - e_2 + m_2) - m_1 m_2}. \tag{7}$$

The cross-multiplier can also be obtained indirectly as

$$\frac{\partial Y_2}{\partial G_1} = \frac{\partial Y_1}{\partial G_1} \cdot \frac{\partial M_1}{\partial Y_1} \cdot \frac{\partial Y_2}{\partial M_1}. \tag{8}$$

The first product in this expression is equal to $\partial M_1 / \partial G_1$. Of course, $\partial M_1 / \partial G_1$ could be obtained directly from the reduced-form equation for own imports, derived as

$$M_1 = m_1 Y_1 = \frac{m_1[(1 - e_2 + m_2)G_1 + m_2 G_2]}{(1 - e_1 + m_1)(1 - e_2 + m_2) - m_1 m_2},$$ (9)

which yields

$$\frac{\partial M_1}{\partial G_1} = \frac{m_1(1 - e_2 + m_2)}{(1 - e_1 + m_1)(1 - e_2 + m_2) - m_1 m_2}.$$ (10)

However, it is convenient to think of $\partial M_1/\partial G_1$ as the product of two properties of the economy being modeled—its own-expenditure multiplier for income, $\partial Y_1/\partial G_1$, and its marginal import propensity, $\partial M_1/\partial Y_1$:

$$\frac{\partial M_1}{\partial G_1} = \frac{\partial M_1}{\partial Y_1} \cdot \frac{\partial Y_1}{\partial G_1}$$

$$= m_1 \left( \frac{1 - e_2 + m_2}{(1 - e_1 + m_1)(1 - e_2 + m_2) - m_1 m_2} \right),$$ (11)

which is seen to equal equation 10. Thus, a country may transmit a sizable impulse abroad as a result of a domestic disturbance either because it has a high domestic expenditure multiplier or because it has a high marginal import propensity, or for both reasons. It is true, of course, that a high import propensity tends itself to reduce the size of the income multiplier, but the latter is also independently affected by other structural parameters such as $e_i$ in the example.

The last term in equation 8 is the foreign-trade (income) multiplier for country 2:

$$\frac{\partial Y_2}{\partial M_1} = \frac{\partial Y_2}{\partial X_2} = \frac{1}{1 - e_2 + m_2},$$ (12)

as may be seen by differentiating equation 2. Hence, the income response in country 2 to an increase in its own exports depends on its internal response characteristics as summarized in equation 12. Finally, the product of the impulse and response multipliers 11 and 12 is equal to equation 7, the directly derived cross-multiplier for real income in response to an autonomous external demand shock, $\partial Y_2/\partial G_1$.

The decomposition of cross-multipliers from the LINK system reported below is analogous to the foregoing exercise for a rudimentary two-country Keynesian income-expenditure model. The principal qualifications with respect to this analogy follow:

• The LINK models are nonlinear in variables and parameters, so the estimated multipliers are not invariant to initial conditions. Because of the nonlinearities, the multipliers are obtained by simulation.

• The national models in LINK are large, disaggregated macroeconometric demand and supply systems including absolute and relative prices as endogenous variables. In many of the national models interest rates and exchange rates are also endogenous, although the latter were treated as predetermined variables in the present set of simulations. Model disturbances are propagated abroad through induced changes in the prices as well as the quantities of tradable goods and services. Hence, the multiplier coefficients and import propensities inferred from the simulations embody relative price effects and are not pure income responses as in the illustrative example.

• Distributed lags figure prominently in most of the national models of Project LINK, so the calculated multipliers are dynamic in contrast to the static relationships in the example.

• Because of the more complex structures of the LINK models, the responses to alternative demand shocks may differ substantially from those reported below for exogenous shifts in government expenditures. Equivalent exogenous changes in tax rates or transfer payments would yield different multipliers, for example.

• Similarly, responses to supply shocks would differ considerably from those reported here for demand shocks.[2]

• Nonaccomodating monetary policies are assumed in the shocked solution, so that some crowding out of private expenditures occurs as a result of rising interest rates. Exchange rates are implicitly managed so as to remain unchanged under the impact of the domestic and foreign disturbances.

• LINK is a multinational system, so the foreign impact of a domestic shock is spread over many trading partners instead of the single recipient of the illustrative model. This makes little difference for the value of the own multiplier $\partial Y_1/\partial G_1$, since the feedback to the exports of country 1 from the rest of the world, represented exclusively by country 2 in expression 6 in the simplified model, now is simply received from many trading partners instead of one and differs from the simpler case only because of second-order compositional effects. Insofar as the cross-multipliers for receiving countries are concerned, however, the impact on any one of them is generally much smaller than if it were the only trading partner of country $i$.

To allow for this attenuation of the cross-multipliers, we may generalize expression 8 to

$$\frac{\partial Y_j}{\partial G_i} = \frac{\partial Y_i}{\partial G_i} \cdot \frac{\partial M_i}{\partial Y_i} \cdot \frac{\partial X_j}{\partial M_i} \cdot \frac{\partial Y_j}{\partial X_j}. \tag{13}$$

In Project LINK the exports of a given country are determined as

$$X_k = \sum_{l=1}^{n} \alpha_{kl} M_l \tag{14}$$

where $\alpha_{kl}$ is the share of exporting country $k$ in the total imports of country $l$ and there are $n$ countries. (The import shares are themselves endogenous functions of relative export prices in the simultaneous solution of the $n$-country system.) This implies that

$$\frac{\partial X_j}{\partial M_i} = \alpha_{ji} + \sum_{\substack{l \\ l \neq i}} \alpha_{jl} \frac{\partial M_l}{\partial M_i}. \tag{15}$$

Thus, the induced increase in $j$'s exports includes the indirect stimulus from the induced expansion of trade in the other recipient countries as well as the direct stimulus from the import expansion of country $i$, equal to $\alpha_{ji}$. The indirect stimulus from any one of $j$'s other trading partners will generally be small, but their summation can be at least as important as the direct stimulus from country $i$. Thus, the magnitude of $\partial X_j / \partial M_i$ depends generally on $j$'s average share in all import markets, or its overall share of world exports. It remains true, however, that $\alpha_{ji}$ has greater weight than the other individual shares in equation 15, so the direct stimulus from a particular country $i$ will be especially large for country $j$ in those instances where $j$'s share in market $i$ is substantially higher than its average share elsewhere.

## Components of the International Multipliers in Absolute and Elasticity Forms

In this section we present an analytical decomposition of own and cross-country income multipliers for unsynchronized expenditure shocks. Time subscripts are omitted for expositional convenience. The multipliers are defined in both absolute and elasticity forms.

The variables are $Y$ (GDP), $G$ (government expenditure), $M$ (merchandise imports), and $X$ (merchandise exports), measured for all countries is constant U.S. dollars. The country in which the shock originates is indexed by $I$, and a country receiving an external shock by $J$. The symbol $D$ is used for the difference operator referring to the absolute change in a variable measured by the difference between the shocked and control solutions in a given period. Then the conventional own multiplier for a government-expenditure shock defined for absolute changes is

$$YIGI = DYI/DGI \tag{16}$$

and the corresponding cross-multiplier is

$$YJGI = DYJ/DGI. \tag{17}$$

In the elasticity form, the shock and the response are measured as a percentage of income:

$$EYIGI = \frac{DYI/YI}{DGI/YI}, \tag{18}$$

$$EYJGI = \frac{DYJ/YJ}{DGI/YI}, \tag{19}$$

where $YI$ and $YJ$ are the real incomes of countries $I$ and $J$ in the control solution.[3]

The own multiplier has the same value in the conventional and elasticity forms, but the corresponding cross-multipliers are related as follows:

$$EYJGI = YJGI \times (YI/YJ). \tag{20}$$

Thus, the conventional and elasticity cross-multipliers differ according to the relative size of the disturbing and disturbed countries. An apparently small multiplier as conventionally measured may imply a large elasticity multiplier when a small country is disturbed by a large one, and vice versa.

The fourfold decomposition of the conventional cross-multiplier is given by

$$YJGI = YIGI \times MIYI \times XJMI \times YJXJ \tag{21}$$

where

$$YIGI = DYI/DGI \tag{22}$$

is the own-income multiplier for government expenditure in country $I$,

$$MIYI = DMI/DYI \tag{23}$$

is the marginal propensity to import of country $I$, *mutatis mutandis*,

$$XJMI = DXJ/DMI \tag{24}$$

is the direct and indirect response of $J$'s exports to the import increment in $I$, and

$$YJXJ = DYJ/DXJ \tag{25}$$

is the foreign-trade multiplier, or the income multiplier for exports in country $J$.

The first two terms of equation 21 govern the size of the external impulse from the shock in country $I$. The impulse is greater the greater the internal instability of the country as measured by its income multiplier and the greater the import response to the income change. The marginal import/income ratio is akin to the usual marginal propensity to import, except that the latter is measured *ceterus paribus*, whereas equation 23 also incorporates the negative effects on imports of the induced increase in the relative price of domestic and imported goods resulting from the demand shock. Similarly, the impulse transmitted abroad includes the induced increase in the price of exports from country $I$ along with the increment in real demand for foreign goods measured in equation 23. The induced substitution effects are of secondary importance insofar as real-income shocks and responses are concerned, however, so the present decomposition is a meaningful interpretative tool for income multipliers.[4]

The last two terms of equation 21 summarize the principal determinants of the response of $J$ to an external trade shock from $I$. The exposure of country $J$ to an external shock from country $I$ depends generally on $J$'s importance in international trade, and particularly on its share in $I$'s imports. For a given degree of exposure to external shocks originating in $I$, however, the income response of country $J$ depends also on its own internal instability as measured by its income multiplier for export shocks (equation 25).[5]

The impulse and response characteristics of the cross-country multipliers may be summarized in two expressions,

$$MIGI = DMI/DGI = YIGI \times MIYI, \tag{26}$$

$$YJMI = DYJ/DMI = XJMI \times YJXJ, \tag{27}$$

which provide an alternate twofold decomposition of the total cross-multiplier:

$$YJGI = DYJ/DGI = MIGI \times YJMI. \tag{28}$$

Corresponding decompositions may be defined for the elasticity multipliers. Thus,

$$EYJGI = EYIGI \times EMIYI \times EXJMI \times EYJXJ \tag{29}$$

where

$$EYIGI = \frac{DYI/YI}{DGI/YI} \tag{30}$$

is the own elasticity income multiplier for a domestic demand shock in country $I$,

$$EMIYI = \frac{DMI/MI}{DYI/YI} \tag{31}$$

is the income elasticity of $I$'s imports, *mutatis mutandis*,

$$EXJMI = \frac{DXJ/XJ}{DMI/MI} \tag{32}$$

is the elasticity of $J$'s exports with respect to $I$'s imports, and

$$EYJXJ = \frac{DYJ/YJ}{DXJ/XJ} \tag{33}$$

is the elasticity foreign-trade multiplier for country $J$.
Similarly, the twofold elasticity decomposition is

$$EYJGI = EMIGI \times EYJMI \tag{34}$$

where

$$EMIGI = EYIGI \times EMIYI \tag{35}$$

summarizes the impulse from $I$ and

$$EYJMI = EXJMI \times EYJXJ \tag{36}$$

summarizes the response in $J$.

Finally, we take note of some definitional relationships between the component expressions for the conventional and elasticity decompositions. The elasticity decomposition may be obtained by adjusting the conventional components by the appropriate ratios. Thus,

$$EYIGI = YIGI \times (YI/YI), \tag{37}$$

so the own multipliers are the same value in either form,

$$EMIYI = \frac{MIYI}{MI/YI}, \tag{38}$$

so the import elasticity equals the marginal propensity divided by the average propensity,

$$EXJMI = XJMI \times (MI/XJ), \tag{39}$$

so the relative size of the external shock to $J$ depends on the direct and indirect response of $J$'s exports to the import increment in $I$ and on the ratio of $I$'s total imports to $J$'s total exports, and

$$EYJXJ = YJXJ \times (XJ/YJ), \tag{40}$$

so the relative internal response to the export shock depends on $J$'s internal foreign-trade multiplier and on the relative importance of exports, or the openness of $J$'s economy.

## Project LINK Multipliers

Let us turn now to empirical estimates of some international income multipliers. These are dynamic multipliers for independent demand shocks in six large OECD countries. The control solution was an *ex ante* forecast of the Project LINK system for 1979–1985. Each of the six large models was disturbed in turn by a sustained exogenous increase of government expenditure, and the new global solution was compared with the control to measure the induced responses in the thirteen LINK OECD nations (Filatov, Hickman, and Klein 1979).

The matrix of own multipliers and cross-multipliers in absolute form is presented in table 1. The own multipliers appear on the main diagonal and exhibit substantial stability in all countries. The highest values obtained are 2.9 in Germany and 2.8 in the United States. Values range between 1.1 and 2.1 in the other countries. The time paths vary according to the response mechanisms of the models. With the exception of Germany, however, there is little evidence of endogenous cyclical responses, except possibly for highly damped inventory fluctuations.

A high degree of international stability is also implied by the cross-multipliers, which are generally small. The biggest cross-multipliers appear in the columns for the major countries (especially Germany and the United States), whereas the smaller countries show little sensitivity to external disturbances in these measures. These facts basically reflect the relative importance of large and small countries in world trade, with the smaller countries simply not supplying much of the imports of the larger ones. Nevertheless, the degree of sensitivity to external shocks is seriously overstated for large countries and understated for small ones in the conventional measures of table 1.

The cross-elasticity multipliers in table 2 are a superior indicator of susceptibility to external disturbances, since they automatically allow for the relative incomes of the disturbing and disturbed countries as shown in formula 20. The relative income conversion factors for moving from the absolute to the elasticity multiplier forms are shown for 1979 in part A of table 3. This correction reduces the values of the cross-multipliers for the larger countries—dramatically and uniformly for the United States and moderately and unevenly for the others—and substantially increases those for the smaller OECD economies. Nevertheless, it remains true that the cross-multipliers, even in elasticity form, are generally low except for small countries that are close trading partners of larger ones. This implies that independent domestic shocks even in large countries are unlikely to lead to synchronized fluctuations in the industrialized world—a point discussed at length and reinforced by other evidence in addition to LINK elasticity multipliers in Hickman and Schleicher 1978. This central point should not be lost from sight as we examine the multipliers in detail in the remainder of this paper.

**Table 1**

International multipliers for real income ($YJGI$) (income change of country in column induced per dollar shock to real government expenditure of country in row).

| Originating country ($I$) | Year | Receiving countries ($J$) | | | | |
|---|---|---|---|---|---|---|
| | | France | Germany | Italy | Japan | U.K. |
| France | 1979 | 1.08 | 0.12 | 0.06 | 0.04 | 0.02 |
| | 1980 | 1.07 | 0.15 | 0.07 | 0.07 | 0.03 |
| | 1981 | 1.06 | 0.25 | 0.10 | 0.10 | 0.04 |
| | 1982 | 1.07 | 0.30 | 0.10 | 0.10 | 0.04 |
| | 1983 | 1.07 | 0.34 | 0.10 | 0.12 | 0.04 |
| | 1984 | 1.08 | 0.34 | 0.11 | 0.12 | 0.04 |
| | 1985 | 1.08 | 0.29 | 0.10 | 0.12 | 0.04 |
| Germany | 1979 | 0.08 | 1.83 | 0.13 | 0.08 | 0.05 |
| | 1980 | 0.08 | 1.87 | 0.17 | 0.15 | 0.06 |
| | 1981 | 0.12 | 2.91 | 0.25 | 0.22 | 0.03 |
| | 1982 | 0.13 | 2.73 | 0.27 | 0.25 | 0.09 |
| | 1983 | 0.13 | 2.37 | 0.25 | 0.26 | 0.08 |
| | 1984 | 0.12 | 1.88 | 0.23 | 0.24 | 0.07 |
| | 1985 | 0.10 | 1.28 | 0.18 | 0.20 | 0.05 |
| Italy | 1979 | 0.05 | 0.14 | 1.61 | 0.04 | 0.02 |
| | 1980 | 0.10 | 0.32 | 1.82 | 0.12 | 0.05 |
| | 1981 | 0.10 | 0.42 | 1.94 | 0.14 | 0.06 |
| | 1982 | 0.12 | 0.59 | 2.07 | 0.18 | 0.07 |
| | 1983 | 0.13 | 0.65 | 2.07 | 0.20 | 0.07 |
| | 1984 | 0.14 | 0.66 | 2.09 | 0.22 | 0.07 |
| | 1985 | 0.14 | 0.52 | 2.04 | 0.19 | 0.07 |
| Japan | 1979 | 0.00 | 0.02 | 0.01 | 1.07 | 0.00 |
| | 1980 | 0.01 | 0.03 | 0.02 | 1.15 | 0.01 |
| | 1981 | 0.01 | 0.04 | 0.02 | 1.23 | 0.01 |
| | 1982 | 0.01 | 0.05 | 0.02 | 1.26 | 0.01 |
| | 1983 | 0.01 | 0.05 | 0.02 | 1.27 | 0.01 |
| | 1984 | 0.01 | 0.05 | 0.02 | 1.27 | 0.01 |
| | 1985 | 0.01 | 0.04 | 0.02 | 1.25 | 0.01 |
| U.K. | 1979 | 0.05 | 0.15 | 0.08 | 0.08 | 1.07 |
| | 1980 | 0.07 | 0.22 | 0.11 | 0.13 | 1.14 |
| | 1981 | 0.08 | 0.35 | 0.14 | 0.16 | 1.16 |
| | 1982 | 0.09 | 0.44 | 0.15 | 0.18 | 1.11 |
| | 1983 | 0.10 | 0.53 | 0.17 | 0.21 | 1.08 |
| | 1984 | 0.11 | 0.57 | 0.19 | 0.24 | 1.09 |
| | 1985 | 0.12 | 0.51 | 0.19 | 0.23 | 1.08 |
| U.S. | 1979 | 0.01 | 0.02 | 0.01 | 0.03 | 0.01 |
| | 1980 | 0.01 | 0.04 | 0.02 | 0.05 | 0.01 |
| | 1981 | 0.01 | 0.07 | 0.02 | 0.06 | 0.01 |
| | 1982 | 0.01 | 0.09 | 0.03 | 0.07 | 0.01 |
| | 1983 | 0.01 | 0.11 | 0.04 | 0.09 | 0.02 |
| | 1984 | 0.02 | 0.13 | 0.04 | 0.10 | 0.02 |
| | 1985 | 0.02 | 0.13 | 0.05 | 0.12 | 0.02 |

| U.S. | Australia | Austria | Belgium | Canada | Finland | Netherlands | Sweden |
|------|-----------|---------|---------|--------|---------|-------------|--------|
| 0.12 | 0.00 | 0.00 | 0.02 | 0.02 | 0.00 | 0.02 | 0.01 |
| 0.24 | 0.00 | 0.01 | 0.03 | 0.02 | 0.01 | 0.03 | 0.01 |
| 0.34 | 0.01 | 0.01 | 0.03 | 0.03 | 0.01 | 0.05 | 0.01 |
| 0.35 | 0.01 | 0.01 | 0.03 | 0.02 | 0.01 | 0.05 | 0.01 |
| 0.34 | 0.01 | 0.01 | 0.03 | 0.03 | 0.01 | 0.06 | 0.01 |
| 0.30 | 0.01 | 0.01 | 0.03 | 0.03 | 0.02 | 0.06 | 0.01 |
| 0.25 | 0.01 | 0.01 | 0.03 | 0.03 | 0.02 | 0.06 | 0.01 |
| 0.23 | 0.01 | 0.02 | 0.05 | 0.03 | 0.01 | 0.05 | 0.02 |
| 0.52 | 0.01 | 0.03 | 0.06 | 0.04 | 0.02 | 0.10 | 0.03 |
| 0.82 | 0.01 | 0.04 | 0.09 | 0.06 | 0.04 | 0.16 | 0.04 |
| 0.90 | 0.02 | 0.04 | 0.09 | 0.06 | 0.04 | 0.18 | 0.04 |
| 0.80 | 0.01 | 0.04 | 0.08 | 0.06 | 0.04 | 0.18 | 0.03 |
| 0.63 | 0.01 | 0.03 | 0.07 | 0.05 | 0.04 | 0.17 | 0.02 |
| 0.37 | 0.01 | 0.02 | 0.05 | 0.04 | 0.04 | 0.15 | 0.01 |
| 0.14 | 0.00 | 0.01 | 0.02 | 0.02 | 0.00 | 0.02 | 0.01 |
| 0.43 | 0.01 | 0.02 | 0.04 | 0.04 | 0.01 | 0.05 | 0.02 |
| 0.60 | 0.01 | 0.02 | 0.04 | 0.05 | 0.02 | 0.08 | 0.02 |
| 0.67 | 0.01 | 0.03 | 0.05 | 0.05 | 0.02 | 0.09 | 0.03 |
| 0.65 | 0.01 | 0.03 | 0.05 | 0.05 | 0.03 | 0.10 | 0.02 |
| 0.59 | 0.01 | 0.02 | 0.05 | 0.05 | 0.03 | 0.11 | 0.02 |
| 0.44 | 0.01 | 0.02 | 0.04 | 0.05 | 0.03 | 0.11 | 0.01 |
| 0.06 | 0.00 | 0.00 | 0.00 | 0.01 | 0.00 | 0.00 | 0.00 |
| 0.12 | 0.00 | 0.00 | 0.00 | 0.01 | 0.00 | 0.00 | 0.00 |
| 0.13 | 0.00 | 0.00 | 0.00 | 0.01 | 0.00 | 0.01 | 0.00 |
| 0.12 | 0.00 | 0.00 | 0.00 | 0.01 | 0.00 | 0.01 | 0.00 |
| 0.10 | 0.00 | 0.00 | 0.00 | 0.01 | 0.00 | 0.01 | 0.00 |
| 0.08 | 0.00 | 0.00 | 0.00 | 0.01 | 0.00 | 0.01 | 0.00 |
| 0.05 | 0.00 | 0.00 | 0.00 | 0.01 | 0.00 | 0.01 | 0.00 |
| 0.23 | 0.01 | 0.01 | 0.02 | 0.05 | 0.01 | 0.03 | 0.02 |
| 0.50 | 0.01 | 0.01 | 0.03 | 0.07 | 0.03 | 0.06 | 0.03 |
| 0.65 | 0.01 | 0.02 | 0.04 | 0.07 | 0.04 | 0.09 | 0.04 |
| 0.67 | 0.02 | 0.02 | 0.04 | 0.07 | 0.05 | 0.10 | 0.03 |
| 0.66 | 0.02 | 0.02 | 0.05 | 0.08 | 0.05 | 0.11 | 0.02 |
| 0.65 | 0.02 | 0.02 | 0.05 | 0.09 | 0.06 | 0.12 | 0.02 |
| 0.57 | 0.02 | 0.02 | 0.05 | 0.09 | 0.06 | 0.13 | 0.02 |
| 1.60 | 0.00 | 0.00 | 0.00 | 0.05 | 0.00 | 0.00 | 0.00 |
| 2.39 | 0.00 | 0.00 | 0.00 | 0.06 | 0.00 | 0.01 | 0.00 |
| 2.73 | 0.00 | 0.00 | 0.01 | 0.06 | 0.00 | 0.01 | 0.00 |
| 2.74 | 0.00 | 0.00 | 0.01 | 0.06 | 0.00 | 0.01 | 0.00 |
| 2.78 | 0.00 | 0.00 | 0.01 | 0.08 | 0.01 | 0.01 | 0.01 |
| 2.75 | 0.00 | 0.01 | 0.01 | 0.09 | 0.01 | 0.02 | 0.01 |
| 2.81 | 0.00 | 0.01 | 0.01 | 0.11 | 0.01 | 0.02 | 0.01 |

**Table 2**
International elasticity multipliers for real income (*EYJGI*) (percentage income change of country in column induced per unit percentage income shock to real government expenditure of country in row).

| Originating country (*I*) | Year | Receiving countries (*J*) | | | | |
|---|---|---|---|---|---|---|
| | | France | Germany | Italy | Japan | U.K. |
| France | 1979 | 1.08 | 0.09 | 0.09 | 0.02 | 0.04 |
| | 1980 | 1.07 | 0.11 | 0.11 | 0.04 | 0.04 |
| | 1981 | 1.06 | 0.18 | 0.14 | 0.05 | 0.06 |
| | 1982 | 1.07 | 0.21 | 0.15 | 0.05 | 0.06 |
| | 1983 | 1.07 | 0.24 | 0.16 | 0.06 | 0.06 |
| | 1984 | 1.08 | 0.24 | 0.16 | 0.07 | 0.06 |
| | 1985 | 1.08 | 0.20 | 0.16 | 0.06 | 0.06 |
| Germany | 1979 | 0.11 | 1.83 | 0.28 | 0.06 | 0.09 |
| | 1980 | 0.12 | 1.87 | 0.35 | 0.11 | 0.12 |
| | 1981 | 0.17 | 2.91 | 0.52 | 0.17 | 0.19 |
| | 1982 | 0.18 | 2.73 | 0.57 | 0.19 | 0.20 |
| | 1983 | 0.18 | 2.37 | 0.54 | 0.19 | 0.18 |
| | 1984 | 0.17 | 1.88 | 0.48 | 0.18 | 0.16 |
| | 1985 | 0.15 | 1.28 | 0.40 | 0.15 | 0.13 |
| Italy | 1979 | 0.03 | 0.07 | 1.61 | 0.02 | 0.02 |
| | 1980 | 0.07 | 0.16 | 1.82 | 0.05 | 0.06 |
| | 1981 | 0.06 | 0.20 | 1.94 | 0.05 | 0.06 |
| | 1982 | 0.08 | 0.28 | 2.06 | 0.06 | 0.07 |
| | 1983 | 0.09 | 0.30 | 2.07 | 0.07 | 0.08 |
| | 1984 | 0.10 | 0.31 | 2.09 | 0.08 | 0.08 |
| | 1985 | 0.09 | 0.23 | 2.04 | 0.07 | 0.07 |
| Japan | 1979 | 0.01 | 0.02 | 0.02 | 1.07 | 0.01 |
| | 1980 | 0.01 | 0.04 | 0.04 | 1.15 | 0.02 |
| | 1981 | 0.02 | 0.06 | 0.05 | 1.23 | 0.03 |
| | 1982 | 0.02 | 0.07 | 0.05 | 1.26 | 0.03 |
| | 1983 | 0.02 | 0.07 | 0.05 | 1.27 | 0.03 |
| | 1984 | 0.02 | 0.07 | 0.05 | 1.27 | 0.03 |
| | 1985 | 0.02 | 0.05 | 0.05 | 1.25 | 0.03 |
| U.K. | 1979 | 0.03 | 0.07 | 0.08 | 0.03 | 1.07 |
| | 1980 | 0.04 | 0.10 | 0.11 | 0.05 | 1.14 |
| | 1981 | 0.05 | 0.16 | 0.13 | 0.05 | 1.16 |
| | 1982 | 0.05 | 0.20 | 0.15 | 0.06 | 1.11 |
| | 1983 | 0.06 | 0.23 | 0.16 | 0.07 | 1.08 |
| | v984 | 0.07 | 0.25 | 0.17 | 0.08 | 1.09 |
| | 1985 | 0.07 | 0.21 | 0.17 | 0.07 | 1.08 |
| U.S. | 1979 | 0.05 | 0.13 | 0.14 | 0.13 | 0.08 |
| | 1980 | 0.06 | 0.21 | 0.21 | 0.20 | 0.12 |
| | 1981 | 0.07 | 0.33 | 0.26 | 0.22 | 0.13 |
| | 1982 | 0.08 | 0.44 | 0.31 | 0.25 | 0.14 |
| | 1983 | 0.10 | 0.55 | 0.37 | 0.32 | 0.18 |
| | 1984 | 0.12 | 0.61 | 0.42 | 0.37 | 0.20 |
| | 1985 | 0.14 | 0.62 | 0.48 | 0.41 | 0.23 |

| U.S. | Australia | Austria | Belgium | Canada | Finland | Netherlands | Sweden |
|------|-----------|---------|---------|--------|---------|-------------|--------|
| 0.02 | 0.01 | 0.04 | 0.12 | 0.02 | 0.05 | 0.09 | 0.04 |
| 0.03 | 0.02 | 0.06 | 0.14 | 0.03 | 0.09 | 0.15 | 0.05 |
| 0.05 | 0.02 | 0.08 | 0.16 | 0.04 | 0.14 | 0.21 | 0.06 |
| 0.05 | 0.03 | 0.08 | 0.16 | 0.04 | 0.17 | 0.23 | 0.06 |
| 0.05 | 0.03 | 0.09 | 0.16 | 0.04 | 0.19 | 0.26 | 0.05 |
| 0.04 | 0.03 | 0.09 | 0.16 | 0.04 | 0.21 | 0.28 | 0.04 |
| 0.04 | 0.03 | 0.08 | 0.15 | 0.04 | 0.21 | 0.29 | 0.03 |
| 0.04 | 0.03 | 0.24 | 0.34 | 0.06 | 0.18 | 0.37 | 0.11 |
| 0.10 | 0.05 | 0.34 | 0.46 | 0.09 | 0.39 | 0.63 | 0.17 |
| 0.16 | 0.08 | 0.50 | 0.63 | 0.13 | 0.66 | 0.99 | 0.25 |
| 0.18 | 0.08 | 0.52 | 0.65 | 0.14 | 0.81 | 1.09 | 0.25 |
| 0.16 | 0.08 | 0.47 | 0.58 | 0.13 | 0.83 | 1.11 | 0.19 |
| 0.13 | 0.07 | 0.39 | 0.49 | 0.12 | 0.83 | 1.06 | 0.11 |
| 0.08 | 0.05 | 0.30 | 0.41 | 0.09 | 0.70 | 0.99 | 0.03 |
| 0.01 | 0.01 | 0.05 | 0.06 | 0.02 | 0.04 | 0.06 | 0.02 |
| 0.04 | 0.02 | 0.13 | 0.14 | 0.04 | 0.11 | 0.16 | 0.06 |
| 0.06 | 0.03 | 0.14 | 0.15 | 0.05 | 0.16 | 0.22 | 0.07 |
| 0.06 | 0.03 | 0.15 | 0.16 | 0.05 | 0.21 | 0.26 | 0.08 |
| 0.06 | 0.04 | 0.15 | 0.16 | 0.05 | 0.23 | 0.30 | 0.06 |
| 0.06 | 0.04 | 0.14 | 0.16 | 0.05 | 0.25 | 0.32 | 0.05 |
| 0.04 | 0.03 | 0.12 | 0.14 | 0.05 | 0.23 | 0.32 | 0.02 |
| 0.01 | 0.01 | 0.02 | 0.02 | 0.02 | 0.02 | 0.02 | 0.01 |
| 0.03 | 0.02 | 0.03 | 0.03 | 0.03 | 0.04 | 0.03 | 0.03 |
| 0.04 | 0.03 | 0.03 | 0.03 | 0.03 | 0.06 | 0.05 | 0.03 |
| 0.03 | 0.03 | 0.03 | 0.03 | 0.03 | 0.06 | 0.06 | 0.02 |
| 0.03 | 0.03 | 0.03 | 0.03 | 0.03 | 0.06 | 0.06 | 0.01 |
| 0.02 | 0.03 | 0.02 | 0.03 | 0.03 | 0.07 | 0.07 | 0.01 |
| 0.01 | 0.03 | 0.02 | 0.03 | 0.03 | 0.06 | 0.06 | 0.00 |
| 0.02 | 0.02 | 0.05 | 0.08 | 0.05 | 0.13 | 0.09 | 0.06 |
| 0.04 | 0.03 | 0.08 | 0.11 | 0.06 | 0.23 | 0.17 | 0.10 |
| 0.06 | 0.03 | 0.10 | 0.13 | 0.07 | 0.32 | 0.24 | 0.10 |
| 0.06 | 0.04 | 0.10 | 0.14 | 0.07 | 0.38 | 0.26 | 0.08 |
| 0.06 | 0.04 | 0.11 | 0.15 | 0.08 | 0.42 | 0.30 | 0.07 |
| 0.06 | 0.04 | 0.12 | 0.16 | 0.09 | 0.48 | 0.34 | 0.06 |
| 0.05 | 0.04 | 0.12 | 0.15 | 0.09 | 0.49 | 0.37 | 0.05 |
| 1.60 | 0.03 | 0.08 | 0.10 | 0.53 | 0.10 | 0.10 | 0.07 |
| 2.39 | 0.06 | 0.14 | 0.17 | 0.63 | 0.22 | 0.20 | 0.12 |
| 2.73 | 0.08 | 0.19 | 0.21 | 0.63 | 0.35 | 0.29 | 0.15 |
| 2.74 | 0.09 | 0.22 | 0.24 | 0.68 | 0.45 | 0.34 | 0.15 |
| 2.78 | 0.10 | 0.26 | 0.27 | 0.83 | 0.54 | 0.43 | 0.16 |
| 2.75 | 0.11 | 0.30 | 0.31 | 0.97 | 0.64 | 0.53 | 0.17 |
| 2.81 | 0.12 | 0.34 | 0.34 | 1.15 | 0.73 | 0.63 | 0.17 |

**Table 3**
Conversion ratios.

| Originating country ($I$) | Receiving countries ($J$) | | | | | |
|---|---|---|---|---|---|---|
| | France | Germany | Italy | Japan | U.K. | U.S. |
| A.  $YI/YJ$ | | | | | | |
| France | 1.00 | 0.72 | 1.49 | 0.55 | 1.50 | 0.14 |
| Germany | 1.40 | 1.00 | 2.08 | 0.77 | 2.10 | 0.19 |
| Italy | 0.67 | 0.48 | 1.00 | 0.37 | 1.01 | 0.09 |
| Japan | 1.81 | 1.30 | 2.70 | 1.00 | 2.72 | 0.25 |
| U.K. | 0.67 | 0.48 | 0.99 | 0.37 | 1.00 | 0.09 |
| U.S. | 7.38 | 5.28 | 10.97 | 4.07 | 11.07 | 1.00 |
| B.  $MI/XJ$ | | | | | | |
| France | | 0.56 | 1.17 | 0.80 | 1.06 | 0.40 |
| Germany | 1.42 | | 1.89 | 1.29 | 1.71 | 0.64 |
| Italy | 0.58 | 0.37 | | 0.53 | 0.70 | 0.27 |
| Japan | 0.68 | 0.44 | 0.91 | | 0.83 | 0.31 |
| U.K. | 0.86 | 0.55 | 1.15 | 0.78 | | 0.39 |
| U.S. | 1.86 | 1.18 | 2.48 | 1.70 | 2.25 | |
| C.  $XJ/YJ$ | | | | | | |
| Any country | 0.19 | 0.22 | 0.22 | 0.12 | 0.24 | 0.06 |

Note: Data are for 1979.

## Impulse and Response Components of the Multipliers

A given cross-multiplier may be substantial either because the impulse from the originating country is large or because the response in another country is large, or for both reasons. Moreover, the dynamic pattern of a cross-multiplier may follow that of the originating impulse or may be modified by the response characteristics of the receiving country. In tables 4 and 5 the cross-multipliers are decomposed into their impulse and response components according to formulas 28 and 34. The multipliers are reported for the first, fourth, and seventh years to provide a partial time profile. The impulse multipliers for each major country are shown in the first column and the response and cross multipliers are reported separately in the remaining columns. For each originating country, the cross-multipliers in the last three lines are the product of the impulse and response multipliers in the first three lines.

In absolute form, the smallest impulse multipliers by far are found for Japan and the United States, with France occupying an intermediate

| Australia | Austria | Belgium | Canada | Finland | Netherlands | Sweden |
|-----------|---------|---------|--------|---------|-------------|--------|
| 3.74      | 8.71    | 5.16    | 1.45   | 13.22   | 4.23        | 4.52   |
| 5.23      | 12.18   | 7.21    | 2.04   | 18.48   | 5.92        | 6.32   |
| 2.52      | 5.86    | 3.47    | 0.98   | 8.89    | 2.85        | 3.04   |
| 6.79      | 15.81   | 9.36    | 2.64   | 23.98   | 7.69        | 8.20   |
| 2.50      | 5.81    | 3.44    | 0.97   | 8.82    | 2.83        | 3.01   |
| 27.64     | 64.35   | 38.10   | 10.75  | 95.59   | 31.29       | 33.37  |
|           |         |         |        |         |             |        |
| 3.86      | 5.56    | 1.57    | 1.30   | 8.99    | 1.60        | 3.33   |
| 6.25      | 9.00    | 2.54    | 2.10   | 14.54   | 2.59        | 5.39   |
| 2.57      | 3.70    | 1.05    | 0.87   | 5.98    | 1.06        | 2.22   |
| 3.02      | 4.35    | 1.23    | 1.02   | 7.02    | 1.25        | 2.60   |
| 3.79      | 5.46    | 1.54    | 1.28   | 8.82    | 1.57        | 3.27   |
| 8.21      | 11.82   | 3.34    | 2.76   | 19.10   | 3.40        | 7.07   |
|           |         |         |        |         |             |        |
| 0.16      | 0.27    | 0.56    | 0.19   | 0.25    | 0.45        | 0.23   |

position and Germany, Italy, and the United Kingdom showing large values. The small absolute impulse multipliers for Japan and the United States are mirrored in small cross-multipliers for the receiving countries. The absolute response multipliers are positively correlated with country size, making for higher cross-multipliers in larger countries and negligible ones for the small nations.

Just as before, however, the absolute multipliers give a seriously misleading impression of the strength of the impulse and response mechanisms in many countries, as may be seen by comparing tables 4 and 5. It is apparent from the elasticity multipliers that the United States can transmit impulses abroad comparable to those emanating from other large countries and that the impulses from Japan are considerably bigger when viewed as elasticities. Similarly, the response multipliers for big countries (especially the United States) are generally diminished in the elasticity measures. Those of the small countries are affected little by the shift from absolute to elasticity measures, however.

**Table 4**
International impulse and response multipliers (absolute form).

| Originating country | Year | Impulse multiplier (*MIGI*) | Response and cross-country multipliers | | | | |
|---|---|---|---|---|---|---|---|
| | | | France | Germany | Italy | Japan | U.K. |
| **France** | | | | | | | |
| *YJMI* | 1979 | 0.20 | | 0.60 | 0.31 | 0.22 | 0.12 |
| | 1982 | 0.19 | | 1.52 | 0.51 | 0.51 | 0.19 |
| | 1985 | 0.17 | | 1.66 | 0.53 | 0.71 | 0.21 |
| *YJGI* | 1979 | | | 0.12 | 0.06 | 0.04 | 0.02 |
| | 1982 | | | 0.29 | 0.10 | 0.10 | 0.04 |
| | 1985 | | | 0.29 | 0.10 | 0.12 | 0.04 |
| **GERMANY** | | | | | | | |
| *YJMI* | 1979 | 0.50 | 0.16 | | 0.27 | 0.17 | 0.09 |
| | 1982 | 0.79 | 0.17 | | 0.34 | 0.31 | 0.11 |
| | 1985 | 0.48 | 0.22 | | 0.38 | 0.42 | 0.11 |
| *YJGI* | 1979 | | 0.03 | | 0.13 | 0.08 | 0.05 |
| | 1982 | | 0.13 | | 0.27 | 0.25 | 0.09 |
| | 1985 | | 0.10 | | 0.18 | 0.20 | 0.05 |
| **ITALY** | | | | | | | |
| *YJMI* | 1979 | 0.23 | 0.20 | 0.60 | | 0.19 | 0.10 |
| | 1982 | 0.48 | 0.25 | 1.21 | | 0.35 | 0.15 |
| | 1985 | 0.42 | 0.33 | 1.22 | | 0.46 | 0.16 |
| *YJGI* | 1979 | | 0.05 | 0.14 | | 0.04 | 0.02 |
| | 1982 | | 0.12 | 0.59 | | 0.18 | 0.07 |
| | 1985 | | 0.14 | 0.52 | | 0.19 | 0.07 |
| **JAPAN** | | | | | | | |
| *YJMI* | 1979 | 0.04 | 0.09 | 0.45 | 0.21 | | 0.10 |
| | 1982 | 0.05 | 0.21 | 0.91 | 0.34 | | 0.19 |
| | 1985 | 0.05 | 0.25 | 0.77 | 0.36 | | 0.18 |
| *YJGI* | 1979 | | 0.00 | 0.02 | 0.01 | | 0.00 |
| | 1982 | | 0.01 | 0.05 | 0.02 | | 0.01 |
| | 1985 | | 0.01 | 0.04 | 0.02 | | 0.01 |
| **U.K.** | | | | | | | |
| *YJMI* | 1979 | 0.41 | 0.12 | 0.35 | 0.19 | 0.19 | |
| | 1982 | 0.54 | 0.16 | 0.82 | 0.29 | 0.33 | |
| | 1985 | 0.66 | 0.18 | 0.77 | 0.28 | 0.36 | |
| *YJGI* | 1979 | | 0.04 | 0.15 | 0.08 | 0.08 | |
| | 1982 | | 0.09 | 0.44 | 0.15 | 0.18 | |
| | 1985 | | 0.12 | 0.51 | 0.19 | 0.23 | |
| **U.S.** | | | | | | | |
| *YJMI* | 1979 | 0.09 | 0.07 | 0.26 | 0.14 | 0.34 | 0.08 |
| | 1982 | 0.13 | 0.09 | 0.70 | 0.23 | 0.53 | 0.10 |
| | 1985 | 0.22 | 0.10 | 0.62 | 0.21 | 0.54 | 0.10 |
| *YJGI* | 1979 | | 0.01 | 0.02 | 0.13 | 0.03 | 0.01 |
| | 1982 | | 0.01 | 0.09 | 0.03 | 0.07 | 0.01 |
| | 1985 | | 0.02 | 0.13 | 0.05 | 0.12 | 0.02 |

| U.S. | Australia | Austria | Belgium | Canada | Finland | Netherlands | Sweden |
|------|-----------|---------|---------|--------|---------|-------------|--------|
| 0.60 | 0.02 | 0.02 | 0.11 | 0.07 | 0.02 | 0.11 | 0.04 |
| 1.82 | 0.03 | 0.05 | 0.16 | 0.13 | 0.07 | 0.27 | 0.06 |
| 1.43 | 0.04 | 0.05 | 0.16 | 0.15 | 0.09 | 0.37 | 0.04 |
| 0.12 | 0.00 | 0.00 | 0.02 | 0.02 | 0.00 | 0.02 | 0.01 |
| 0.35 | 0.01 | 0.01 | 0.03 | 0.02 | 0.01 | 0.05 | 0.01 |
| 0.25 | 0.01 | 0.01 | 0.03 | 0.03 | 0.02 | 0.06 | 0.01 |
| 0.46 | 0.01 | 0.04 | 0.09 | 0.06 | 0.02 | 0.13 | 0.04 |
| 1.15 | 0.02 | 0.05 | 0.11 | 0.08 | 0.06 | 0.23 | 0.05 |
| 0.77 | 0.02 | 0.05 | 0.11 | 0.09 | 0.08 | 0.31 | 0.01 |
| 0.23 | 0.01 | 0.02 | 0.05 | 0.03 | 0.01 | 0.06 | 0.02 |
| 0.90 | 0.02 | 0.04 | 0.09 | 0.06 | 0.04 | 0.18 | 0.04 |
| 0.37 | 0.01 | 0.02 | 0.05 | 0.04 | 0.04 | 0.15 | 0.01 |
| 0.60 | 0.02 | 0.04 | 0.07 | 0.08 | 0.02 | 0.09 | 0.03 |
| 1.39 | 0.03 | 0.05 | 0.10 | 0.11 | 0.05 | 0.19 | 0.05 |
| 1.03 | 0.03 | 0.05 | 0.10 | 0.11 | 0.06 | 0.25 | 0.02 |
| 0.14 | 0.00 | 0.01 | 0.02 | 0.02 | 0.00 | 0.02 | 0.01 |
| 0.67 | 0.01 | 0.03 | 0.05 | 0.05 | 0.02 | 0.09 | 0.03 |
| 0.44 | 0.01 | 0.02 | 0.04 | 0.05 | 0.03 | 0.11 | 0.01 |
| 1.37 | 0.05 | 0.02 | 0.05 | 0.17 | 0.02 | 0.05 | 0.03 |
| 2.23 | 0.08 | 0.03 | 0.07 | 0.17 | 0.05 | 0.13 | 0.05 |
| 1.07 | 0.09 | 0.03 | 0.06 | 0.20 | 0.05 | 0.15 | 0.00 |
| 0.00 | 0.00 | 0.00 | 0.00 | 0.01 | 0.00 | 0.00 | 0.00 |
| 0.12 | 0.00 | 0.00 | 0.00 | 0.01 | 0.00 | 0.01 | 0.00 |
| 0.05 | 0.00 | 0.00 | 0.00 | 0.01 | 0.00 | 0.01 | 0.00 |
| 0.57 | 0.02 | 0.02 | 0.05 | 0.12 | 0.03 | 0.08 | 0.05 |
| 1.25 | 0.03 | 0.03 | 0.08 | 0.14 | 0.09 | 0.18 | 0.05 |
| 0.87 | 0.03 | 0.03 | 0.07 | 0.14 | 0.09 | 0.20 | 0.03 |
| 0.23 | 0.01 | 0.01 | 0.02 | 0.05 | 0.01 | 0.03 | 0.02 |
| 0.67 | 0.02 | 0.02 | 0.04 | 0.07 | 0.05 | 0.10 | 0.03 |
| 0.57 | 0.02 | 0.02 | 0.05 | 0.09 | 0.06 | 0.13 | 0.02 |
|  | 0.01 | 0.01 | 0.03 | 0.53 | 0.01 | 0.03 | 0.02 |
|  | 0.03 | 0.03 | 0.05 | 0.51 | 0.04 | 0.09 | 0.04 |
|  | 0.02 | 0.03 | 0.04 | 0.52 | 0.04 | 0.10 | 0.02 |
|  | 0.00 | 0.00 | 0.00 | 0.05 | 0.00 | 0.00 | 0.00 |
|  | 0.00 | 0.00 | 0.01 | 0.06 | 0.00 | 0.01 | 0.00 |
|  | 0.00 | 0.01 | 0.01 | 0.11 | 0.01 | 0.02 | 0.01 |

**Table 5**
International impulse and response multipliers (elasticity form).

| Originating country | Year | Impulse multiplier (*EMIGI*) | Response and cross-country multipliers | | | | |
|---|---|---|---|---|---|---|---|
| | | | France | Germany | Italy | Japan | U.K. |
| **France** | | | | | | | |
| *EYJMI* | 1979 | 1.20 | | 0.07 | 0.08 | 0.02 | 0.03 |
| | 1982 | 1.18 | | 0.18 | 0.13 | 0.05 | 0.05 |
| | 1985 | 1.18 | | 0.17 | 0.13 | 0.05 | 0.05 |
| *EYJGI* | 1979 | | | 0.09 | 0.09 | 0.02 | 0.04 |
| | 1982 | | | 0.21 | 0.15 | 0.05 | 0.06 |
| | 1985 | | | 0.20 | 0.16 | 0.06 | 0.06 |
| **Germany** | | | | | | | |
| *EYJMI* | 1979 | 2.57 | 0.04 | | 0.11 | 0.03 | 0.04 |
| | 1982 | 4.28 | 0.04 | | 0.13 | 0.04 | 0.05 |
| | 1985 | 2.63 | 0.06 | | 0.15 | 0.06 | 0.05 |
| *EYJGI* | 1979 | | 0.11 | | 0.28 | 0.06 | 0.09 |
| | 1982 | | 0.18 | | 0.57 | 0.19 | 0.20 |
| | 1985 | | 0.15 | | 0.40 | 0.15 | 0.13 |
| **Italy** | | | | | | | |
| *EYJMI* | 1979 | 1.35 | 0.02 | 0.05 | | 0.01 | 0.02 |
| | 1982 | 3.26 | 0.02 | 0.09 | | 0.02 | 0.02 |
| | 1985 | 3.05 | 0.03 | 0.08 | | 0.02 | 0.02 |
| *EYJGI* | 1979 | | 0.03 | 0.07 | | 0.02 | 0.02 |
| | 1982 | | 0.08 | 0.28 | | 0.06 | 0.07 |
| | 1985 | | 0.09 | 0.23 | | 0.07 | 0.07 |
| **Japan** | | | | | | | |
| *EYJMI* | 1979 | 0.56 | 0.01 | 0.04 | 0.04 | | 0.02 |
| | 1982 | 0.79 | 0.03 | 0.08 | 0.07 | | 0.04 |
| | 1985 | 0.65 | 0.03 | 0.07 | 0.07 | | 0.04 |
| *EYJGI* | 1979 | | 0.01 | 0.02 | 0.02 | | 0.01 |
| | 1982 | | 0.02 | 0.07 | 0.05 | | 0.03 |
| | 1985 | | 0.02 | 0.05 | 0.05 | | 0.03 |
| **U.K.** | | | | | | | |
| *EYJMI* | 1979 | 1.65 | 0.02 | 0.04 | 0.05 | 0.02 | |
| | 1982 | 2.19 | 0.02 | 0.09 | 0.07 | 0.03 | |
| | 1985 | 2.40 | 0.03 | 0.09 | 0.07 | 0.03 | |
| *EYJGI* | 1979 | | 0.03 | 0.07 | 0.08 | 0.03 | |
| | 1982 | | 0.05 | 0.20 | 0.15 | 0.06 | |
| | 1985 | | 0.07 | 0.21 | 0.17 | 0.07 | |
| **U.S.** | | | | | | | |
| *EYJMI* | 1979 | 1.92 | 0.02 | 0.07 | 0.07 | 0.07 | 0.04 |
| | 1982 | 2.71 | 0.03 | 0.16 | 0.11 | 0.12 | 0.05 |
| | 1985 | 3.78 | 0.04 | 0.16 | 0.13 | 0.11 | 0.06 |
| *EYJGI* | 1979 | | 0.05 | 0.13 | 0.14 | 0.13 | 0.08 |
| | 1982 | | 0.08 | 0.44 | 0.31 | 0.34 | 0.14 |
| | 1985 | | 0.14 | 0.62 | 0.48 | 0.41 | 0.23 |

| U.S. | Australia | Austria | Belgium | Canada | Finland | Netherlands | Sweden |
|------|-----------|---------|---------|--------|---------|-------------|--------|
| 0.01 | 0.01 | 0.03 | 0.10 | 0.02 | 0.04 | 0.08 | 0.03 |
| 0.04 | 0.02 | 0.07 | 0.14 | 0.03 | 0.15 | 0.19 | 0.05 |
| 0.03 | 0.02 | 0.03 | 0.13 | 0.03 | 0.18 | 0.25 | 0.03 |
| 0.02 | 0.01 | 0.04 | 0.12 | 0.02 | 0.05 | 0.09 | 0.04 |
| 0.05 | 0.03 | 0.08 | 0.16 | 0.04 | 0.17 | 0.23 | 0.05 |
| 0.04 | 0.07 | 0.08 | 0.15 | 0.04 | 0.21 | 0.29 | 0.03 |
| | | | | | | | |
| 0.02 | 0.01 | 0.09 | 0.13 | 0.02 | 0.07 | 0.14 | 0.04 |
| 0.04 | 0.02 | 0.12 | 0.15 | 0.03 | 0.19 | 0.26 | 0.06 |
| 0.03 | 0.02 | 0.12 | 0.15 | 0.04 | 0.27 | 0.38 | 0.01 |
| 0.04 | 0.03 | 0.24 | 0.34 | 0.06 | 0.18 | 0.37 | 0.11 |
| 0.18 | 0.08 | 0.53 | 0.65 | 0.14 | 0.81 | 1.09 | 0.25 |
| 0.08 | 0.05 | 0.30 | 0.41 | 0.09 | 0.70 | 0.99 | 0.03 |
| | | | | | | | |
| 0.01 | 0.01 | 0.04 | 0.04 | 0.01 | 0.03 | 0.04 | 0.02 |
| 0.02 | 0.01 | 0.05 | 0.05 | 0.02 | 0.06 | 0.08 | 0.02 |
| 0.01 | 0.01 | 0.04 | 0.05 | 0.02 | 0.08 | 0.10 | 0.01 |
| 0.01 | 0.01 | 0.05 | 0.06 | 0.02 | 0.04 | 0.06 | 0.02 |
| 0.06 | 0.03 | 0.15 | 0.16 | 0.05 | 0.21 | 0.26 | 0.08 |
| 0.04 | 0.03 | 0.12 | 0.14 | 0.05 | 0.23 | 0.32 | 0.02 |
| | | | | | | | |
| 0.02 | 0.02 | 0.03 | 0.03 | 0.03 | 0.04 | 0.03 | 0.02 |
| 0.04 | 0.04 | 0.04 | 0.04 | 0.03 | 0.08 | 0.07 | 0.03 |
| 0.02 | 0.05 | 0.03 | 0.04 | 0.04 | 0.09 | 0.09 | 0.00 |
| 0.01 | 0.01 | 0.02 | 0.02 | 0.02 | 0.02 | 0.02 | 0.01 |
| 0.03 | 0.03 | 0.03 | 0.03 | 0.03 | 0.06 | 0.06 | 0.02 |
| 0.01 | 0.03 | 0.02 | 0.03 | 0.03 | 0.06 | 0.06 | 0.00 |
| | | | | | | | |
| 0.01 | 0.01 | 0.03 | 0.05 | 0.03 | 0.08 | 0.06 | 0.09 |
| 0.03 | 0.02 | 0.05 | 0.06 | 0.03 | 0.18 | 0.12 | 0.04 |
| 0.02 | 0.02 | 0.05 | 0.06 | 0.04 | 0.21 | 0.15 | 0.02 |
| 0.02 | 0.02 | 0.05 | 0.08 | 0.05 | 0.13 | 0.04 | 0.06 |
| 0.06 | 0.04 | 0.10 | 0.14 | 0.07 | 0.38 | 0.26 | 0.03 |
| 0.05 | 0.04 | 0.12 | 0.15 | 0.09 | 0.49 | 0.37 | 0.05 |
| | | | | | | | |
| | 0.02 | 0.04 | 0.05 | 0.28 | 0.05 | 0.05 | 0.04 |
| | 0.03 | 0.08 | 0.09 | 0.25 | 0.17 | 0.12 | 0.06 |
| | 0.03 | 0.09 | 0.09 | 0.30 | 0.19 | 0.17 | 0.04 |
| | 0.03 | 0.08 | 0.10 | 0.53 | 0.10 | 0.10 | 0.07 |
| | 0.09 | 0.22 | 0.24 | 0.68 | 0.45 | 0.34 | 0.15 |
| | 0.12 | 0.34 | 0.34 | 1.15 | 0.73 | 0.63 | 0.17 |

## Decomposition of International Impulse Multipliers

As shown in formulas 26 and 35, both forms of international impulse multipliers can be factored into two components, one representing the internal income response to a domestic demand shock and the other representing the import response to the income change. Thus, the impulse transmitted abroad as the result of a domestic shock is larger the larger is the own-income multiplier and the larger is the marginal import propensity or elasticity. The quantitative decomposition for both the absolute and elasticity versions of the dynamic impulse multipliers is given in table 6.

Turning first to the absolute form of the impulse multipliers, we observe that the smallest values are found for Japan, and that this is due to both a small income multiplier and a low import propensity. The import propensity of the U.S. economy is comparably low, but the U.S. impulse multiplier is raised considerably even in absolute form because of a relatively high income multiplier. The highest import propensity appears in the U.K. model, but the destabilizing potential for U.K. trading partners is mitigated by the low U.K. income multiplier. In contrast, the moderately high import propensities for Germany and Italy are reinforced by sizable income multipliers.

Converting to the elasticity form considerably narrows the discrepancies among the impulse multipliers because the range of import elasticities is smaller than that of the import propensities. The highest import elasticities are found in Germany, Italy, and the United Kingdom, with resulting high impulse multipliers (especially for Germany and Italy, where the effect is reinforced by high income multipliers). Because the income elasticity of U.S. imports approximates unity despite the very low marginal propensity to import in this country, the high income multiplier translates into a high elasticity impulse multiplier. In contrast, Japan exhibits the lowest import elasticity and one of the three lowest income multipliers of the major countries, resulting in an elasticity impulse multiplier that is much lower than even France's.

## Decomposition of International Response Multipliers

The two primary factors governing the sensitivity of one country to a trade shock from another are the internal response mechanism of the

# Table 6
Decomposition of international impulse multipliers.

| Originating country | Absolute form | | | | | | | Elasticity form | | | | | | |
|---|---|---|---|---|---|---|---|---|---|---|---|---|---|---|
| | 1979 | 1980 | 1981 | 1982 | 1983 | 1984 | 1985 | 1979 | 1980 | 1981 | 1982 | 1983 | 1984 | 1985 |
| **A. Own Income Multipliers** | | | | | | | | | | | | | | |
| | YIGI | | | | | | | EYIGI | | | | | | |
| France | 1.08 | 1.07 | 1.06 | 1.07 | 1.07 | 1.08 | 1.08 | 1.08 | 1.07 | 1.06 | 1.07 | 1.07 | 1.08 | 1.08 |
| Germany | 1.83 | 1.87 | 2.91 | 2.73 | 2.37 | 1.88 | 1.28 | 1.83 | 1.87 | 2.91 | 2.73 | 2.37 | 1.88 | 1.28 |
| Italy | 1.61 | 1.82 | 1.94 | 2.07 | 2.07 | 2.09 | 2.04 | 1.61 | 1.82 | 1.94 | 2.07 | 2.07 | 2.09 | 2.04 |
| Japan | 1.07 | 1.15 | 1.23 | 1.26 | 1.27 | 1.27 | 1.25 | 1.07 | 1.15 | 1.23 | 1.25 | 1.27 | 1.27 | 1.25 |
| U.K. | 1.07 | 1.14 | 1.16 | 1.10 | 1.08 | 1.09 | 1.08 | 1.07 | 1.14 | 1.16 | 1.10 | 1.08 | 1.09 | 1.08 |
| U.S. | 1.60 | 2.39 | 2.73 | 2.74 | 2.78 | 2.75 | 2.81 | 1.60 | 2.39 | 2.73 | 2.74 | 2.78 | 2.75 | 2.81 |
| **B. Import Propensities or Elasticities** | | | | | | | | | | | | | | |
| | MIYI | | | | | | | EMIYI | | | | | | |
| France | 0.19 | 0.18 | 0.19 | 0.18 | 0.17 | 0.16 | 0.16 | 1.12 | 1.11 | 1.11 | 1.10 | 1.11 | 1.10 | 1.09 |
| Germany | 0.27 | 0.29 | 0.27 | 0.29 | 0.29 | 0.31 | 0.37 | 1.40 | 1.58 | 1.46 | 1.57 | 1.59 | 1.68 | 2.06 |
| Italy | 0.14 | 0.26 | 0.22 | 0.23 | 0.22 | 0.22 | 0.21 | 0.84 | 1.57 | 1.42 | 1.53 | 1.62 | 1.60 | 1.50 |
| Japan | 0.04 | 0.05 | 0.05 | 0.04 | 0.04 | 0.04 | 0.04 | 0.52 | 0.71 | 0.65 | 0.62 | 0.58 | 0.54 | 0.52 |
| U.K. | 0.39 | 0.45 | 0.47 | 0.49 | 0.53 | 0.57 | 0.61 | 1.56 | 1.78 | 1.85 | 1.98 | 2.05 | 2.15 | 2.23 |
| U.S. | 0.06 | 0.05 | 0.04 | 0.05 | 0.05 | 0.06 | 0.08 | 1.20 | 1.05 | 0.96 | 0.99 | 1.09 | 1.20 | 1.35 |
| **C. International Impulse Multipliers** | | | | | | | | | | | | | | |
| | MIGI | | | | | | | EMIGI | | | | | | |
| France | 0.20 | 0.19 | 0.20 | 0.19 | 0.19 | 0.18 | 0.17 | 1.20 | 1.19 | 1.18 | 1.18 | 1.19 | 1.20 | 1.18 |
| Germany | 0.50 | 0.55 | 0.78 | 0.79 | 0.70 | 0.58 | 0.48 | 2.57 | 2.96 | 4.23 | 4.28 | 3.77 | 3.15 | 2.63 |
| Italy | 0.23 | 0.48 | 0.44 | 0.48 | 0.47 | 0.45 | 0.42 | 1.35 | 2.86 | 2.75 | 3.26 | 3.35 | 3.33 | 3.05 |
| Japan | 0.04 | 0.06 | 0.06 | 0.05 | 0.05 | 0.05 | 0.05 | 0.56 | 0.82 | 0.80 | 0.79 | 0.74 | 0.68 | 0.65 |
| U.K. | 0.41 | 0.51 | 0.54 | 0.54 | 0.57 | 0.63 | 0.66 | 1.66 | 2.03 | 2.15 | 2.19 | 2.21 | 2.34 | 2.40 |
| U.S. | 0.09 | 0.12 | 0.12 | 0.13 | 0.15 | 0.18 | 0.22 | 1.92 | 2.51 | 2.62 | 2.7 | 3.02 | 3.29 | 3.78 |

**Table 7**
Decomposition of international response multipliers for 1979.

| Originating country (I) | Receiving countries (J) | | | | | | | | | | | | |
|---|---|---|---|---|---|---|---|---|---|---|---|---|---|
| | France | Germany | Italy | Japan | U.K. | U.S. | Australia | Austria | Belgium | Canada | Finland | Netherlands | Sweden |
| **Absolute form** | | | | | | | | | | | | | |
| A. Trade-response coefficients (XJMI) | | | | | | | | | | | | | |
| France | | 0.40 | 0.14 | 0.22 | 0.12 | 0.35 | 0.03 | 0.02 | 0.16 | 0.05 | 0.01 | 0.15 | 0.05 |
| Germany | 0.21 | | 0.13 | 0.16 | 0.09 | 0.17 | 0.02 | 0.04 | 0.13 | 0.04 | 0.01 | 0.18 | 0.05 |
| Italy | 0.27 | 0.40 | | 0.19 | 0.10 | 0.34 | 0.03 | 0.04 | 0.10 | 0.05 | 0.01 | 0.13 | 0.04 |
| Japan | 0.14 | 0.24 | 0.07 | | 0.11 | 0.74 | 0.09 | 0.02 | 0.06 | 0.10 | 0.01 | 0.08 | 0.05 |
| U.K. | 0.15 | 0.24 | 0.08 | 0.19 | | 0.33 | 0.03 | 0.02 | 0.08 | 0.08 | 0.03 | 0.12 | 0.06 |
| U.S. | 0.09 | 0.17 | 0.06 | 0.33 | 0.08 | | 0.03 | 0.01 | 0.04 | 0.36 | 0.01 | 0.05 | 0.03 |
| B. Foregin-trade multipliers (YJXJ) | | | | | | | | | | | | | |
| France | | 1.49 | 2.17 | 1.01 | 1.00 | 1.74 | 0.54 | 1.02 | 0.71 | 1.48 | 1.42 | 0.71 | 0.78 |
| Germany | 0.77 | | 2.10 | 1.02 | 1.00 | 1.74 | 0.53 | 1.00 | 0.71 | 1.47 | 1.40 | 0.71 | 0.78 |
| Italy | 0.73 | 1.51 | | 1.01 | 0.99 | 1.76 | 0.53 | 1.03 | 0.73 | 1.50 | 1.47 | 0.69 | 0.76 |
| Japan | 0.63 | 1.91 | 2.85 | | 0.87 | 1.85 | 0.53 | 1.09 | 0.83 | 1.67 | 1.59 | 0.66 | 0.65 |
| U.K. | 0.77 | 1.45 | 2.32 | 1.02 | | 1.74 | 0.54 | 1.01 | 0.72 | 1.44 | 1.39 | 0.70 | 0.80 |
| U.S. | 0.73 | 1.51 | 2.19 | 1.02 | 0.98 | | 0.53 | 1.02 | 0.74 | 1.47 | 1.46 | 0.68 | 0.74 |
| C. International-response multipliers (YJMI) | | | | | | | | | | | | | |
| France | | 0.60 | 0.31 | 0.22 | 0.12 | 0.60 | 0.02 | 0.02 | 0.11 | 0.07 | 0.02 | 0.11 | 0.04 |
| Germany | 0.16 | | 0.27 | 0.17 | 0.09 | 0.46 | 0.01 | 0.04 | 0.09 | 0.06 | 0.02 | 0.13 | 0.04 |
| Italy | 0.20 | 0.60 | | 0.19 | 0.10 | 0.60 | 0.02 | 0.04 | 0.07 | 0.08 | 0.02 | 0.09 | 0.03 |
| Japan | 0.09 | 0.45 | 0.21 | | 0.10 | 1.37 | 0.05 | 0.02 | 0.05 | 0.17 | 0.02 | 0.05 | 0.03 |
| U.K. | 0.12 | 0.35 | 0.19 | 0.19 | | 0.57 | 0.02 | 0.02 | 0.05 | 0.12 | 0.03 | 0.08 | 0.05 |
| U.S. | 0.07 | 0.26 | 0.14 | 0.34 | 0.08 | | 0.01 | 0.01 | 0.03 | 0.53 | 0.01 | 0.03 | 0.02 |

**Elasticity form**

### A. Trade-response coefficients (EXJMI)

| | France | Germany | Italy | Japan | U.K. | U.S. |
|---|---|---|---|---|---|---|
| France | 0.16 | 0.24 | 0.12 | 0.07 | 0.25 | 0.12 |
| Germany | 0.24 | 0.46 | 0.21 | 0.08 | 0.33 | 0.35 |
| Italy | 0.10 | 0.14 | 0.07 | 0.05 | 0.10 | 0.14 |
| Japan | 0.13 | 0.10 | 0.10 | 0.10 | 0.07 | 0.10 |
| U.K. | 0.20 | 0.18 | 0.22 | 0.10 | 0.12 | 0.12 |
| U.S. | 0.22 | 0.16 | 0.15 | 1.00 | 0.13 | 0.15 |

### B. Foreign-trade multipliers (EYJXJ)

| | France | Germany | Italy | Japan | U.K. | U.S. |
|---|---|---|---|---|---|---|
| France | 0.18 | 0.32 | 0.35 | 0.28 | 0.40 | 0.27 |
| Germany | 0.18 | 0.32 | 0.35 | 0.28 | 0.39 | 0.27 |
| Italy | 0.17 | 0.31 | 0.37 | 0.28 | 0.41 | 0.27 |
| Japan | 0.15 | 0.30 | 0.40 | 0.32 | 0.46 | 0.29 |
| U.K. | 0.18 | 0.32 | 0.34 | 0.27 | 0.40 | 0.27 |
| U.S. | 0.17 | 0.31 | 0.36 | 0.28 | 0.41 | 0.27 |

### C. International-response multipliers (EYJMI)

| | France | Germany | Italy | Japan | U.K. | U.S. |
|---|---|---|---|---|---|---|
| France | 0.03 | 0.03 | 0.04 | 0.02 | 0.10 | 0.03 |
| Germany | 0.04 | 0.15 | 0.07 | 0.02 | 0.13 | 0.09 |
| Italy | 0.02 | 0.04 | 0.03 | 0.01 | 0.04 | 0.04 |
| Japan | 0.02 | 0.03 | 0.04 | 0.03 | 0.03 | 0.03 |
| U.K. | 0.04 | 0.06 | 0.08 | 0.03 | 0.05 | 0.03 |
| U.S. | 0.04 | 0.05 | 0.05 | 0.28 | 0.05 | 0.04 |

first country and the importance of its trade with the second. Quantitative measures of these two components and their product, the cross-country-response multiplier, are shown in table 7. The absolute forms are computed from formulas 24, 25, and 27, and the elasticity versions from 32, 33, and 36. Because a $6 \times 13$ matrix is required for each of these sets of cross-country coefficients, we confine ourselves to presenting the measures for 1979, the first year of the multiplier simulations.

The first point about the trade response coefficients relating $J$'s exports to $I$'s imports is that they are generally small. Thus, a given increase in $I$'s imports is spread over so many trading partners that the impact on any but the most important partners is small. This is the basic reason for the generally small cross-multipliers in table 1.

Second, the degree of exposure of large countries such as Germany and the United States to external trade shocks is seriously overstated when the trade-response coefficients are measured in absolute form, whereas the reverse is true for the smaller OECD economies. As shown in formula 39, the relative magnitude of an external shock from $I$ to $J$ depends not only on $J$'s marginal export response to $I$'s import increase ($XJMI$) but also on the ratio of $I$'s total imports to $J$'s total exports ($MI/XJ$). These conversion ratios are given in table 3. When converted to the elasticity form, the trade-response coefficients in table 7 are sharply reduced for Germany and the United States and substantially increased for the smaller nations. The column average of these coefficients may serve as an index of the overall degree of exposure of the country in the column to shocks from the six large countries.

The foreign-trade-impact multipliers, measuring the income responses to export shocks in the receiving countries, range between 0.5 for Australia and 1.75 for the United States when calculated in absolute form. For a given receiving country, the foreign-trade multiplier may vary somewhat according to the country of origin of the trade shock. This minor variation reflects the differing composition of trade between the given receiving country and its trading partners, since total trade is disaggregated into four commodity classes in the LINK system.

Conversion to elasticity form greatly narrows the differences among the foreign-trade multipliers in the receiving countries. In the elasticity form, the absolute-income multiplier for exports ($YJXJ$) is weighted by the importance of exports to $J$'s economy ($XJ/YJ$), as shown in formula 40. For a given mechanism of response to export shocks, the more open the economy in terms of export trade the larger is the foreign-trade-elasticity multiplier. The export shares of the various economies are given in table 3. The small export shares of Japan and the United States make for low foreign-trade-elasticity multipliers, whereas the reverse is true for Belgium and the Netherlands.

## Conclusions

Our method of decomposing international multipliers is designed to highlight key parameters of the transmission process. The principal determinants of the strength of transmission impulses are the domestic multiplier and the import propensity of the initiating country. Neither a highly open, domestically stable economy nor a nearly closed, unstable economy can propagate a powerful impulse abroad in response to its own domestic disturbance. Transmission responses depend primarily on the openness of an economy and its importance in world trade, which together govern its exposure to external shocks, and on its own internal instability as reflected in its foreign-trade multiplier. Neither an open, domestically stable economy nor a nearly closed, unstable economy can be disturbed much from abroad.

Impulse, response, and complete cross-multipliers can be defined either in dollar units or as elasticities. The dollar cross-multipliers can be badly misleading as measures of potential international instability. They are positively correlated with country size simply because large countries tend to be important traders in world markets. When converted to elasticity form the dispersion among the cross-multipliers for large and small countries is greatly reduced, since the foreign shocks and responses are now scaled according to country size. Insofar as impulses are concerned, the misleadingly low conventional multiplier for the United States, due to a low import propensity, is raised to a level comparable to that of Germany when the comparison is based on elasticities, whereas the dollar multiplier for the United Kingdom, which is high because of a high import propensity, is correspondingly reduced in elasticity form. Similarly, when measured as elasticities, the range of the trade-response coefficients is narrowed among the large and small countries and the foreigh-trade multipliers for large, comparatively closed economies such as Japan and the United States are sharply reduced relative to the more open smaller economies.

The elasticity cross-multipliers are much smaller than the own multipliers for all countries, owing primarily to the extensive dispersion of trade among the OCED nations. Shocks from Germany and the United States can be relatively large and affect many countries, but even in these cases domestic shocks in other countries will generally swamp an independent disturbance from one of the trading giants. Apart from its general level of sensitivity to external disturbances, any given country may be particularly susceptible to an impulse from an especially close trading partner, as in the case of Canada from the United States, or of Austria, Belgium, and the Netherlands from Germany. The cross-multipliers for Australia and Japan are generally rather low, since much of their trade is with Pacific Basin neighbors instead of the European and North American countries included in this empirical study.

Our theoretical decomposition could be implemented for any multinational model with the requisite structural detail. The general method could also be applied to other aspects of the transmission mechanism, such as responses to supply shocks.

## Notes

1. For a history of Project LINK see Hickman and Klein 1979. The principal papers from the project are contained in Ball 1973, Waelbroeck 1976, and Sawyer 1979, and the last volume includes an extensive bibliography of other LINK publications.

2. See Hickman and Lima 1979 for LINK multipliers in response to supply (wage) shocks.

3. The elasticity multipliers could be defined with respect to the percentage change in government expenditures, as in $(DYI/YI)/(DGI/GI)$. As noted in Hickman 1974, however, the present formulation is preferable because it standardizes the shock according to the size of GDP and is unaffected by differences among originating countries in their government-expenditure shares.

4. Similarly, the feedback effects on the exports of $I$, which amplify the own multiplier $YIGI$ as explained in the preceding section, are partly nullified by the induced increases in the export price of $I$ accompanying the demand shock.

5. Again there is a small substitution effect because $J$'s import price is raised by $I$'s export-price increase.

## Bibliography

Ball, R. J., ed. 1973. *The International Linkage of National Economic Models*. Amsterdam: North-Holland.

Filatov, V., B. G. Hickman, and L. R. Klein. 1982. Long run simulations with the Project LINK system 1978–85. In B. G. Hickman, ed., *Global International Economic Models*. International Institute of Applied Systems Analysis, Austria.

Hickman, B. G. 1974. International transmission of economic fluctuations and inflation. In Albert Ando et al., eds., *International Aspects of Stabilization Policies*. Boston: Federal Reserve Bank.

Hickman, B. G., and L. R. Klein. 1979. A decade of research by Project LINK. *Items* (Social Science Research Council, New York) 33 (no. 3/4): 49–56.

Hickman, B. G., and A. Lima. 1979. Price determination and transmission of inflation in the LINK system. In Sawyer 1979.

Hickman, B. G., and S. Schleicher. 1978. The interdependence of national economies and the synchronization of economic fluctuations: Evidence from the LINK Project. *Weltwirtschaftliches Archiv* 114 (no. 4): 642–708.

Sawyer, J. A., ed. 1979. *Modelling the International Transmission Mechanism*. Amsterdam: North-Holland.

Waelbroeck, J. L. 1976. *The Models of Project LINK*. Amsterdam: North-Holland.

# 18 The Transmission of World Economic Expansion to an Open Economy: Some Experiments for Canada

J. A. Sawyer
D. P. Dungan
G. V. Jump

There have been a number of studies in recent years on both theoretical and empirical aspects of the international transmission of economic fluctuations, with particular attention paid to the differences between fixed- and flexible-exchange-rate regimes. Analyses with a substantial theoretical content include those by Buiter (1978, 1979), Casas (1975), Dornbusch (1976), Helliwell (1975), Kenen (1978a), Mussa (1979), Nyberg and Viotti (1979), Purvis (1979), Saidi (1980), and Scarfe (1977). Artus and Young (1979) have reviewed the arguments for fixed and flexible exchange rates and discussed the adjustment process to external shocks. Descriptive papers on some of the recent empirical evidence have been written by Fieleke (1978) and Ripley (1978). Bonomo and Tanner (1972) have examined Canada's sensitivity to economic cycles in the United States. Helliwell (1974) has linked econometric models of Canada and the United States to study trade, capital flows, and migration as channels for the international transmission of stabilization policies. Fair (1979) has surveyed a number of these bilateral linkages and commented on modeling problems. Econometric studies of the United Kingdom, a very open economy, have been done by Jonson (1976) and by Ball, Burns, and Laury (1977). The Project LINK system of linked national econometric models has been used for several studies. Hickman (1974) and Hickman and Lima (1979) have studied the international transmission of inflation. Klein, Su, and Beaumont (1979) have simulated the effects of different international fiscal policies and exchange-rate revaluations. Weinberg (1979) has compared various policies to stimulate the world economy.

The last two studies mentioned provided part of the incentive for the present chapter. They were both concerned with the slowdown in world economic expansion that began in the mid-1970s. Fiscal stimulation in the major industrialized countries was suggested as one means of getting the world back onto an expansionary path. The impact of world expansion on a particular country will depend, however, on the transmission mechanism, its strength in transmitting these expansionary effects, the exchange-rate regime, monetary and fiscal policy, and the degree of slack in resource utilization in the domestic economy at the time world expansion occurs. In this chapter, the effect on Canada of a sustained 3 percent increase in real output in other major industrialized countries is simulated over a five-year period using the FOCUS model of the Canadian economy under various assumptions about the economic environment in Canada.[1]

It was decided to restrict the study to the effect of an increase in real output and to exclude the effects of changes in the rate of inflation and interest rates in the rest of world in order to concentrate on a particular aspect of the transmission mechanism and to simplify the separation of various effects.[2] The analysis is also incomplete in that feedbacks from Canada to the expanding countries are excluded. Ultimately, a set of simulation experiments with the complete LINK system, in which the same rules concerning monetary and fiscal policy, exchange-rate regimes, and degree of resource utilization are applied to each country, might provide sets of country multipliers that would give some indication of the differing effects under alternative economic environments.[3] Another respect in which the study is incomplete is that it assumes no change in fiscal policy. An adaptive fiscal policy could, depending on the policy targets, amplify or dampen the outcomes.

## The FOCUS Model

The FOCUS model is a quarterly macroeconometric model of the Canadian economy, developed and maintained at the Institute for Policy Analysis of the University of Toronto.[4] Its name is an acronym for FOreCasting and User Simulation. Some care has been taken in developing the model's structural equations to ensure that they embody desirable long-run properties as well as plausible short-run dynamics. There are four features of the model's domestic sectors that are somewhat distinctive and deserve explanation.

First is the way inflation expectations are modeled in the labor and domestic financial markets.[5] FOCUS utilizes "synthetic" expectations series to represent expected rates of price inflation 90 days, one year, and two years into the future. These series were constructed by regressing actual rates of price inflation on a set of lagged explanatory variables, which would seem to come closer to the kinds of variables on which market participants actually base expectations than distributed lags of past rates of change in prices. For example, 90-day expectations are specified to depend upon recent observations of money-supply growth, unemployment rates, foreign prices, and the exchange rate in addition to the actual past rates of price inflation. The use of synthetic expectations series permits the modeling of expectations in an internally consistent manner. The same expected rate of price inflation that influences nominal interest rates appears as an explanatory varible in the key wage equation. Thus, labor-market participants are assumed to form expectations in the same manner as participants in financial markets. Variations in expectations will simultaneously alter both interest rates and wage settlements.[6]

Second, FOCUS contains an integrated supply side. Factor demand equations for labor and machinery-and-equipment capital are derived from a common production function so that labor-capital ratios are responsive to relative prices. This is not unique to the FOCUS model, but the nature of the production function is. The private sector of the economy is viewed as consisting of $N$ nearly identical plants. Each plant is assumed to have an optimal size. Production is constrained to follow a Cobb-Douglas production function with factor inputs of production labor and machinery and equipment. Investment in new nonresidential structures is identified with the time rate of change in $N$. Positive net investment occurs whenever $\dot{N} > 0$, and is stimulated by a positive differential between the internal rate of return on structures and the real, after-tax rate of interest on government bonds. This internal rate of return is determined endogenously as the ratio of after-tax corporation profits to the replacement cost of the capital stock. When the ratio of profits to replacement cost is high, investment in structures increases and the number of firms expands. The profit rate also determines the level at which the existing stock of plant capacity is utilized. Labor and machinery-and-equipment stock are viewed partly as "overhead" to plants and partly as variable inputs to the production process. Because of the production-function constraint they are substitute factors of production; a rise in wage rates relative to the service price of machinery and equipment will reduce the demand for the former and increase the demand for the latter. When relative prices are stable, both variable factors are complementary to structures investment; that is, an increase in $N$ will normally lead to increased demand for both labor and machinery and equipment. When profits are high, the number of firms entering the industry increases, driving down prices and thereby reducing profitability and moderating the incentives for further entry. Thus, the specifications bridge the short and the long run.

Third, the model offers two alternative methods of determining its key price variable, the implicit price index for privately produced gross national product (PGNPP). A "cost markup" regime may be specified in which PGNPP is determined by a behavioral equation with labor, import, tax, and petroleum costs as explanatory variables. Alternatively, a neoclassical "market-clearing" regime may be specified in which PGNPP equates separate calculations of supply and demand for aggregate output within the model. The latter specification produces a "perfectly flexible" price level, and PGNPP responds not only to changes in unit labor costs and capital goods prices (which are supply-side variables) but also directly to variations in aggregate demand. Thus, an exogenous increase in aggregate demand will lead to increases in both prices and profit margins in model solutions. The real wage rate will decline as a result, moving the economy down the labor-demand schedule to a higher level of employment.

A fourth distinctive feature of FOCUS is the wide range of policy levers embedded throughout its structure. This enables the user to perform a variety of simulations under different policy assumptions.

## Trade, Capital Flows, and the Exchange Rate in the FOCUS Model

Canada is modeled as an open economy that is a price taker for imported goods but not for export goods.[7] Table 1 presents the elasticities of the principal trade variables of the model.

An important empirical finding of the model, which has implications for the simulation results reported below, is the relatively low interest-rate sensitivity of net capital flows (table 2). That is, in contrast to the assumptions of some theoretical models, on balance capital does not appear to be highly mobile. In response to a 1-percentage-point increase in the domestic interest rate, long-term flows increase on average by $3.6 billion over a year while short-term flows decrease by $2.3 billion, for a net increase of $1.3 billion.[8] A number of authors, among them Goldstein (1980), Mussa (1979), and Saidi (1980), have stressed the relation between the degree of capital mobility and the insulating properties of flexible exchange rates.

**Table 1**
Long-run price, exchange-rate, and activity elasticities of the principal trade equations of the FOCUS model.

| | Activity | Domestic price | Foreign price | Exchange rate |
|---|---|---|---|---|
| Exports of goods (excluding petroleum and natural gas and motor vehicles to U.S.) (XGO) | 1.22 (4)[a] (foreign industrial production) | −1.60 (8) | 1.60 (8) | 1.60 (8) |
| Exports of motor vehicles to U.S.[b] (XGAUS) | 0.46 (3) (U.S. real motor-vehicle consumption) | −1.33 (6) | 1.33 (6) | 1.15 (7) |
| Exports of services (excluding capital service receipts) (XSO) | 0.53 (6) (U.S. GNP) | −0.37 (6) | 0.37 (6) | 0.37 (6) |
| Imports of goods (excluding petroleum and motor vehicles from U.S.) (MGO) | 1.00 (4) (import-weighted average of GNP components) | 0.91 (7) | −0.90 (1) | −1.01 (5) |
| Imports of motor vehicles from U.S. (MGAUS) | 0.40 (4) (Canadian real motor-vehicle consumption) | 1.13 (5) (relative Canadian and U.S. wage rates) | −1.13 (5) | −1.06 (6) |
| Imports of services (excluding capital service payment) (MSO) | 0.34 (3) (Canadian real private GNP) | 0.69 (4) | −0.69 (4) | −0.68 (4) |

a. Length of lag (including the current quarter) is given in parentheses.
b. Includes also effects on imports of motor vehicles from U.S.; elasticity of motor vehicles exports with respect to motor vehicle imports is 0.75.

**Table 2**
Interest-rate sensitivity of principal capital in flows in the FOCUS Model.

| Capital-flow variable | 1975–1979 average value (billions of Canadian dollars) | Change in flow due to one-percentage-point increase in interest rate[a] |
|---|---|---|
| Direct investment in Canada (BPDIL) | 0.34 | 0.085 (1.8%) (4): Canadian rate of return on new investment |
| Canadian direct investment abroad (BPDIA) | −1.21 | −0.049 (1.1%) (4): U.S. return on capital |
| Net new issues of provincial and municipal bonds (BPLPMN) | 2.83 | 2.014 (43.7%) (4): differential of Canadian and U.S. provincial/state and local bond rates (multiplied by Canadian nonfederal government spending) |
| New issues of corporate bonds (BPLCH) | 1.70 | 0.607 (13.2%) (4): differential of Canadian and U.S. corporate bond rates (multiplied by Canadian private GNP) |
| Trade in outstanding bonds and stocks (BPLCBS) | 0.28 | 0.438 (9.5%) (4): differential of Canadian and U.S. 3–5-year bond rates (multiplied by sum of U.S. and Canadian GNP(s). 0.462 (10.0%) (4): change in differential of Canadian 90-day paper rate and Eurodollar rate (multiplied by sum of Canadian and U.S. GNP(s) |
| Short-term flows[b] and errors and omissions (BPSN) | 2.09 | 0.455 (10.0%): differential of Canadian 90-day paper rate and weighted average of U.S. 3-month treasury bill rate and Eurodollar rate |

a. Changes reported are 1975–1979 averages, in billions of Canadian dollars at annual rates and as a percent of the average (absolute) value of the Canadian current-account deficit in those years ($4.61 billion). The lengths of all lags, including the current quarter, are given in parentheses. All equations are in levels form.
b. Short-term flows also offset 0.753 of the net long-term-flow balance.

The relatively low sensitivity of capital flows to interest-rate changes has the effect that an expansionary fiscal policy in Canada leads to a depreciation of the Canadian dollar in the foreign-exchange market, in contrast to the appreciation that would result if capital were highly mobile. Hence, fiscal policy may be more effective, given the elasticities of the FOCUS model, under flexible than under fixed exchange rates.

The model is capable of determining the U.S.-Canadian dollar exchange rate as the rate that equates the current and capital account balances without official intervention. To achieve this result required an interactive simulation-regression analysis for estimating the parameters of the sector. Various equations were estimated individually and then simulated in concert with other equations in the sector. Specifications that led to erratic behavior in the exchange rate were replaced with alternatives until, after repeated simulations, a balance-of-payments sector that produced a smoothly responsive (but by no means sluggish) exchange rate was obtained.

## Direct Transmission Channels in the FOCUS Model

Increases in the level of real output in the rest of the world directly affect four variables, which enter as exogenous inputs into five behavioral equations of the model. These channels are shown in table 3, which also shows the share of total exports and of GNP of each component of Canada's exports, and the elasticities of exports and capital flows with respect to the four world activity variables.

For the simulation experiments reported below, each of the four world activity variables was increased by 3 percent over its control solution value.

## Alternative Economic Environments

The control solution was basically the actual historical path of the Canadian economy over the period 1975–1979. For the main set of experiments, the level of employment was adjusted to be 2 percentage points above the natural rate of unemployment[9] and the capacity-utilization rate was set at 80 percent. Hence, the world economic expan-

**Table 3**
Transmission channels for world economic expansion in the FOCUS model.

| Exogenous world activity variable | Behavioral equation(s) affected | Share of total exports[a] / Share of GNP | Elasticities[b] One-quarter / Long-run |
|---|---|---|---|
| Weighted industrial production index of six major Canadian export markets (UWQIND)[c] | Exports (real) of goods (excluding petroleum, natural gas, and motor vehicles to U.S.) (XGO) | $\frac{56.8}{13.1}$ | (L) $\frac{0.07\ (4)}{1.22}$ |
| U.S. GNP (current U.S. dollars) (USCNPV) | Exports (real) of services (excluding capital services receipts) (XSO) | $\frac{15.9}{3.6}$ | (L) $\frac{0.15\ (6)}{0.53}$ |
| | Long-term capital flows: trade in outstanding bonds and stocks (BPLCBS) | — | (A) $\frac{0.69\ (3)}{1.38}$ |
| U.S. consumer expenditure (real) on motor vehicles and parts (USCDA) | Exports (real) of motor vehicles to U.S. (XGAUS) | $\frac{22.7}{5.2}$ | (L) $\frac{0.32\ (3)}{0.46}$ |
| U.S. net exports (current U.S. dollars) (USBPM) | Canadian direct investment abroad (BPDIA) | — | (A) $\frac{0.22}{0.22}$ |

a. Average shares, 1975–1979. Shares of total exports do not add up to 100 because one category—exports (real) of petroleum and natural gas—is exogenous in the experiments.

b. Elasticities are simply the appropriate equation coefficients if a log specification (L) was used, and are evaluated using 1975–1979 average values for equations with arithmetic (A) specifications. Long-run elasticities are sums across all lags. The lengths of the lag (including the current quarter) are given in parentheses.

c. The six trading partners are France, Italy, Japan, the United Kingdom, the United States, and the Federal Republic of Germany.

**Table 4**
Effects of world economic expansion on real aggregate demand in Canada.

| | | Experiment | | | | | | | |
|---|---|---|---|---|---|---|---|---|---|
| | | 1 | 2 | 3 | 4 | 5 | 6 | 7 | 8 |
| Utilization rates | | Low | Low | Low | Low | Low | Low | High | High |
| Exchange-rate regime | | Fix | Flex | Fix | Flex | Fix | Man | Fix | Flex |
| Monetary policy | | Bres | Bres | Int | Int | Part | Adap | Bres | Bres |
| Variable[a] | Year | Percentage change | | | | | | | |
| Gross national product (GNP) | 1 | 0.22 | 0.15 | 0.24 | 0.16 | 0.27 | 0.33 | 0.16 | 0.10 |
| | 2 | 0.42 | 0.11 | 0.52 | 0.19 | 0.69 | 0.83 | 0.25 | 0.03 |
| | 3 | 0.40 | −0.10 | 0.60 | −0.03 | 0.92 | 0.98 | 0.19 | −0.16 |
| | 4 | 0.32 | −0.09 | 0.64 | −0.19 | 1.01 | 1.11 | 0.06 | −0.14 |
| | 5 | 0.23 | −0.04 | 0.64 | −0.39 | 1.16 | 1.43 | −0.02 | −0.10 |
| Personal consumption (C) | 1 | 0.08 | 0.09 | 0.08 | 0.09 | 0.09 | 0.10 | 0.08 | 0.09 |
| | 2 | 0.27 | 0.23 | 0.31 | 0.25 | 0.37 | 0.43 | 0.30 | 0.24 |
| | 3 | 0.38 | 0.15 | 0.47 | 0.20 | 0.62 | 0.67 | 0.43 | 0.16 |
| | 4 | 0.45 | 0.11 | 0.60 | 0.13 | 0.80 | 0.82 | 0.47 | 0.11 |
| | 5 | 0.53 | 0.13 | 0.73 | 0.03 | 0.96 | 1.07 | 0.49 | 0.11 |
| Business gross fixed capital formation (IFB) | 1 | 0.13 | −0.01 | 0.24 | 0.08 | 0.45 | 0.83 | 0.14 | −0.01 |
| | 2 | 0.51 | 0.02 | 1.08 | 0.33 | 2.16 | 2.85 | 0.56 | 0.05 |
| | 3 | 0.57 | −0.10 | 1.60 | 0.01 | 3.06 | 2.91 | 0.62 | −0.06 |
| | 4 | 0.20 | −0.25 | 1.48 | −0.89 | 2.59 | 2.76 | −0.06 | −0.32 |
| | 5 | −0.18 | −0.08 | 0.98 | −1.61 | 2.46 | 3.49 | −0.88 | −0.29 |

| | | | | | | | | |
|---|---|---|---|---|---|---|---|---|
| Exports of goods and services (X) | 1 | 1.50 | 1.44 | 1.50 | 1.45 | 1.50 | 1.51 | 1.37 | 1.38 |
| | 2 | 2.53 | 2.08 | 2.54 | 2.12 | 2.54 | 2.53 | 2.19 | 1.96 |
| | 3 | 2.20 | 1.14 | 2.18 | 1.21 | 2.14 | 2.11 | 1.64 | 1.01 |
| | 4 | 1.90 | 1.26 | 1.89 | 1.19 | 1.88 | 2.02 | 1.23 | 1.18 |
| | 5 | 1.72 | 1.56 | 1.81 | 1.32 | 2.00 | 2.15 | 1.24 | 1.56 |
| Imports of goods and services (M) | 1 | 0.75 | 0.90 | 0.79 | 0.91 | 0.86 | 0.98 | 0.90 | 1.00 |
| | 2 | 1.84 | 2.07 | 2.03 | 2.12 | 2.42 | 0.63 | 2.29 | 2.30 |
| | 3 | 1.91 | 1.59 | 2.15 | 1.62 | 2.47 | 2.21 | 2.34 | 1.75 |
| | 4 | 1.77 | 1.49 | 1.88 | 1.32 | 1.76 | .63 | 1.94 | 1.55 |
| | 5 | 1.72 | 1.77 | 1.63 | 1.36 | 1.51 | 1.71 | 1.57 | 1.77 |

a. All variables in this table are in constant 1971 dollars. The figures show percentage changes between a particular simulation and the control solution.

**Table 5**
Effects of world economic expansion on prices, utilization rates, and government balance in Canada.

| | Experiment | | | | | | | |
|---|---|---|---|---|---|---|---|---|
| | 1 | 2 | 3 | 4 | 5 | 6 | 7 | 8 |
| Utilization rates | Low | Low | Low | Low | Low | Low | High | High |
| Exchange-rate regime | Fix | Flex | Fix | Flex | Fix | Man | Fix | Flex |
| Monetary policy | Bres | Bres | Int | Int | Part | Adap | Bres | Bres |
| Variable | Year | | | | | | | |
| Percentage change | | | | | | | | |
| GNP implicit price index | | | | | | | | |
| (PGNP) | 1 | 0.32 | 0.15 | 0.35 | 0.19 | 0.40 | 0.49 | 0.62 | 0.30 |
| | 2 | 0.77 | −0.06 | 0.86 | 0.07 | 1.03 | 1.07 | 1.42 | 0.20 |
| | 3 | 1.10 | −0.59 | 1.20 | −0.50 | 1.29 | 1.13 | 1.83 | −0.36 |
| | 4 | 1.42 | −0.99 | 1.43 | −1.18 | 1.31 | 1.25 | 1.99 | −0.83 |
| | 5 | 1.70 | −1.34 | 1.55 | −2.08 | 1.39 | 1.42 | 1.78 | −1.26 |
| Foreign-exchange rate | | | | | | | | |
| (RXUS) | 1 | 0.00 | −1.16 | 0.00 | −1.03 | 0.00 | 0.00 | 0.00 | −1.18 |
| | 2 | 0.00 | −2.70 | 0.00 | −2.39 | 0.00 | 0.00 | 0.00 | −2.64 |
| | 3 | 0.00 | −2.99 | 0.00 | −2.92 | 0.00 | 0.00 | 0.00 | −2.82 |
| | 4 | 0.00 | −3.60 | 0.00 | −4.17 | 0.00 | 0.00 | 0.00 | −3.40 |
| | 5 | 0.00 | −4.15 | 0.00 | −5.35 | 0.00 | 0.00 | 0.00 | −3.94 |
| Terms of trade (goods) | | | | | | | | |
| (PTTG) | 1 | 0.19 | 0.36 | 0.19 | 0.37 | 0.25 | 0.37 | 0.46 | 0.46 |
| | 2 | 0.65 | 0.95 | 0.73 | 0.93 | 0.84 | 0.93 | 1.18 | 1.18 |
| | 3 | 0.86 | 0.91 | 0.99 | 0.90 | 1.10 | 1.06 | 1.52 | 1.06 |
| | 4 | 1.29 | 0.86 | 1.26 | 0.87 | 1.21 | 1.16 | 1.74 | 0.91 |
| | 5 | 1.43 | 0.99 | 1.31 | 0.83 | 1.24 | 1.24 | 1.51 | 0.98 |

Percentage points

| Unemployment rate (RU) | | | | | | | | |
|---|---|---|---|---|---|---|---|---|
| 1 | -0.09 | -0.07 | -0.10 | -0.08 | -0.11 | -0.13 | -0.12 | -0.08 |
| 2 | -0.28 | -0.12 | -0.32 | -0.16 | -0.40 | -0.46 | -0.31 | -0.12 |
| 3 | -0.32 | 0.01 | -0.39 | -0.03 | -0.51 | -0.50 | -0.27 | 0.02 |
| 4 | -0.31 | 0.05 | -0.40 | 0.10 | -0.48 | -0.47 | -0.19 | 0.07 |
| 5 | -0.30 | 0.02 | -0.39 | 0.22 | -0.49 | -0.59 | -0.09 | 0.05 |

| Capacity-utilization rate (RHO) | | | | | | | | |
|---|---|---|---|---|---|---|---|---|
| 1 | 0.36 | 0.21 | 0.38 | 0.24 | 0.42 | 0.51 | 0.00 | 0.00 |
| 2 | 0.59 | 0.03 | 0.68 | 0.13 | 0.86 | 0.95 | -0.04 | -0.28 |
| 3 | 0.34 | -0.27 | 0.45 | -0.25 | 0.59 | 0.52 | -0.21 | -0.44 |
| 4 | 0.11 | -0.11 | 0.22 | -0.32 | 0.30 | 0.41 | -0.36 | -0.20 |
| 5 | -0.03 | -0.00 | 0.07 | -0.29 | 0.25 | 0.40 | -0.01 | -0.01 |

Billions of current dollars

| Government balance (GBAL) | | | | | | | | |
|---|---|---|---|---|---|---|---|---|
| 1 | 0.35 | 0.18 | 0.37 | 0.22 | 0.40 | 0.47 | 0.45 | 0.23 |
| 2 | 0.69 | 0.13 | 0.76 | 0.22 | 0.90 | 0.94 | 0.75 | 0.13 |
| 3 | 0.70 | -0.09 | 0.78 | -0.09 | 0.85 | 0.71 | 0.54 | -0.16 |
| 4 | 0.79 | -0.02 | 0.83 | -0.31 | 0.75 | 0.77 | 0.41 | -0.11 |
| 5 | 0.97 | 0.02 | 0.93 | -0.68 | 0.97 | 1.17 | 0.32 | -0.08 |

Note: The exchange rate is the number of Canadian dollars per U.S. dollar. Hence, a negative sign means a lower price for foreign currency.

**Table 6**
Effects of world economic expansion on money and interest rates in Canada.

| | | Experiment | | | | | | | |
|---|---|---|---|---|---|---|---|---|---|
| | | 1 | 2 | 3 | 4 | 5 | 6 | 7 | 8 |
| Utilization rates | | Low | Low | Low | Low | Low | Low | High | High |
| Exchange-rate regime | | Fix | Flex | Fix | Flex | Fix | Man | Fix | Flex |
| Monetary policy | | Bres | Bres | Int | Int | Part | Adap | Bres | Bres |
| Variable | Year | | | | | | | | |
| **Percentage change** | | | | | | | | | |
| Money supply | 1 | −0.06 | −0.06 | 0.48 | 0.28 | 1.48 | 3.07 | −0.05 | −0.06 |
| (MONMI) | 2 | −0.12 | −0.10 | 1.13 | 0.19 | 3.25 | 2.72 | −0.13 | −0.09 |
| | 3 | −0.16 | −0.03 | 1.55 | −0.45 | 3.02 | 2.94 | −0.18 | −0.03 |
| | 4 | −0.17 | −0.01 | 1.64 | −1.08 | 3.61 | 5.56 | −0.18 | −0.01 |
| | 5 | −0.16 | −0.03 | 1.62 | −1.84 | 5.22 | 5.64 | −0.13 | −0.02 |
| **Percentage points** | | | | | | | | | |
| Rate on 90-day | 1 | 0.13 | 0.08 | 0.00 | 0.00 | −0.26 | −0.64 | 0.18 | 0.10 |
| finance paper | 2 | 0.30 | 0.04 | 0.00 | 0.00 | −0.49 | −0.34 | 0.40 | 0.08 |
| (RMF) | 3 | 0.37 | −0.14 | 0.00 | 0.00 | −0.28 | −0.29 | 0.49 | −0.10 |
| | 4 | 0.43 | −0.23 | 0.00 | 0.00 | −0.50 | −0.99 | 0.50 | −0.21 |
| | 5 | 0.47 | −0.30 | 0.00 | 0.00 | −0.94 | −1.02 | 0.43 | −0.29 |
| Rate on 1–3-year | 1 | 0.13 | 0.05 | 0.07 | 0.02 | −0.03 | −0.22 | 0.18 | 0.08 |
| government bonds | 2 | 0.30 | 0.11 | −0.02 | −0.01 | −0.55 | −0.86 | 0.37 | 0.14 |
| (RMBGI) | 3 | 0.37 | −0.11 | −0.10 | −0.07 | −0.41 | −0.44 | 0.44 | −0.08 |
| | 4 | 0.43 | −0.19 | −0.10 | 0.05 | −0.58 | −0.83 | 0.50 | −0.16 |
| | 5 | 0.47 | −0.24 | −0.05 | 0.11 | −0.76 | −1.39 | 0.50 | −0.23 |

| | | | | | | | | | |
|---|---|---|---|---|---|---|---|---|---|
| Real rate on 1–3-year government bonds (RMRGI) | 1 | −0.05 | 0.21 | −0.21 | 0.07 | −0.52 | −0.98 | −0.09 | 0.19 |
| | 2 | −0.05 | 0.25 | −0.42 | 0.12 | −1.06 | −0.95 | −0.15 | 0.20 |
| | 3 | 0.06 | 0.23 | −0.41 | 0.40 | −0.78 | −0.72 | 0.03 | 0.21 |
| | 4 | 0.24 | 0.27 | −0.22 | 0.77 | −0.66 | −1.16 | 0.39 | 0.32 |
| | 5 | 0.35 | 0.07 | −0.10 | 0.92 | −1.04 | −1.21 | 0.61 | 0.15 |
| Real rate of return on investment (RRIFN) | 1 | 0.12 | 0.15 | 0.12 | 0.14 | 0.12 | 0.14 | 0.09 | 0.13 |
| | 2 | 0.35 | 0.32 | 0.40 | 0.35 | 0.48 | 0.56 | 0.26 | 0.27 |
| | 3 | 0.19 | 0.06 | 0.27 | 0.09 | 0.39 | 0.38 | 0.04 | 0.00 |
| | 4 | 0.06 | 0.12 | 0.17 | 0.09 | 0.28 | 0.31 | −0.13 | 0.08 |
| | 5 | −0.01 | 0.24 | 0.13 | 0.14 | 0.32 | 0.50 | −0.21 | 0.20 |

**Table 7**
Effects of world economic expansion on Canada's balance of payments.

| | | Experiment | | | | | | | |
| | | 1 | 2 | 3 | 4 | 5 | 6 | 7 | 8 |
| Utilization rates | | Low | Low | Low | Low | Low | Low | High | High |
| Exchange-rate regime | | Fix | Flex | Fix | Flex | Fix | Man | Fix | Flex |
| Monetary policy | | Bres | Bres | Int | Int | Part | Adap | Bres | Bres |
| Variable | Year | | | | | | | | |
| Exports of goods and | | Percentage change | | | | | | | |
| services | 1 | 1.73 | 1.03 | 1.75 | 1.13 | 0.73 | 1.88 | 1.89 | 1.11 |
| (XV) | 2 | 3.11 | 0.87 | 3.19 | 1.15 | 1.53 | 3.37 | 3.37 | 1.02 |
| | 3 | 3.08 | −0.49 | 3.14 | −0.31 | 1.66 | 2.99 | 3.12 | −0.36 |
| | 4 | 3.10 | −0.90 | 3.07 | −1.36 | 1.83 | 3.03 | 2.90 | −0.77 |
| | 5 | 3.11 | −1.05 | 3.03 | −2.35 | 2.35 | 3.25 | 2.66 | −0.91 |
| Imports of goods and | 1 | 0.73 | −0.04 | 0.77 | 0.03 | 0.39 | 0.98 | 0.90 | 0.05 |
| services | 2 | 1.77 | −0.38 | 1.97 | −0.03 | 1.18 | 2.56 | 2.22 | −0.11 |
| (MV) | 3 | 1.84 | −1.12 | 2.08 | −0.58 | 1.37 | 2.14 | 2.24 | −0.84 |
| | 4 | 1.69 | −1.17 | 1.81 | −1.59 | 1.15 | 1.59 | 1.85 | −1.48 |
| | 5 | 1.63 | −1.94 | 1.56 | −2.77 | 1.21 | 1.69 | 1.46 | −1.75 |
| Current account balance | | Billions of current dollars | | | | | | | |
| (BPC) | 1 | 0.37 | 0.44 | 0.36 | 0.43 | 0.35 | 0.32 | 0.36 | 0.43 |
| | 2 | 0.56 | 0.60 | 0.50 | 0.56 | 0.38 | 0.29 | 0.45 | 0.53 |
| | 3 | 0.59 | 0.38 | 0.48 | 0.42 | 0.33 | 0.38 | 0.38 | 0.28 |
| | 4 | 0.81 | 0.58 | 0.73 | 0.73 | 0.72 | 0.85 | 0.59 | 0.51 |
| | 5 | 1.07 | 0.76 | 1.08 | 0.94 | 1.19 | 1.16 | 0.86 | 0.73 |

|  |  |  |  |  |  |  |  |  |  |
|---|---|---|---|---|---|---|---|---|---|
| Net short-term | 1 | 0.04 | −0.41 | 0.00 | −0.39 | −0.08 | −0.20 | 0.04 | −0.42 |
| capital flows | 2 | −0.16 | −0.63 | −0.14 | −0.53 | −0.09 | 0.24 | −0.28 | −0.66 |
| (BPSN) | 3 | −0.36 | −0.25 | −0.09 | −0.22 | 0.47 | 0.64 | −0.53 | −0.26 |
|  | 4 | −0.63 | −0.24 | −0.00 | −0.52 | 0.76 | 0.75 | −0.86 | −0.28 |
|  | 5 | −0.93 | −0.03 | 3.07 | −0.70 | 1.09 | 1.63 | −1.14 | −0.09 |
| Net long-term | 1 | 0.02 | −0.03 | −0.00 | −0.04 | −0.04 | −0.11 | 0.06 | −0.01 |
| capital flows | 2 | 0.39 | 0.03 | 0.19 | −0.03 | −0.18 | −0.53 | 0.62 | 0.13 |
| (BPLN) | 3 | 0.71 | −0.14 | 0.12 | −0.20 | −0.80 | −1.03 | 1.00 | −0.03 |
|  | 4 | 1.10 | −0.34 | 0.00 | −0.21 | −1.30 | −1.59 | 1.44 | −0.23 |
|  | 5 | 1.52 | −0.73 | −0.09 | −0.24 | −2.02 | −2.73 | 1.77 | −0.64 |
| Change in official | 1 | 0.43 | 0.00 | 0.36 | 0.00 | 0.22 | 0.00 | 0.46 | 0.00 |
| reserves | 2 | 0.79 | 0.00 | 0.54 | 0.00 | 0.11 | 0.00 | 0.79 | 0.00 |
| (BRES) | 3 | 0.93 | 0.00 | 0.51 | 0.00 | 0.00 | 0.00 | 0.85 | 0.00 |
|  | 4 | 1.28 | 0.00 | 0.73 | 0.00 | 0.18 | 0.00 | 1.17 | 0.00 |
|  | 5 | 1.65 | 0.00 | 1.06 | 0.00 | 0.26 | 0.00 | 1.49 | 0.00 |

sion takes place in an environment of economic slack in the Canadian economy. For two of the experiments, however, the slack was removed by setting the unemployment rate 1 percentage point below the natural rate and setting the capacity-utilization rate at 94 percent (which corresponds historically to maximum utilization).

With respect to the exchange rate, three different assumptions were made. The two basic alternatives were fixed and flexible (cleanly floating) exchange rates. In one experiment, however, it was assumed that there was a managed floating regime and that the object of monetary policy was to maintain the existing (control solution) exchange rate; that is, the monetary authorities were assumed to adjust monetary aggregates in such a manner as to maintain a target value for the exchange rate with no change in official reserves.

With respect to monetary policy, two principal alternatives were used. The first was the assumption that commercial bank reserves (ARRCB) are controlled by the central bank and held at target levels.[10] This implies in the fixed-exchange-rate regime that the effect on the money supply of foreign-exchange transactions by the central bank is completely offset ("sterilized") by transactions in the bond market.[11] One experiment was also performed assuming only 50 percent sterilization. The second alternative assumed that a nominal short-term interest rate (the rate on 90-day finance company paper; RMF) is held by the central bank at target levels.[12]

Finally, a choice had to be made concerning price behavior in the model. Because the shock in the Canadian economy was an increase in aggregate demand, it seemed reasonable to assume that prices respond in a market-clearing manner to this increase. Thus, prices rise to equate quantity supplied to quantity demanded. The alternative would have been to use the markup-pricing equation in the FOCUS model. In the latter case, prices would not have responded as quickly to the excess demand for Canadian output, since the markup is on normal unit costs.[13]

Eight experiments were performed, each involving the same increase in world economic activity but with different combinations of assumptions about the three determinants of the economic environment. The different environmental assumptions are shown at the head of each column in tables 4–7, in which the results are shown. The abbreviations are defined as follows.

## Utilization Rate

Low: unemployment rate 2 percentage points above natural rate; capacity utilization 80 percent.
High: unemployment rate 1 percentage point below natural rate; capacity utilization 94 percent.

## Exchange-Rate regime

Fix: fixed (pegged) exchange rate.
Flex: flexible (cleanly floating) exchange rate.
Man: floating rate managed through monetary policy in such a way that exchange rate is held at a target level.

## Monetary policy

Bres: commercial bank reserves held at target level (complete sterilization).
Int: short-term interest rate held at target level.
Part: partial (50 percent) sterilization
Adap: adaptive; i.e., bank reserves and interest rates adjust to keep exchange rate at target level.

# Effects on Canada of World Economic Expansion

Tables 4–7 present the first five years' results for simulation experiments in which the real output of the major industrialized countries is increased by 3 percent over the control-solution levels. The quarterly output from the FOCUS model was converted to annual figures for these tables. All figures are differences between a particular simulation and the control solution. Because capital formation and labor-force participation are endogenous and change in response to the shocks, the results are neither the textbook static results nor long-run equilibrium growth results.

As can be seen in table 4, the short-run (one year) impact effect of the increase in world economic activity is to increase Canada's real exports, when the utilization rates are low, by an average of 1.48 percent over the control-solution levels and by 1.38 percent when the utilization rates are high. These effects reflect not only the effects of the exogenous change in foreign activity levels but also the effects of induced price and exchange-rate changes.

In the first experiment, which assumes there is some slack in the economy, the exchange rate is fixed and monetary policy is such that commercial bank reserves are held at target levels. The results are moderate increases in price levels (table 5) and in the terms of trade and in nominal interest rates (table 6). As table 6 also shows, there is a very slight decrease in the money supply (narrowly defined) as the general public changes its composition of asset holdings, and a slight short-run decrease in the real rate of interest. The real rate of return on business investment in structures also increases, so there is an increase in business capital formation. This, together with the increase in exports, induces increases in both personal consumption and imports. The increase in the price level also stimulates imports but fails to choke off the general stimulus to demand, so there is a sustained increase in real GNP over the control-solution level (table 4).

As table 7 indicates, there is an increase in official international reserves. Some net capital inflows are induced by increased real investment and higher nominal interest rates, but, as noted above, net capital flows in the FOCUS model are not highly sensitive to interest-rate changes. Therefore, in this experiment, the current account remains the chief contributor to the sustained balance-of-payments surplus (the direct stimulus to exports outweighs the negative effects of the increase in the terms of trade and the increased income). The continued balance-of-payments disequilibrium does not, however, lead to any modification in monetary policy. The government deficit is reduced from control-solution levels (see table 6, where the difference in the government balance is positive). Again, in these experiments, any possible repercussions on fiscal policy are ignored. With fiscal policy unchanged, the government is acting as the traditional "automatic stabilizer."

Under flexible exchange rates (experiment 2) the story is rather different. The exchange rate appreciates steadily (table 5) over the five-year period. In the short run the GNP price index rises, but thereafter the exchange-rate effect dominates and prices fall relative to the control solution. The major difference with respect to the fixed-rate case is the intermediate-term effect on business capital formation. The small changes in nominal interest rates imply an increase in real interest rates. Thus, in the short run there is virtually no change in capital formation, and there is a decline in later years.

Hence, under a flexible exchange rate the effects on real GNP and the unemployment rate are smaller and mixed in sign compared with the fixed-rate case. The domestic economy is not insulated from foreign shocks, but the magnitude of the effects is reduced. They are more compositional than aggregative insofar as total output is concerned. Exports increase, but in the main are offset by increased imports. There is little change in the government account and less likelihood, therefore, of any indirect changes in fiscal policy for budgetary reasons.[14]

Where the central bank controls nominal interest rates rather than bank reserves (experiments 3 and 4), the main difference in the flexible-exchange-rate case is the much larger increase in the real rate of interest in later years and the consequent larger decrease in capital formation. In the fixed-rate case, the declines in the real rates of interest are larger than when bank reserves were controlled, and the increase in capital formation is therefore larger. Hence, real GNP increases more in the later years. Because there is little if any change in nominal interest rates, there is little effect on capital flows, and the change in official reserves reflects almost entirely the current-account balance.

When only partial sterilization (50 percent) occurs (experiment 5), there are much larger increases in the money supply (table 6). Hence, the increases (which are not anticipated by economic agents) produce decreases in nominal interest rates in each year and corresponding decreases in real interest rates. Thus, capital formation is stimulated, as is overall economic activity. The rate of return on investment also rises, providing further stimulus. Although the 50 percent sterilization figure was chosen arbitrarily, it comes close to producing balance in international payments. This indicates that, even with partial sterilization, the classical "specie-flow" mechanism is still at work under fixed rates.

The last variation in monetary policy tried (experiment 6) was to assume that the central bank is controlling the exchange rate (a regime of managed flexibility) and that its target is to maintain the exchange rate at the control-solution levels. This gives rise to increases in the money supply that are, on balance, slightly larger than in the partial-sterilization case. The stimulus to aggregate demand and real output is therefore slightly larger.

In the final set of experiments (7 and 8), the first two experiments were repeated under conditions of high utilization rates. In the fixed-rate case the damping effect of rising prices is more pronounced, but the effect on real GNP does not disappear until the fifth year. Compositional changes similar to those in the first experiment still occur. Real output increases in the early years (contrary to what static analysis might lead one to expect when a shock occurs in a situation of full employment) because labor-force participation increases and the net stock of capital increases as a result of the decline in real interest rates. Hence, the supply of factors of production increases.[15] In the flexible-exchange-rate case, however, there are no significant increases in capital formation because of the different behavior of nominal interest rates as a result of the appreciation of the exchange rate. In general, variables do not behave qualitatively any differently than in the low-utilization-rate case (experiment 2); the chief impact of the high-utilization assumption is in the relative degree to which variables respond. As expected, real effects are diminished and price effects magnified in the high-utilization case.

## Conclusion

The major difference between the fixed- and flexible-exchange-rate regimes arises from the appreciation of the Canadian dollar that occurs when the exchange rate is flexible. This results in higher real interest rates than in the fixed-exchange-rate case, while the real rate of return on investment in plant and equipment tends to be lower. Hence, capital formation increases more in the fixed-exchange-rate case. The increase in productive capacity (to which changes in labor-force participation also contribute) enables real output to expand even when the utilization rates are high, although the proportionate impact on prices is greater. Thus, there are distinctive compositional and aggregate effects on total real output depending on the exchange-rate regime.[16]

Experiments 5 and 6 suggest that, when there is slack in the economy, a monetary policy that not only accommodates the increase in foreign demand but also offsets the tendency for the foreign-exchange rate to appreciate produces the largest increase in real GNP (although at the cost of an increase in the price level). Indeed, experiment 6 suggests a policy of managing a floating exchange rate to take advantage of opportunities for export-led growth or to create such opportunities.[17] This supports Goldstein's (1980, p. 54) contention that "the fact that flexible rates can provide less insulation than was previously supposed means that, on balance, the case for active policy against foreign disturbances (including the use of exchange-market intervention) has been strengthened," particularly in the case of smaller, open economies. The International Monetary Fund discourages managed floating regimes (which can be interpreted as "beggar thy neighbor" policies), but experiments 5 and 6 demonstrate that essentially the same results as with intervention in the foreign exchange market can be achieved by an appropriately chosen monetary policy.[18]

## Acknowledgment

Research for this paper was done under the auspices of the Policy and Economic Analysis Program of the Institute for Policy Analysis of the University of Toronto.

## Notes

1. Carr, Jump, and Sawyer (1976) used the TRACE model to simulate the effects of a "no growth" situation in the U.S. economy on Canada.

2. T. A. Wilson, in an unpublished study, has used the FOCUS model to analyze Canada-U.S. wage and price linkages. Rao and Whillans (1980) have used the CANDIDE model of the Economic Council of Canada to study the impact of foreign prices and interest rates on the Canadian economy. Ripley (1980) has used the IMF World Model of Merchandise Trade to do simulation studies of the impact of changes in the levels of economic activity in the industrial countries (including Canada) on their foreign-trade balances.

3. The FOCUS model is the Canadian model in the LINK system. (It replaced the TRACE model in 1979.) For a discussion of the standardization of the "economic environment" for the calculation of multipliers from different models, see de Bever et al. 1979.

4. A full description of the FOCUS model is contained in G. V. Jump et al., *FOCUS: Forecasting and User Simulation Model.*

5. Adaptive expectations (involving distributed lags) are used in the trade and capital-flow equations.

6. See Jump 1979 for a fuller discussion of interest rates and monetary policy in the FOCUS model.

7. This procedure has been confirmed by the recent work of Applebaum and Kohli (1979). Calmfors and Herin (1979) have concluded similarly for the Swedish economy that domestic and foreign products are imperfect substitutes.

8. Short-term flows do not respond perversely to interest rates; in fact, short-term flows will increase by $0.5 billion in response to a 1-percentage-point increase in the domestic interest rate. However, historically, Canadian net short-term flows have offset changes in long-term flows, and it is this offset factor—currently estimated at 75 percent—that accounts for the net decrease in short-term flows.

9. The series on the natural rate of unemployment is from Dungan and Wilson 1980. The natural rate of unemployment in the period 1975–1979 is close to 6 percent. The long-run Phillips curve in the FOCUS model is vertical.

10. *Fixed* (or *constant*) means held at the same level as in the control solution. Constancy of commercial bank reserves is not equivalent to constancy of the money supply, since small induced changes do occur in the ratio of public holdings of currency to deposits.

11. The ability of the central bank to control the money supply under a fixed-exchange-rate regime reflects the low interest-sensitivity of capital flows.

12. Historically, given that Canada is an economically small country beside a large neighbor (the U.S.) and that capital flows freely between the two countries, the assumption that Canadian interest rates may move independent of those in the U.S. may be unrealistic in a fixed-exchange-rate regime. As table 2 indicates, however, the interest-elasticity of capital flows is not high.

13. Indeed, in the very short run the average market price would have been lower than in the control solution, since the increased weight of exports, (on which there are no excise or sales taxes) in final output would have lowered average prices.

14. The partial insulation from the foreign shock is similar to that found by Kenen (1978b) in his experiment.

15. Also at work in the short run are lagged adjustment mechanisms in the employment and wage equations which temporarily reduce real wages and raise labor productivity (the converse of the labor hoarding effect in the downswing).

16. Compositional shifts in demand will require the redistribution of productive resources among industrial sectors, while short-run wage and price stickiness and sector-specific capital stocks may prevent the reallocation from working smoothly and cause short-term unemployment in declining industries and upward wage and price pressure in expanding industries. Naturally, these effects cannot be fully captured in a single-sector model.

17. In commenting on a suggestion made by Lord Kaldor, Ball et al. (1977) point out that the major objection to this strategy is the effect on the inflation rate. Our simulation experiments also indicate that the cost is an increase in the inflation rate.

18. A similar point has been made by Henderson (1980). In a recent paper Buiter (1979) shows that optimal reserve-management and exchange-rate management are generally superior to either freely floating or fixed-exchange-rate regimes. Roper and Turnovsky (1980) have also analyzed some optimal intervention rules to provide maximum insulation of the domestic economy from foreign shocks.

## Bibliography

Applebaum, E., and U. R. Kohli. 1979. Canadian–United States trade: Tests for the small-open-economy hypothesis. *Canadian Journal of Economics* 12 (February): 1–14.

Artus, J. R., and J. H. Young. 1979. Fixed and flexible exchange rates: A renewal of the debate. *International Monetary Fund Staff Papers* 26 (December): 654–698.

Ball, R. J., T. Burns, and J. S. E. Laury. 1977. The role of exchange rate changes in balance of payments adjustment: The United Kingdom case. *Economic Journal* 87 (March): 1–29.

de Bever, L., et al. 1979. Dynamic properties of four Canadian macroeconomic models: A collaborative project. *Canadian Journal of Economics* 12 (May): 133–194.

Bonomo, V., and J. E. Tanner. 1972. Canadian sensitivity to economic cycles in the United States. *Review of Economics and Statistics* 54 (February): 1–8.

Buiter, W. 1978. Short-run and long-run effects of external disturbances under a floating exchange rate. *Economica* 45 (August): 251–272.

Buiter, W. 1979. Optimal foreign exchange market intervention with rational expectations. In J. P. Martin and A. Smith, eds., *Trade and Payments under Flexible Exchange Rates*. London: Macmillan.

Calmfors, L., and J. Herin. 1979. Domestic and foreign price influences: A disaggregated study of Sweden. In Assar Lindbeck, ed., *Inflation and Employment in Open Economies*. Amsterdam: North-Holland.

Carr, J. L., G. V. Jump, and J. A. Sawyer. 1976. The operation of the Canadian economy under fixed and flexible exchange rates: Simulation results from the TRACE model. *Canadian Journal of Economics* 9 (February): 102–120.

Casas F. R. 1975. Efficient macroeconomic stabilization policies under floating exchange rates. *International Economic Review* 16 (October): 682–698.

Dornbusch, R. 1976. The theory of flexible exchange rate regimes and macroeconomic policy. *Scandinavian Journal of Economics* 78 (no. 2): 253–275.

Dungan, D. P., and T. A. Wilson. 1980. Potential GNP—Performance and Prospects. Study done for Economic Council of Canada, Ottawa.

Fair, R. C. 1979. On modeling the economic linkages among countries. In R. Dornbusch and J. A. Frenkel, eds., *International Economic Policy: Theory and Evidence*. Baltimore: Johns Hopkins University Press.

Fieleke, N. S. 1978. The international transmission of inflation. In Managed Exchange-Rate Flexibility: The Recent Experience. Federal Reserve Bank of Boston.

Goldstein, M. 1980. Have Flexible Exchange Rates Handicapped Macroeconomic Policy? Special Paper in International Economics no. 14, International Finance Section, Princeton University.

Helliwell, J. F. 1974. Trade, capital flows, and migration as channels for international transmission of stabilization policies. In International Aspects of Stabilization Policies. Federal Reserve Bank of Boston.

Helliwell, J. F. 1975. Adjustment under fixed and flexible exchange rates. In P. Kenen, ed., *International Trade and Finance*. Cambridge University Press.

Henderson, D. W. 1980. In R. Hinshaw, ed., *Domestic Goals and Financial Interdependence: The Frankfurt Dialogue*. New York: Marcel Dekker.

Hickman, B. G. 1974. International transmission of economic fluctuations and inflation. In International Aspects of Stabilization Policies. Federal Reserve Bank of Boston.

Hickman, B. G., and A. Lima. 1979. Price determination and transmission of inflation in the LINK system. In J. A. Sawyer, ed., *Modelling the International Transmission Mechanism: Applications and Extensions of the Project LINK System*. Amsterdam: North-Holland.

Jonson, P. 1976. Money and economic activity in an open economy: The United Kingdom, 1880–1970. *Journal of Political Economy* 84 (October): 979–1012.

Jump, G. V. 1979. The Financial Sector of the FOCUS Econometric Model of the Canadian Economy. Working Paper 7912, Institute for Policy Analysis, University of Toronto.

Jump, G. V., et al. FOCUS: Forecasting and User Simulation Model (a reference manual updated annually). Institute for Policy Analysis, University of Toronto.

Kenen, P. B. 1978a. New views of exchange rates and old views of policy. *American Economic Review* 68 (May): 398–406.

Kenen, P. B. 1978b. *A Model of the U.S. Balance of Payments*. Lexington, Mass.: Lexington.

Klein, L. R., V. Su, and P. Beaumont. 1979. Coordination of international fiscal policies and exchange rate revaluations. In J. A. Sawyer, ed., *Modelling the International Transmis-*

*sion Mechanism: Applications and Extensions of the Project LINK System.* Amsterdam: North-Holland.

Mussa, M. 1979. Macroeconomic interdependence and the exchange rate regime. In R. Dornbusch and J. A. Frenkel, eds., *International Economic Policy: Theory and Evidence.* Baltimore: Johns Hopkins University Press.

Nyberg, L., and S. Viotti. 1979. Unemployment, inflation, and the balance of payments: A dynamic analysis. In A. Lindbeck, ed., *Inflation and Employment in Open Economies.* Amsterdam: North-Holland.

Purvis, D. D. 1979. Wage responsiveness and the insulation properties of a flexible exchange rate. In A. Lindbeck, ed., *Inflation and Employment in Open Economies.* Amsterdam: North-Holland.

Rao, P. S., and J. D. Whillans. 1980. Impact of Foreign Prices and Interest Rates on Canadian Economy under Alternative Monetary and Exchange Rate Regimes. Discussion Paper 170, Economic Council of Canada, Ottawa.

Ripley, D. M. 1978. The transmission of fluctuations in economic activity: Some recent evidence. In Managed Exchange-Rate Flexibility: The Recent Experience. Federal Reserve Bank of Boston.

Ripley, D. M. 1980. The world model of merchandise trade: Simulation applications. *International Monetary Fund Staff Papers* 27 (June): 285–319.

Roper, D. E., and S. J. Turnovsky. 1980. Optimal exchange market intervention in a simple stochastic macro model. *Canadian Journal of Economics* 13 (May): 296–309.

Saidi, N. H. 1980. Fluctuating exchange rates and the international transmission of economic disturbances. *Journal of Money, Credit and Banking* 12 (November), part I: 575–591.

Scarfe, B. L. 1977. *Cycles, Growth, and Inflation: A Survey of Contemporary Macrodynamics.* New York: McGraw-Hill.

Weinberg, C. B. 1979. Comparisons of policies to stimulate the world economy. In J. A. Sawyer, ed., *Modelling the International Transmission Mechanism: Applications and Extensions of the Project LINK System.* Amsterdam: North-Holland.

# 19 How do European Short-Term Forecasters Predict? An Evaluation of Two Sets of GNP Forecasts

J. Waelbroeck
D. De Roo

There is by now a large literature evaluating the accuracy of short-term economic forecasts (for some of the early work, see Christ 1951 and Theil 1966). Some of the more recent studies, such as McNees 1978, have evaluated these forecasts from the viewpoint of the theory of rational expectation. Here the goal is not only to test whether the forecasts are accurate; an attempt is also made to find out whether the information available to the forecaster has been used efficiently.

Another important strand of thought is the role of expectations in the international transmission of economic fluctuations. Here a point of departure is the finding that present business-cycle models cannot explain why economic fluctuations appear to be transmitted from country to country by rather strong forces (see, for example, Hickman 1975 and Dramais 1977). These papers, based on the simulations of Project LINK's model and of other linked short-term models, suggest that macro models of the type generally built today, linked in the usual way by trade equations, imply that price and quantity shocks are transmitted quite weakly from country to country. When Project LINK was at an early stage, Waelbroeck (1973) foresaw this finding and suggested that there should be a search for the "missing links" that relate business trends in different countries and are not accounted for in current models; contagion of expectations might be one of those.

In a world of mass media, expectations in different countries might be positively correlated because the world reads the same news and believes in the same fads. Synchronized shifts of the general business climate might be one of the forces that synchronize business cycles. This idea has been advanced by other authors. Batchelor (1982) has found some confirmation by analyzing data on expectations of businessmen, gathered in the EEC Business Survey.

A third idea, which has not received as much attention as might be desirable, is that it may be worthwhile to look for the specific biases of different types of forecasters. A "rational" forecast is the forecast that is optimal in terms of the self-interest of the forecaster. A speculator who is putting his money on the line should predict in the way described by the theory of rational expectations; Idi Amin Dada's chief planner would have been wise to predict imminent prosperity. Other short-term forecasters lie somewhere between these two extremes. They have no money riding on their prediction, but they cannot afford to be too far off the mark as this would damage their prestige, their research funding, and possibly their consulting fees. They will also be mindful that Cassandra was not the most popular girl in Troy, and will be tempted to shade forecasts to make them more attractive to whomever supports their research.

The biases of official forecasts are well known, and users allow for them automatically. For years, the Belgian budget always balanced *ex ante*, but the bias was on the same few figures, so it was possible to reconstruct the truth fairly accurately. The UN's estimate of future growth of developing countries goes up by 1 percent every "development decade," whereas actual growth is constant. There is probably no official forecast that is completely free of political bias, though the bias may be small, or apparent in some years only.

Private forecasters are affected by more subtle pressures. The problem here is the perishability of their work. It gets published in the press, where it gets far less attention than the major events of the day. It is distributed to subscribers to forecasting services, who throw it away when the next forecast comes along. There is no real day of reckoning, except on the rare occasions when someone takes the trouble to undertake a *post mortem* evaluation of past predictions. As a result, the best strategy may be to announce something halfway between what the forecaster expects and what his public is prepared to believe. When the unexpected does happen the forecaster's clients will convince themselves that they had seen it coming, but if it does not they will castigate and ridicule him without mercy. Only when an event is truly extraordinary and the forecaster very sure of his judgment is it worthwhile to risk to announce something that runs contrary to general opinion.

As is suggested by much evidence, to the extent that the public tends to be slow in recognizing the implications of new developments it would be expected that private forecasters would mimic this tendency, as they bow to public-acceptability bias.

This chapter examines, in the spirit of these remarks, the forecasts for Western European countries of OECD and of the institutes grouped in the AIECE. AIECE stands for Association des Instituts Européens de Conjoncture Economique (Association of European Institutes of Business Cycle Research), an European federation of institutes specializing in short-term forecasting and business cycle analysis.[1]

## Data

Forecasts of gross national products have been compiled from information gathered by two international institutions, the OECD and the AIECE.[2] Twice a year each of these organizations issues a general report based on questionnaires mailed to members. Consistency of assumptions across countries is not necessarily ensured, because these forecasts are made before the meeting. It would still be erroneous to assume complete independence; the institutes maintain many informal contacts, and the AIECE achieves some consistency during premeeting workshops.

Differences in the natures of the participating institutions must be kept in mind in interpreting the national forecasts. Some of them are closely linked with governments, as for example the Central Planning Bureau of the Netherlands, the INSEE in France, or the ISCO in Rome. Others have business ties, such as the Chambre de Commerce de Paris or the IFO in Munich, or are academic institutes, like the DULBEA and the IRES in Belgium and the ETH in Zurich. It is thus clear that for some institutes the forecasts are to some extent normative. In addition there are differences in methodology; for example, the Central Planning Bureau uses sophisticated econometric methods, while ISCO does not. Finally, some institutes (like the NIESR of London) traditionally provide conditional forecasts taking official economic policy commitments as given, whereas others may feel more free to take government policy announcements with a grain of salt.

The OECD forecasters are in close contact with the countries for which they are responsible, but may be a little more "outsiders" than the AIECE forecasters. On the other hand, they have an advantage in that they can more easily keep track of what is happening in other countries; a coffee-break conversation is to them the equivalent of a trip abroad for an AIECE forecaster. The latter are a highly traveled lot, however, and some of the AIECE institutes have an international dimension. Two of the "wise five" German institutes, Kiel and Hamburg, are involved in worldwide economic assessments, and so are the NIESR in London and the Central Planning Bureau in the Netherlands.

Another difference that we feel may be important is in the continuity of the forecasting process. Most of the AIECE forecasters have to make known their numerical predictions on an almost continuous basis at various gatherings. The OECD commits itself to numbers every six months only. This, we feel, is an advantage: There is a greater chance that the forecast will not be tainted by reluctance to acknowledge a past error of judgment.

Real-GNP forecasts are available for 1968–1978 for the following AIECE countries: Austria, Belgium, Finland, France, Germany, Italy, Norway, Switzerland, the Netherlands, and the United Kingdom. Several forecasts exist for France, Belgium, and the Federal Republic of Germany. Since some of the institutes did not join the AIECE until quite recently, we have taken for these countries an average of the forecasts of participating institutes.

OECD forecast data for 1968 and 1969 were not available for some of the countries considered, so we will compare AIECE and OECD forecasts only for the period 1970–1978.

In appraising results, it is important to take account of the fact that OECD forecasts are made two months later than those of the AIECE (December, July, and December versus October, May, and October). Since the accuracy of predictions increases rapidly over time, this will affect the performance of the two groups. It should also be noted that the second and third forecasts published are made after the beginning of the predicted year.

We will report on results from pooled regressions (in which all forecasts made for all countries are lumped together in one sample) and on regressions of "aggregated forecasts" (which give the average percentage change of GNP in Western European countries covered, weighted by trade shares). There does not seem to be much point in reporting the large mass of individual-country results, which confirm the overall results reported. Extensive calculations were made also for the main components of GNP. No calculations were made for the price forecasts, because those reported by the AIECE are not sufficiently homogeneous; different institutes predict different indices and often the same institutes predicts different indices in different years.

## Accuracy of Forecasts

Our first task is to evaluate the accuracy of the forecasts. It is convenient to use for this purpose the well-known coefficient introduced by Theil. This provides a convenient decomposition of the forecasting error that reflects different types of errors in judgment.

**Table 1**
Accuracy appraisals.

| Theil's statistic | AIECE | | | OECD | | |
|---|---|---|---|---|---|---|
| | Oct. $t-1$ | May $t$ | Oct. $t$ | Dec. $t-1$ | July $t$ | Dec. $t$ |
| **Forecasts pooled (9 × 9 observations)** | | | | | | |
| $U$ | 0.619 | 0.446 | 0.241 | 0.600 | 0.340 | 0.243 |
| $U^m$ | 0.051 | 0.016 | 0.000 | 0.019 | 0.003 | 0.012 |
| $U^s$ | 0.240 | 0.268 | 0.042 | 0.161 | 0.194 | 0.016 |
| $U^c$ | 0.709 | 0.716 | 0.957 | 0.821 | 0.803 | 0.972 |
| **Forecasts aggregated (1 × 9 observations)** | | | | | | |
| $U$ | 0.577 | 0.357 | 0.108 | 0.536 | 0.190 | 0.126 |
| $U^m$ | 0.067 | 0.082 | 0.001 | 0.045 | 0.053 | 0.066 |
| $U^s$ | 0.446 | 0.564 | 0.027 | 0.286 | 0.502 | 0.056 |
| $U^c$ | 0.487 | 0.354 | 0.972 | 0.669 | 0.445 | 0.878 |

Notes: $U^2 = \sum (F_t - A_t)^2 / \sum A_t^2$.
$U^m$ = Fraction of $U^2$ accounted for by mean bias.
$U^s$ = Fraction of $U^2$ accounted for by variance bias.
$U^c$ = Fraction of $U^2$ accounted for by covariance bias.

Let $A_t$ and $F_t$ be the actual and forecasted values of a variable. Then the Theil coefficient is

$$U^2 = \sum (F_t - A_t)^2 / \sum A_t^2.$$

$U^2$ can be decomposed into shares accounting for different types of errors as follows:

$$1 = U^m + U^s + U^c$$

$$= \frac{(F - A)^2}{\sum (F_t - A_t)^2 / n} + \frac{(S^f - S^a)^2}{\sum (F_t - A_t)/n} + \frac{2(1 - r)S^f \cdot S^a}{\sum (F_t - A_t)^2 / n}$$

where $U^m$ is the part of the prediction error accounted for by a wrong estimate of the mean, $U^s$ is the part accounted by an erroneous estimate of the variance, and $U^c$ reflects errors due to incomplete covariation of forecasts and actual values. $S^f$ and $S^a$ are the standard errors and $\overline{S}$ and $F$ the means of $F_t$ and $A_t$, and $r$ is the correlation coefficient between these variables (see, for example, Theil 1976).

As table 1 shows, the overall accuracy of the OECD and AIECE forecasts is similar, whether judgment is based on the results of pooled data or on weighted aggregates of data. The accuracy improves strikingly over time. The OECD is more accurate than the AIECE, but it forecasts two

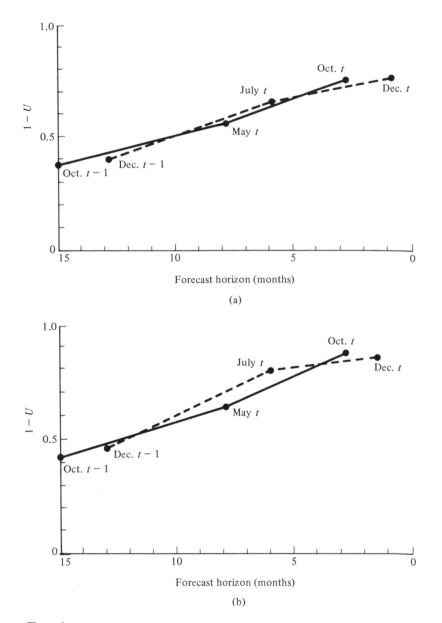

(a)

(b)

**Figure 1**
Comparisons of accuracy of AIECE (solid lines) and OECD (dashed lines) forecasts,
allowing for improvement of accuracy over time. (a) Forecasts for individual countries;
(b) forecasts aggregated by trade weights.

months later than its competitor, so this does not mean that its forecasts are truly better.

Figure 1 suggests a way of comparing the performance of the two groups. Assuming that the accuracy of forecasts grows linearly over time between two publication dates, then if the OECD is more accurate than the AIECE the broken line should lie above the solid line. According to this criterion, there is not much of a basis for a choice between the groups of forecasters. This finding parallels the conclusions reached by other researchers who have pitted forecasts against each other. The equality is an equality in mediocrity rather than in excellence. It is disappointing that in the initial forecasts, which are the only ones made before the beginning of the year, the variance of prediction errors is three-fifths of the variance of the rate of growth of GNP. This is not due to the fact that the rate of growth of GNP was stable over the period; 1970–1978 covers a major cycle.

It is interesting that the accuracies of the two institutions' forecasts for the same countries seems to be rather similar (table 2). Predictions are poor for Italy and Switzerland, better than average for France and Norway. Whether this is because forecasters draw inspiration from each other's work or because particular major changes happen to be easy or difficult to predict is hard to say.

**Table 2**
Appraisal of accuracy at country level (Theil's statistic, 1970–1978).

| | AIECE | | | OECD | | |
|---|---|---|---|---|---|---|
| | Oct. $t-1$ | May $t$ | Oct. $t$ | Dec. $t-1$ | July $t$ | Dec. $t$ |
| Austria | 0.56 | 0.45 | 0.19 | 0.56 | 0.36 | 0.17 |
| Belgium | 0.60 | 0.45 | 0.31 | 0.59 | 0.29 | 0.25 |
| France | 0.46 | 0.32 | 0.18 | 0.43 | 0.26 | 0.17 |
| Germany | 0.64 | 0.44 | 0.21 | 0.56 | 0.26 | 0.21 |
| Italy | 0.73 | 0.47 | 0.25 | 0.79 | 0.45 | 0.26 |
| Netherlands | 0.61 | 0.44 | 0.25 | 0.59 | 0.33 | 0.23 |
| Norway | 0.46 | 0.24 | 0.10 | 0.38 | 0.19 | 0.16 |
| Switzerland | 0.85 | 0.62 | 0.36 | 0.77 | 0.45 | 0.39 |
| United Kingdom | 0.68 | 0.61 | 0.31 | 0.80 | 0.46 | 0.39 |

Note: Theil's statistic

$$\left(\frac{\sum(F_t - A_t)^2}{\sum A_t^2}\right)^{1/2} = U$$

where $F_t$ and $A_t$ are forecasted and actual values of GNP, respectively.

## Are Expectations One of the Links that Account for the Transmission of Business Cycles Between Countries?

Paul Samuelson has remarked that forecasters are like six Eskimos in the same bed; all that one can be sure of is that they will all turn together. This expresses picturesquely something both forecasters and their readers perceive vividly. Whether this is a good or a bad thing is not clear. Perhaps, as Samuelson hints, there is interaction as each forecaster cribs from the others; perhaps each of them is processing and drawing conclusions efficiently from the same information. It is of course important to distinguish the two hypotheses. Copying each other's errors will, if the forecasts are believed, trigger artificial fluctuations as economic agents are impressed by a consensus of expert views that has no solid basis. On the other hand, there is no reason to criticize several economists for drawing the same conclusions from the same facts; one hopes that economic science will become mature enough so that such agreement becomes the rule rather than the exception. Thus, we will replace Samuelson's image by two of our own: Forecasters can be like a school of minnows, flittering aimlessly in a lake, but never far from each other; or they can be like the Three Kings at the coming of Christ, responding in the same way to an evident truth.

Both AIECE and OECD forecasters do change their views together, and the correlations between changes of predicted rates of growth of GNP are surprisingly high.[3] (In table 3 correlations between the May–October revisions are listed above the diagonal, those between October–May revisions below it. We give the results only for the AIECE. The results for the OECD are quite similar.)

Do forecasters behave like the Three Kings, or do the gregarious habits of their kind lead them to behave like minnows? The only sure way of distinguishing between the two possibilities would be to have a complete record of the process involved in generating forecasts, from guesses about exogenous variables to the model used to convert these into forecasts of endogenous variables. The record should record reasonings such as "I can't put down 4 percent when my readers (or my division chief) are convinced that 2 percent is right." Such a record is of course not available. But we know that in each country an important exogenous variable is changes in world demand. This can be represented by various proxies. We assume that the forecasters' Star of Bethlehem is the OECD

**Table 3**
Correlation across countries of AIECE forecast revisions, 1968–1978.

| | Revision between May $t$ and October $t-1$ | | | | | | | | | |
|---|---|---|---|---|---|---|---|---|---|---|
| | Austria | Belgium | France | Italy | Norway | Netherlands | U.K. | Switzerland | Germany | Aggregate |
| Austria | — | 0.88 | 0.65 | 0.73 | 0.26 | 0.70 | 0.06 | 0.74 | 0.64 | 0.66 |
| Belgium | 0.83 | — | 0.80 | 0.81 | 0.04 | 0.71 | 0.02 | 0.75 | 0.64 | 0.69 |
| France | 0.91 | 0.86 | — | 0.77 | 0.20 | 0.66 | 0.23 | 0.81 | 0.76 | 0.80 |
| Italy | 0.02 | 0.10 | 0.06 | — | 0.28 | 0.69 | 0.18 | 0.70 | 0.75 | 0.83 |
| Norway | 0.42 | 0.37 | 0.43 | 0.29 | — | 0.04 | 0.08 | 0.43 | 0.52 | 0.33 |
| Netherlands | 0.88 | 0.88 | 0.85 | 0.22 | 0.42 | — | 0.22 | 0.61 | 0.50 | 0.64 |
| U.K. | 0.72 | 0.56 | 0.72 | 0.43 | 0.45 | 0.63 | — | 0.14 | 0.60 | 0.65 |
| Switzerland | 0.47 | 0.59 | 0.39 | 0.16 | 0.13 | 0.51 | 0.36 | — | 0.78 | 0.71 |
| Germany | 0.91 | 0.80 | 0.82 | 0.20 | 0.48 | 0.79 | 0.66 | 0.52 | — | 0.96 |
| Aggregate | 0.93 | 0.84 | 0.92 | 0.28 | 0.50 | 0.82 | 0.82 | 0.50 | 0.95 | — |

Revision between October $t$ and May $t$

industrial-production index. This ought to be lagged, as it takes time to compile and publish the index. Here we assume that a lag of three months is adequate. This leads to a regression between changes in successive forecasts of GNP and six-month changes of this index, which would mimic the correct forecasting model if GNP was generated by a reduced-form equation relating each country's GNP to the OECD production index as follows:

$$\Delta GNP_i = a_0^i + a_1^i \Delta Y + e_i$$

where $\Delta Y$ is the change in the OECD production index and $e_i$ is a non-autocorrelatéd disturbance reflecting factors specific to country $i$. (We drop time indices from variables to lighten notations.)

This specification, it is clear, is a very incomplete representation of the set of exogenous variables whose common impact on different countries could account for the high correlations between revisions of forecasts. Other variables would be world inflation, the Eurodollar rate, and the the price of oil. It would surely be desirable to test for such influences in the pooled regression, if the number of degrees of freedom was adequate.

There is a methodological problem, as expectations both determine and are determined by output. Irrational swings in expectations may be self-fulfilling, so that the direction of causation between expectations and production changes is uncertain. As we have lagged production changes by three months, we do not feel that this is a serious problem.

Again we give only results for the AIECE, as those for the OECD are quite similar. Table 4 provides, we feel, weak evidence in favor of the minnows theory, and confirms the similarly weak evidence produced by Batchelor (1982). Correlations across countries are indeed weaker after allowance is made for the influence of world business trends on changes in expectations; a number of coefficients are even negative (the number of positive ones remains highly significant according to a test based on the binomial distribution). We have not attempted to check whether this result would remain robust after allowing for the common influence of other world variables.

## Rationality of the Forecasts

As is emphasized by the theory of rational expectations, forecasts should be equal to the mathematical expectations of the predicted variable,

**Table 4**
Correlation across countries in forecast revisions after a linear correction for available information, 1968–1978 (AIECE forecasts).

| | Revision between May $t$ and October $t-1$ | | | | | | | | | |
| --- | --- | --- | --- | --- | --- | --- | --- | --- | --- | --- |
| | Austria | Belgium | France | Italy | Norway | Netherlands | U.K. | Switzerland | Germany | Aggregate |
| Austria | — | 0.66 | −0.03 | 0.28 | 0.11 | 0.49 | 0.09 | 0.34 | 0.16 | 0.23 |
| Belgium | 0.77 | — | 0.11 | 0.25 | −0.49 | 0.55 | 0.01 | 0.15 | 0.12 | 0.12 |
| France | 0.83 | 0.80 | — | 0.24 | −0.03 | 0.39 | 0.41 | 0.46 | 0.40 | 0.53 |
| Italy | −0.46 | −0.39 | −0.30 | — | 0.13 | 0.46 | 0.31 | 0.17 | 0.38 | 0.60 |
| Norway | 0.30 | 0.25 | 0.31 | 0.19 | — | −0.23 | 0.08 | 0.38 | 0.51 | 0.22 |
| Netherlands | 0.91 | 0.84 | 0.82 | −0.50 | 0.33 | — | 0.26 | 0.31 | 0.15 | 0.39 |
| U.K. | 0.33 | 0.28 | 0.41 | 0.23 | 0.34 | 0.46 | — | 0.20 | 0.86 | 0.92 |
| Switzerland | 0.50 | 0.59 | 0.36 | −0.26 | −0.20 | 0.48 | 0.33 | — | 0.51 | 0.35 |
| Germany | 0.78 | 0.70 | 0.63 | −0.13 | 0.39 | 0.74 | 0.22 | 0.57 | — | 0.91 |
| Aggregate | 0.83 | 0.80 | 0.84 | −0.04 | 0.44 | 0.83 | 0.56 | 0.57 | 0.89 | — |
| | Revision between October $t$ and May $t$ | | | | | | | | | |

Note: The correlation matrix has been computed from

$$u_j^i = (P_j^i - P_{j-1}^i) - (a_0^i + a_1^i \Delta Y)$$

where $i = 1, \ldots, 9$ (countries), $j = 2, 3$ (forecasts), and $Y$ is a monthly total of OECD industrial-production index (time indices are dropped to lighten notation).

conditional on the information available to their author. Formally, if $F_t$ and $A_t$ are the forecasted and realized values of a variable, $I$ is the information set of the agent, and $E$ is the expectations operator, it should be true that

$$F_t = E(A_t | I_t).$$

This condition has been shown to have extremely subtle implications for macroeconomic analysis. What is relevant from the viewpoint of this paper is, however, quite straightforward.

A first implication, understood long ago (see, for example, Theil 1966, pp. 33–36) is that the coefficients $a_0$ and $a_1$ of the regression

$$A_t = a_0 + a_1 F_t + e_t$$

should be equal to 0 and 1, respectively. This unbiasedness condition can be tested by an $F$ test. It is convenient also to calculate $t$ values indicating to what extent $a_0$ and $a_1$ differ from 0 and 1, respectively.

Only recently has it come to be realized that rationality also implies that forecasting errors should be uncorrelated with the components of the information set $I$. This would be a very strong test of rationality if the information used to draw up forecasts could be ascertained, as unfortunately it cannot. To the extent that some of the information used is known, this orthogonality condition does make it possible to detect some deviations from rationality.

The OECD and the AIECE pass the unbiasedness test satisfactorily for the second and third forecasts, but not for the first, the only one that is purely a look into the future. (In the second and third forecasts part of the year is already known.) Unbiasedness could be due to mutually canceling errors involving different biases for different countries. To test for this, pooled regressions were run with separate intercepts for different countries, and separate regressions for separate countries. These led us to accept the validity of the pooled regression. This result may be related to that obtained by McNees (1978), who concluded that these forecasts were not unbiased. His study described quarterly forecasts produced by models, whereas the OECD and most of the AIECE institutes do not use models to produce their yearly forecasts. McNees's test procedure also differs from ours.

We test next for orthogonality. As there is no way of knowing what information was used to draw up the forecasts, all that is possible in practice is to test for autocorrelation of successive forecasting errors. Intuitively, a forecaster who comes to realize that the procedures he uses lead him to make errors that are correlated over time should be able to use this information to produce more accurate predictions. Indeed, past errors are part of his information set, and future errors should be uncorrelated with respect to them.[4]

We are happy to note in table 5 that there is no strong evidence of autocorrelation of residuals. This particular form of irrationality does not seem to be present

The next hurdle is more of a problem. The orthogonality condition obviously requires that the forecasting error be uncorrelated with the change in the forecast with respect to the last forecasting date. As table 6 shows, this condition is not satisfied by the AIECE forecasters. The OECD is free of this tendency for its third forecast, but not for the second. This indicates that the AIECE forecasters especially tend to be timid in assessing the implications of the information obtained between two prediction dates. This probably reflects what we have referred to above as public-acceptability bias—a tendency to avoid jarring the beliefs of users by sudden revisions of predicted changes in the GNP.[5]

It is amusing to discover that an outsider can predict how an AIECE forecaster is going to change his mind. Indeed, it turns out that the change between the second and the third forecasts is significantly related to the preceding forecast revision (see table 7). This strengthens the impression of overcautionusness in evaluating data, or of unwillingness to change forecasts so quickly that users will lose faith in them. As table 7 shows, every one of the institutes suffers from this defect to some extent, the highest correlations being those for France, Austria, and Germany. British forecasters are the most rational of all from this point of view, or perhaps their stop-and-go economy is so unpredictable that the defect is swamped by the large random element in economic growth.

Another, more constructive interpretation of table 7 is that it is the lack of linkage of AIECE forecasts that causes our results. According to this interpretation, each institute calculates the impact of outside events on its country without realizing that the same events will affect that country's exports via their effect on its neighbors. It is only at the AIECE meeting that forecasters become aware of what is happening elsewhere, and their next forecast reflects this information. This interpretation is suggested by the strong positive correlation between the revision for each country and

**Table 5**
Results of ordinary least-squares regression for 1970–1978.

| Forecast | AIECE | | | | | | OECD | | | | | |
|---|---|---|---|---|---|---|---|---|---|---|---|---|
| | $a_0$ | $a_1$ | $F$ | $R^2$ | $\rho$ | D.W. | $a_0$ | $a_1$ | $F$ | $R^2$ | $\rho$ | D.W. |
| **Pooled ($N = 81$)[a]** | | | | | | | | | | | | |
| 1 | 0.42 (0.8) | 0.73 (0.2) | 3.1[b] | 0.15 | ... (0.1) | 2.0 | 0.73 (0.6) | 0.70 (0.2) | 2.5 | 0.19 (0.1) | ... | 1.9 |
| 2 | −0.73 (0.5) | 1.14 (0.1) | 1.4 | 0.54 | −0.1 (0.1) | 2.1 | −0.45 (0.3) | 1.11 (0.1) | 1.2 | 0.73 | −0.1 (0.1) | 2.0 |
| 3 | 0.00 (0.2) | 1.00 (0.0) | ... | 0.86 | −0.2 (0.1) | 2.2 | 0.19 (0.2) | 0.97 (0.0) | 0.7 | 0.86 | ... (0.1) | 2.0 |
| **Aggregated ($N = 9$)** | | | | | | | | | | | | |
| 1 | −0.30 (3.9) | 0.93 (1.0) | 0.3 | 0.10 | −0.2 (0.4) | 2.4 | −0.05 (2.4) | 0.89 (0.7) | 0.2 | 0.21 | −0.1 (0.4) | 2.2 |
| 2 | −2.54 (1.2) | 1.62 (0.3) | 2.2 | 0.77 | −0.6 (0.3) | 2.9 | −1.00 (0.4) | 1.26 (0.1) | 2.7 | 0.94 | −0.6 (0.4) | 2.8 |
| 3 | 0.15 (0.3) | 0.95 (0.1) | 0.2 | 0.97 | 0.1 (0.4) | 1.7 | 0.32 (0.3) | 0.93 (0.1) | 0.7 | 0.96 | 0.1 (0.4) | 1.7 |

$A_t = a_0 + a_1 F_t + e_t.$

Standard errors are given in parentheses.
Dots mean nil or negligible.
a. In the pooled regressions, terms relating the last residual for a country and the first residual for the following country are dropped in calculating the D.W. and $\rho$ statistics. The denominator of these statistics is adjusted appropriately.
b. Significant at the 5 percent level.

**Table 6**
Linear dependence between errors of forecasts and revisions of forecasts (OLS estimates).

| | AIECE | | | | OECD | | | | |
|---|---|---|---|---|---|---|---|---|---|
| | $a_0$ | $a_1$ | $R^2$ | | $a_0$ | $a_1$ | $R^2$ | | |
| **Pooled** | | | | | | | | | |
| May t / Oct. t − 1 | −0.06 (0.2) | 0.49 (0.2) | 0.10 | −0.1 (0.1) | ··· (0.2) | 0.28 (0.1) | 0.10 | −0.1 (0.1) | July t / Dec. t − 1 |
| Oct. t / May t | 0.03 (0.1) | 0.04 (0.1) | ··· | −0.2 (0.1) | 0.09 (0.1) | −0.10 (0.1) | 0.01 | ··· (0.1) | Dec. t − 1 / — / July t |
| **Aggregated** | | | | | | | | | |
| May t / Oct. t − 1 | −0.19 (0.3) | 1.10 (0.3) | 0.63 | −0.5 (0.3) | −0.01 (0.2) | 0.37 (0.1) | 0.56 | −0.5 (0.3) | July t / Dec. t − 1 |
| Oct. t / May t | −0.01 (0.2) | −0.06 (0.1) | 0.03 | 0.1 (0.3) | −0.05 (0.2) | −0.26 (0.2) | 0.19 | ··· (0.3) | Dec. t − 1 / July t |

$A − F_j = a_0 + a_1(F_j − F_{j-1})$ with $j = 2, 3$.

October t − 1, May t, and October t = 1, 2, 3 for AIECE.
Dec. t − 1, July t, Dec. t = 1, 2, 3 for OECD.
Dots mean nil or negligible.
Standard errors are given in parentheses.

**Table 7**
Correlation matrix for revisions in successive AIECE forecasts: (October $t$ − May $t$) versus (May $t$ − October $t$ − 1).

|            | Austria | Belgium | France | Italy | Norway | Netherlands | U.K. | Switzerland | Germany | Aggregate |
|------------|---------|---------|--------|-------|--------|-------------|------|-------------|---------|-----------|
| Austria     | 0.84 | 0.84 | 0.78 | 0.81 | 0.46 | 0.59 | 0.05 | 0.93 | 0.71 | 0.67 |
| Belgium     | 0.52 | 0.56 | 0.70 | 0.76 | 0.67 | 0.30 | 0.08 | 0.74 | 0.66 | 0.59 |
| France      | 0.74 | 0.73 | 0.71 | 0.77 | 0.46 | 0.32 | 0.07 | 0.81 | 0.66 | 0.60 |
| Italy       | 0.29 | 0.50 | 0.22 | 0.34 | 0.45 | 0.19 | 0.09 | 0.15 | 0.10 | 0.27 |
| Norway      | 0.43 | 0.43 | 0.09 | 0.31 | 0.47 | 0.07 | 0.12 | 0.40 | 0.41 | 0.25 |
| Netherlands | 0.61 | 0.55 | 0.53 | 0.67 | 0.67 | 0.31 | 0.02 | 0.80 | 0.64 | 0.54 |
| U.K.        | 0.60 | 0.80 | 0.57 | 0.57 | 0.01 | 0.26 | 0.18 | 0.58 | 0.40 | 0.39 |
| Switzerland | 0.10 | 0.31 | 0.37 | 0.53 | 0.07 | 0.37 | 0.36 | 0.39 | 0.09 | 0.14 |
| Germany     | 0.74 | 0.84 | 0.77 | 0.93 | 0.38 | 0.63 | 0.14 | 0.85 | 0.80 | 0.80 |
| Aggregate   | 0.78 | 0.88 | 0.78 | 0.90 | 0.34 | 0.51 | 0.00 | 0.82 | 0.73 | 0.72 |

**Table 8**
Theil statistic indicating whether the forecast for year $t$ is a good "predictor" of the growth achieved in year $t - 1$ (9 × 9 observations).

|  | AIECE | OECD |  |
|---|---|---|---|
| Oct. $t - 1$ | 0.64 | 0.71 | Dec. $t - 1$ |
| May $t$ | 0.62 | 0.70 | July $t$ |
| Oct. $t$ | 0.82 | 0.83 | Dec. $t$ |

$$V = \left( \frac{\sum (F_t - A_{t-1})^2}{\sum A_{t-1}^{\,2}} \right)^{1/2}.$$

the preceding revision announced by other AIECE members at the preceding meeting. The implication of this hypothesis would be that each institute should take the trouble of revising its forecast thoroughly at the end of each meeting. (Formal linkage would be an even better solution, but would require that each institute use a model rather than—as is mostly the case—rely on judgmental estimates.) OECD economists, who are sitting in neighboring rooms, can of course take account of such cross-impacts via coffee-break chats as well as more formal forecast-coordination meetings.

One idea worth testing is that the autocorrelation in forecast revision is due to the fact that predictions are generated adaptively, as arithmetic averages of the most recent change of GNP and of the GNP change suggested by recent data. (Such a pattern would be rational if forecasters were capable of predicting rationally the implications of recent events but were reluctant to predict drastic trend changes to avoid losing the faith of their readers.) To test for this, table 8 calculates the values of the Theil coefficients of predicted changes of GNP with respect to the growth observed one year before the forecast year. As expected, the values of the statistic rise over time. The extrapolative element is stronger in early than in later forecasts. This is not an indication of lack of rationality, for business fluctuations do tend to exhibit continuity, and forecasters are justified in using this fact in building up their estimates of GNP changes. The Theil coefficient for the first forecast is quite high, so forecasters cannot be accused of producing mere mechanical extrapolations of past trends.[6]

As a last means of identifying the nature of the bias, we regress the change between forecasts 2 and 3 on the preceding forecast revision, as before, and add to the regression the percentage increase of the OECD

**Table 9**
Regressions of forecast revisions on earlier forecast revisions and on the lagged change of the OECD industrial production index.

|                     | $a_0$   | $a_1$   | $a_2$  | $R^2$ | $\rho$ |
|---------------------|---------|---------|--------|-------|--------|
| **Pooled data**     | $-0.69$ | 0.04    | 0.19   | 0.33  | 0.15   |
| AIECE               | (0.18)  | (0.13)  | (0.04) |       |        |
| OECD                | $-0.56$ | $-0.13$ | 0.14   | 0.20  | 0.08   |
|                     | (0.18)  | 0.09    | (0.03) |       |        |
| **Aggregated data** | $-0.81$ | 0.30    | 0.20   | 0.68  | $-0.23$ |
| AIECE               | (0.43)  | (0.48)  | (0.10) |       |        |
| OECD                | $-0.82$ | $-0.27$ | 0.20   | 0.52  | 0.23   |
|                     | (0.39)  | (0.32)  | (0.10) |       |        |

$F_3 - F_2 = a_0 + a_1(F_2 - F_1) + a_2 \Delta Y$ where $F_j$ $(j = 1, 2, 3)$ is one of the three forecasts published by AIECE and OECD and $\Delta Y$ represents the six-month change of the industrial production index of OECD, lagged by three months with respect to the publication date of forecast 3.
$\rho$ is first-order autocorrelation of errors.
Standard errors are given in parentheses.

industrial-production index, lagged three months as in the last section. This regression is meant to detect whether the cause of the autocorrelation is a failure to assess accurately the evolution of business trends outside the AIECE countries. This leads to table 9, which describes the results obtained for AIECE forecasts as a whole, and table 10, which describes the results obtained for individual countries. In table 9 we also give results for OECD.

Table 9 suggests that the autocorrelation of forecast revisions is indeed the result of poor forecasts of business trends in the world as a whole. The introduction of the OECD production-growth variable wipes out the significance of the previous forecast revision in the regression. Table 10, which gives results for individual countries of the AIECE, leads to a similar conclusion.

## Conclusions

We have surveyed the GNP forecasts of the diverse institutes that are members of the AIECE, and those of the OECD. Their performance is remarkably uniform. However, the accuracy of these forecasts is not very good. As has been increasingly realized recently, this does not mean that the forecasters are not doing a competent job. The problem may be that, as emphasized by the work on rational expectations, production will tend

**Table 10**
Correlation matrix for revisions in successive forecasts, adjusted for available information: (October $t$ − May $t$) versus (May $t$ − October $t − 1$).

| | Austria | Belgium | France | Italy | Norway | Netherlands | U.K. | Switzerland | Germany | Aggregate |
|---|---|---|---|---|---|---|---|---|---|---|
| Austria | 0.30 | 0.17 | 0.12 | 0.20 | 0.26 | 0.13 | −0.06 | 0.44 | 0.14 | 0.09 |
| Belgium | −0.09 | −0.32 | 0.13 | 0.26 | 0.50 | −0.17 | −0.09 | 0.25 | 0.17 | 0.07 |
| France | 0.21 | 0.04 | 0.09 | 0.23 | 0.27 | −0.16 | −0.08 | 0.33 | 0.13 | 0.07 |
| Italy | 0.00 | 0.40 | −0.20 | 0.04 | −0.57 | −0.03 | 0.08 | −0.71 | −0.25 | 0.00 |
| Norway | 0.07 | −0.09 | −0.03 | 0.18 | 0.36 | −0.44 | −0.12 | −0.14 | 0.07 | −0.16 |
| Netherlands | 0.18 | −0.11 | −0.13 | 0.25 | 0.53 | −0.08 | 0.03 | 0.47 | 0.24 | 0.11 |
| U.K. | 0.01 | 0.20 | −0.17 | −0.13 | −0.19 | −0.23 | −0.19 | −0.04 | −0.25 | −0.24 |
| Switzerland | 0.31 | −0.12 | 0.08 | 0.38 | −0.03 | 0.18 | −0.37 | 0.15 | −0.28 | −0.20 |
| Germany | 0.13 | 0.15 | 0.08 | 0.41 | 0.18 | 0.17 | 0.13 | 0.29 | 0.27 | 0.28 |
| Aggregate | 0.12 | 0.12 | 0.01 | 0.27 | 0.12 | 0.02 | 0.01 | 0.18 | 0.10 | 0.10 |

The table lists correlation coefficients between $u_3^i$ and $u_2^i$, where $u_j^i = (F_j^i - F_{j-1}^i) - (a_0^i + a_1^i \Delta Y)$ $(j = 2, 3; i = 1, \ldots, 9$ countries). $\Delta Y$ is the six-month change of the OECD total industrial production index, lagged by three months.

to respond immediately to any change of demand forecasted for the future, so that changes of output are inherently difficult to predict.

What is perhaps more serious is that the forecasts do not seem to be optimal in a mean-square sense. They could be improved by an outsider with no information on the economy apart from knowledge of past forecasted and actual values. We have tried to identify the biases that lead to this result. Forecasters seem reluctant to change their forecasts as sharply as they ought to, perhaps because they do not want to seem inconsistent in the eyes of their public. There is some (weak) evidence of simultaneous swings of optimism and pessimism in the various countries. Finally, there is evidence of a lag in taking account of the implications of forecast revisions in other countries for each of the countries concerned. Some type of procedure to link the various forecasts formally might make it possible to take account without delay of changes of expectations in other countries.

## Acknowledgments

This research has been supported by the Ford Foundation under its International Economic Order research program (grant 775 0022). We are grateful for comments from W. Branson, D. Laidler, M. C. Adam, A. Farber, V. Ginsburgh, J. Gunning, and P. Barten.

## Notes

1. This study covers forecasts of the following AIECE members:
Bureau d'Information et de Prévisions Economiques, Paris
Central Bureau of Statistics, Oslo
Centre d'Observation Economique de la Chambre de Commerce et d'Industrie de Paris
Centraal Plan Bureau, The Hague
Deutsches Institut für Wirtschaftsforschung, Berlin
Département d'Economie Appliquée de l'Université Libre de Bruxelles
The Economic Council, Copenhagen
Rheinisch-Westphälisches Institut für Wirtschaftsforschung, Essen
Institut für Wirtschaftsforschung an der ETH, Zurich
Institut für Wirtschaftsforschung, Hamburg
Institut für Wirtschaftsforschung, Munich
Institut National de la Statistique et des Etudes Economiques, Paris
Institute Nazionale per lo Studio della Congiuntura, Rome
Institut für Wirtschaftsforschung an der Universität, Kiel

2. Forecasts are available for the main national accounts aggregates evaluated at constant prices and for prices. The AIECE price forecasts cannot unfortunately be used, as the price forecasts do not always refer to the same price for different years and countries. As to constant price aggregates, we discuss only those for GNP.

3. Batchelor (1982) has found a similar very high correlation between expectations of businessmen in different EEC countries; this is higher than the correlation between realized changes in industrial production. His interpretation that this favors what we have called the minnows hypothesis is doubtful, for it could easily happen that the systematic part of changes of production in different countries, which is what is captured by correlations between expectations, tend to move together to a greater extent than the purely random factors, which cannot be predicted.

4. It is not quite true that past forecasting errors are known when a forecast is made for the following year. In October of year $t - 1$, when the first AIECE forecast is made, there is only a provisional estimate of GNP of year $t - 2$, and a (pretty good) forecast for year $t - 1$.

5. L. Dupriez, the first president of the AIECE, used to tell that a business friend had complained that forecasters usually announced that a little cloud was coming only when rain was already pouring hard.

6. As already mentioned, forecasters do not know the rate of growth in year $t$ when making the first prediction for year $t + 1$. It would have been more correct therefore to calculate Theil coefficients between the forecasted growth for year $t$ at each prediction date and the assessment of growth in year $t - 1$ made at the same date.

## Bibliography

Batchelor, R. 1982. Expectations, output and inflation, the European experience. *European Economic Review* 17, no. 1: 1–26.

Christ, C. 1951. A test of an econometric model of the United States, 1921–47. Conference on Business Cycle Analysis, National Bureau of Economic Research, New York.

Dramais, A. 1977. Transmission of inflationary pressures between the EEC members. *European Economic Review* 9, no. 1: 21–42.

Hickman, B. 1975. International transmission of economic fluctuations. In R. Herring and R. Marston, eds., International Aspects of Stabilization Policies. Federal Bank of Boston.

McNees, S. K. 1978. The "rationality" of economic forecasts. *American Economic Review* 68, no. 2: 301–305.

Theil, H. 1966. *Applied Economic Forecasting*. Amsterdam: North-Holland.

Theil, H. 1976. *Economic Forecasts and Policy*. Amsterdam: North-Holland.

Waelbroeck, J. 1973. The methodology of linkage. In R. J. Ball, ed., *The International Linkage of National Economic Models*. Amsterdam: North-Holland.

# Contributors

F. Gerard Adams
University of Pennsylvania

T. W. Anderson
Stanford University

Albert Ando
University of Pennsylvania

R. J. Ball
London Graduate School of Business

Jere R. Behrman
University of Pennsylvania

D. DeRoo
Centre D'Economie Mathematique et d'Econometrie
Université Libre de Bruxelles

Phoebus J. Dhrymes
Columbia University

D. P. Dungan
Institute for Policy Analysis
University of Toronto

Victor Filatov
Morgan Guaranty Trust
New York

John F. Helliwell
University of British Columbia

Alan W. Heston
University of Pennsylvania

Bert G. Hickman
Stanford University

G. V. Jump
Institute for Policy Analysis
University of Toronto

Irving B. Kravis
University of Pennsylvania

Wilhelm Krelle
Institut für Gesellschafts- und Wirtschaftswissenschaften
University of Bonn

Naoto Kunitomo
University of Tokyo

Lawrence J. Lau
Stanford University

Nissan Liviatan
Hebrew University of Jerusalem

Michael Margolick
University of British Columbia

Jaime R. Marquez
University of Pennsylvania

Michael D. McCarthy
Wharton Econometric Forecasting Associates
Philadelphia

Chikashi Moriguchi
Institute of Economic Research
Kyoto University

Mitsuo Saito
Kobe University

Paul A. Samuelson
Massachusetts Institute of Technology

Takamitsu Sawa
Kyoto Institute of Economic Research
Kyoto University

J. A. Sawyer
Institute for Policy Analysis
University of Toronto

Stefan Schleicher
University of Graz

Robert Summers
University of Pennsylvania

Paul Taubman
University of Pennsylvania

J. Waelbroeck
Centre d'Economie Mathematique et d'Econometrie
Université Libre de Bruxelles

# Index